TEACHER'S MANUAL

to

CONTRACTS: TRANSACTIONS AND LITIGATION

Third Edition

■ ■ ■

By

George W. Kuney

*W.P. Toms Distinguished Professor of Law and
Director of the Clayton Center for Entrepreneurial Law
The University of Tennessee College of Law*

Robert M. Lloyd

*Lindsay Young Distinguished Professor of Law
The University of Tennessee College of Law*

AMERICAN CASEBOOK SERIES®

WEST®

A Thomson Reuters business

Mat #41060115

© 2011 Thomson Reuters

    610 Opperman Drive
    St. Paul, MN 55123
    1–800–313–9378

Printed in the United States of America

ISBN: 978–0–314–26747–4

About the Authors

George Kuney is a W.P. Toms Distinguished Professor of Law at The University of Tennessee College of Law. Prior to becoming the Director of The Clayton Center for Entrepreneurial Law at The University of Tennessee College of Law in 2000, was a partner in California's Allen Matkins Leck Gamble & Mallory LLP where he concentrated his practice on business law, insolvency, and reorganization matters, and before that he practiced with the Morrison Foerster and Howard, Rice firms in San Francisco. Professor Kuney is the author of *Mastering Appellate Advocacy and Procedure* (with Donna C. Looper, Carolina Academic Press), *Secured Transactions: UCC Article 9 and the Bankruptcy Code* (with Robert M. Lloyd, Clayton Center for Entrepreneurial Law), *Mastering Legal Drafting* (with Donna C. Looper, Carolina Academic Press), *The Elements of Contract Drafting* (3d ed. West), *Legal Drafting: Process, Techniques, and Exercises* (with Thomas Haggard, West), *Legal Drafting in a Nutshell* (with Thomas Haggard, West), *California Contract Law* (with Donna C. Looper, CEB), *Mastering Bankruptcy* (Carolina Academic Press), *Mastering Intellectual Property* (with Donna C. Looper, Carolina Academic Press), *Chapter 11-101* (with coauthors, ABI), *Mastering Legal Analysis and Drafting* (Carolina Academic Press), and a number of articles dealing with contracts, business acquisitions, corporate governance, and reorganization matters. He holds a J.D. from the University of California's Hastings College of the Law, an M.B.A. from the University of San Diego, and a B.A. from the University of California at Santa Cruz.

Robert Lloyd is the Lindsay Young Distinguished Professor of Law at The University of Tennessee College of Law. He joined the faculty in 1983 after a career in commercial law with the Los Angeles firm of Sheppard, Mullin, Richter & Hampton. He helped to develop the college's Concentration in Business Transactions and served as the first Director of the college's Clayton Center for Entrepreneurial Law. Professor Lloyd has had numerous articles on commercial lending transactions published. He holds a J.D. from the University of Michigan and a B.S.E. from Princeton University.

TABLE OF CONTENTS

I. Introduction

We structured this text to promote organized thinking about contract law. We basically reject the "hide the ball" method of teaching contracts in favor of a three step process, which each of the casebook chapters follows: (1) provide a description of the subject matter at issue and the potentially applicable rules, (2) examine the cases to illustrate application (or not) of the rules, (3) reinforce this understanding through questions and problems that require application of the rule in new situations. Kuney augments this process with periodic drafting assignments and midterm examinations, two in the first semester and one in the second, to evaluate performance mid-course and provide feedback.

Chapter 1 introduces the objective theory of contracts, which underlies all the materials. In contract law, we are generally not concerned with the parties' innermost subjective intent, but by the so-called "objective," reasonable meanings to be ascribed to their public words and conduct, as informed by custom and practice in any particular industry or practiced between the parties. Kuney finds it helps to be explicit in telling the students that we are not talking about "objective like a ruler," but rather a notion of "objective" based upon the "collective subjective interpretation by the fact finders involved," which may vary depending upon custom, location, time, and all other aspects of the context of the dispute and its resolution. Chapters 2 through 4 explore the nature of offers, acceptance, and termination of offers. The alternative rules from the CISG and UNIDROIT are presented here and elsewhere in the text to round out the issues and provide an international perspective and to allow students to compare and contrast similar but distinct standards relevant to the same issue. Passing from offer and acceptance, Chapters 5 through 8 examine whether or not the purported contract is supported by consideration or an accepted consideration substitute. These doctrines are the ones that separate promises that the law will enforce from those gratuitous promises that, though they may be morally binding, are not enforceable through legal action.

Chapters 9 to 13 present the basic formation defenses of mistake, misrepresentation, duress, unconscionability, and the statute of frauds. Even if the objective theory of contracts would indicate that an offer was made and was accepted prior to termination, and the resulting agreement was supported by consideration or an acceptable consideration substitute, these formation defenses and others like them, if proved up, will prevent a finding that a contract exists to be enforced.

Chapters 14 and 15 examine the parol evidence rule and the use of extrinsic evidence to interpret written contracts. This is some of the most confusing material for students of the common law and most of it is rejected by countries other than the United States.

Chapters 16 and 17—new with this edition of the book—cover UCC warranty liability and defenses to that liability.

Chapters 18 to 22 present doctrines concerning the recovery of contract damages and other remedies. In other words, if one party is found to be in breach, what may the other party recover? These chapters emphasize problem solving and are supported by on-line problem sets at the Clayton Center for Entrepreneurial Law's website on the University of Tennessee College of Law's web server. Damages are, after all, the point of the costly and time-consuming business of litigation.

Chapters 23 and 24 address express and implied conditions and, secondarily, discuss representations, warranties, and other types of clauses that are a transactional lawyer's stock in trade and that allow planning for and against future litigation. Implied conditions, which govern the order and necessity of performance, year in and year out, prove to be the second most difficult subject for students to master.

Chapter 25—also new with this edition of the text—covers contract performance under the UCC, specifically the perfect tender rule, cure, acceptance, rejection, and revocation of acceptance.

Chapters 26 and 27 address the excuses for non-performances of a contract such as anticipatory repudiation, impracticability, and frustration of purpose. Chapter 28 addresses the amorphous concept of the duty of good faith and fair dealing, which may also be employed as an affirmative defense or excuse for non-performance.

Assignment and delegation and third party beneficiary contracts are covered in Chapter 29. The cases in this chapter were selected not only to illustrate the rules that are the subject matter of the chapter, but to review and reprise concepts covered previously in the materials.

Throughout the text are some observations that are intended to undermine the common distinction that is drawn between the knowledge and skills needed to be a litigator and those needed as a transactional attorney. Fact development for litigation builds upon the documentation and the record produced when the transaction is negotiated, structured, entered into, and carried out by the parties. The most successful practitioners in the contracting field can play on both sides of the street and run circles around the less well-rounded "other side" at contract negotiation, documentation, supervision of performance, modification, and litigation.

Comments on the text and related matters are welcomed and encouraged.

Prof. George W. Kuney
gkuney@utk.edu
Clayton Center for Entrepreneurial Law
The University of Tennessee College of Law

1505 W. Cumberland Ave.
Knoxville, TN 37996

II. Principle Goals and Techniques

A. Case Analysis

Because Contracts is generally taught as a first year law school course, its goals are broader than simply teaching substantive contract law. It is also intended to teach, among other things, case analysis. Judicial opinions are working documents, not entertaining stories or objective reports to be uncritically swallowed. They must be analyzed to determine their holdings and announced rules and the reasoning employed to reach those ends. They should be critically analyzed to determine whether or not the court was following or making law and whether or not the writing judge had a "thumb on the scale" in weighing the facts and law. Facts are not objective, they are conclusions.

Further, as we try and emphasize in the text, once a case has been analyzed, its rules and reasoning should be incorporated into plans for future dealings and transactions. Transactional work provides the opportunity to plan for the future, including future performance, renegotiation, and litigation between the parties. Documents should be drawn up with this in mind. Pure litigation work generally involves confronting a cold record of facts that, while they can be developed and shaped through advocacy, cannot be created or destroyed. Transactional work, on the other hand, provides the opportunity to take one's knowledge of the law and design documents that either avail themselves of law or avoid its application. If a safe harbor or a prohibited or unenforceable provision has been identified by a case or statute, it should be drafted into or around as appropriate. The factual record should be developed along the way to provide admissible evidence to benefit the client in later litigation, should that come to pass.

In each case, after understanding the court's presentation of the facts, students should be encouraged to understand what rule the court applied, whether there were any alternate rules that could have been applied, and whether (and, if so, how) it would matter if a different rule had been applied. Beyond that, students should be thinking of how the dispute could have been prevented in the first place and what transactional mechanisms are available to accomplish that end.

Contract law involves the study of rules governing relationships among people and other entities. When things do not go well and a dispute arises, or where there has been a failure to plan, the law steps in with a set of default rules to resolve the dispute. Those rules are contract law. They are rules of general applicability and, thus, even if flexible, are not specifically tailored to the parties or their circumstances. The result of these default rules is most often *not* what either of the parties would have negotiated or intended had they addressed the issue in their contract.

Briefing and case analysis helps students learn the process of legal reasoning, to see how cases fit together to form bodies of legal rules, and to allow them to compare the facts, rules, and reasoning of cases that have already been decided to a new problem or issue facing a client. This is why this casebook relies so heavily at times upon problems that follow the cases, which are themselves used to illustrate the various rules of black-letter law. Knowing how to better structure the transaction involving the transport of the mill shaft in *Hadley v. Baxendale* is all well and good, but being able to use that knowledge to provide for recovery of consequential damages if defective software shuts down a company's operations is far more valuable.

All of this is generally a new way of thinking for first-year law students. As a result, it bears some emphasis and repetition, especially in the beginning of their first semester. It is generally not sufficient to rely upon a legal research and writing class to cover case analysis and briefing. Just as professors ask their students to break down the facts and law of the cases, those professors may want to break down the skills and tasks that the students are being asked to use. Even for those that teach first-year law students on a regular basis, it is hard to remember how little exposure first year students have to these skills and to rigorous, precise reading and writing prior to law school. Put another way, it is difficult to imagine how little they generally know about law in general and contracts in particular.

Basic Form of Case Brief

Case Name and Citation: *(The parties names and citation).*

Facts: *(These are the pertinent, legally significant, historical facts – not the procedural facts).*

Procedural History: *(The procedural facts).*

Issue(s): *(The question that the court must answer, or the error asserted by the appellant in the lower court decision).*

Holding(s): *(The answer to the issues).*

Judgment: *(What happens to the litigants, precisely).*

Reasoning: *(The rules the court applied, how it fit them together, etc.).*

Dissenting or Concurring Opinions: *(If these are included, what was their point?).*

Other Thoughts and Comments: *(Either the student's or the professor's).*

Students have to tear a case apart in order to find these components. Often, it is easier to take them out of order.

Case analysis also feeds the IRAC form of presentation. This is a key skill to successful legal reasoning and argument. Unfortunately, many law students come to law school with less than rigorous training in critical reading and writing. They often have been encouraged to express themselves in whatever personal, creative form they please. This is not the way for them to succeed in law school, at least not at first. We stress the fundamentals as building blocks for later success.

We repeatedly remind students that IRAC (Issue, Rule, Analysis, Conclusion) is the model that they should follow in presenting their analysis of legal problems. There are facts that come from clients or from law professors that need to be parsed into the legally significant facts, contextual facts, and those that are irrelevant. This should then lead to identification of the legal issues involved, broken down into the smallest divisible set of issues and, for each one, identification of the governing legal rules and how they are to be applied, leading to a conclusion. The conclusion, if reasonable, is often the least important part of the exercise. Emphasizing (and re-emphasizing) this format brings students up to speed more quickly, improves the quality of classroom discussion, and, hopefully, leads to better and easier to read exam answers.

B. Elements vs. Factors

The casebook uses the terms "elements" and "factors" to describe the components of many of the legal rules and standards that students will encounter in the course. In the notes, questions, introductory material, and problems, we have been careful to use the terms in a specific way. "Elements" denotes required showings that trigger a rule or result; "Factors" denotes non-mandatory showings that should be considered, usually presented in a non-exclusive, open-ended list, when determining whether a standard has been met. The courts and commentators do not always follow this convention in the use of these terms. We have forced the distinction for our own teaching purposes; students need to be cautious when they run into these terms "in the wild" and ask themselves what is actually being stated.

One of the basic legal skills for Contracts students is to isolate and break down the rules and standards employed by the courts into their constituent parts. Although this skill is elemental and there may be the temptation to gloss over it, our experience is that the more explicit the instructor is, the better. This is especially true at the inception of the course. Getting the elements and factors stated with precision and up on the board (or overhead, or PowerPoint, etc.) so that the students can then debate whether the relevant legally significant facts support checking them off is critical. This approach, although somewhat mechanical, is not anti-intellectual. Rather, it is disciplined. The checklist approach allows students to focus their discussion and analysis on the precise concepts that are at issue and whether or not various conclusions are adequately supported by the record. It also allows the instructor to draw a distinction between questions of fact, questions of law, and mixed questions of law and fact. That, in turn, can lead to a discussion of the standards for deciding various potentially dispositive motions and standards of appellate review. Failure to focus the students on the structure and interrelationship of the elements and factors involved tends to lead to a lot of unstructured discussion about "justice," "fairness," and "equity." It is not that those notions have no place in Contracts–they do–but to be meaningful, they should be seen as conclusions—forgone or not—that result from purposeful application of detailed rules and standards.

C. Litigation Problem-Solving

In teaching Contracts to first year law students, we believe that there are some fundamental skills that go beyond mere doctrinal contract law and provide training in basic litigation skills and analysis. To this end, we emphasize the critical evaluation of the rule or standard of law that is at issue in the case, as well as identifying its "flex points," often adjectives like "material," "prompt," and "reasonable." With these targets in mind, we work the students through the cases and problems (to illustrate the application of the rule). Importantly, these problems are contained in the text of the casebook, so that students can prepare them before class rather than wasting time figuring them out "on the fly" in class—an exercise that has little or no relationship to actual practice. The problems emphasize the litigation skill of ferreting out the legally significant facts that are known and unknown and also emphasizes the importance of the context of a dispute and the relationship that gave rise to it. Litigation is largely concerned with after the fact, *post mortem* examination and development of the facts and their application to a legal rule or rules that will establish or defeat liability. Our goal is to simulate that process, to one degree or another, in the classroom.

We find that when the students have had the opportunity to work up the problems in advance, rather than being hit by a surprise hypothetical in class, the discussion keeps moving ahead at full speed. It is always possible to vary the problem in a hypothetical in class if we feel the need to introduce additional topics, bring additional pressure to bear, or work a student through the analytical process "live." Little is gained, in our experience, by doing this all the time, however.

D. Transactional Problem-Planning

Beyond the somewhat traditional litigation-focused approach, however, a contracts course provides the opportunity to discuss what some studies indicate that over 70% of law school graduates will engage in: out-of-court transactional practice. Transactional lawyers assist clients with establishing and maintaining relationships and providing for the termination of those relationships when necessary, all with an eye toward protecting the client's interests. To this end, then, we examine the cases and problems in the book with an eye to how the parties or their lawyers could have behaved differently prior to the litigation that gave rise to the reported case and could have either avoided litigation entirely or have produced a stronger record for their client to use in court. Facts are what you make of them, both when making a record and when rolling it out in court.

Transactional lawyers should be thinking through the relationship from start to finish. They should be making sure that they advise the client at any one juncture in a way that takes into account both the present issue but also as many future potential issues as possible. One professor has likened this sort of thinking to time travel. Although clients, largely, live in the moment and want to know what to do now, the transactional lawyer should be looking all the way down the line to predict the likely ramifications of any action and what can be done to change the likely results or provide the client with additional options.

Further, transactional practice is not divorced from litigation. First, as noted above, it is the job of the transactional lawyer to be thinking about the record as it is being created in terms of later litigation. This influences the way that correspondence is worded and how negotiations take place, who is the bearer of particular pieces of news, and whether a vague, ambiguous, or unaddressed issue or term should be cleaned up in advance, etc. Second, the vast majority of all litigation ends in settlement, and often those settlements are structured to take place over time. Many involve the continued or renewed relationship of the parties. Thus, the conclusion of litigation is often itself transactional in nature. It is what we think of as transactional skills that guide counsel to propose a late payment *penalty* in writing to address the other side's concerns over prompt or timely payment, knowing that this may lay the groundwork for a later claim that the provision is an unenforceable penalty rather than an enforceable liquidated damages clause. The settlement relationship is being structured to work and, if not, to provide a useful record for the next round of litigation.

E. Modes of Jurisprudence: Formalism vs. Realism; Economic Analysis of the Law

Contracts is a particularly good course for teaching students the way styles of judging have evolved. Lloyd requires his students to read Grant Gilmore's *The Ages of American Law* as part of the course. It's a short, entertaining book with a lot of information on the way our legal system evolved. Even if you don't require the students read the book, which is Kuney's approach, it's worth acquainting them with the basic theme (which is actually explained better, though at much more length, in a number of other books, including Karl Llewellyn's *The Common Law Tradition*). The gist of it is summarized in the following paragraphs.

The way courts in the United States decide cases has gone through three distinct phases. During the first phase, which began as the colonies were being settled and extended until approximately the time of the Civil War, courts engaged in what we today sometimes call "frontier justice." There were few precedents, law books were scarce, and judges (like lawyers) were poorly trained. So courts felt free to decide cases on their own perceptions of the equities. After the Civil War, in the spirit of industrialism and the incipient period of statism, there began a period of what has been called "formalism." During the formalist period, courts developed a comprehensive system of rules derived from a few basic principles. The courts purported to apply these rules rigidly and without being influenced by sympathy, politics, and the like. The American "legal realism" movement, which began after World War I, tried to bring more discretion back into judging. The realists advocated replacing rigid rules with flexible standards. They tried to do away with rules like the statute of frauds, the parol evidence rule, and the plain meaning rule, all of which took cases away from the jury.

The essence of formalism was expressed in the teaching and writing of Christopher Columbus Langdell, who in 1870 became the first dean of the Harvard Law School. Langdell is famous (or infamous) for introducing the Socratic method to American law schools, but this was only part of a broader philosophy which regarded law as a science, similar to chemistry and physics. (It also appears to be a method to spread faculty resources as thinly over as many students as possible, thus maximizing tuition revenues while minimizing the cost of providing educational services.)

The formalists thought that law was a unified system and that all legal rules could be deduced from a few general principles. A good example of this philosophy is the pre-existing duty rule covered in Chapter 6 of this casebook. Because an agreement to modify a contract is in actuality another contract, the formalists felt it must have the same rules as all other contracts. Therefore, where a modification of the contract changed only the duties of one party, the modification was unenforceable because there was no consideration for it. But if there was even nominal consideration for the modification, the bargain, however one-sided it might be in actuality, was enforceable.

As a corollary of the idea that the law was a unified system, the formalists also embraced the idea that judges did not make new rules to fit new situations. Instead, the formalists claimed, the judge found the correct rule by deduction from more general rules and principles, in the same way that the physicists of the time derived most of their learning from Newton's laws of motion and his law of universal gravitation. Thus, the courts developing the forerunner of the doctrine of impracticability did not say: "Our rules don't cover this situation, we need to analyze the problem and develop a new rule that covers it." Instead, they "discovered" a rule providing that
where the existence of a thing is necessary for a party to perform its contractual obligations, there is an implied condition that this thing be in existence at the time for performance. (See *Taylor v. Caldwell*, the first case in Chapter 24.)

The realists took issue with these ideas. The realists believed that in any close case a good judge could find two different rules that seemingly applied to the case and would give different results. The judge would then pick the rule that gave the result he or she deemed most equitable. This, argued the realists, brought into the law the very uncertainty the formalists were trying to avoid. To remedy this, the realists proposed a number of solutions.

One solution was "narrow-issue thinking," the idea that legal rules should be pragmatic rules developed for specific situations, rather than broad rules derived from general principles without regard for the impact they would have on specific situations. Examples of such narrow-issue thinking is the realist approach to contract modification embodied in section 2-209(1) of the UCC, which provides that no consideration is necessary for contract modification, and section 89 of the Restatement (Second) of Contracts, which validates modifications without consideration made under certain circumstances.

Another realist solution was the adoption of flexible standards. This gave judges some leeway in evaluating cases but still purported to constrain them to consider only those facts the law deemed relevant. Judges were not to take into account sympathy and what Karl Llewellyn called "fireside equities."

(Recent years have seen some development of neoformalism completed with attacks on "activist judges," But that is a story for another day).

As the course progresses, students begin to see the influence of the different schools of thought in the opinions they read, and they see how different judges might approach the same problem in different ways. We talk about the need to consider these differences when litigating and when doing deals. In litigation, the lawyer needs to frame his or her argument in terms that the judge will relate to. A judge who looks at things from a formalist perspective will respond to different arguments than one who takes a realist approach.

When doing deals, the lawyer needs to remember that judges don't always think like transactional lawyers. Most lawyers in transactional practice tend to have a formalist mind set. They spell out the terms of the deal in what they think is unmistakable language and expect the courts to enforce the bargain as agreed to by competent parties. Students going into this type of practice need plenty of reminders that the judges and jurors who may be enforcing their documents don't think the same way they do. Many of them will want to ignore the language of the document in order to carry out their own notion of justice in the particular case. To make sure their documents get enforced, lawyers need to build in extra protection using recitals, representations, warranties, covenants, express conditions, events of default and remedies—protections that wouldn't be necessary if everyone were a formalist. Just as the legal standards provide a framework for later narrative development and storytelling in litigation, transactional documents provide a record of the facts from which the narrative is to be drawn.

We also try to give students a brief introduction to the law and economics movement. Law and economics practitioners apply economic reasoning, primarily neoclassical microeconomics, to legal problems. They use economic analysis both to explain why certain legal rules came about and to propose improvements to existing rules.

Classical law and economics theory begins with the basic tenet that humans are rational maximizers of their individual satisfactions (monetary and otherwise). As such, they respond to incentives. Thus, a main goal of law and economics theorists is to structure legal rules in such a way that they provide individuals and organizations with incentives to act in a way that is best for society as a whole. This is relatively uncontroversial. More controversial is the position of many law and economics theorists that the goal of the legal system should be the most efficient allocation of resources (as opposed to, say, the most "equitable" allocation).

While much of the scholarly writing in law and economics now relies on advanced economic theories which are beyond the grasp of most law faculty, let alone most law students, the average student can still get a lot from learning to apply some very basic economic concepts to legal problems. Many of these concepts are so basic that they seem intuitive to most law teachers. Nevertheless, students need to be reminded of them and supplied with shorthand names for them. For instance, economics has sometimes been defined as the study of the way society allocates scarce resources. So in our policy discussions we remind students that the law doesn't operate in a world of unlimited resources. We have to consider not only the benefits of a proposed legal rule, but the costs as well. We also introduce the concept of the market as a method of allocating these resources and as a method of determining value. This can be done in simple ways, such as pointing out the inconsistency when a party claims a high value for an item but the facts show that she was unable to sell it in the market for that price. The notion of the "least cost insurer" is also useful, especially when discussing the allocation of risk using representations and warranties.

The casebook includes a number of opinions by Circuit Judges Frank Easterbrook and Richard Posner. These judges are not only leaders in the law and economics movement, but are also former law professors as well. Their opinions are usually entertaining. Rather than using economics jargon, they make commonsense economic arguments in a conversational style. Easterbrook opinions are often quite opinionated, but Posner, unlike most American judges, often presents both sides of the issue and doesn't treat difficult questions as if they were slam dunks.

III. Sample Lecture Notes & Considerations

The following lecture notes are provided to help instructors formulate their class presentations. As a result, they are not universal, complete or "correct" for all classes. They do, however, give you an idea of what Kuney and Lloyd think is important about the materials and provide model "answers" or discussion points for the casebook's problems, questions, and notes.

CHAPTER 1

THE OBJECTIVE THEORY OF CONTRACTS— STANDARDS, ELEMENTS, AND FACTORS

— ♦ —

Go over structure of a contract from the introduction so that students can see one "for real." Talk about the provisions and their purpose. Then let them know that the Contracts I course is not about whole, real contracts. Rather, much of the course is about the legal doctrines that will apply when the parties have not addressed terms or circumstances in their documentation. But keep the contract in mind as it shows the transactional structure to which this course material relates.

Suggestions for How to Succeed in this Course:

1.   **Be prepared. Do the reading.** Actively. *Either brief or book brief the cases.* You should be able to respond to the following questions regarding each case you read:

   a.   What are the **facts**? Who are the parties? Who did or did not do what to or for whom, when? This is all the pre-suit stuff.

   b.   What is the **procedural history** of the case? What was the court below doing?

   c.   What is the **holding** and **disposition** of the case itself? The disposition is the easy part: affirmed, reversed, in whole or in part, remanded with instructions, etc. The holding is the rule of law that, when applied to the facts, leads to the disposition.

   d.   Is there **anything else important** here? Reasoning? Policy? Collection of cases? Majority and minority rules? Anything? But this comes last!

   e.   How could I use the rule of law discussed here when planning for a client or drafting a contract? Think ahead.

Do not wait for the end of the semester to cram—the undergraduate formula—largely based upon regurgitation of memorized information—that got you here will not work with the same degree of success. You all got good grades before. Some of you are going to get C's or perhaps lower grades this semester. This is not a reflection on you, personally and absolutely - *it is a reflection on your performance in this course on particular examinations, on particular days, relative to that of the others in the section.* We grade your work product, not you. But you are responsible for your work product.

2. *This course is more about thinking, reasoning, and analysis than black letter law.* Keep that in mind for guidance. But, make no mistake, extracting the rules from the cases, understanding them, and synthesizing them so you can apply them to new problems and situations is important. Knowing the black letter law is a necessary but not sufficient condition for success. It is critical to master effective *deployment* of that black letter law.

3. *At the end of each chapter, review the material and your notes, and try to pull together the rules and analyses applicable to that chapter.* You can outline if you want to—it works for some, not for others. Some benefit from organizing the material into graphical flow charts. Some make flash cards. Some benefit from extended discussion. Find what works for you.

4. *Study and do the reading independently but then discuss it with a friend or two.* Try *teaching* each other the material. If you can't explain it to them so that they understand, you don't get it either.

5. *See me early on if you are having difficulty with the material.* There is no shame in doing so. If you want to be sure of getting me, please make an appointment by e-mailing my assistant. I will also respond to e-mail inquiries, usually within 24 hours.

6. I expect you to reason and apply your knowledge from day one. People will soon be paying you for your judgment and knowledge—time to gain and exercise them now.

Any Questions?

What is a contract and how is it different from an agreement or an arrangement in general?

Digging for "a promise that the law will enforce."

There must be an offer and an acceptance. Usually not an issue, but sometimes it really is in practice and it *often* is in law school. Kuney once litigated a case for 2 years that was about whether or not there was an offer and an acceptance in a purported $52 million real estate transaction in which both sides were represented by sophisticated counsel.

The Objective Theory of Contracts—What is that?

Dig for "objective" = reasonable person's understanding of the circumstances. Probe "objective"; is it really objective in a universal sense? Like a ruler? (no.) Or is there cultural subjectivity built-in? (necessarily). In other words, is the "reasonable person" that is the key to the "objective" theory of contracts him or herself a "subjective" construct based on prevailing social norms within the decision maker's cultural norm? Is the "objective" theory of contract really more of a "collective subjective, context specific" standard? Would a "wise latina woman" use the same reasonable person contract as Oliver Wendell Holmes?

♦ - - ♦

Introductory Exercise

Go over Restatement (Second) of Contracts section 24. Students break R2d § 24 into three elements and then apply it to the examples.

a.   "I'll sell you my car for $1,000." *Yes. A reasonable person would believe that this is an offer to exchange the car for $1,000.*

b.   "I'm thinking of selling my car for $1,000." *No. A person could not reasonably believe that this is an offer. The speaker is merely stating what he is thinking about doing.*

c.   "I'm going to sell my car for $1,000." *No. A person could not reasonably believe that this is an offer. The speaker is merely stating what he is planning to do.*

d.   "Would you give me $1,000 for my car?" *Maybe. On its own, the statement may indicate that the speaker is trying to feel out whether his price is reasonable, which would not be an offer to sell. This is the kind of statement that might be used if people were bargaining, however, and could be construed as an offer or counteroffer in that context.*

So, what is the objective theory of contract? What is the alternative?

The subjective theory of contract - which crept in a bit in the "meeting of the minds" standard that is sometimes mentioned. **Is that workable?** (Maybe, but it is pretty difficult. Especially once we allow parties to testify on their own behalf; which means allowing the parties to shade the truth on their own behalf or lie).

♦ - - ♦

Lucy v. Zehmer
Supreme Court of Virginia
196 Va. 493, 84 S.E.2d 516 (1954)

IRAC & Classic Brief Categories, below.

Facts: See text - what is the story? Let's see what each witness testifies to and *put it on the board.* Note how everybody involved has a slightly different view of the facts.

13

Procedure: Court below took evidence at trial and apparently concluded that there was no contract and refused to grant specific performance to Lucy. [para. 4].

Disposition: Reversed and remanded with instructions to order Specific Performance (what is that?) [para. 34].

Holding/Rule/Reasoning: A contract was formed. Objective theory of contract is used here. There is no need for a subjective meeting of the minds in actuality. Reasonable interpretation of words and actions is enough. [paras. 27 and 30].

Note that once legislatures started allowing parties to testify, the potential for perjury makes a subjective intent standard all but impossible to administer. In *Lucy v. Zehmer*, the only witness other than the parties was the waitress and her testimony is neither here nor there, really.

Conclude: Contract = an agreement the law will enforce. Bottom Line: Whether there is a contract is determined with reference to the "Objective Theory of Contract," which asks whether a reasonable and disinterested person watching and listening to the parties would conclude that a contract was formed, and if so, the law will conclude it was.

NOTES AND QUESTIONS

1. **What facts and circumstances led the court to conclude that Lucy and Zehmer had a contract?**

The facts which led the court to conclude that a contract had been made included:

(1) Zehmer claimed to be drunk, but attempted to testify in great detail about the events of the evening, which the court found to be inconsistent [para. 21];

(2) the final agreement was written in the plural and was signed by Mr. & Mrs. Zehmer, and there were no readily apparent spelling errors [para. 22];

(3) the forty minute discussion which led to the contract, rewriting of the first draft of the document, discussion of what was to be included in the sale provision for title examination, the completeness of the document; and

(4) the fact that Lucy took the document without any demand from Zehmer that he return it [para. 23].

2. **What facts and circumstances could be used to argue they did not have a contract?**

That Lucy had offered to purchase Zehmer's farm on more than one previous occasion, and Zehmer had always refused or backed out [para. 5, 10]; that during deliberations, Zehmer seemed to doubt that Lucy had $50,000 [para. 6, 11]; that the parties were drinking [para. 7, 10]; and that Zehmer told his wife that it was just a joke [para. 13] may be used to argue that a contract was not formed.

3. At what point in the discussion were Lucy and Zehmer bound to a contract?

When Lucy said he would give $50,000 for the farm, after Lucy said, "I bet you wouldn't take $50,000 for that place," and Zehmer said, "Yes, I would, too. You wouldn't give fifty." [para. 5]. Or, when the document was signed by both Zehmer and his wife? The later is particularly true if the statute of frauds applies, as it did, but we haven't covered that yet.

4. Is what Lucy and Zehmer said and did on Sunday and Monday relevant to the question of whether or not they had formed a contract on Saturday night?

No, what each party did the next day has no bearing on whether the contract was formed. The contract was already formed (or not) by that time. Each party's behavior may help to indicate whether he thought the contract was a serious business transaction, but it has nothing to do with whether the contract was actually formed the night before.

5.& 6. The quotes from *Kabil* and *Hotchkiss*.

The circumstances described in each quote are different. In the Kabil quote, the court describes a situation in which each party thinks that the other party does not want to form a contract. There are no secret intentions in this case, because each party's intention is known to the other party.

In the Hotchkiss quote, neither of the parties believes that the other party means to agree. However, the other party does not mean to form a contract, even though his outward behavior indicates that he does.

Learned Hand's statement is a reflection of the objective theory of contracts. It doesn't matter what a person is secretly thinking if the other person is reasonable in believing that the other wants to enter a contract.

◆ - - ◆

Embry v. Hargadine, McKittrick Dry Goods Co.
Court of Appeals of Missouri
127 Mo. App. 383 (1907)

"Go ahead, you're alright. Get your men out, and don't let that worry you."

Who is the appellant? The employee. **So, who won at trial?**
Employer, as this is an intermediate appellate court, this is an automatic. But
this is kind of interesting—the jury evidently believed the employer more than
they believed the employee. They observed the witnesses and were in the best
position to evaluate their credibility. **Why is the Appellate court wading in
to change the result?** They do it by focusing on the instruction that required a
finding of actual, subjective intent by both parties—a question of law—and they
reverse.

What was going on here—state the facts.

Written contract of employment for managing the sample department of
the dry goods company. $2,000 per year. Set to expire December 15, 1903.

Plaintiff claims that he was re-engaged by respondent (what happened to
appellee? Ct. changes nomenclature), by its president (all corporations have to
act through people).

But then he was discharged in March, received notice in February.
President blames the board of directors (what is that, how does that work, do a
little corporate law and a little practical reality about limited authority and how
it can be used to provide excuses and to shield individuals from criticism and
responsibility).

So, what is plaintiff's theory of recovery?

Based on the objective theory of contract, the contract was renewed. He
had been requesting renewal from the president for some time and was being put
off. Thus, when the president said, "Go ahead, you're all right. Get your men out,
and don't let that worry you"—an objective, reasonable third party, viewing the
transaction as a whole, would have concluded that there was a contract. End of
story.

Did the trial court agree? No. It issued an instruction to the jury to
the effect that it had to find, not only that the conversation occurred as
plaintiff/appellant stated, *but that both parties intended through the conversation
to contract with each other!* [para. 3]. This is issue #1 in the case.

**Did the parties disagree as to the terms of the contract that was
either entered into or not entered into?** No. Thus, before the appellate court
is no question of fact, just of law. Was the subjective intent of both parties
required to make a contract? No.

What is the holding of the case on issue #1? The secret, subjective
intent of the parties is not the test of whether or not they had a contract. The test
is whether an objective observer, a "reasonable person" would think that the
parties made the contract. [para. 4, second half].

Why? **Why should we not care about secret intent? Why should we not require a subjective meeting of the minds?** Objective standard is necessary for administration of justice, esp. once we allow the parties to testify themselves. Dangers of perjury and lies, lies, lies! **Other reasons?**

What is issue #2 in this case? Whether or not, Embry, as a reasonable man, might consider himself employed for another year based upon the conversation. Court says he could and should. **What do you think?**

So, what does the court do? Reverses and remands to the trial court. **What will that court do?** Retrial. **Really? Actually, won't the parties settle? Why or why not?**

If you were Mr. Embry, would you have thought you were employed for another year?

NOTES AND QUESTIONS

1. B sues A for breach of contract. B testifies as follows: "A said to me: 'I'll sell you my car for $1,000.' I told him 'It's a deal.'" A testifies that what he said was "I'm thinking of selling my car. **Do you think I can get $1,000 for it?" Is there a contract?**

According to the *Embry* court, should the question of whether there was a contract be decided by the judge or by the jury? Is it a question of fact or a question of law? What is the difference, both in terms of who makes the original determination on the question and in terms of the standard of review that may be employed on appeal?

The question of whether there was a contract here depends on which of the parties' testimony is adopted as "the truth." This is a question of fact that should be decided by a jury (or a judge in a bench trial). The question of fact here will involve assessing witness credibility and any other factual matters introduced as evidence. If A's version of events is accepted as true, there is no contract. If B's version prevails, there is. A question of fact determined by a jury generally may not be reviewed by an appellate court assuming there is supporting evidence in the record. A question of fact determined by a judge in a bench trial is reviewed under a narrow standard, generally "abuse of discretion" or "substantial evidence." Questions of law are broadly reviewable on appeal, generally under a "de novo" standard whether or not a jury is involved—after all, if it is a question of law, it doesn't depend upon the evidence and the appellate court is in as good a position as the trial judge to answer the legal question. Maybe even a better position, being away from the passion and drama (such as it is) of trial!

2. "I think we may have a deal." **Offer? Acceptance?**

Neither. But a useful question to foreshadow acceptance as well as offer under the objective theory of contracts.

PROBLEM 1-1

Bobby hears that Andy and Sylvia have broken up, so he asks Sylvia for a date. Needing someone to talk to, Sylvia says yes. Wanting to make a great impression, Bobby spends $600 for a new suit, $400 for two floor-level tickets for the Knicks game, $175 for a limo and $75 for a bottle of champagne. He also has his apartment cleaned for the first time since his girlfriend moved out four months ago. Two hours before she is supposed to meet Bobby, Sylvia reconciles with Andy. She calls Bobby and tells him she can't go out with him. Bobby threatens to sue her for breach of contract.

Does he have a case?

What would a reasonable person think, in terms of the R2d § 24 standard? Bobby might have a case if he can prove that Sylvia knew he was going to spend all that money and they made the deal with that in mind, but it's probably not a very strong case. On the other hand, people don't usually go to court when someone breaks a date. If they did, the courts would be a lot busier than they already are. It may be that no reasonable person would ever conclude that an agreement to go on a date was a contract, or at least a contract that was irrevocable and not subject to cancellation. Does it matter what year it is when all this occurs? "Dating rules" change over time. Does this matter?

A New Jersey judge, when presented with a similar case said: "This is a question for Miss Manners, not for the courts of this state. That case involved a teen who sued her ex-boyfriend for the cost of an unused prom dress ($244). The court held that "law and sound public policy limit legal remedies in cases involving a social agreement." The judge further observed that "[e]ven a promise for the ultimate 'date'—a wedding—can be broken without legal liability. Miss Manners, Not Court, Forum for Spurned Date, The National Law Journal A 23, June 22, 1998.

PROBLEM 1-2

Rex and Teresa LeGalley of Albuquerque, New Mexico executed a 16-page "contract" governing virtually all aspects of their marriage. Among other things (many other things) the document provides:

(1)   Shoes will be left in the garage when entering the house.

(2)   Lights will be turned out at 11:30 p.m. and the parties will rise promptly at 6:30 a.m.

(3)   Lunches will be taken to work (not bought) whenever possible.

(4)   Gas tanks in vehicles owned by the parties will not be allowed to go below half full, and only premium grade gasoline will be used in these vehicles.

(5)   When driving, the parties will maintain a separation from the vehicle in front by a distance of at least one car length for each 10 miles per hour of speed.

Suppose that Ms. LeGalley has been tailgating and letting the gas run to a quarter tank or less lately. **Can Mr. LeGalley go to court and get an injunction requiring her to keep a safe distance and fill up more often?**

If the contract has a typical "events of defaults and remedies" section, can Mr. LeGalley give Ms. LeGalley a notice of default, opportunity to cure the default, and then exercise remedies, which include assessing monetary fines and imposing additional household chores on her?

The parties in this situation explicitly agreed in writing to behave in a certain way. One of the parties is now failing to meet those requirements in blatant violation of that agreement. But what's supposed to happen if they don't behave the way they agreed to in the contract? Is it a condition of their marriage? Does that mean they automatically get divorced if they don't follow their rules? Why does Mr. LeGalley need to go to court to get an injunction? Couldn't he just ask his wife to follow the rules?

This was a negotiated deal. The LeGalleys may have been motivated by issues that had arisen in their prior marriages. The "contract" also provided that:

We will engage in "healthy sex" three to five times a week. Teresa will stay on birth control for two years after we are married and then will try to get pregnant. Teresa can have. . . a maximum of three pregnancies. After the third pregnancy, we will both get sterilized.

We won't raise voices or get snappy.

We will count to 10 first, if we get angry.

Nothing will be left on the floor overnight, unless packing for a trip.

If Robert and/or Brandon (their children from previous marriages) elect to live with us, they will have a bedroom even if they share one.

While Robert and Brandon don't live with us, they will be treated as guests when they come to visit. Sleeping arrangements will be on an availability basis. They will be expected to help out around the house and obey the house rules.

Allowances should be $10/week per child for their school lunches - if they choose to pack their lunch, they can keep the money. Each child can earn an additional $10/week to supplement their allowance.

Robert and Brandon shall be referred to as "our boys" or "my kids."

The children shall have a free ride through college – resident tuition, books, transportation, room, and meal ticket at the cafeteria.

If they keep good grades (3.0/4.0), they may have a part-time job.

We will take the children on one good vacation per year.

Reproduced in Icon Thoughtstyle Magazine, September/October 1998.

As to an events of default provision and a remedies section—more on that in later chapters but be thinking about it a little now.

♦ - - ♦

Leonard v. Pepsico, Inc.
United States District Court, Southern District, New York
88 F. Supp. 2d 116 (1999)

Facts? See Case. Judge Kimba Wood lays them out well.

Procedural Context? Motion for Summary Judgment by Defendant (Pepsico) in an action seeking specific performance of an alleged offer of a Harrier Jet from the Pepsi Stuff ads.

Hold on. What is a motion for summary judgment? Explain and identify the standard for granting it: [paras. 14 and 15]. Civil Procedure less probably will not have covered this yet.

General: Viewing the evidence in the light most favorable to the non-moving party, there are no genuine issues of material fact and movant is entitled to judgment as a matter of law.

Specific: The question of whether or not a contract was formed is appropriate for resolution on summary judgment when words and actions that allegedly formed the contract are so clear themselves that reasonable people could not differ over their meaning.

What is Summary Judgment all about? Efficient administration of justice and positioning the case so that it is amenable to resolution. This requires breaking down plaintiff's causes of action to their elements, doing discovery (what is that?) to establish either the existence or non-existence of facts to meet each element, and then packaging that as a motion and supporting documents to present the substantive issues in a procedural device to the judge, who then functions, in theory, like a little machine and spits out an order and possibly an opinion that either grants or denies, in whole or in part, the motion brought.

On the defense side, if you can't position your client to win on summary judgment, most of the time, your client has, in some sense, already lost.

20

Issue? Was the "Pepsi Stuff" commercial an offer that was capable of acceptance?

Holding? No. Dismiss case. [para. 16] – nice thesis paragraph. No objective person could reasonably have concluded that the commercial actually offered consumers a Harrier Jet. If it is clear that an offer was not serious, then no offer has been made.

Was this a jury question like the sexual harassment case [para. 20]? No. Federal judges are competent re: commercials and contracts, but their jobs are somewhat isolating – their knowledge of acceptable interpersonal contacts and communications in the modern workplace may be more limited.

Note structure of opinion – this is good writing! Point it out. Map it on the board. Show IRAC. Show IRAC. Show IRAC. Walk through the reasoning of the case starting even with the sections that have been edited out – just to note the omitted issues, note the structure.

Requests for additional discovery. What was that about? (1) evidence of subsequent changes to ad to increase points needed and then to add "(just kidding)" – not pertinent to seriousness of the offer at the time it was communicated; and (2) discovery re: how defendant itself understood the offer is irrelevant – subjective intent does not govern (note plaintiff's strategy here is to keep the matter open and uncertain and generate a question of fact by taking depositions and finding some peg to hang a hat on to boost settlement value or, maybe, get the matter to a jury).

NOTES AND QUESTIONS

1. When Leonard tried to accept the "offer," he was represented by counsel. **Should the court then determine whether a reasonable person would have thought his assent to the bargain is invited and would conclude it, or should the standard be whether a reasonable person represented by a reasonable lawyer would have thought so?**

The general rule is not what a reasonable person with a reasonable lawyer would believe, but what a reasonable person would believe. Also, the offer (if there is one) is not being made to a lawyer, but to the viewer of the commercial. The viewer's lawyer wouldn't accept the offer, the viewer would. However, the involvement of a lawyer at an early stage in the process seems to indicate that Leonard knew he might have trouble getting Pepsi to provide him with a Harrier jet. If Leonard really believed that the offer was legitimate, why did he hire a lawyer before he even turned in his order form?

2. One professor has suggested that the court should have found a contract in *Leonard* in order to discourage deceptive advertising. Ignore, for purposes of this question, how that is impractical for a variety of reasons and assume for

purposes of this question that the ad was deceptive. **Should the court then have found there to be a contract?**

In this case, it was not up to the court to determine that the ad was deceptive, or that deceptive advertising should be discouraged. Leonard apparently had not brought such a cause of action. He brought a breach of contract action. The court's task was to determine only whether a contract had been formed i.e., to determine the controversy presented to it by the parties. Unlike some civil law or other systems, the American judiciary is not generally impressed with a license to ride the range doing "justice" as it sees fit. Rather, its function is to determine justiciable issues presented to it by parties with standing; the court would be overstepping the bounds to find a contract where there legally isn't one just to punish a practice it doesn't like. One can explore the role of the judiciary vs. that of the legislative and executive branches at this juncture.

3. Mr. Leonard would not have ended up with a working jet even had the court found an offer. In 1997, the Pentagon announced that the Harrier was not for sale in flying condition. Before any of the Marine aircraft could be offered to the public, they would have to be "demilitarized" which would have meant removal of all weapons and weapons systems as well as disabling the ability to take off and land vertically, which would make flying one impossible.

◆ - - ◆

PROBLEM 1-3

Jodee Berry sued the owners of the restaurant at which she worked for breach of contract. According to the complaint filed in the case, her manager told the waitresses that whoever sold the most food and beverages at each participating location during the month of April would be entered in a drawing for a new Toyota. Over the course of the month, the manager allegedly told the waitresses that he didn't know whether the prize would be a Toyota car, truck, or van, but the winner would have to pay the registration fees on the vehicle. In May, the manager informed Ms. Berry that she was the lucky winner. He blindfolded her and led her to the parking lot. Waiting for her there was a doll of the Star Wars character "Yoda." Ms. Berry was informed that she was the proud winner of a "toy Yoda."

Ms. Berry was unable to see the humor in the situation. She sued. **Should she win?** *See* Keith A. Rowley, *You Asked For It, You Got It...Toy Yoda: Practical Jokes, Prizes, and Contract Law,* 3 NEV. L. J. 526 (2003).

The manager was misleading by telling the waitresses that the winner would have to pay the registration fees for the prize (Star Wars action figures do not need registration), and by saying it would be a car, truck, or van.

The manager appears to have had a secret intention that was not obvious to Ms. Berry. If Ms. Berry was reasonable in believing that the contest was for a

Toyota and not for a toy Yoda, then the manager should be held to that offer, which she accepted by performance.

Jodee Barry settled her lawsuit on undisclosed terms. Her attorney told the press that, while he could not disclose the settlement's details, his client could now go to the dealership and "pick out whatever type of Toyota she wants." Former Hooters waitress settles Toyota suit, USA TODAY, May 9, 2002.

PROBLEM 1-4

Read UNIDROIT article 4.2. **Is that standard consistent with the "objective theory of contract" that is the topic of this chapter?**

UNIDROIT article 4.2 is largely consistent with the objective theory of contracts. Section 2 is essentially the theory. Section 1 applies to what a party DID know or MUST HAVE known about the other party's intentions. If the party knew what the other party was thinking, it is not a secret intention.

Note how UNIDROIT article 4.2 begins with the narrow private meaning and makes the broad exception the understanding of a reasonable person.

However, whether a party knew something or could not have been unaware of something is somewhat suggestive of a subjective standard. How do you show that someone else "had to have been thinking" something? We don't have thought bubbles hovering around our heads like in the cartoons. (Too bad. It would make class time more interesting to say the least.) "What a party is actually thinking" isn't the "reasonable person" standard described in the objective theory of contracts.

PROBLEM 1-5

Consider an American importer that contracts with a German company to supply it with commercial quantities of chickens, which it intended to resell to restaurant supply companies for resale to their customers. The contract is governed by U.S. law and simply provides for the supply of chicken at various rates for various sizes of birds (e.g., 2.5 to 3 lbs, $120 per 100 lbs.). When the chickens arrive in the U.S., the importer discovers that they are what it would call "old, stewing chickens" and it claims that it had meant young chickens, suitable for broiling and frying. It claims the German company is in breach of its contract. The German company protests that it has supplied just what the contract called for – chickens. **How will this dispute be resolved under the objective theory of contracts?**

This is, of course, the Frigaliment Importing *case from chapter 15, and most of the various arguments that can be made are found in that case. Foreshadowing issues of interpretation in addition to formation under the objective theory of contracts is the point of this problem. The issue is taken up starting in chapter 14, dealing with the parol evidence rule, and then in chapter 15, dealing with the four-corners rule, ambiguity, and interpretation, but it is nice to raise it now.*

Lawyering Skills Problem: Summarizing and Synthesizing

1. Summarize. If you have not done so already, boil down the holdings of each of the cases and problems in this chapter to no more than five, and preferably three, sentences of ordinary length written in plain English. These summaries should be generalizations that can be separated from the specific facts of the cases and problems so you can use them to analyze other sets of facts.

2. Synthesize. Take the summaries from the first part of this exercise and blend them together into a coherent statement of the law of the objective theory of contract. You should aim to be able to do this in no more than six to ten sentences of ordinary length written in plain English.

If you have students turn this assignment in, you can evaluate their skills in this area and give them both a head start in their legal drafting or legal process classes and a hint that such classes are perhaps the most important class of their first year, given their overlap with the rest of the curriculum, outlining, and exam taking.

♦ - - ♦

Summing up Chapter 1, should you choose to do so rather than leaving the students with the Lawyering Skills Problem above: What do we have here, in these three cases? What are our "take away points"? Work these up on the board. (This is a good thing to do for Chapter 1 — but make it clear you are going to turn this all over to the students in subsequent chapters. Show once and relinquish responsibility to the students.)

Title: Objective Theory of Contracts

Black Letter Law:

1. A contract is an agreement that the law will enforce.

2. **Lucy v. Zehmer:** The law does not look into the subjective, secret heart of the parties but instead uses what we call an "objective test": a reasonable person standard. We ask whether a reasonable and disinterested person watching and listening to the parties would conclude that a contract was formed; if so, the law will conclude that it was.

3. **Embry v. Hargadine, McKittrick Dry Goods Co.:** The subjective, secret intent of the parties does not matter in the inquiry as to whether there was a contract or not. The applicable test is that of an objective observer, a reasonable person. Note a little bit of the concept of "reasonable reliance" working its way into this opinion – this will show up later in doctrines called detrimental reliance or promissory estoppel – just note it for now.

4. **Leonard v. Pepsico:** Objective Person Standard applied to a television commercial and a finding that there was no offer if there was no way that a reasonable, objective person could reasonably have concluded that the commercial actually offered consumers a Harrier Jet.

CHAPTER 2

HAS AN OFFER BEEN MADE?

— ♦ —

Factors and Elements – comment to reinforce these methods of structuring a legal standard and how it fits with legal reasoning as a model of IRACing. The key is to break the facts down, lay them out, and match them (or not) to the standard—that is a major part of the "practice of law" and "thinking like a lawyer."

FACTORS v. ELEMENTS

Lonergan v. Scolnick
District Court of Appeal, Fourth District, California
129 Cal. App. 2d 179, 276 P.2d 8 (1954)

Among other things, the case illustrates the principle that where a person sends a communication to multiple recipients, but has only one thing to sell, a reasonable person receiving the communication would not expect it to be an offer.

The opinion is strange—Trial court says Apr 8 letter is an offer (paragraph beginning "the matter was submitted") and next to last sentence of opinion says that was "the most reasonable" interpretation. But the appellate court seems to have thought it wasn't. Elsewhere they seem to say there was no offer.

March ?	Ad published
March 26	Seller (defendant) writes letter describing property, giving directions, rock bottom price --(good pun Joshua tree is a rock-climbing center) $2500-- "This is a form letter."
April 7	Buyer (plaintiff) writes saying he's not sure he found the property, asking for legal description (explain), asking if bank is OK for escrow agent "Should I desire to purchase."
April 8	Seller writes "you have found property. Bank is OK for escrow agent." "If you are really interested, you will have to move fast as I expect to have a buyer in the next week or so."
April 12	Seller sells property to someone else.
April 14	Buyer gets Seller's letter of April 8.
April 15	Buyer writes saying he will put the money into escrow "in conformity with your offer."
April 17	Buyer opens escrow.

27

Trial Court finds that April 8 letter was a conditional offer, the condition being prompt acceptance, plaintiff did not meet the condition, thus, no contract.

Court of Appeals affirms, but for a different reason: it finds that the April 8 letter was merely an extension of the prior advertisement, *which was not an offer but an invitation to receive offers.* Thus, no offer, no ability to accept, no contract, no specific performance.

Let's do the facts and look for offers. And let's look at the parties' actions as they do this commercial courtship dance – for that is what it is, with a little bit of "checking each other out," a little bit of "tease," and a little bit of attempted "gottcha" going on.

NOTES AND QUESTIONS

1. The way to analyze a case like *Lonergan v. Scolnick* is to look at each communication and determine whether or not it was an offer. Make a table with column headings *Date/Time, From, To, Substance,* and *Analysis.* List each of the communications about the Joshua Tree land on this chart. Make sure that you can explain why each communication here either was or was not an offer using the standards of R2d § 24 and UNIDROIT Article 2.2. Be prepared to explain why each communication was or was not an offer under either standard.

March 1952	*Defendant places advertisement.*
Unknown Date	*New York resident (plaintiff) writes to ask for more information.*
March 26	*Defendant responds, briefly describing the property, giving directions, stating that his rock bottom price . was $2,500 cash and further stating that this was a form letter.*
April 7	*Plaintiff writes back asking for legal description, asking whether it was all level land or included some jutting rocks, and suggesting a certain bank as escrow agent.*
April 8 *This is the trial court's "conditional offer" and the court of appeals' "further invitation to receive offers."*	*Defendant writes back "from your description you have found the property: and that the specified bank is "Ok for escrow agent," that the land was fairly level, giving the legal description, and then saying "if you are really interested, you will have to decide fast, as I expect to have a buyer in the next week or so."*
April 12	*Defendant sells to another for $2,500.*
April 14	*Plaintiff get April 8 letter.*
April 15	*Plaintiff says thanks for confirming land location, I will immediately open escrow and deposit $2,500 and please forward deed with instructions to the escrow agent.*
April 17	*Plaintiff opens escrow.*

An alternative, more detailed format follows:

Date	To	Substance	Analysis – Restatement	Analysis - UNIDROIT
March 1952	Readers of LA Paper	"Joshua Tree vic. 40 acres...need cash, will sacrifice."	Not an offer. Another person would not be justified in thinking that assent to the bargain would conclude it.	Not an offer. Insufficiently definite: leaves out price, location.
March ?	Defendant	Inquiry about property mentioned in advertisement	Not an offer. Merely a request for information. No reason to think that assent would conclude the bargain.	Not an offer. Merely a request for information. Insufficiently definite.
March 26	Plaintiff	Description of property, directions to property, lowest price, "This is a form letter."	Not an offer. Provides information, does not indicate that assent will conclude the bargain.	Not an offer. "Form letter" indicates that the defendant send the same information to more than one person.
April 7	Defendant	Request for verification that property had been found, legal description, suggesting an escrow agent "Should I desire to purchase the land."	Not an offer. "Should I..." indicates that more action would be needed from both parties to conclude the bargain.	Not an offer. Specifically indicates that the plaintiff is not bound and does not intend to be bound by the document, with the "Should I desire to purchase the land" statement.
April 8	Plaintiff	Confirmation on that property found, approval of escrow agent, "You will have to decide fast, as I expect to have a buyer in the next	Maybe an offer. Defendant manifested willingness to enter a bargain. However, a person would not be justified in	Maybe an offer. The specific terms have been established in previous documents. The defendant indicated

		week."	thinking that mere assent would conclude the matter – a person would have to be the FIRST person to assent.	willingness to be bound, either to plaintiff or a third party, by "next week."
April 12		Sells property to third party.		
April 14	Plaintiff receives April 8 letter.			
April 15	Defendant	Thanks for letter confirming that he was on the right land, notification that plaintiff was opening an escrow account, request for defendant to send deed.	Not an offer. This is a manifestation of willingness to enter into a bargain, but doesn't justify another person in understanding that his assent will conclude it. The letter assumes that assent has already been given and the contract has already been formed.	Not an offer. The terms are sufficiently definite, and does indicate the intention of the plaintiff to be bound. However, the letter does not invite an acceptance in response, it assumes that the bargain has already been made.

2. Did the trial court think that the letter of April 8 was an offer? Did the Court of Appeals think it was?

The Trial Court concluded that the April 8 letter was an offer with the condition that the plaintiff accept the offer promptly, which he didn't do [para. 5].

The Appeals Court did not conclude that the April 8 letter was an offer, "The letter of April 8 added nothing in the way of a definite offer" [para. 8].

♦ - - ♦

Lefkowitz v. Great Minneapolis Surplus Store, Inc.
Supreme Court of Minnesota
251 Minn. 188, 86 N.W.2d 689 (1957)

Ads for $1 minks and other coats for first to appear. Store claims according to "house rules" it is for ladies only.

Trial court, for plaintiff, in part. Disallows claim on the first ad as the coat values were not stated so damages would be speculative and uncertain, but on the second ad, where value was given, give judgment to the plaintiff for value stated less the $1 purchase price.

Court of appeals affirms.

But I thought advertisements were just invitations to receive offers, not offers themselves, which would be capable of acceptance. What gives?! "Reward" case or offer of unilateral contract accepted by performance (showing up first).

QUESTION

What was it that allowed the advertisement in *Lefkowitz* to be an offer when the advertisement in *Lonergan* was not an offer?

The ads in Lefkowitz were clear, definite, and explicit, and left nothing open for negotiation [para. 10]. A person could reasonably expect that by being the first person to show up and ask for it, he could purchase the fur coat for the amount listed in the ad, i.e., his performance would constitute assent to the deal and conclude it. R2d §24.

The ad in Lonergan was not clear, definite, or explicit. It merely stated that some land was for sale for cash and that the owner was willing to sell the land for a relatively low price [Lonergan, para. 4]. It did not say what that price was or where exactly the land was. A person wishing to "accept" such an offer would have to get more information before being able to reasonably believe that her assent to the bargain was invited and would conclude it.

The Test from Williston [para. 8]: *Whether the facts show that some performance was promised in positive terms in return for something requested. If so, then it is not an invitation to make an offer but an offer itself capable of acceptance.*

♦ - - ♦

Courteen Seed Co. v. Abraham
Supreme Court of Oregon
129 Ore. 427 (1929)

Trial court found contract and found for plaintiff; this court reverses finding no offer and thus no acceptance, no contract, no damages. Let's do the facts carefully. Who did a timeline? Check hands and consider asking those with hands up to construct the time line on the board. You can also hand one out later.

Courteen Seed.

Note that the facts are out of order in the opinion.

Sep. 21	Seller (defendant) mails out samples in envelopes with words: "Red clover, like sample. I am asking 24 cents per, f.o.b., Amity Oregon."
unspecified	Buyer (plaintiff) responds saying it has plenty and will wait.
Oct. 4	Seller needs buyers and writes plaintiff. (Court doesn't tell us exact language.)
Oct. 8	Buyer wires: "Your price too high. Wire firm offer, naming absolutely lowest f.o.b."
Oct. 8	Seller wires back--"I am asking 23 cents per pound for the car of red clover from which your sample was taken . . . Have an offer 22 ¾ per pound, f.o.b. Amity."

NOTES AND QUESTIONS

1. The court makes much of the fact that the seller used the word "asking" instead of the word "offer." It should be clear by now that you do not have to use the word "offer" to make an offer. Nobody used that word in *Lucy* or in *Embry*. In fact, in some contexts, "ask" and "offer" are considered synonyms. For instance, stock traders use the term "asked price" for the price at which people are offering to sell a stock. **There is something in this case that makes the ask/offer dichotomy important. What is it?**

*In the telegram that was allegedly the offer, the defendant stated that it was "asking 23 cents per pound," and referred to "an offer of 22 3/4 per pound." Because they are different words, and used in the same telegram, the court concludes that the writer of the telegram must have meant to convey two different concepts [para. 7]. This is a tough principle -- using the same words to mean the same thing every time as different words suggest a different meaning – to get right, even for lawyers. **Is it fair to use this principle to interpret the communications of lay persons?***

32

2. It is often useful to make a timeline showing the facts of the case in chronological order, together with the date on which each event occurred. This is especially useful when the facts are complex or when (as in *Courteen Seed*) the court, parties, or witnesses relate them out of chronological order. *Use overhead of Courteen Seed timeline.*

> *Sept. 21.*   *Defendant mails samples of seed to several people, including plaintiff [para. 8].*
>
> *Oct. 4.*   *Rain. Defendant writes to plaintiff, looking for seed buyers [para. 9].*
>
> *Oct. 8.*   *Plaintiff sends telegram to defendant: "Price too high. Wire firm offer." [para. 9].*
>
> *Oct. 8.*   *Defendant sends telegram to plaintiff: "Asking 23 cents per pound." [paras. 5, 9].*

3. Practicing lawyers always prepare timelines or chronological summaries when litigating complex business cases. In the real world, you are not told the facts in the order in which they happen. You learn them bit by bit as you prepare for trial (and, unfortunately, you too often learn some of them during the trial). Putting them down in chronological order makes it easier to see relationships you might otherwise overlook.

4. This case may have been wrongly decided. There is one crucial fact that the court does not discuss in context. A timeline will make it easier for you to see what that fact is. **Do you think the court got it right?**

The case may be wrongly decided because the court of appeals did not discuss the first October 8 wire, which requested a firm offer, which tends to suggest that a response to it, if ambiguous as to whether it was an offer or not, was an offer as requested.

The defendant was trying to sell its seed, and wrote to the plaintiff in the hope that plaintiff would buy. The plaintiff sent a telegram for the lowest price, and the defendant responded by telegram. It seems that the parties might have been trying to finalize the deal on Oct. 8. They were communicating by slower methods until that day, and then sent two telegrams on Oct. 8.

◆ - - ◆

Southworth v. Oliver
Supreme Court of Oregon
284 Ore. 361 (1978)

Land and grazing permits in Bear Valley, Oregon for sale.

Trial court: Orders specific performance for plaintiff, finding that letter that followed discussions with information, including price, was an offer.

This court: Affirmed.

[Question in footnote 12—suppose A then says, "It's a deal." Is there then a contract? If so, who made the offer and who accepted?—Eds.In that case, there would be a contract. B would have made the offer to buy the car for $500, and A would have accepted the offer.]

Rules to take from the case:

- A contract includes not only what the parties said, but also what is necessarily to be implied by what they said.

- Although a price quotation, standing alone, is not an offer, there may be circumstances where a price quotation, considered with the other circumstances, may constitute an offer. The fact that the price quotation is sent to more than one person does not require a finding that there is no offer.

- People very seldom express themselves either accurately or in complete detail, thus, we have some guidelines to help us determine what they mean:

  - Objective test: What would a reasonable person think was meant?

  - If there are no words of promise, undertaking, or commitment, the tendency is to construe the expression to be an invitation for an offer or mere preliminary negotiations in the absence of strong, countervailing circumstances.

  - If the expression definitely names a party or parties, it is more likely to be construed as an offer. If the addressee is an indefinite group, it is less likely to be an offer. This is the general rule re: circulars and advertisements, the exception is in the reward cases.

  - In general, the more definite the proposal, the more reasonable it is to treat it as an offer.

NOTES AND QUESTIONS

1.   When you have only one thing to sell and you send out a communication to a number of people, that's a powerful fact in favor of finding the communication is *not* an offer. **Why wasn't that the case in *Southworth v. Oliver*?**

The court mentions the "surrounding circumstances" under which the letter was prepared, and determines that they would have led a reasonable person to believe that defendants were making an offer [para. 21]. Also, defendant didn't send the letter to many people, just the three or four neighbors who already owned land near the land for sale.

2. **Was the use of the word "information" and the failure to use the word "offer" significant in determining whether or not the communication was an offer?**

Again, the courts says that the facts & circumstances of the case would have led a reasonable person to come to the conclusion that an offer had been made. That the letter said "information" and did not say "offer" is not controlling as to whether an offer has been made. [para. 27]. The use or absence of the words is important in considering the reasonableness of the plaintiff, but isn't the key factor in whether there was an offer [para. 26].

3.   **What factors went into the determination that the June 17 letter was an offer?**

(a) The letter did not show up unsolicited.

(b) The parties had met to discuss the possibility of plaintiff purchasing defendant's land, with the understanding that the defendant would get specific price information worked out, and the plaintiff would arrange financing.

(c) There was a later phone call that confirmed this understanding was accurate [para. 22].

(d) The letter was definite, and included specific price information [para. 24] and was sent to a small group of people.

4.   Suppose Holliday or one of the other two neighbors who received the letter wanted to buy the land. **Does it necessarily follow that the letter would have been an offer as to them?**

The basis of the court's finding that there was an offer was the specific circumstances surrounding the letter in this case. We don't know if the circumstances were the same for the other neighbors. If they were largely the same, the court would probably conclude that an offer had been made to the other neighbors as well. However, the acceptance would have to be on a first come, first served basis as in Lefkowitz.

5. Do you think the Olivers drafted the letter of June 24, 1976, themselves? Why or why not? What was the purpose of the letter?

The Olivers may have drafted the June 24 letter, but it doesn't have quite the same voice as the June 17 letter. Also, the June 24 letter seems to use terms like "misconstrued," "firm offer of sale," "memorandum," and "constitute an enforceable contract," that were probably not in the everyday writing vocabulary of a cattle rancher. It suggests the involvement of a lawyer or someone with a command of legalese (not a great accomplishment). The letter attempts to establish that an offer was not made in the June 17 letter. The letter may have been a last ditch effort to get out of selling the land or an attempt to scare the plaintiff with big legal terms to get him to back out of buying the land.

6. Is the Supreme Court of Oregon, which decided both *Courteen Seed* and *Southworth v. Oliver*, being consistent in the two opinions? Or has the law changed between 1929 and 1978? Can the two decisions be harmonized? Or is one of these decisions wrong?

In each case, the court looked to the specific facts surrounding the alleged offer to determine whether an offer had actually been made. It seems the court may have done a more in-depth analysis of the surrounding circumstances in Southworth than it did in Courteen Seed. Also, the sale in Southworth was of land, and the sale in Courteen Seed was of seeds. This may have had something to do with the different results, though it is difficult to say why. The applicable legal standard does not appear to have changed. In each case, the court interpreted the situation around the offer as well as the alleged offer itself. When this occurs, it is possible for two reasonable people (or courts) to reach two different conclusions even if using the same standard.

◆ - - ◆

Continental Laboratories v. Scott Paper Co.
United States District Court, Southern District, Iowa
759 F. Supp. 538 (1990)

Negotiation of supply and distribution agreement for hospitality supplies (the "free stuff" in hotel rooms). Continental to make, Scott to distribute. Never fully documented and signed by all parties. Summary judgment for Scott, the defendant. No contract. No offer or acceptance.

May 1987:	Scott produces 5 discussion drafts of the Supply and Distribution Agreement, rounds of negotiations. (Note manner of negotiation, oral, then reduce to writing, review, oral, reduce to writing.)

July 19:	Scott announces internally that Scott and Continental have reached an agreement in principle.
August 25/26:	Continental representatives believed that a binding oral contract was reached on a telephone call. Scott, however, never intended to be bound by the oral agreements and only by a written contract executed by both sides.
September 2:	Draft written agreement circulates and Scott representative signs it; Continental never does.
	More dickering.

September 16, 1987: The Madrid meeting. Scott calls it all off.

Continental files suit alleging there was a contract already. Filed in state court, Scott removes to Federal District Court (why?) (Originally filed in Boone Country Iowa State Court, Continental's headquarters is located in Madrid, Iowa, in the heart of Boone County. Discuss effect of different venues and broader federal district jury venues when compared to state county courts.)

Scott moves for summary judgment on ground that there was no binding contract or, alternatively, that if there was, it was subject to a condition precedent to Scott's performance, a written, executed agreement, that never occurred, thus making the contract cancellable.

NOTE THE OPINION'S STRUCTURE – Especially paragraphs 9 et seq. Good explicit IRACs, even if you don't agree with the decision.

– intent of the parties standard – objective theory of contract.

– court employs a 7 factor test:

1. Whether the contract is of a sort normally found in writing.

2. Whether it is of a type needing a writing for its full expression.

3. Whether it has few or many details.

4. Whether the amount is large or small.

5. Whether the contract is common or unusual.

6. Whether all details have been agreed upon or some remain unresolved.

7. Whether the negotiations show a writing was discussed or contemplated.

Here, court goes down the list and finds insufficient evidence to show a contract, so find for Scott [paras. 12 to 16]. (Note that this is not a list to memorize, per Notes and Questions that follow). Although oral contracts can be binding, even if parties intend to later execute them in written form, this was not the case here.

NOTES AND QUESTIONS

1. In the first sentence of paragraph 10 under the heading "Discussion," the court says: "It is the parties' intent that will determine the time of their contract formation." **Is that a correct statement of the law?**

No, back to objective theory of contract again. A reasonable person standard. The court probably meant to say that it is the parties' manifestation of intent that would be interpreted by a reasonable person as an offer or acceptance.

2. The list of seven factors that the court gives is a good example of the type of list NOT to memorize. It's pretty much common sense, and, if you want to spend time doing it, you could probably come up with a better list. It all comes down to the basic idea of the objective theory of contracts -- what would a reasonable person take into account in deciding whether she was bound before the terms of the deal had been reduced to writing and signed in a big meeting with lawyers running around as if they thought the world was coming to an end? In *Pennzoil v. Texaco*, the fact that a toast had been drunk to celebrate the deal was a major factor leading the jury to decide the parties had made a contract for a multi-billion dollar deal. In that case, all seven of the factors listed in the *Continental Laboratories* opinion would have argued for finding there was no contract, but the jury thought this was apparently outweighed by the Texas tradition of making deals on the basis of a handshake.

3. Review the *Embry* case in Chapter 1. **What was the offer there? What was the acceptance?**

In paragraph 1 of Embry, *the appellant said that he would quit if his contract were not renewed. His boss told him to get back to work and not to worry about it.*

Embry's (the appellant's) statement could be construed as an offer to renew the contract that his boss accepted by telling him to go back to work. This is bolstered by the fact that he was working after expiration of his prior contract.

It could also be construed as an offer to quit which was rejected by his boss. (But would this renew the contract for a year?)

♦ - - ♦

Metro-Goldwyn Mayer v. Scheider
Supreme Court of New York
347 N.Y.S.2d 755 (1972)

MGM sues Scheider seeking an injunction preventing him from working during a period of time during which they assert he is obligated to work for MGM.

Trial Court: Finds a contract and would issue the injunction, but for the statute of frauds issue, not discussed, on which it is reversed on appeal anyway.

The Munich Project—Pile Made; Basic agreement terms are there [para. 3], but the billing status was left open, resolved orally, but not put in writing. Other terms—including the starting date for performance and ending date.

Court turns to custom and practice to help interpret the contract [paras. 8-9], note how this is a logical extension of the objective theory of contract. Educating the reasonable person. Enough has been shown to allow custom and usage in. So there is a contract.

♦ - - ♦

PROBLEM 2-1

Scarlett sends a letter to Rhett in which she says: "If you submit a written offer to buy Tara for $250,000 or more, I will accept your offer." Rhett submits a written offer to buy Tara for $275,000. Scarlett says: "Rhett, I've changed my mind."

Do they have a contract? [Look carefully at R2d § 24 and UNIDROIT article 2.1.2 before you answer.] Is the answer the same under both standards?

Scarlett's first letter may be the offer, and Rhett's letter may be the acceptance.

This interpretation might fail under the Restatement. Scarlett has manifested willingness to enter into a bargain, and Rhett would be justified in thinking that his assent is invited. However, he might not be justified in thinking that his assent will conclude the matter. Scarlett will still have to accept his offer to buy Tara before the deal can conclude. So her opening letter may well just be an invitation for Rhett to make an offer.

The analysis is more clearly in Rhett's favor under UNIDROIT. The proposal is definite (specific item, price, and addressee), and indicates Scarlett's intention to be bound if Rhett offers more than $250k for Tara.

But, still, Scarlett's first letter may be a solicitation for an offer, Rhett's letter may be an offer, and Scarlett's statement may be a rejection of that offer. In this interpretation, Rhett is manifesting his willingness to enter into a bargain, and Scarlett is justified in thinking that her assent is invited and will conclude it. This satisfies the Restatement. Under UNIDROIT, Rhett's proposal is definite, and indicates his intent to be bound if Scarlett accepts, so it is an offer.

PROBLEM 2-2

Read carefully UCC § 2-328, especially subsection (3). **In an auction "with reserve," who is the offeror? In an auction "without reserve," who is the offeror and what are the terms of the offer?**

In an auction with reserve, the bidders are making offers to buy the item that the seller may reject. In an auction without reserve, the seller is making an offer to sell the item to the bidders.

Note the structure of UCC § 2-328: Breakdown structure of an auction and lay out the rules in plain English.

Cover the summation materials at the end of the chapter as briefly as possible. It is self-explanatory.

PROBLEM 2-3

A rural landlord wants to convince his tenant to locate more cattle on the land the tenant rents because the rent is measured in terms of cows on the land and goes up as the size of the herd increases. He says to the tenant, "I will see that there will be plenty of water because it never failed here before." The tenant relied upon the statement and acquired more cattle. The water failed. The tenant sued.

Had the landlord made an offer – to see that there will be enough water—and, if so, what were the terms of the offer?

See Anderson v. Backlund, 199 N.W. 90 (Minn. 1924) *(held: remark was in the nature of a prediction, not a representation, warranty, or other contract term).*

The landlord was not making an offer: He wasn't promising to do anything, just stating a fact or an opinion in the hope that the tenant would get more cattle and pay more rent.

The landlord was making an offer: He was making a promise to tend to the water supply so that his tenant could have more cattle on the ranch and the landlord would have more rent money.

♦ - - ♦

OFFERS – AN ORIENTATION *(Self-explanatory)*

♦ - - ♦

In terms of negotiation leverage and being in control of the substance and structure of a transaction, **is it better to be the offeror or the offeree? Is there one right answer to this question? Why or why not?**

This is wide open for discussion and there is no single answer, although it provides an opportunity for discussion of the offeror as "master" of the offer if she exercises that mastery.

Lawyering Skills Problem

Your client has received the following letter from a person they have never met who appears to have gotten your client's name and address by searching the city's real property tax records (available online):

Client O. Yours
2525 Elmwood Glen Drive
Anytown, Anystate 55512

RE: 1305 Bridge Avenue; Assessor's Parcel no. 05–24116–008

Dear Mr. or Ms. Yours:

[1] I am interested in acquiring the above-referenced property, which you are listed as owning in the county clerk's records. This letter is an offer to purchase the property from you for $1,100,000.

[2] The property appears to be improved with approximately 50 3–bedroom/2–bathroom apartment units, an onsite laundry facility, and at least 50 standard-sized parking spaces. I estimate, therefore, that there are approximately 150 bedrooms and, estimating rental revenue of $450 per bedroom per month for this sort of low income, itinerant, or student housing, a rent revenue stream of approximately $67,500 per year, assuming 100% occupancy. Deducting $17,500 for operating expenses and a vacancy allowance, then, your property should yield $50,000 per year in net operating income. Given that apartment complexes locally have been recently selling with an imputed capitalization rate of 5%, this means your property is worth $1,000,000.

[3] Because I have some capital that I wish to deploy in the local real estate market in the very near term, I am willing to pay you $1,100,000 for your property, subject to your being able to convey marketable title that is free and clear of all but customary encumbrances. If you accept this offer, the full purchase and sale agreement will include all the standard terms and conditions. No brokerage commission will be paid.

[4] If you accept this offer, please indicate that you do so by signing below where indicated and returning the original to:

IMA Investor, LLC
721 Old Colony Drive

I thank you for your time and consideration in this matter.

Very truly yours,

Dan Gelling

Dan Gelling
President
IMA Investor, LLC

I accept the offer stated above.

Signed: _____   Dated: _____
Name: Client O. Yours
Title: Owner, 1305 Bridge Avenue

(a) Your client has come to you because, although he does not need to sell the property, being able to sell for more than it is worth is of interest. The client's first question is if this is "for real"—*i.e.*, is this an offer capable of immediate acceptance and, if he signs and returns the letter, will there be a binding contract? Is this an offer under the standards employed in the previous cases and in the R2d? Articulate those standards as a series of factors or elements and indicate what facts support a finding that those factors or elements have or have not been satisfied to support your conclusion.

(b) Is this an offer under the standards of CISG article 14 (assuming it applied to this transaction)?

(c) Is this an offer under the standards of UNIDROIT article 2.1.2?

(d) What is the legal significance of paragraph 2 of the letter, if any? Do you need to understand its details and critically analyze its argument regarding value and the like in order to answer your client's question of whether this letter is an offer?

(e) What is the legal significance of paragraph 3 of the letter, if any? Do you need to understand its details in order to answer your client's question as to whether this is an offer?

(f) There are many issues raised by this letter, whether it is an offer or not. What are these issues? Be sure to break them down to their constituent parts.

Which issues that you have identified are legal issues? Which are business issues? Are there other issues and, if so, how would you categorize them if they are not legal or business issues?

(g) In order to accept the offer, must your client sign off on the letter and return it to the sender? If they are not required to accept by doing so, but want to accept, how would you advise them to do so?

CHAPTER 3

HAS THE OFFER BEEN ACCEPTED?

— ♦ —

Two issues: Was the offer accepted? Was the offer valid when purportedly accepted?

Restatement (Second) of Contracts, section 50, Acceptance:

Acceptance of an Offer Defined; Acceptance by Performance; Acceptance by Promise

(1) Acceptance of an offer is a [a] manifestation of assent to the terms thereof [b] made by the offeree [c] in a manner invited or required by the offer.

(2) Acceptance by performance requires that [a] at least part of what the offer requests be performed or tendered and [b] includes acceptance by a performance which operates as a return promise.

(3) Acceptance by a promise requires that [a] the offeree complete every act essential to the making of that promise.

Break these standards into elements with the students (see the bracketed letters above). Get them in the habit of doing this automatically. Kuney uses overheads or projections for this purpose.

As an aside and a re-drill, what is the Restatement? Is it binding anywhere? What about the UCC. What is it? Where is it binding? UNIDROIT? The CISG? This is a good time to ask "does the UCC apply to the sale of a racehorse?" And sort out the students' confusion working with the UCC definition of "goods." The answer is "yes"—but it is always interesting to see who is confused by UCC § 2-105's reference to include the unborn young of animals and whether that creates a negative inference regarding already-born animals. Sometimes the argument is ventured that a racehorse is a "thing in action," which provides a nice opportunity to discuss choses in action or claims and the ability to buy, sell, or encumber same.

♦ - - ♦

Ever-Tite Roofing Corp. v. Green
Court of Appeal of Louisiana
83 So. 2d 449 (1955)

Roof repair contract

6/10   Parties signed an "instrument" saying it would only be binding upon written acceptance by an authorized officer of the contractor or upon commencing performance of the work.

The contractor checked the homeowner's credit, which took time.

6/18 or 19   Contractor loaded trucks and went to the homeowners' home. The homeowners said they had already contracted with somebody else.

Trial Court: For defendant, homeowner. The contract said it could only be accepted by written acceptance by principal or authorized officer of the contractor or upon commencing performance of work. The trial court finds that work not commenced and not accepted prior to rejection.

Court of Appeals: Reversed (and judgment ordered for plaintiffs). The reasoning is muddled a bit. Not clear what standard that they are using. One possibility is the "reasonable time" standard from the Restatement. The second is "commencement of work" from the contract. Both are met in the court's opinion. The contract language standard should control, but belt and suspenders makes sense. The Court addresses the issue of what constitutes commencement of performance vs. preparation to perform.

But "what is a reasonable time?" is a fact question. Doesn't the trial court get a little deference here? Or were the facts undisputed so it is really just a question of law?

NOTES AND QUESTIONS

1. Read R2d § 30(1). This section reiterates in more formal language the generally-accepted rule that "the offeror is master of her offer." It is mirrored in R2d § 50(1). Suppose A says to B: "I hereby offer to sell you my car for $1,000. You can accept this offer only by standing on your head and whistling The Star-Spangled Banner." B can't accept the offer by saying "It's a deal." B can't accept the offer by paying A $1,000. B can accept the offer only by standing on his head and whistling The Star-Spangled Banner.

2. Read R2d § 30(2). **What was the offer in *Ever-Tite*? How was it accepted? How else could it have been accepted?**

The offer in Ever-Tite was the June 10 document, which described the services to be performed and the price to be paid [para. 2]. It was accepted by commencement of performance on June 18 or 19, when the plaintiff's workmen loaded the trucks and went to defendant's house to begin work [para. 4]. The offer could also have been accepted in writing [para. 2].

3. The court ignores a powerful argument for the defendants. **What is it?** (Hint: Remember that we've been talking about the importance of characterizing the facts in a way most favorable to our client. You should also start looking at alternative ways of interpreting language.) **Could "commencing performance of work" have a meaning other than the one the court gave it?** Many attorneys start billing for their time when travel to an engagement starts.)

The alternative view would be that loading the trucks was merely preparation to perform and was not sufficient to constitute acceptance. The case is a "wobbler" as it could go either way. When does performance begin?

4. **In Ever-Tite, whom did the court regard as specifying how the offer could be accepted? Who really determined how the offer could be accepted? Was the court therefore wrong in the way it decided the case?**

It seems that the court regarded the defendant as being the one who specified how the offer could be accepted. However, the plaintiff probably drafted the document, which would mean that the plaintiff actually specified the manner in which the offer could be accepted and put those words in the mouth of the defendant. The court paid a great deal of attention to the idea that the offeror is the master of the offer. The court did not seem to focus on the idea that the offeror in this case was (probably) not the person who drafted the contract. Still, the defendant agreed to the terms of the document, even though the defendant could have made a different offer. Drafters not being the ones to issue the drafted document is a repeated theme in the cases.

5. UNIDROIT article 2.1.6 corresponds to R2d section 50(1). **Are the standards the same?** *(Overheads help discuss this one). Restatement § 50(1) defines acceptance as a manifestation of assent to the terms of the offer in a manner invited by the offer. UNIDROIT 2.1.6 defines acceptance as a statement or other conduct indicating assent to an offer. Unlike the Restatement, UNIDROIT does not require that assent be in a manner invited by the offer. Can this be implied? Is it better or worse to lose the "mastery" of the offeror over the offer?*

♦ - - ♦

PROBLEM 3-1

A writes B a letter:

Dear B:

I hereby offer to sell you my Collection of Marilyn Monroe Memorabilia for $1,000.

Please advise me by mail whether you accept this offer.

Sincerely,

A

B gets the letter and telephones A telling him she accepts the offer. **Has a contract been formed?**

What if B gets the letter and *e-mails* A telling him she accepts the offer? *See* R2d § 60.

Whether a contract had been formed depends on whether the described manner of acceptance is a permitted manner or a prescribed manner. If it is a permitted manner, then that does not exclude other manners of acceptance. If it is a prescribed manner, then that manner must be used to accept the offer and form a contract. The examples in R2d indicate that to prescribe a manner of acceptance, the offer must make it clear that no other method of acceptance is permitted. See, e.g., R2d § 60, ill. 1-5. The letter does not use the term "must" or "only;" it uses the less restrictive, polite, and therefore ambiguous term, "please," which may indicate that the manner of acceptance is a permitted one rather than the only one.

Beard Implement Co. v. Krusa
Appellate Court of Illinois
208 Ill. App. 3d 953 (1991)

12/23	Farmer signs order. Form says it's subject to acceptance by Dealer
12/26	Farmer tells dealer's rep he doesn't want to go through with the deal.
12/27	According to Farmer's testimony, Dealer said he would let him out of the deal.

Note the check that was left undated, apparently in the expectation that it was no good until dated.

Dealer's people testify basically the same, except they say Farmer said "I'll take the deal," and they say they never agreed to let him out of the deal.

Contract? T.C. said yes. But this court reverses.

Ct. endeavors to find the offeror and the offeree, and goes to Calamari & Perillo [para. 19], which states that when A solicits offers on purchase orders that are subject to A's rep's approval, B has made the offer and A is the offeree (who must accept).

The court looks at similar cases for this proposition and discusses them in some serial case analysis [paras. 20-25]. Discuss difference between serial case analysis and integrated discussion analysis.

Thus, the result is reversal of the normal presumption; farmer is offeror, dealer is offeree, even though dealer's form is being used.

Look at the UCC concepts:

Course of Performance

No. No sequence of conduct between the parties. No repeated occasions for performance.

What is the idea behind course of performance? It allows us to educate and specialize the reasonable person in the objective theory of contracts. *See* UCC § 1-303(d) or § 1-205(1), depending upon the version being used.

Course of dealing

No. No previous transactions (or are there? Do we know?).

What is the idea behind course of performance? Ditto. *See* UCC § 1-303(d) or § 1-205(1), depending upon version being used.

Usage of Trade

No. Not proved and Farmer Brown seems to have contrary facts well in hand.

What is the idea behind usage of trade? Ditto. *See* UCC § 1-303(d) or § 1-205(2), depending upon version being used.

NOTES AND QUESTIONS

1. The dealer argued that an oral contract had been formed before the purchase order was signed. **If that had been the case, would it matter whether the "dealer" ever signed the purchase order?**

If there were truly an oral contract, then it shouldn't matter whether the written purchase order was signed by the dealer. The purchase order would just be a "confirming memorandum" stating again what the parties were already obligated to do. The contract was already made.

2. In a case involving facts very similar to the facts of this case, the Los Angeles Rams lost the services of a Heisman Trophy winner because the National Football League's standard player contract form provided that there was no contract until the deal was approved by the league's commissioner. The player, Billy Cannon, signed the Rams' document, but before the commissioner approved, Cannon informed the Rams he was taking a better deal from the Houston Oilers of the newly-formed American Football League (AFL). The court held that Cannon didn't have a contract with the Rams. His signing the form was the offer and it was not accepted until the commissioner gave his approval. *Los Angeles Rams Football Club v. Cannon*, 185 F. Supp. 717 (S.D. Cal. 1960). Because the AFL was able to sign stars like Cannon, it was able to become a competitor to the National Football League (NFL). The two leagues later merged to create the present NFL.

3. Suppose that in the Billy Cannon case, Mr. Cannon had said before he signed the form: "I don't want to hang around waiting for some bureaucrat to approve this. I want to know right now whether we have a contract. So let's just cross out the part that says it has to be approved by the commissioner."

(a) If they had then just signed the form, would they have a contract?

The player is making an offer to the NFL. If the NFL accepts the player's different terms then a contract is made.

(b) Suppose the League had a rule that no player contract is valid without the signature of the commissioner. Would that affect the outcome?

This would affect whether a contract was formed based on the limited authority of the NFL representative. We could go into the distinctions and ramifications of "actual" and "apparent" authority, but that is generally a waste of class time at this stage of the students' studies.

Essentially, there is no contract without the commissioner's signature. The player is the offeror, and can determine the terms of the contract. However, the player is making an offer that, essentially, only the commissioner can accept.

Sometimes students raise the possibility that the player could cross out the clause requiring the commission to sign. Crossing the clause wouldn't change the fact that the commissioner would still have to sign it to make it a contract under the NFL's rules. The NFL doesn't want to be bound without the commissioner saying it's OK.

♦ - - ♦

Davis v. Jacoby
Supreme Court of California
1 Cal. 2d 370, 34 P.2d 1026 (1934)

The trip from Canada to California based on promise of taking under a will. Cover the facts, esp. the communications [paras. 3-8].

March 18   Mr. Whitehead writes Caro saying Blanche wants to see her.

March 24   Frank, at Caro's request, telegraphs, saying Caro can come in about 2 weeks. "IF you think it advisable."

March 30   Mr. Whitehead writes Frank a long letter laying out all their problems and saying that under his will everything would go to his wife and HE THINKS under her will practically everything will go to Caro.

April 9   Mr. Whitehead again writes saying he thinks he can save $150,000 and having Frank there "would be a big thing."

April 12   This is the letter that the court says is "a definite offer." Addressed to them both. "So if you can come, Caro will inherit everything." Also says "let me hear from you soon." ·

April 14   Frank writes back saying they are coming on the 25th after his court appearance as executor.

April 15   Mr. Davis sends waffling letter.

April 17   Frank wires, "Cheer up-- we will soon be there."

April 22   Mr. Whitehead commits suicide.

April 24ish   Frank and Caro arrive and start caring for Mrs. Whitehead.

May 31   Mrs. Whitehead dies.

Her will leaves everything to her husband; his leaves it to her for life then to his nephews. His will was written just a few weeks before this all happened.

Note in paragraph 8, that one of the nephews was apparently named after Mr. Whitehead. Were his parents trying to get in the graces of the rich uncle?

Focus on the April 12 letter from Whitehead to Davis – hey wait a second, this is Davis v. Jacoby – who is Jacoby? (Executor).

That April 12 offer – was it an offer of a bilateral or unilateral contract? If unilateral, would it be accepted upon completion of duties (when the Whiteheads are dead), upon arrival in California, or upon preparation to set out (like the *Ever Tight* roofers in Louisiana)?

Do the procedure. Suit for quasi specific performance. What is that? Note that SP is unavailable, as the Whiteheads are dead, so this suit seeks imposition of a trust with the actual beneficiaries of the Whitehead will to act as "trustees." You will see this in remedies – it is a "constructive trust." Discuss the notion of "legal fiction."

What did the trial court find, and why? No acceptance. April 12 letter was offer, and the April 14 letter was a purported acceptance, but the offer was of a unilateral contract that could only be accepted by performance (full, partial, otherwise), but that performance had not been accomplished by the time Whitehead died, and upon death (or insanity) the offer is withdrawn by operation of law.

What did the appeals court do and why? Reversed. Discusses the difference between unilateral and bilateral contracts, and notes the presumption of bilateral contracts, which saves the Davis claim. Assisted by the fact that performance would not be complete until the Whiteheads were dead, at which point they could not perform (although at least one of us thinks the Whiteheads' wills could contain conditional bequests or a claim in probate could be made that would solve this problem). **What seems to be going on here? A little legal realism? Or maybe result-oriented jurisprudence?** Note how the court works the facts in order to make the trip from Canada worthwhile for Mr. and Mrs. Davis.

QUESTIONS

1. **According to the court, what was the offer and what was the acceptance?**

The offer was in the letter of April 12, 1931 from Mr. Whitehead to the Davises [para. 3, 11, 22]. It was accepted in the letter of April 14, 1931 from Mr. Davis to Mr. Whitehead [para. 4, 22].

2. **If, after Frank sent the April 14 letter, he and Caro had decided they couldn't leave Canada, would they have been in breach of contract? If, under those circumstances, Mr. Whitehead had sued them, would he have been successful?** (This is the sort of thing you should think of before you accept a court's, or your opponent's, or your supervising attorney's characterization of the facts.)

If you accept the appellate court's reasoning that a bilateral contract was formed, the Davises would have been in breach. They made a promise to come to California in exchange for a promise of money and assets. Mr. Whitehead sent another letter to the Davises on April 15, 1931 in which he seemed to leave some allowance for Mr. Davis to stay to tend to his own business. This doesn't change the fact that they already entered a contract. (Although, Mr. Whitehead probably hadn't received the April 14 acceptance letter yet, as we will cover later, the "mailbox rule" would make the acceptance effective upon deposit in the mail.). Could Whitehead sue for breach of contract? (Probably not, right? Common sense. But why, legally speaking?). Does this mean that the offer was not really one of a bilateral contract?

3. The court discusses the fact that by leaving his business in Canada, Frank lost $8,000. Is this important? Why or why not?

This is part of the damage that Mr. Davis suffered as a result of relying on Mr. Whitehead's promise. I think it's a fact irrelevant to the law (a "fireside equity") thrown in to show that the outcome was fair. I don't think it's relevant to damages because it looks like the trial court is being told to grant specific performance.

♦ - - ♦

Additional Question (Teacher's Manual Only)

What is the purpose of paragraph 2? How is it relevant? Is it perhaps the most relevant paragraph in the opinion?

♦ - - ♦

PROBLEM 3-2

Queen Victoria's pet Welsh Corgi slips out of the palace and begins to try to make it back home to Wales. Heartbroken, the Queen places an advertisement offering a $100,000 reward to anyone who finds the cuddly little thing and returns him to her. Sherlock Holmes sees the ad and writes the following letter:

Your Majesty:

I promise to find your pet and return it to you.

Your servant,

Sherlock

(a) Under the rule articulated in R2d §§ 30(2) and 32, has a contract been formed?

There is no contract under the Restatement, only an offer to enter a unilateral contract. The Queen wants her dog back, not a promise to get her dog back. So, it's not "reasonable in the circumstances," as required by Restatement § 30(1), that Sherlock's letter could be an acceptance that the Queen is looking for. The Queen's offer is not of the sort that can be accepted by either performance or a promise, only by performance, so Restatement § 32 doesn't apply.

(b) Under the rule articulated in *Davis v. Jacoby*, has a contract been formed?

The court found a bilateral contract in Davis v. Jacoby. Mr. Whitehead had to rely on Mr. & Mrs. Davis' promise to care for Mrs. Whitehead after he died. Queen Victoria doesn't have the same problem. Sherlock can only accept her offer by finding and returning her dog.

Sherlock hasn't done that, so there isn't a contract. Also, in Davis, the court reiterated that the offeror can specify the mode & means of acceptance [para. 20], which Queen Victoria did: "finds the cuddly little thing and returns him to her."

(c) Under the rule articulated in CISG article 18 (assuming it applied), has a contract been formed?

Under CISG article 18(1), there may actually be a contract. Sherlock has responded to Victoria's offer with a statement indicating assent to the offer, which meets the definition of acceptance. Assuming, of course, that Sherlock and the Queen have not had prior dealings that trigger CISG article 18(3).

(d) Under the rule articulated in UNIDROIT article 2.1.6?

Sherlock's letter meets the requirements of UNIDROIT article 2.1.6(1). Sherlock has indicated his assent to the offer. However, article 2.1.6(3) is applicable as well. The offer is of the sort that the offeree can indicate assent without notice to the offeror, so the acceptance is effective when the act is performed. In this case, the performance is the finding & returning of the dog to Victoria.

PROBLEM 3-3

MercMart, Inc. ("The Company") publishes a mail order catalogue in which it advertises "everything today's mercenary needs to be 100% combat effective." Among other things, the catalogue includes weapons, eavesdropping equipment, and how-to manuals on fighting, breaking and entering, and other criminal activities. You are general counsel for The Company and "The Boss" has asked your advice on the following matters.

(a) Colonel "Mad Mark" Slutzky entered into a contingent fee contract to carry out a revolution in Amerigo, an island nation. On March 1, he ordered 10,000 land mines from The Company, requesting immediate delivery. The land mines were shipped on March 5. That night the colonel had a dream in which an apparition told him "land mines are bad." He immediately called The Company and canceled the contract. The Company told him "Tough. We got a contract." True to The Company's culture, the person who talked to the colonel spoke first and thought about it later. Now she wants to know whether there is in fact a contract obligating the colonel to take the mines. Consult UCC § 2-206 and advise her.

The catalogue is not an offer, just an invitation for offers. Under UCC § 2-206(1)(b), an order (offer) to buy goods invites acceptance either by a prompt promise to ship or a prompt shipment. The mines were shipped four days after the order (offer) was placed, requesting immediate shipment. If that qualifies as prompt, then the order was accepted and there is a contract. However, UCC § 2-206(2) states that if an offeror has not been notified of acceptance within a reasonable time may treat the offer as having lapsed before acceptance. Depending on what is standard in the bulk landmines trade, four days may or may not be reasonable. If it is not reasonable, then there is not a contract because the offer was not timely accepted. Still, Mad Mark didn't act like the offer had lapsed, since he made a phone call to try to cancel the contract. If the offer had lapsed, there wouldn't be a contract.

(b) When Mad Mark's order came in, The Boss immediately called Amerigo's government and offered to sell them 50,000 AK-47 assault rifles. The conversation got nowhere because the Boss and the Minister of Defense couldn't agree on the amount of the Minister's bribe. A short time later, the Minister of Defense sent in a written purchase order for 50,000 AK-47 rifles at MercMart's catalogue price "for immediate delivery." Because of materials shortages, The Company was unable to obtain 50,000 AK-47 assault rifles. Based on what Mad Mark had told The Company, The Boss knew that the government needed weapons immediately, so he shipped the American counterparts of the AK-47, the AR-15 (also known as the M-16). When the rifles arrived at Amerigo's secret warehouse in the United States, the government refused to accept them. The Company took them back and thought no more about it until it was served by Amerigo with a summons and complaint for breach of contract. The Boss says you should explain to the judge that there was no contract to breach because the Company never accepted the government's offer. **What is your assessment of the strength of the Boss's position?** *See* UCC § 2-206(1)(b).

The order to buy AK-47s may have been accepted by The Company's shipment of AR-15s. If AK-47s and AR-15s are interchangeable, then Amerigo is in breach of contract for refusing to accept them. However, this might have been a shipment of non-conforming goods, if the rifles were substantially different. A shipment of non-conforming goods does not constitute an acceptance if the seller notifies the buyer that the shipment is only an accommodation.

Whether the offer was accepted depends on whether The Company notified Amerigo that it was shipping AR-15s as an accommodation. If The Company notified Amerigo, then there was no acceptance and so there is no contract. If The Company didn't, then it accepted the order and is in breach of contract.

(c) If you concluded in Part (b) that The Company is in breach, how would you advise The Boss to avoid similar problems in the future?

The Company could have avoided the possibility of being in breach of contract if it simply notified Amerigo that it could only send AR-15s instead of AK-47s and requesting assent to the substitution. By doing this, they would not be accepting Amerigo's offer, but making a new offer which Amerigo could then accept or reject. They could also have notified the buyer that the AR-15s were provided as an accommodation.

PROBLEM 3-4

Law Student has her first call-back interview on Friday. On Monday, she walks into the dry-cleaning establishment she normally patronizes and lays her best conservative, dress-for-success suit on the counter. The cheery clerk says: "Hi, Ms. Student. How are you today?"

Figuring it would be impolite to say that she's three weeks behind in all of her courses, she doesn't even know what's going on in a couple of them, and she thinks she's coming down with the flu, she lies and says: "Pretty good. How are you?"

"Great," says the clerk. "Wednesday OK?"

"That's fine," says Ms. Student as she walks out wondering if she'd be happier working there instead of a law office.

On Thursday, just before closing time, Ms. Student walks into the dry cleaners and the same friendly clerk is on duty. She returns Ms. Student's suit in the same condition it was in on Monday. Noting the startled look on Ms. Student's face, the clerk says: "The boss got sued last week, and now he hates all lawyers. He says we aren't going to do any cleaning for lawyers any more, and I guess that includes law students as well."

Ms. Student goes to the interview in her second-best outfit, one she knows is a little too trendy for the stodgy law firm where she wants to work. A few weeks later she hears that the people who interviewed her were impressed with her credentials but they thought the way she dressed indicated she "wouldn't fit in here."

Does she have a breach of contract action against the dry cleaner? If so, what was the offer and what was the acceptance?

Open discussion. Kuney has used this as a writing assignment to help build IRAC skills.

♦ - - ♦

Carlill v. Carbolic Smoke Ball Co.
Court of Appeal
1 Q.B. 256 (1892)

Do the facts.

Was this advertisement intended to be a promise at all? Or just a puff?

Not a puff to Lord Lindley. The reward being on deposit seems pretty dispositive for him.

But it was just made generally, to all, like all ads, and those are held not to be offers.

Ah, but this is a classic "reward" case, and that is the exception to the rule that ads are not offers; it is an offer of a unilateral contract that can (only) be accepted by performance [para. 6].

But what about the need for notice of acceptance?

General rule would be yes – for a bilateral contract. But here it is a unilateral contract and notice of completed performance is all that is needed. The offer was never revoked [para. 7].

Wasn't it too vague to be a legal promise?

Not to this court. Use the balls according to instructions and imply reasonable use and reasonable duration of protection.

Why does Lord Bowen opine separately?

He is pointing out that the reasonable duration language is not part of his opinion. To him, protection lasts while using the ball.

Why does Lord Smith opine separately?

Not sure what he wanted to add. He does make it clear that he sees it as an offer intended to be acted upon (unilateral contract offer) by purchasing the ball and, when conditions of use and sickness met, the contract was to pay the sum stated.

NOTES AND QUESTIONS

1. In paragraph 4, Lord Justice Lindley states: ". . . as a general proposition, when an offer is made, it is necessary in order to make a binding contract, not only that it should be accepted, but that the acceptance should be notified." **Is this the rule under R2d § 54? Under UCC § 2-206? Under CISG article 18? UNIDROIT article 2.1.6?**

It is not the rule under Restatement § 54, which requires notification only if the offer requests it. If the offeree has reason to know that the offeror has no means of learning of acceptance, then the offeree must exercise reasonable diligence to notify the offeror.

It is similar to the rule in UCC § 2-206(2), which requires notification to the offeror of acceptance within a reasonable time, or else the offeror may treat the offer as lapsed.

It is the rule under CISG article 18.

It is the rule under UNIDROIT article 2.1.6.

Which approach do you favor? Why? *(Discuss)*

2. *Means of Acceptance vs. Conditions of Performance.* In many contracts books, the Carbolic Smokeball case is in the chapter on determining what is an offer. The *Leonard* case (the plaintiff who wanted to buy the Harrier jet) served that purpose in this book. Our interest in the Carbolic Smoke Ball case is in the method of acceptance of the offer.

What were the terms of the offer, and how could it be accepted? There are a couple of different ways of analyzing these questions. The judges don't really address what had to be done to accept because the case comes out the same way no matter how one analyzes these issues, but it might be important if the offer had been withdrawn between the time the plaintiff bought the smoke ball and the time she got sick. Consider the following interpretations of the Carbolic Smoke Ball ad:

Interpretation One

Accept the offer by purchasing a smoke ball. The terms of the contract are that the user gets the hundred pounds if they (1) use the ball according to directions and (2) get sick within a reasonable time thereafter.

Interpretation Two

Accept the offer by purchasing a smoke ball and using it according to directions. The terms of the contract are that the user gets the hundred pounds if they get sick within a reasonable time thereafter.

Interpretation Three

To accept the offer, the user must (1) purchase the smoke ball, (2) use it according to directions, and (3) get sick within a reasonable time thereafter.

Assume the offer was withdrawn on January 1. (For purposes of this question, assume that an offer which can be accepted by performance can be revoked at any time before performance is complete. As we'll see later, this is no longer the law in most jurisdictions.)

A purchased the ball on November 15, used it according to directions, completing her two week minimum use on November 29, and got the flu on December 15. **Under which of these interpretations would she be allowed to recover the 100 pounds?** *All three.*

B purchased the ball on December 15, used it according to directions, completing her two week minimum use on December 29, and got the flu on January 15. **Under which of these interpretations would she be allowed to recover the 100 pounds?** *Interpretations 1 and 2.*

C purchased the ball on December 20, used it according to directions, completing her two week minimum use on January 4, and got the flu on January 7. **Under which of these interpretations would she be allowed to recover the 100 pounds?** *Interpretation 1.*

All three interpretations would allow for recovery for A. The smoke ball was purchased, used as required, and the person got sick before the offer was revoked.

Interpretations one and two allow for B to recover. B purchased and used the ball as required before the offer was revoked. B did not get sick before the offer was revoked. If B had to get sick in order to accept the offer, as required in interpretation three, it was too late on January 15.

C may only recover under interpretation one. C purchased the ball before the offer was revoked. He did not get sick or complete use of the ball before the offer was revoked. If either of those are required to accept the offer, as in interpretations two and three, he was too late on January 4 and January 7.

3. *Making a silk purse out of a sow's ear.* The *Carbolic Smoke Ball* case is well known and a staple of Contracts courses. Less well known is the company's next move. In a subsequent advertisement, on February 15, 1893, the company renewed and increased its offer, albeit with some careful drafting and limitations, both legal and practical, on liability:

100£ REWARD was recently offered by the CARBOLIC SMOKE BALL CO. to anyone who contracted influenza [or various other diseases] after having used the Carbolic Smoke Ball according to the printed directions. Many thousand Carbolic Smoke Balls were sold, but only three persons claimed the reward of 100£, thus proving conclusively that this invaluable remedy will prevent and cure the above-mentioned diseases.

THE CARBOLIC SMOKE BALL CO., Ltd., now offers 200£ REWARD to the person who purchases a Carbolic Smoke Ball and afterwards contracts any of the following diseases, . . . INFLUENZA . . . . or any disease caused by taking cold while using the Carbolic Smoke Ball.

This offer is made to those who have purchased a Carbolic Smoke Ball since January 1, 1893, and is subject to conditions to be obtained upon application, a duplicate of which must be signed and deposited with the Company in London by the applicant before commencing the treatment specified in the conditions [including having to take the three doses each day at corporate headquarters]. This offer will remain open only until March 31, 1893.

♦ - - ♦

PROBLEM 3-5

(Use overhead of R2d § 54 and UNIDROIT article 2.1.6)

Jeff had a boathouse on a remote lake. He heard there had been several incidents of vandalism in the area, so, on January 10, he wrote to a contractor he knew in a small town near the lake:

> Marcia,
>
> I need a chain link fence with a locked gate around my boathouse. If you can do it for less than $2,500, please start immediately and send me the bill. Use your own judgment as to things like height, placement, etc.
>
> *Jeff*

Marcia began construction on January 12, as soon as she got the letter (business at the lake is slow in the winter), and she finished two days later. Marcia had become a contractor because she liked building things more than she liked doing paperwork, so she hadn't gotten around to sending a bill (or otherwise telling Jeff she had done the job) before she received his fax on January 30 telling her not to build the fence because he was going to sell the boathouse and didn't want "an ugly fence" around it.

There are a number of issues here, so don't jump to conclusions.

(a) Do the parties have a contract? *See* R2d § 54 and UNIDROIT article 2.1.6.

Probably. No notification is necessary under Restatement § 54(1) unless it is requested in the offer. If Marcia had reason to know that Jeff didn't get to the remote boathouse very often, and might not know about performance, it could be argued that she had to notify him under Restatement § 54(2)(a).

No, under UNIDROIT article 2.1.6(2), the offer is accepted when the indication of assent reaches the offeror, so there would not be a contract, as the offer would have been revoked before the notification was received. However, it appears the parties know each other and may have had prior dealings and the offer instructed Marcia to start immediately if she accepted, and makes no mention of notice. Under UNIDROIT article 2.1.6(3), this would indicate that acceptance had occurred before the offer was revoked.

(b) If the parties do have a contract, does Jeff have to pay?

Jeff made an offer for a unilateral contract that Marcia accepted by building the fence. He didn't want Marcia to promise to build the fence; he wanted her to just build the fence. When Marcia performed, Jeff became obligated to pay the price for the fence. However, Jeff may have had to receive notification or else his obligation would be discharged. This could be satisfied by Marcia using reasonable diligence to notify Jeff (which she didn't seem to do), or by Jeff learning of the performance within a reasonable time. At the earliest, Jeff would have found out about acceptance 20 days after he sent the offer, 16 days after performance was complete.

♦ - - ♦

THE "MAILBOX RULE"

A very important, but very basic rule of contract law is the so-called "mailbox rule" or the rule of *Adams v. Lindsell*. Emphasize that the mailbox rule is only a default rule when the parties don't specify otherwise. If they specify, that controls!

♦ - - ♦

PROBLEM 3-6

Seller writes Buyer: "I will sell you my Franklin Mint plate commemorating The Life of Elvis for $400. This offer will expire at noon on July 4." Buyer writes back: "I accept your offer." Buyer's letter is mailed on July 4 at 11 a.m., but because the post office is closed on July 4, it is not postmarked until 2 p.m. on July 5. **Do the parties have a contract?**

Buyer mailed his acceptance before the offer expired. Following the mailbox rule, the offer was accepted when the acceptance was deposited at the post office. This is so even if the buyer knew that the letter wouldn't even be touched by the post office until the next day, although there may be problems of proof due to the late post mark.

PROBLEM 3-7

Seller writes Buyer: "I will sell you my Sammy Sosa rookie card for $100. This offer will expire on September 18. Your answer must be in my hands by that date." Buyer mails her acceptance on September 17. Seller receives it on September 19. **Do they have a contract?**

The Seller specified that the mailbox rule would not apply by stating that the acceptance had to be in his hands by a certain date. When that date passed and the acceptance had not been received, the offer expired. There is no contract. The mailbox rule is only a default rule and the parties, specifically the offeror, are free to change it.

PROBLEM 3-8

Mr. Kenge sends John Jarndyce an e-mail message offering to convert his fee arrangement in *Jarndyce v. Jarndyce* from hourly billing to a contingency fee. The message states: "This offer will expire at noon tomorrow." At eleven the next morning, Mr. Jarndyce, having cogitated on the offer whilst he took his tea, boots up his computer and sends Mr. Kenge a message purporting to accept the offer. Unfortunately, though neither party knew it, Mr. Jarndyce's internet provider, England On-Line, has suffered a server crash. As a result the message is not delivered for three days. In the meantime, Kenge & Carboy, assuming that Jarndyce has rejected their offer and that they will therefore be able to bill *Jarndyce v. Jarndyce* as they always had, hires a new associate. **Does Jarndyce have a contract to change the billing arrangement?** *See* R2d §§ 63, 64, 67.

Section 15(a) of the Uniform Electronic Transactions Act provides:

Unless otherwise agreed between the sender and the recipient, an electronic record is sent when it:

(1) is addressed properly or is otherwise directed properly to an information processing system that the recipient has designated or uses for the purpose of receiving electronic records or information of the type sent and from which the recipient is able to retrieve the electronic record;

(2) is in a form capable of being processed by that system; and

(3) enters an information processing system outside the control of the sender or of a person that sent the record on behalf of the sender or enters a region of the information processing system designated or used by the recipient which is under the control of the recipient.

*Jarndyce probably has a contract to change the billing. Restatement §
63(a) provides that an acceptance completes the contract as soon as it is put out of
the offeree's possession, without regard to whether it ever reaches the offeror.
UETA § 15(a) is in accord. Jarndyce properly dispatched the acceptance, which
was effective when he mailed it at 11 a.m., before the noon deadline.*

Our apologies to Charles Dickens.

PROBLEM 3-9

On March 1, Farmer writes Developer: "I hereby offer to sell you the
property known as the 'Jones Farm' for a price of $500,000." Developer receives
the letter on March 4. On March 5, Farmer changes her mind and mails (by the
U.S. Postal Service) Developer the following:

"My offer to sell the farm is hereby revoked." On March 6, Developer mails
(by the U.S. Postal Service) a letter purporting to accept the offer. On March 7,
Developer receives Farmer's revocation letter. On March 8, Farmer receives
Developer's acceptance letter.

Do the parties have a contract? *See* R2d § 42; UNIDROIT article 2.1.4.

*Under Restatement § 42, the revocation of an offer is effective when it is
received by the offeree. UNIDROIT article 2.1.4 provides that an offer may be
revoked if the revocation reaches the offeree before he has dispatched an
acceptance. Developer mailed his acceptance before he received the revocation.
Under both the Restatement and UNIDROIT, the offer was accepted and the
contract completed on March 6 when Developer mailed the acceptance.*

PROBLEM 3-10

B has been admiring A's collection of baseball cards. B tells. A
[communication #1]: "If you ever decide to get rid of your Johnny Bench rookie
card, I'll trade you my Hank Aaron signed bat." A says he wouldn't part with the
Johnny Bench rookie card for a million dollars *[communication #2]*. A couple of
weeks later, however, A changes his mind and sends B the following e-mail
[communication #3]: "I've changed my mind. I'll trade the Bench rookie card on
the terms you suggested. If I don't hear otherwise by two weeks from today, I'll
assume we have a deal and I'll ship."

B gets the e-mail and decides she's no longer so interested in baseball
cards. She plans to e-mail A rejecting the offer, but forgets to do so. On the day
he said he would, A mails the rookie card to B (insured for $10,000)
[communication #4]. Immediately upon receiving the card, B re-wraps it for
mailing and encloses a letter saying that she never agreed to the swap. Once
again she gets sidetracked with other projects and it's three more weeks until she
gets around to mailing the package *[communication #5]*. When A gets the

package he is irate. He thought he had a contract, and he sues B for breach of contract. A wants that bat.

How should the court decide the case? Consider R2d § 56 and 69, UCC § 2-206, CISG article 18, UNIDROIT articles 2.1.2-2.1.7. *How the court should decide the case depends on what it determines the offer (that ultimately formed/didn't form the contract that led A to send the baseball card) to be. If the court determines B's statement to A in communication #1 to be the offer, then it should find for A. If the court determines that A's email to B, communication #3, is the offer, then the court should find for B.*

Under R2d § 56, acceptance by promise requires reasonable diligence in attempting to inform or actual reasonable acceptance. UCC § 2-206 focuses on acceptance being reasonable under the circumstances and presumes a need for prompt notice and shipment of goods. Under CISG article 18, an oral offer must be accepted immediately unless circumstances indicate otherwise; UNIDROIT article 2.1.7 is in accord for oral offers.

If communication #1, B's statement, was an offer to trade the card for the bat, it may have expired immediately upon rejection by A. However, B used the phrase "ever decide" when making the offer, which may indicate that B intended it to be a standing offer that A could accept at any time although it probably takes more than this to make "evergreen" offer that survives rejection.

If communication #1 is the offer and it was not terminated by communication #2, A's initial rejection, then A accepted it by sending the e-mail. As long as this method of acceptance is reasonable, the contract was formed when A sent the e-mail. B was in breach of contract when she failed to send the bat in exchange for the card.

If communication #1 was an offer and A rejected it, then communication #3, A's e-mail to B is the operative offer. A specified that he would assume a contract after two weeks unless he heard otherwise. Under the Restatement § 69(1)(b), silence and inaction do not indicate acceptance where the offeror has given the offeree reason to understand that assent may be manifested by silence unless the offeree intends to accept by remaining silent. B did not intend to accept the offer, and therefore the parties did not form a contract. B was not in breach because there was no contract.

Lawyering Skills Problem

Sherri was a senior partner in a large law firm. After 25 years of practicing law, she was very wealthy. But she was also burned-out and totally fed up with the practice of law. She wasn't ready to retire, but she wanted to find another career. She had always enjoyed skiing, so she decided that a ski resort would be the ideal business for her.

Among her many contacts was Mario, who was a business broker. He was in the business of helping people like Sherri find businesses to buy. On

November 5, when she was cleaning up her desk after a hard day of negotiating on behalf of clients, Sherri wrote Mario the following e-mail:

> Mario:
>
> How's my favorite broker? Doing any deals lately?
>
> I've decided to hang it up with the practice of law. I'm going to buy a ski resort. You can make a quick hundred grand if you can find me one that meets my needs. I can pay as much as ten million for the right place if I can get the financing I need.
>
> If you find me the right property, I'll pay you a commission of up to $100,000. I know this is less than you're used to getting, but we're old friends, and I promise that I'll be easy to deal with.
>
> If this is OK, let me know. I'm not going to work with any other brokers, just you. You don't have to commit to spend a lot of time on the deal. Just check out the market and you may earn a quick hundred grand.
>
> *Sher*
>
> BTW—Disregard the stuff below this. The firm's server puts that on all the e-mails. Don't you just love paranoid lawyers? ;-)
>
> This communication was sent by the law firm of Cardozo, Gonzales, Chang & Weinstein. It may contain confidential information protected by the attorney-client privilege. If you believe you have received this communication in error, destroy all copies and immediately telephone the sender.
>
> This communication does not reflect an intention by the sender or the sender's client to conduct a transaction or make any agreement by electronic means. Nothing contained in this message or in any attachment shall satisfy the requirements for writing and nothing contained herein or therein shall constitute a contract or a signature.

When Mario got the e-mail, he ignored it because he wasn't interested in ski resorts. He had a couple of hot bio-tech deals going and he wasn't going to be distracted from them for a deal that could only bring him a hundred grand.

About a week later, however, (November 15 to be exact) the weather turned cold and Mario's mind turned to snowboarding. He decided that he would play around with Sherri's idea. He began an intensive study of the winter resort industry. It was mostly to satisfy his own curiosity, but he was thinking there was the possibility he might by chance run across something that would be suitable for Sherri. As sometimes happens, he got carried away with the project and he began spending an inordinate amount of time looking for a deal for Sherri. Finally, he discovered a resort that was exactly what Sherri was looking for. It was a small resort that drew customers from a nearby city. It didn't have much challenging terrain. In fact, it didn't have much terrain at all. But what can you expect for a lousy ten million? Mario first learned of the availability of the resort on November 22, after spending all of that day and most of the previous two days searching on the Internet, telephoning real estate brokers in the mountainous areas of seven states, and checking out a lot of resorts that turned out to be unsuited to Sherri's needs.

On November 23, he sent the following e-mail to Sherri:

Sher:

Found a great property for you. The owner wants too much for it, of course. They always do. But I'm confident we can get him down to your max price and probably a bit below. The geezer is getting old and he wants to retire to Mexico.

Details to follow by snail mail.

Best,
Mario

In the meantime, on November 22, Sherri, infuriated by Mario's lack of response to her earlier e-mail and wanting to have tangible written confirmation of her position, Sherri sent the following letter to Mario by the United States Postal Service (registered mail):

Dear Mr. O'Riley:

You have failed to respond as requested to my electronic mail message of November 5. Accordingly, I hereby withdraw any offer which I may have made to you in that message or any other way.

Please direct all future communications to the attorney representing me in this matter, Ralph J. Cardozo, Esq.

Very truly yours,

S. Weinstein, Esq.

Mario received the letter on November 25.

Mario, of course, demanded his $100,000.

Sheri has come to you seeking advice as to whether or not she owes the $100,000 commission. Although Mr. Cardozo has given her his opinion that she does not, she wants someone who will not be paid to litigate the case and is thus more unbiased to give her a legal opinion.

This is likely your students' first exposure to a traditional final exam style problem.

ANALYSIS OF THE PROBLEM

The first issue is whether Sherri's message is an offer. It has some characteristics that would indicate it is an offer. It promises to pay a commission if he finds a ski resort for her. It tells him that he doesn't have to commit to spending a lot of time on the deal, just to take a look at the market. Telling him to disregard the disclaimer is a pretty clear indication that Sherri intends to be bound. If she only intended this as a prelude to an offer, she wouldn't have to be concerned about the disclaimer, and as a lawyer, she would know that.

On the other hand, she doesn't say the exact amount of the commission. She says she'll pay up to $100,000. If this is an indication she has left this very important term up for negotiation, then the message is not an offer. But the language could also be interpreted to mean that she will pay the normal commission (either the going rate in the business or Mario's normal rate) with a cap of $100,000. Given that Sherri is a sophisticated lawyer (senior partner in a large firm) and apparently a friend of Mario, she likely knows the going rate. More troublesome for finding the message to be an offer is that it doesn't say how it can be accepted. One can certainly argue that a senior partner in a law firm would, if she intended to make an offer, spell out how it can be accepted. On the other hand, in determining whether this is an offer, we have to look at it from the point of a reasonable person in Mario's position. Mario is a broker and may be used to doing deals in a much more informal manner. On the other hand, in Continental Labs the court decided that a pair of uptight corporations weren't bound until they had all the details worked out and formal documents signed. The big question seems to be if, in the current context, people do deals this way.

The apparent friendship (she says they're "old friends") between Mario and Sherri cuts both ways. On one hand, it can be argued that Mario could see it as indicating that Sherri intends to be bound without being more formal and complete in her offer because she can depend on their relationship to allow them to work out the details as they go. Moreover, it might be awkward for people who normally communicate on friendly and familiar terms to suddenly become formal. On the other hand, the fact that they are familiar might lead Mario to understand that Sherri is asking him to get started on the deal as a favor and that he should depend on her to make a legal commitment sometime later.

The fact that Sherri later wrote a very formal letter also cuts both ways. On one hand, it can be argued that it shows that when she wanted to write something that had a legal effect she wrote in a formal manner, so the implication is that when she wrote in an informal manner it indicated she did not intend to be

legally bound. On the other hand, the fact that she did write a formal letter revoking "any offer I may have made" is an acknowledgment that there is at least some argument she made an offer. Of course, we have said that what she does later is not technically relevant. It is only what a reasonable person in Mario's position would have thought
at the time he received the message.

Based on all of the foregoing we would conclude that the letter was an offer.

If the letter was an offer, there is the question of how it can be accepted. The common law rule was that an offer was either one that could be accepted by a promise or one that could be accepted by performance and the court must make a determination which it is. In case of doubt, the preference is for finding it can be accepted by a promise. The R2d rule is that an offer can be accepted in any manner that is reasonable under the circumstances.

The offer can be analogized to an offer for a reward, an offer that can be accepted only by performance. A promise would not be sought because there is no way Mario can promise that he will find a "suitable" property. That is the way most open listing real estate brokerage contracts are construed, and this deal is very closely analogous to an open listing real estate brokerage contract. On the other hand, the statement that Sherri is not going to work with other brokers is an indication that she wants a commitment (promise) from Mario. Her statement that he doesn't have to commit to spending a lot of time could imply that he does have to make a minimum commitment of taking a look at the market, or it could be construed as saying that before he commits to anything he should look at the market, and then they can make commitments to one another based on the results of his preliminary survey. Because we think Sherri wants some assurance that Mario is going to work on this deal, we think this offer can be accepted only by a promise.

If the offer is one that can be accepted only by a promise, there is a question whether Mario's letter constitutes such a promise. It says that he has performed or at least that he thinks he has performed. He apparently thinks he has found a suitable property, but the final determination is of course not his to make. (Whether Sherri gets to determine what is suitable or whether she is bound to take what a reasonable person in her position would think is suitable is an issue we don't have to determine to answer this question.) Mario's message was sent before he received Sherri's revocation letter, so the revocation letter doesn't affect it. I think that if Sherri's message is construed as asking for a promise, Mario's message sent in response to it implies a promise to do what is necessary to complete a deal with this seller ("we can get him down") as well as a promise to look for other properties if this one doesn't work out. But it could also be construed as saying "I've done this and that's all I'm going to do." The latter interpretation would not be an acceptance if the offer can be accepted only by a promise.

We think that Mario's letter constitutes an acceptance if the offer is one that can be accepted by a promise.

If the offer is one that can be accepted by performance (either because it can be accepted only by performance or because it can be accepted either by a promise or by performance), there is the question of when it can be revoked. The old common law rule is that an offer for a unilateral contract can be revoked any time before performance is complete. If that rule is applied, there is still the question of whether Mario has completed performance. It can be argued that performance was not complete until Sherri had indicated that the company is "suitable" or perhaps even not until she has entered into a deal. That interpretation, however, would make it too easy for people like Sherri to cheat their brokers, so I think the better interpretation would be that performance was complete when Mario found the company, or at least when he informed Sherri of it. Either of these interpretations would mean that performance was complete before Sherri revoked the offer.

The R2d provides that if the offer is one that can be accepted only by performance, the beginning of performance makes the offer irrevocable; and that if the offer is one that can be accepted either by a promise or by performance, the beginning of performance constitutes acceptance. In either case, Sherri's attempted revocation would be ineffective.

There is also the question of whether the offer expired because it was not accepted within a reasonable time. If Mario's message of November 23 was the acceptance, 18 days elapsed between the time Sherri first messaged him and the time he responded. It can be argued that Mario accepted within a reasonable time because the offer was not the sort of thing that required prompt action. Sherri was making a major life change, and this is the sort of thing that should be done only after considerable thought spread over some time. He might have reasonably thought that he was doing her a favor by giving her time to change her mind. Moreover, Sherri does not ask for a fast reply, and Mario could reasonably have expected that as a lawyer Sherri would know to do that if she wanted a fast reply. In fact, there is nothing in Sherri's message that directly indicates she is in any hurry. It is possible that Mario assumed that because Sherri was asking him to take on the search at less than his usual fee she was giving him time to decide whether he wanted to do her that favor. On the other hand, it can be argued that if all Mario had to do was give a simple yes or no answer, he should have done so much faster. Also, the fact that Sherri is committing not to use another broker means that she needs a relatively fast response so that she can engage another broker if Mario turns her down. I find this latter reasoning persuasive, and if the offer was one that could be accepted only by a promise, I think it elapsed before Mario sent his message.

If the offer was one that could be accepted only by performance, then it would seem that the offer did not expire because 18 days is a very short time to find a business meeting Sherri's requirements.

If Mario accepted the offer by rendering performance, Sherri might be able to argue that her contractual duty is discharged under R2d section 54(2). Her argument would be that Mario accepted by beginning to study the industry on November 15 and did not notify her until November 23. While this is a relatively *short time, Sherri could argue that the R2 speaks of "reasonable diligence" and because he easily could have sent an e-mail, he should have done that so that Sherri would know she didn't have to look for another broker. I don't think this argument would be successful because the time was so short.*

Generally, classes are pretty evenly split between those who think that the offer could only be accepted by a promise, people who think it can be accepted only by performance, and those that think it can be accepted either way. The most common mistake made when addressing this problem is to only address one of the alternatives, not all three.

CHAPTER 4

HAS THE OFFER TERMINATED?

— ◆ —

Minnesota Linseed Oil Co. v. Collier White Lead Co.
Circuit Court, District of Minnesota
17 F. Cas. 447 (1876)

Seller--Plaintiff--Minnesota Linseed Oil Co.
Buyer--Defendant--Collier White Lead Co.

July 29, 1875 – Plaintiff Seller to Defendant – please wire best offer for round lot of one hundred barrels.

July 30, 1875 – Defendant to Plaintiff Seller– three hundred barrels, 55 cents here, thirty days, no commission, August delivery, Answer.

July 31, 1875 – Plaintiff Seller to Defendant – Will accept 58 cents on terms in your telegram. [This was sent at 9:15 p.m. Saturday night and gets delivered to the defendant on Monday morning, August 2, between 8 and 9 a.m.]

Aug. 3, at 8:53 a.m. – Defendant deposits acceptance for 300 barrels in the telegraph office. *[This is the response that the court feels is too late to be reasonable.]*

Aug. 3, later that day, Plaintiff Seller to Defendant – withdraw our offer.

Aug. 3, later, Defendant to Plaintiff – no way, we have a contract, ship. *This was a period of market volatility.*

Issues:

Note that buyer/defendant is the one saying they have a contract. The defendant is saying they have a contract to have a counterclaim against a bill for a previous sale. Buyer is apparently seller's local agent in St. Louis. Seller sues for some money due from prior dealings, and buyer counterclaims for breach of this contract.

Operative communication was buyer's wire of 31 July counter-offering to buy at 58 cents a gallon. It was transmitted 31 July at 9:15 PM (Saturday evening) and received Monday morning (2 Aug) between eight and nine.

Acceptance was transmitted Tuesday at 8:53 AM.

After acceptance was transmitted, a withdrawal of the offer was transmitted.

Price was fluctuating from day to day between 55 and 75 cents per gallon.

Seller makes a halfhearted attempt to argue that the mailbox rule doesn't apply ("The rule is not strenuously dissented from on the argument"--beginning of paragraph). But the mailbox rule does not wipe out the "reasonable time" requirement. Here, that was not met.

Court indicates it's important that the offer was made by telegraph, the "instaneous means of communication of the day."

Procedure is convoluted. Defensive counterclaim to give rise to a right of set off to avoid paying a bill. The Plaintiff, trying to collect the bill, denies the contract was formed.

♦ - - ♦

Kempner v. Cohn
Supreme Court of Arkansas
47 Ark. 519, 1 S.W. 869 (1886)

30 Jan	John Kempner writes offering to sell the property letter is sent care of A. Kempner
2 Feb	Cohn gets letter
5 Feb	Cohn tells A. Kempner "he would take the property"
7 Feb	Cohn mails acceptance letter at 9 PM
7 Feb	John Kempner writes revoking offer

Question of reasonable time was submitted to the jury and they said it was within a reasonable time. On appeal, the defendant is asking the court to determine as a matter of law it was not within a reasonable time. Court distinguishes cases of things fluctuating in price and says five days is not unreasonable.

Sale of a lot in the city of Little Rock. Disappointed buyer sues.

January 28 – plaintiff Cohn writes defendant inquiring terms for sale.

February 2 – Defendant's reply specifies $10k price, 50% down, with 50% as a note with 10% interest. Sent care of A. Kempner, the defendant's uncle (a special, not general agent), and was not delivered to Cohn until February 2.

Feb. 5 – Cohn tells Kempner that he will take the property and asks him to tell the defendant.

Feb. 7 – Follows up with confirming letter on February 7 enclosing deed and asking that it be signed and returned. Deposited prior to any notice of withdrawal and postmarked Feb. 7, arrives on Feb. 9.

Feb. 7 – Defendant being informed by Agent Kempner that Cohn is interested, writes letter declining to sell, a purported rejection.

Inquiry – what is going on here? Talk about sellers feeling around for how high a price the buyer will pay by looking like they are making offers but not really doing so or attempting to withdraw offers before they are accepted.

Held: Contract. The acceptance was mailed before the plaintiff had knowledge of the withdrawal. The mailbox rule does not apply to a withdrawal as it does to an acceptance. As long as the acceptance was mailed in a reasonable time, before knowledge of the offer's withdrawal, it is effective.

◆ - - ◆

PROBLEM 4-1

Suppose that Tom [Wolfe (the famous author)] wrote a letter to Ted Kaczynski (the mathematician who attempted to assassinate public figures by mailing them bombs, dubbed "the Unabomber" by the press) offering to ghostwrite Mr. Kaczynski's autobiography in return for half the royalties earned by the book. Suppose further that Mr. Kaczynski wrote Mr. Wolfe a letter accepting the offer and (Mr. Kaczynski) mailed the letter back to Mr. Wolfe along with a bomb. **If the bomb exploded and killed Mr. Wolfe before he read the acceptance letter, would they have a contract?** (Recall that the death of the offeror or the offeree terminates the offer.)

Acceptance is effective upon deposit; bombs are effective upon detonation. No need for Tom to read.

Under the mailbox rule, the offer is accepted as soon as the acceptance is put out of the offeree's control. Here, this occurred when Kaczynski shipped the package to Wolfe. The acceptance occurred before Wolfe's death, and was therefore valid to form a binding contract.

However, was Kaczynski truly expressing assent to the terms of the offer? Wolfe can't write a book if he's dead, and Kaczynski must have been aware of this. Though he may have sent a manifestation of assent to the bargain in the letter, he also sent a manifestation of the intent to kill Wolfe at the same time. Of course, that assumes he intended to kill rather than just scare or maim.

◆ - - ◆

Dickinson v. Dodds
Court of Appeal, Chancery Division
2 Ch. D. 463 (1876)

(R2d § 43)

Seller (Defendant Dodds) delivers to Dickinson a letter offering to sell his property. "This offer to be left over until Friday 9 o'clock AM".

On Thursday morning, the buyer decides to accept the offer.

According to the statement of facts in paragraph [3]: "On Thursday afternoon the buyer was informed by a Mr. Berry that the seller 'had been offering or agreeing to sell the property to Thomas Allen.'"

According to the first sentence in paragraph [13]: "Dickinson is informed by Berry that the property has been sold by Dodds to Allan".

On Thursday evening at 7:30, buyer goes to home of Mrs. Burgess, the mother-in-law of seller and delivers to her formal acceptance of the offer. Mrs. Burgess testifies she forgot to give it to seller.

On Friday morning, buyer and his agent give acceptances to seller, but he says he has already sold the property.

Court states that even though the parties thought the offer had to be kept open, it's very clear it could be revoked. Court also states that it's very clear that buyer knew seller was no longer intending to sell the property to him.

Held: No contract. There was no consideration for the keeping the offer open as part of the deal, so it was a naked offer unless and until a full acceptance was received.

When plaintiff had knowledge of behavior that was inconsistent with an exclusive offer then this knowledge will serve as notice of withdrawal. Notice of the impossibility of performance serves as withdrawal.

NOTES AND QUESTIONS

1. Read R2d § 43, which states the generally accepted rule on indirect revocation of acceptance. **If the *Dickinson* court had applied that rule, would the offer have been revoked?**

The offeror took a definite action inconsistent with entering a contract with plaintiff [para. 3]. Plaintiff received information to that effect [para. 3]. If this information was reliable, then there was an indirect revocation and no contract was formed, according to Restatement § 43. If the information was unreliable, then there was not a revocation, and there may have been a contract. The letter that was left with defendant's mother-in-law may have been the acceptance, issue there is authority and agency, even though it never reached the defendant, assuming that the mailbox rule is applicable here.

2. Note how casually in paragraph 13 Lord Justice Mellish says the law may be wrong. American judges are much less willing to make such a statement.

♦ - - ♦

OPTION CONTRACTS *(Self-explanatory)*

♦ - - ♦

PROBLEM 4-2

When Bill's Software, Inc. was a small, struggling company, Bill recruited seven star programmers by offering them each an option to buy 100,000 shares of stock in the company at a price of $5 a share. The stock was then selling at $6 a share. The options were exercisable (i.e., the offer could be accepted) any time within the next three years. Since that time, Bill's Software, Inc. has done very well. The stock is now selling for $150 a share.

You are the general counsel for Bill's Software, Inc. (you don't have any stock options. Lawyers are easier to get than programmers.) One day Bill comes into your office and says he has bad news. You notice, however, that he is having trouble suppressing a smile. He tells you that six of the seven programmers were helicopter skiing in British Columbia and were killed in an avalanche. Bill says he knows the death of the offeree terminates an offer, and he wants your confirmation that he isn't going to have to sell any cheap stock to the estates of the programmers.

What do you tell him? *See* R2d §§ 37 and 48.

Under R2d § 48, the death of an offeree terminates the offer. However, this case concerns an option contract and there is a carve-out for option contracts. Under R2d § 37, the death of the offeror (Bill or his company) does not terminate the power of acceptance under an option contract. But it is the programmers—the offerees—that died. In light of the fact that R2d § 48 refers to both offerees, and R2d § 37 refers only to termination upon the death of the offeror, we may draw the negative inference that the offeree's death does not terminate the option.

♦ - - ♦

UCC Notes and Problem 4-3 (Teacher's Manual Only)

Section 2-205 UCC firm offers. Go over statute on board and suggest that students (1) parse it for elements and (2) do problem 4-3 on p. 111 to test their knowledge. Same for CISG article 16(2) and problem 4-4 on p. 112.

♦ - - ♦

PROBLEM 4-3

Read carefully UCC § 2-205 dealing with so called "firm offers." Do not ignore definitional cross-references.

John wrote Mary the following letter:

September 15, 2003

Dear Ms. Roe:

I hereby offer to sell you the items on the attached list for a total price of $850,000.

This offer will remain open until November 15 of this year.

Sincerely,
J. Doe

Mary gave no consideration to John for his promise to keep the offer open.

Would the offer be irrevocable if:

(a) The "items on the attached list" were pieces of heavy construction machinery and John and Mary were dealers in used construction machinery?

Irrevocable. John, a merchant in the sense of being a dealer in the contract's subject matter, made the offer to leave the offer open in a signed writing, which satisfies UCC § 2-205.

(b) The "items on the attached list" were comic books and John and Mary were brokers on the New York Comic Book Exchange?

Irrevocable. John is a broker in the industry, and so has (or should have) knowledge peculiar to the industry, which makes him a merchant for the purposes of the UCC. (UCC § 2-104(1)).

(c) The "items on the attached list" were lots on which homes could be constructed and John and Mary were real estate developers?

Revocable. UCC § 2-205 applies to goods. Real estate lots are not moveable and are not goods as defined in UCC § 2-105(1).

(d) The "items on the attached list" were stocks and bonds and John and Mary were stockbrokers?

Revocable. 2-105(1) excludes investment securities from the definition of goods.

(e) The "items on the attached list" were antique automobiles and John was a dealer in antique automobiles while Mary was the lead singer in a rock group?

Irrevocable. UCC § 2-205 requires that the offeror be a merchant. It doesn't matter who the offeree is.

(f) The "items on the attached list" were antique automobiles and Mary was a dealer in antique automobiles while John was the lead singer in a rock group?

Revocable. The offeror is not a merchant as required by UCC § 2-205.

(g) The "items on the attached list" were pieces of heavy construction machinery and John and Mary were dealers in used construction machinery, but John typed his name rather than writing it manually in script?

Irrevocable, if you apply UCC § 1-201(39). The key here is John's intent: did he execute or adopt the typewritten name "John" with "the present intent to authenticate a writing"? Why else sign your name?

(h) The "items on the attached list" were pieces of heavy construction machinery and John and Mary were dealers in used construction machinery, but the letter stated that the offer would remain open for six months?

The offer would either be revocable because the stated time period is too long, or be irrevocable for the time limit of 3 months. UCC § 2-205. The question is what remedy is appropriate as well as whether the offer contained a boilerplate savings clause that was up to the task.

PROBLEM 4-4

Read carefully CISG article 16(2) (firm offers). **Under the CISG, which of the prior offers would be irrevocable?**

a.   *Irrevocable. As above.*

b.   *Irrevocable. As above.*

c.   *Revocable. The CISG limits the contract to goods.*

d.   *Revocable. The CISG limits the contract to goods.*

e.   *Irrevocable. As above.*

f.   *Irrevocable. The CISG does not have the requirement that the offeror be a merchant.*

g.   *Irrevocable. The CISG does not have the requirement that the option offer be signed.*

h.   *Irrevocable. The CISG does not specify a time limit.*

◆ - - ◆

Petterson v. Pattberg
Court of Appeals of New York
248 N.Y. 86, 161 N.E. 428 (1928)

Discounted payoff proposal (explain this sort of transaction).

Creditor (defendant Pattberg) writes:

I hereby agree to accept cash for the mortgage which I hold against premises 5301 6th Ave., Brooklyn, N.Y.

It is understood and agreed as a consideration I will allow you $780 providing said mortgage is paid on or before May 31, 1924, and the regular quarterly payment due April 25, 1924, is paid when due.

This is a $780 discount off of a principle balance of $5,450, a 14% discount.

Debtor (plaintiff Petterson) pays the quarterly payment (which he already had a duty to pay). In the latter part of May, he presents himself at creditor's house and knocks at the door. Creditor asks who it is and he says: "It's Mr. Petterson. I've come to pay off the mortgage." Creditor partly opens the door and debtor shows him the cash. Creditor refuses to take it. Prior to this time, Creditor had sold the bond and mortgage to a third person.

So, issues are: offer, announcement of intent to accept by performance, revocations, tender of performance, in that order.

Held: Traditional harsh rule that the offer can be revoked at a time before performance – court sees it as an offer of a unilateral contract.

But hadn't performance already started by making the April payment? Pre-existing duty implications. Side-step for now.

Note, if you say that the announcement is a promise, then a bilateral contract could have been formed, then no cancellation – this is where the dissent is going.

Note, if the offer had been stated as "I agree to accept," then it would have been binding when the offer to pay is made [Dissent para. 11]. Do you agree?

Note, if he had mailed in the money, the mailbox rule might have protected him?

NOTES AND QUESTIONS

1. **Did the majority think the offer was one that could be accepted (i) only by a promise, (ii) only by the performance of an act, or (iii) either by a promise or the performance of an act? If it could be accepted by the performance of an act, what was the act?**

The majority thought that it was an offer that could be accepted only by performance of an act [para. 3]. The act was to pay the mortgage by May 31.

2. **Did Judge Lehman think the offer was one that could be accepted (i) only by a promise, (ii) only by the performance of an act, or (iii) either by a promise or the performance of an act? If it could be accepted by the performance of an act, what was the act?**

The minority thought that it was an offer that could be accepted only by performance of an act [para. 8]. The act was to offer to pay, to tender payment, or to pay the mortgage by May 31 [para. 10]. Judge Lehman was willing to excuse formal tender of performance and stress the need for good faith.

3. Judge Lehman, in paragraph 11, considered the letter in question: "The thought behind the phrase proclaims itself misread when the outcome of the reading is injustice or absurdity." Contrast this with Lord Justice Mellish's statement in *Dickenson v. Dodds* that the law might be wrong. **Do you see the different underlying paradigms for thinking about legal and factual issues?**

It seems that Lehman is trying to fit the facts into the law. It seems that Mellish looked at the facts, thought they wouldn't fit into the law, and then said that the law might be wrong.

♦ - - ♦

REVOCATION OF OFFERS FOR UNILATERAL CONTRACTS
(Self-explanatory)

♦ - - ♦

Minneapolis & St. Louis Railway v. Columbus Rolling-Mill Co.
Supreme Court of the United States
119 U.S. 149, 75 Ct. 168, 30 L. Ed. 376 (1886)

Series of telegrams: Was there a contract?

December 5 – Plaintiff: quote me price for iron rails, 2000 to 5000 tons.

December 8 – Defendant: Quote w/ force majure clause.

December 16 – Plaintiff: Purported Acceptance as to 1,200 tons.

December 16 – Plaintiff: We ordered 1,200, can you sell us splices?

December 18 – Defendant: We cannot book your order.

December 19 – Plaintiff: Alright, give me 2000 tons at the quoted price.

December 22 – Plaintiff: Did you enter my order?

Defendant denies contract.

Held: No contract. The December 16 "acceptance" varied the quantity and thus was a rejection of the offer and the offer was never recessitated. Do make sure the students understand what was going on: The buyer was inflating its destined quantity to get a lower quoted price per unit and got hoisted by its own petard, here a purported acceptance that the court found to be a rejection.

Good summary of the law in paragraph 13.

♦ -- ♦
Livingstone v. Evans
Alberta Supreme Court
4 D.L.R. 769 (1925)

Defendant seller writes plaintiff buyer offering to sell him land (we aren't told terms of the offer).

Buyer wires back "Send lowest cash price. Will give $1800 cash."

Seller's agent wires back: "Cannot reduce price."

Buyer writes back, accepting offer.

Court says "Cannot reduce price" was a renewal of the original offer.

The key fact here is that it was in response to something that asked for the lowest cash price

Plaintiff: I accept the offer.

Held: It was a renewal, thus there was a contract.

◆ -- ◆

Those are the common law rules – but now we get to the battle of the forms and modern practice. Problems 4-3 and 4-4 are the set up for that as they ask you to apply the common law rules: which set up the "last shot problem" – since all the forms are non-conforming, they each are a rejection/counteroffer and the last one before performance will "win."

That is why the UCC includes 2-207, to eliminate the last-shot advantage. Look at the statute. (Use overhead -- be frank with the students: 2-207 is a failure if its goal was to provide a "simple" set of rules to eliminate the last shot advantage. It is, however, a great teaching tool for statutory interpretation and application).

Select and discuss Problem 4-5; have 4-6 for students to work through to set up the "battle of the forms" and the "last shot advantage."

◆ -- ◆

PROBLEM 4-5

Apply the law of counteroffers as set forth in the two cases above to the following fact situation. Buyer asks Seller to send Buyer a written proposal for the sale of 1,000 heavy-duty stainless steel widgets. Seller sends a written proposal which constitutes an offer to sell 1,000 heavy-duty stainless steel widgets.[1] The fine print on the back of proposal form says "all sales are final" (along with a lot of other terms that are not relevant to our problem). Buyer responds to the proposal with a form headed "Purchase Order." This form contains terms identical to those of the proposal, except that on the reverse side it says "Buyer reserves the right to return any merchandise for full credit within thirty days after delivery." Shortly after receiving the purchase order, Seller ships the widgets. Buyer accepts delivery of the widgets and pays for them. Twenty days after the widgets are delivered, Buyer decides it doesn't need them and ships them back to Seller. They arrive on Seller's loading dock the next day, but Seller refuses to take them back and refuses to give Buyer credit for their price.

Buyer sues. **Who wins?** *Buyer.*

---

[1] For those unfamiliar with the term, a "widget" is a generic, general purpose term, or placeholder name, for an unspecified device or product. It is commonly used for textbook and other examples where the identity of the product or function is irrelevant and could be distracting.

81

We are looking at the common law rules and the last-shot advantage, not UCC 2-207. The written proposal from the Seller was an offer. The purchase order from the Buyer was a purported acceptance of the offer, but, because it was not a mirror image of the offer, was really a rejection and counter-offer. The parties had no contract at this point. When the Seller shipped, he may have accepted the Buyer's counter-offer. If he did, then the terms of the Buyer's form control and the Buyer should win, due to the last-shot advantage.

♦ – – ♦

PROBLEM 4-6

Apply the law of counteroffers as set forth in the cases above to the following fact situation. Buyer asks Seller to send Buyer a written proposal for the sale of 1,000 heavy-duty stainless steel widgets. Seller sends a written proposal which constitutes an offer to sell 1,000 heavy-duty stainless steel widgets. The fine print on the back of proposal form says "all sales are final" (along with a lot of other terms that are not relevant to our problem). Buyer responds to the proposal with a form headed "Purchase Order." This form contains terms identical to those of the proposal, except that on the reverse side it says "Buyer reserves the right to return any merchandise for full credit within thirty days after delivery." Shortly after receiving the purchase order, Seller sends Buyer a form called "Confirmation." The form is pretty much the same as the proposal except that it has a different heading and begins "We have entered your order for the following merchandise." It then reiterates the terms of the proposal. Like the proposal, it has fine print on the back saying "all sales are final." Shortly thereafter, Seller ships the widgets. Buyer accepts delivery of the widgets and pays for them. Twenty days after the widgets are delivered, Buyer decides it doesn't need them and ships them back to Seller. They arrive on Seller's loading dock the next day, but Seller refuses to take them back and refuses to give Buyer credit for their price.

Buyer sues. **Who wins? Why?** *Seller.*

The written proposal from the seller was an offer. The purchase order from the buyer was a counter-offer. The confirmation form from the seller was another counter-offer. There was no contract at this point. When the Buyer accepted the widgets, he may have accepted the Seller's counter-offer. If he did, then the terms of the Seller's last form control and the Seller should win. This time the Seller has the "last-shot" advantage.

♦ – – ♦

PROBLEM 4-7

Buyer (a merchant) asks Seller (also a merchant) to send Buyer a written proposal for the sale of 1,000 heavy-duty stainless steel widgets. Seller sends a written proposal which constitutes an offer to sell 1,000 heavy-duty stainless steel widgets. The fine print on the back of proposal form says "all sales are final" (along with a lot of other terms that are not relevant to our problem). Buyer responds to the proposal with a form headed "Purchase Order." This form contains terms identical to those of the proposal, except that on the reverse side it says "Buyer reserves the right to return any merchandise for full credit within thirty days after delivery."

(a) Under the law of the two cases above, would the parties have a contract at this time?

No. The parties would not have a contract at this time under the law of Minnesota Railway *and* Livingstone. *There was an offer which was rejected by the counter-offer. The counter-offer has not been accepted by a "mirror image" acceptance.*

(b) Under UCC § 2-207(1), would the parties have a contract at this time? (Don't worry about what the terms of the contract might be, and don't worry about subsections (2) and (3) of Section 2-207. They don't apply to the question asked.)

Yes. The parties would have a contract under UCC § 2-207(1). The purchase order is an acceptance, even though it contains a different term.

(c) Under CISG Article 19, would the parties have a contract at this time?

Under Article 19(1), the non-conforming acceptance operates as a rejection unless the terms are not material under Article 19(2), in which case there is a contract. Note the opposite presumption in CISG article 19(1) from UCC § 2-207(1) - Where you end up often depends upon where you begin and whether you get a presumption in your favor or are faced with the burden of rebutting one. Thus, the importance of initial presumptions, burden of proof or persuasion, and standard of review.

(d) Shortly after Seller receives the purchase order, it ships the widgets. **Does Buyer have a right to return the widgets?** *See* Section 2-207(2).

It depends. Additional terms become part of a contract between merchants (which is the situation here) unless the offer limits acceptance to its terms (which doesn't seem to be the situation here), the terms materially alter the offer, or the other party objects. But these are "different" not "additional" terms, so section 2-207(2) may not apply to them. Under the "California" or minority rule, 2-207(2) does apply and "different" terms are treated just like "different" terms. The majority approach distinguishes between "additional" and "different" terms and holds that 2-207(2) does not apply to the different ones, only the additional ones.

If 2-207(2) applies to the different term, if changing the right to return is a material alteration, then Buyer doesn't have the right to return. If the Seller objects, or if Seller's original form stating a different term constitutes an objection, then Buyer doesn't have the right to return. If it's not a material alteration and there is no objection, the Buyer does have the right to return.

The "materiality" trigger is one of the weaknesses of the 2-207 solution to the "last-shot" advantage. The determination of what is material is often difficult to make with any degree of certainty. Reasonable minds can differ. What would you look to in order to determine materiality?

♦ -- ♦

C. Itoh & Co. v. Jordan International Co.
United States Court of Appeals, Seventh Circuit
552 F.2d 1228 (1977)

Jordan is selling to Itoh, which in turn is selling to Riverview.

Itoh sends Jordan a Purchase Order.

Jordan sends acknowledgment with arbitration clause. Acknowledgment says it's "expressly conditional." Note how Jordan's document is drafted to mirror 2-207(1)'s language. But the Riverview arbitration clause excluded quality issues.

Riverview refuses delivery--says steel is defective and delivery is late.

Itoh sues both.

Jordan asks for stay pending arbitration

Trial Court: Denies stay based on notions of efficiency after concluding that Riverview arbitration clause did not apply due to quality carve-out. As that dispute was not arbitrable, court did not enforce either arbitration clause.

Appellate Court: Affirms on different grounds.

(1) First, if arbitration clause there, you *shall* stay the action and compel arbitration. No discretion. Federal Arbitration Act policy favoring arbitration when contracted for is very strong.

(2) Second, the battle of the forms here on expressly conditional material terms prevents the formation of a contract based on the writing. But the parties performed anyway, so there must be a contract under UCC § 2-207(3). What are the terms? All agreed upon plus supplementary terms (meaning the gap filling terms of the UCC, not the arbitration clause). So, no arbitration clause in the contract. Do not issue the stay.

Consider discussing arbitration pros and cons, briefly, so students can understand the materiality of the dispute resolution term. Kuney presents this with an emphasis on critically evaluating whether or not arbitration is desirable

84

for your client at the time of contracting. Having seen clients get burned, badly, by arguably biased arbitrators whose rulings are tantamount to pronouncements from heaven given the limited appellate review afforded arbitration, he is a fan of arbitration in certain circumstances and not in others. Sometimes the ADR movement gets over-emphasized in law school. It should at least be critically evaluated in context, like any legal tool.

◆ -- ◆

PROBLEM 4-8

Buyer sends Acme Foundries a written purchase order (PO) for 10,000 cast iron widgets. The PO does not specify when payment is to be made. Acme sends back a written confirmation with this notation: "Terms: net 30/2% in 10." In business lingo, this means that the net amount of the price is due 30 days after the date of shipment or invoice and, if paid in 10 days, a 2% discount will apply. Buyer does not protest, and the widgets are shipped the next day.

(a) Do the parties have a contract under UCC § 2-207 or CISG Article 19?

Yes. The parties have a contract. The second form contains a new term, but is an acceptance. UCC § 2-207(1). This is not a material change and even appears to be, or may be, "market" or what is standard in the industry. Same result under CISG Article 19.

(b) If so, when does payment have to be made?

In 30 days. Buyer didn't object, so the new term becomes part of the contract, so long as the payment date does not materially alter the contract, and parties are merchants under UCC 2-207. Same result under CISG Article 19.

PROBLEM 4-9

Purchaser sends Vendor a written PO for 15,000 stainless steel widgets. The PO provides: "Terms net 45." Nadir sends back a written confirmation which contains the same terms as the PO except that it provides: "Terms: Net 30/2% in 10." Apogee does not protest, and the widgets are shipped in due course.

(a) Is there a contract? *Yes. The parties have a contract. The forms contain different terms, but the second one is an acceptance.*

(b) If so, when does payment have to be made?

Applying only § 2-207(1) only, it would seem that payment is probably due in 45 days, as that was in the original offer. If § 2-207(2) applies to different as well as additional terms, then payment is probably due in 30 days unless this change is material. (How do we figure out if it is material? It is part of the payment terms, and, at bottom, cash flow is king in business. But it is only a 15-day difference, and they can get a discount . . .).

PROBLEM 4–10

Customer sends Manufacturer a written PO for 20,000 fiberboard widgets. The PO says nothing about the time in which the seller must be notified of defects in the goods. Manufacturer sends back a confirmation which states: "All claims for defects in the goods sold must be made within 5 days after delivery." The norm in the business is that the buyer has at least 30 days in which to give notice of defects.

Is there a contract?

Yes. 2-207(1) acceptance with different terms, not expressly conditioned.

(a) If so, what is the deadline for claims of defects?

Since we have a contract, we must ask what is the term relating to defects? The 5 day period is not knocked out by 2-207(2)(a) as the offer did not limit acceptance to its terms. Similarly, under 2-207(2)(c), there is no knock out as there have been no prior exceptions. This leaves us with 2-207(2)(b) – is this a material alteration? If so, the 5 day term is out; if not, it is in.

PROBLEM 4-11

Developer sends Bank a written offer to purchase the land and building where a soon-to-be-closed branch of the bank is located. Bank writes back: "We accept your offer, but we must be allowed to take with us the chandelier in the lobby." Developer, who has changed her mind, writes back: "The deal is off."

(a) Do the parties have a contract?

Probably not. The acceptance of the offer was made conditional on assent to the new term. The other party did not consent to the new term. Also UCC § 2-207 applies to goods, not real estate, so you are back to the mirror image rule.

(b) If so, who gets the chandelier?

Bank, assuming there was a contract, then not a material term, so Bank gets it. Both may be "merchants" but the UCC does not apply to real estate.

PROBLEM 4–12

Buyer sends Seller a purchase order for 20,000 composite widgets. The PO does not specify when payment is to be made. Seller sends back a written confirmation with the notation: "Terms: net 10." Buyer sends Seller a fax saying:

"We object to your 10-day payment terms." Seller ignores the fax, and the widgets are shipped in due course.

(a) Do the parties have a contract? *Yes.*

(b) If the parties have a contract, when was this contract formed? *When confirmation is sent. 2-207(1).*

(c) If the parties have a contract, when does payment have to be made? *See* UCC § 1-303 (especially subsection (d)) [if you are using the pre-2001 version of Article 1, use 1-205 rather than 1-303], 2-309 and 2-310(a). *Because the buyer's order did not say anything about payment terms the seller is proposing an "additional" term. Because the buyer objects, the seller's term does not become part of the contract. The payment terms will be provided by the UCC. .The default rule is that payment will be due when the buyer receives the goods. UCC § 2-310(a).*

PROBLEM 4–13

Grain Exporter calls Corn Broker and orally enters an order for 100,000 bushels of corn at $4.50 per bushel, the then-current market price. Broker tells her: "You got it." Broker sends a written confirmation. The confirmation provides: "All disputes arising out of this contract shall be settled by arbitration in accordance with the rules of American Arbitration Association." When the corn is delivered, it contains an unacceptably high moisture content. Exporter sues Broker over the high moisture content, and Broker moves to dismiss the suit on the basis that Exporter agreed to arbitrate the dispute.

(a) Is there a contract? *Yes. They entered into an oral contract on the phone. 2-207(1).*

(b) If so, is Exporter compelled to arbitrate? *2-207(2). Merchants, so term comes in unless one of the exceptions applies. Here, materiality is the issue.*

The analysis here is really interesting. The Broker's confirmation proposes an additional term. Per UCC § 2-207(2), that term does not become part of the contract if it materially alters the oral contract. Suppose that in the grain industry, it is the norm for contracts to include an arbitration clause. In that case, the Broker's proposed term is the industry standard. Comment 4 states that a clause that "materially alters" the terms of an offer or oral contract is one that would "result in surprise or hardship, for example, if incorporated without express awareness by the other party. . . ." If arbitration is the prevailing practice in an industry, is the inclusion of an arbitration clause a cause for surprise or hardship? New York courts have held that there is no surprise in this circumstance, so the Exporter would have to arbitrate.

On the other hand, if arbitration were not the general practice in the grain industry, the cases generally hold that inclusion of an arbitration clause would constitute a "material alteration," so the clause would not become part of the contract between the Exporter and Broker. See, generally, James J. White and Robert S. Summers, Uniform Commercial Code, 5th ed., vol. 1 (2002), p. 77.

PROBLEM 4–14

Salesperson calls Homeowner, to whom she has previously given a quote for the installation of vinyl siding on his home. (The quote said nothing about when payment was due, and there is no "industry standard" that would be binding on Homeowner.)

Salesperson: "Do you want to take the siding on the terms of my quote?"

Homeowner: "It's a deal."

Salesperson: "Good. I'll send you a confirmation."

The confirmation that Homeowner receive says "Ten per cent deposit due in 15 days, balance on completion of job." Homeowner does not respond to it.

It's not clear whether Article 2 applies to this transaction, so you need to answer the following questions under the common law and under Article 2.

(a) **Is there a contract?** *Yes, they made an oral contract under both the common law and UCC Article 2. The confirmation proposes an additional term. Under 2-207(2), the additional term does not become part of the contract because the homeowner is not a merchant.*

(b) **If so, when is payment due?** *Because the contract is already made, the confirmation is a proposal for a modification. The default payment term would be provided by R2d § 234(2). Payment due upon completion of the job.*

PROBLEM 4–15

Buyer sends Seller a PO for two boxcar loads of sunflower seeds. The PO provides that freight costs will be paid by the seller. Seller sends back an acknowledgment that provides freight costs will be paid by the buyer. Buyer does not respond to the acknowledgment and the seeds are shipped and accepted. **Who has to pay the freight costs?**

There is a contract. Seller's acknowledgment proposes a different term. Even if UCC § 2-207(2) treated a "different" term in the same way as an "additional" term, the proposed term in the seller's acknowledgement would materially alter the terms of the Buyer's purchase order. So the seller would appear to be stuck with the shipping costs because the buyer's purchase order defines the content of the contract vis a vis the cost of shipping.

PROBLEM 4–16

Seller (a merchant) sends Buyer (a non-merchant) an offer to sell an antique knife. The offer provides that Buyer may return the knife for a full refund within 30 days. Buyer sends a letter saying she accepts the offer but she needs 45 days to determine whether to return the knife because she will be out of the country for the entire 30 days following the anticipated date of delivery. Seller does not respond but instead ships the knife. Buyer attempts to return the knife after 35 days. **Is she entitled to do so?**

Subsection (1) provides that Buyer's letter is an acceptance even though it states terms different from those of the offer. (Subsection (1) applies to all sales of goods, regardless of whether the parties are merchants.) Subsection (2)'s provision that terms not objected to become part of the contract, however, only applies "between merchants" (i.e., when BOTH parties are merchants). It is therefore inapplicable and Buyer is bound by the terms of the original offer. She has only 30 days to return the knife and is (to use traditional legal terminology) s.o.l.

◆ -- ◆

Hill v. Gateway 2000, Inc.
United States Court of Appeals, Seventh Circuit
105 F.3d 1147 (1997)

A very entertaining Easterbrook opinion. But, in our view, he misconstrues UCC § 2-207. His strong and direct style obscures the faulty assumption that he makes that § 2-207 requires more than one form or confirming memorandum. The more forceful the argument, the more we should be suspicious about its accuracy! Note the dismissive tone the court uses for the RICO claim in federal court; perhaps Easterbrook is communicating his disdain for these sorts of suits. Could this be driving the outcome on the merits?

Gateway puts terms on a sheet in the box of its computer, including an arbitration clause (not in the case, but, as reported elsewhere, the term requires the arbitration to take place in Chicago, so you have to come there; this and other costs and fees provided for appear to be an attempt to increase customer's transaction costs in bringing a suit or complaint. It is all part of "the grind down" program. And you thought Kafka was fiction.) Acceptance if you keep the machine for more than 30 days.

The Hills keep the machine, then have problems, then sue. District court does not enforce arbitration clause finding no valid agreement to arbitrate.

This court: Reverse.

The death knell for the Hills is first rung in paragraph 3: "If [the in the box terms] constitute the parties' contract because the Hills had an opportunity to return the computer after reading them, then they must be enforced" (and of course they had the opportunity).

Court states that UCC § 2-207 apples to the battle of the forms and here there are no battling forms, just one form, the in the box terms. Since only one form, 2-207 does not apply. (Sounds good. But, look at UCC § 2-207 – Does it say anything about the battle of the forms or the need for two forms? Any forms at all? Wouldn't it apply to a single non-conforming written confirmation of an oral contract (like one made on the phone)? Could Easterbrook have made a mistake? Or was this just the best way to intentionally side step the 2-207 issue? It sounds good and goes down smoothly on the first reading.

Court reviews *ProCD* and *Carnival* and speaks of freedom of contract, etc. Court knocks down the other three grounds suggested [paras. 5 (limit *ProCD* to software), 6 (limit *ProCD* to executory contracts), and 8 (limit *ProCD* to boxes that give notice that additional terms are within) – the discussion in paragraph 5 is key – *there is no law of software, there is the law of contract as applied to software.* All this talk about "Space Law" and "Computer Law" is silly unless you identify specific statutes on these subject matters, like the Lanham Act, the Copyright Act, etc. that give us "Intellectual Property Law"].

NOTES AND QUESTIONS

Is the court right when it says the UCC § 2-207 requires more than one form in order to be applicable? Or is the battle of the forms a subset of more general matters addressed by § 2-207? If the latter, how would you describe the larger set of matters?

See above.

◆ -- ◆

Klocek v. Gateway, Inc.
United States District Court for the District of Kansas
104 F. Supp. 2d 1332 (2000)

Klocek sues Gateway and HP on warranties that its computer would be generally compatible. Gateway, again, points to the "Standard Terms" and arbitration clause in its notice in the box and the opportunity to return the computer within 5 days to get out of them.

Court goes over the two lines of authority, and Gateway urges that it follow the 7th Cir. Hill/ProCD line of cases. The court then goes out of its way to reverse offeror and offeree analysis from Hill/ProCD [para. 15], casting Klocek as the offeror so it can apply § 2-207, even if there is only one form in the battle (after all, the last shot advantage would apply even if the first shot is the last shot . . . Further, § 2-207 is drafted more broadly than just the two or more competing forms context). Because Klocek is not a merchant, the additional terms do not get presumptively included and they are a material change to the deal anyway (§ 2-207(2)(b)).

90

Finding no assent, it "overrules" – the better term is probably "denies" – Gateway's motion to dismiss.

NOTES AND QUESTIONS

1. The court, after casting the consumer as the offeror and Gateway as the offeree, states "As an expression of acceptance, the 'standard terms' would constitute a counteroffer only if Gateway expressly made its acceptance conditional on plaintiff's assent to the additional or different terms." **How could Gateway accomplish this task?**

Open ended discussion. Require acknowledgment and signature of acceptance? Post them on the website? Include them and a statement to this effect on the e-mail confirmation of the order sent back to the customer, with an "I accept" button . . . . Basically the C.Itoh approach to drafting into the law by using the statutory wording.

2. The rate of change in commercial contracts and practices is accelerating due, in large part, to the growth of the Internet and other information-science technology. Shrink-wrap, in-the-box, and click-to-accept contracts are increasingly used at all levels of the commercial world. As has historically been the case, the law lags behind these developments for the practical reason that legislatures and courts do not address disputes and other problems until after they arise. Then, typically, the legislature addresses the situation unless a strong constituency favors the status quo and opposes change, which may force the judiciary to address the situation by "making law." Whichever branch of government addresses the problem, a variety of rules and solutions are proposed, only a few of which survive to become the dominant or applicable rule. As the preceding cases indicate, things are still working themselves out in this area of law and § 2-207 may prove ill-suited to address box-top licenses and in-the-box terms, both largely unknown when it was drafted.

3. The following case represents a turnaround of the usual situation. Here, the party using boilerplate and a contract of adhesion is the consumer, not BigCo. The "turn about is fair play" attitude of the court to the "form" contract at issue is interesting.

♦ -- ♦

Cook's Pest Control, Inc. v. Rebar
Supreme Court of Alabama
852 So. 2d 730 (2002)

Customers slip an addendum to their pest control agreement with their renewal payment. Cook's cashes the check and is held to have accepted the addendum. Simple offer and acceptance reasoning.

This is a good place to talk about the uneven playing field that self-regulated, industry-dominated arbitration can create, the "repeat player" advantage, and the like.

Lawyering Skills Problem

You are a member of the General Counsel's office at Bell Computer, a producer and retailer of personal computer systems and related products. You have been asked to design the legal aspects of an order-taking and product shipping system that will ensure that, in a later dispute with a customer, the court will find that the customer was the offeree and Bell was the offeror, and that Bell's "in the box" terms—including a mandatory arbitration clause—were part of Bell's offer, which was accepted by the customer when they received their order and retained the product for thirty days without protest. What is your design? Is it practical and workable in the real world of business? Is it legally effective and foolproof?

This problem can be the subject of open ended discussion as students advance proposals and the class critiques them.

◆ -- ◆

Additional 2-207 Problems
(Teacher's Manual Only)

1. Buyer sends Seller a purchase order (PO) for 2,000 pounds of flour. The PO says nothing about when claims for defective goods have to be made. Seller returns an acknowledgment that specifies all claims for defective goods must be made within 30 days after delivery. Buyer does not respond to the acknowledgment. The flour is delivered, accepted, and paid for. Thirty-eight days after delivery Buyer informs Seller it wants a partial refund because some of the flour had weevils in it. **Does Seller have to give a refund?** (UCC § 2-607(3) provides that claims have to be made within a reasonable time.)

Under subsection 2-207(1), the acknowledgment is an acceptance. The requirement that all claims be made within 30 days is an additional term. Subsection 2-207(2) says that between merchants the additional term becomes part of the contract unless the offer limits acceptance to the terms of the offer, the additional term materially alters the offer, or the additional term is objected to. If the requirement that claims be made within 30 days materially alters the offer, then Buyer has a reasonable time to make a claim. If the requirement does not materially alter the offer, then Buyer must make claims within 30 days, and it's out of luck here. I don't think the requirement materially alters the terms of the offer, but I don't know enough about the flour business to say for sure.

2. Buyer sends Seller a PO for 1,000 pairs of shoes. The PO says nothing about arbitration. Seller responds with an acknowledgment that provides all disputes involving the transaction will be settled by arbitration. Immediately upon receipt of the acknowledgment, Buyer sends Seller a fax stating that it refuses to be bound by arbitration. **Do the parties have a contract? Will disputes concerning the contract be settled by a judge or an arbitrator?**

Under subsection 2-207(1), the acknowledgment is an acceptance. The requirement that all disputes be settled by arbitration is an additional term. Subsection 2-207(2) says that between merchants the additional term becomes part of the contract unless the offer limits acceptance to the terms of the offer, the additional term materially alters the offer, or the additional term is objected to. Here the additional term was objected to, so it does not become part of the contract.

3. Seller sends Buyer an offer to sell a used printing press. The offer provides that the press is sold without any warranties whatever. Buyer sends a letter stating that it accepts the offer but "this acceptance is expressly made conditional upon your agreement that the press is warranted for a period of one year." Seller does not respond but ships the press. Buyer accepts the press. **Do the parties have a contract? If so, what warranties, if any, does the press carry?**

The letter is not an acceptance under subsection 2-207(1) because it expressly says it is conditional on the warranty. If subsection 2-207(1) doesn't apply, then neither does subsection 2-207(2), and we go right to subsection (3). Subsection (3) says you get whatever warranties are provided for in the UCC.

4. Buyer sends Seller a PO for two carloads of sunflower seeds. The PO provides that freight costs will be paid by the seller. Seller sends back an acknowledgment that provides freight costs will be paid by the buyer. Buyer does not respond to the acknowledgment and the seeds are shipped and accepted. **Who has to pay the freight costs?**

Under subsection 2-207(1), the acknowledgment is an acceptance. The requirement that the buyer pay the freight is a "different term." There are four ways to treat this different term, depending on how one reads subsection (2).

(a) If the language of subsection (2) is taken literally, that subsection applies only to "additional terms," not to "different terms" (i.e., terms that change the offer, rather than merely adding to it). Under this reading the acknowledgment's requirement that the buyer pay freight costs has no effect (unless of course Buyer should for some reason expressly agree to it). Seller has to pay the freight costs.

(b) If the words "additional terms" in subsection (2) are taken to mean "additional or different terms" (which is the way most courts read it, then there are three ways to analyze the problem:

(i) The requirement that the buyer pay the freight was not objected to, so Buyer has to pay the freight unless the requirement that the buyer pay the freight "materially alters" the offer. Whether the term materially alters the offer would probably depend on how large the freight charges were in relation to the total price.

(ii) The PO's provision that the seller would pay the freight is an objection (made in advance) to the requirement that the buyer pay the freight. Therefore the provision that the buyer pays the freight doesn't get in under subsection (2) and Seller has to pay the freight.

(iii) The contradictory terms in the PO and the acknowledgment cancel each other out (the so-called "knockout rule") so the freight is paid by whomever would pay the freight if the contract were silent on that point. (It's the buyer, but you're not responsible for knowing that.)

CHAPTER 5

CONSIDERATION: THE BARGAIN REQUIREMENT

— ♦ —

"Supported by Consideration" – Put up R2d § 71. A screening devise for agreements the law will enforce.

Old formulation (still repeated in case law), of "benefit to the promisor or detriment to the promisee." We (and most other law professors) don't like that formulation. We like the formulation that focuses on "bargained for" – not haggled over – but that each side either changed its position or promised to change its position in exchange for the other's change in position.

R.2d § 71(1) – see how this is the change in position formulation?

R.2d § 71(2) – covers bargained for.

R.2d § 71(3) – covers what the performance can be (anything).

R.2d § 71(4) – ok for third party beneficiary contracts (put that off for later).

Let's take a look at Problem 5-1 and Problem 5-2.

♦ - - ♦

PROBLEM 5-1

The owners of a major league baseball team were thinking about moving the franchise. A group of civic boosters wanted a team in their city. The boosters told the team owners, "if you'll move the team to Salt Lake, we'll build a new stadium." The parties agreed to this, and a formal document was executed in which the team agreed to move to Salt Lake City and remain there for at least five years and the city agreed to build a new stadium in accordance with certain specifications set forth in the document.

(a) What was the consideration flowing from the city to the team?

The consideration flowing from the city is the city's promise to build a new stadium.

(b) What was the consideration flowing from the team to the city?

The consideration flowing from the team is the promise to move the team.

PROBLEM 5-2

The owners of the professional football team were thinking about moving the franchise. A group of civic boosters wanted a team in their city. The boosters told the owners "if you'll move the team to Portland, we'll build a new stadium." The owners said "we're keeping our options open. If you build a new stadium, that will make your city very attractive to us." Over the opposition of citizens who thought the city had needs more pressing than a new stadium, the city government built a new stadium. When the stadium was completed, the team sent the city a letter promising to move the team. The mayor replied with a letter thanking the team but making no promises. (An earlier draft had the city promising all sorts of things, but someone showed it to the city attorney, who edited out all commitments of any kind by the city, saying the mayor had no authority to promise these things without the approval of the city council.)

(a) Is the team's promise to move binding?

The team's promise is not binding because it is not supported by consideration. The team is promising to move, but the city isn't promising to do anything in return, because the stadium has already been built.

(b) If so, what is the consideration that makes the promise binding?

If the stadium had not yet been built, the promise to build it might have been consideration. Or, if the earlier draft containing the mayor's promises had been sent, there might have been consideration. However, for either of those to be consideration, it must be something that the team wanted in return for its promise to move. The team didn't bargain for the stadium and kept matters open and then promised to move after the city had already built the stadium, so there's no consideration.

♦ -- ♦

NOTES

♦ -- ♦

Hamer v. Sidway
Court of Appeals of New York
124 N.Y. 538 (1891)

If you will refrain from drinking, smoking, swearing and playing cards until you are 21, I will pay you $5,000.

Once the nephew gets to be 21, Uncle puts him off and says I will hold the money, you can consider it to be at interest.

Probate estate. Claim? Yes. No need for the promisor to be benefitted by the performance contracted for. That is not the law. It is enough if another does or refrains from doing something that they are otherwise entitled to do.

NOTES AND QUESTIONS

1. Willie was not the litigious sort. After his uncle's death, when money did not seem to be forthcoming from the estate, he sold the right to the money, his claim, to a third party who, it appears, sold it as well, and so on, until it reached the plaintiff. Discounting and transferring contract claims -- taking less than their face amount for them and transferring them on -- is an old business that continues today. One of the most powerful inventions of modern business is the ability to slice, dice, and sell contract rights, debt, equity, and other entitlements to payment streams into different tranches with different priorities and different risks and rates of return. These are the techniques used to "securitize" something. So, remember, if you or your client has a contract claim, there are more than the two alternatives of pursuing it or dropping it; you may also be able to sell it, subject to some restrictions. The sale of personal tort claims is generally prohibited and the purported sale or assignment of those claims will generally have no legal effect.

2. Suppose the uncle had said, "I'll give you $5,000, no strings attached, but hope that out of gratitude you'll refrain from drinking." **Would there have been a contract?**

There would not have been a contract. The uncle is promising to pay $5,000, but the nephew is not promising to do anything in return. The uncle might hope that his nephew will refrain from drinking, but that's not something the nephew has to do to get the $5,000. Also, the uncle is blatantly stating that there's no consideration by saying, "No strings attached."

3. Suppose the uncle had said, "I'll give you $5,000 right now if you'll promise not to drink until you're 21?" **Would there have been a contract?**

The nephew has to promise to not drink until he's 21 and then, as soon as he promises, he will get the $5,000. He doesn't have to actually refrain from drinking, just say that he will to get the money. If all the uncle wants is a promise, then that may be consideration.

4. **What is wrong with the argument that there was no consideration because Willie was benefitted rather than harmed by doing what his uncle wanted?**

Harm or benefit doesn't have anything to do with the legal definition of consideration. Usually, there will be a harm/benefit of some sort, but what matters is that one person did (or didn't do) something that he otherwise didn't have to do (or could have done) in return for the other person's promise. So, the idea that Willie benefitted is irrelevant to the question of whether there was consideration. (A number of our students have expressed the sentiment that years without drinking, smoking, and swearing sounds horrible and would not, on the best of days, be considered a benefit; others disagree.)

◆ -- ◆

Stonestreet v. Southern Oil
Supreme Court of North Carolina
226 N.C. 261 (1946)

Lease with option to buy.

Later joint K to dig a well.

Then gratuitous promise to reimburse for the well if the option to purchase is exercised.

Option exercised but Oil Co. refuses to reimburse.

Held: No contract. No consideration.

Discuss option contract to purchase land and diagram various contracts.

QUESTIONS

1. **Did Stonestreet have to pay for half the cost of digging the well? If not, why wasn't his making the payment consideration for their promise to reimburse him?**

Stonestreet did pay for its half of the well. He was not entitled to reimbursement from Southern Oil because there was no consideration for its promise to pay Stonestreet's half. Stonestreet's making payment could not have been in consideration for the company's promise to reimburse because he already had an obligation to pay for half of the well. It wasn't part of the separate promise to reimburse.

2. **If Stonestreet wasn't required to pay half the cost of the well, could he get his money back on the basis that there was no consideration for his (Stonestreet's) promise to pay half the cost?**

No. The agreement to split the cost of the well was separate from the lease and each parties' provision to pay ½ the cost supported the counter promise to do the same.

◆ -- ◆

Batsakis v. Demotsis
Court of Civil Appeals of Texas
226 S.W.2d 673 (1949)

Suit to recover $2,000 plus interest that was said to be a loan. Actually a sale of 500,000 drachmae (about 25 USD at the time) to the defendant who was seeking funds to escape the Nazi invasion.

Held: Enforceable. Mere inadequacy of consideration will not void a contract.

QUESTIONS

1. The court says "mere inadequacy of consideration will not void a contract." **What does that mean?**

The court may mean that just because the consideration doesn't seem like a lot, doesn't mean it isn't consideration. A person may have several different reasons for entering a bargain which make it reasonable (to him at least) to give what he is giving in exchange for what he is getting. In this case, the borrower was unable to get to her money because of the war, which probably played a big part in motivating her to offer to pay $2,000 on Tuesday for a $25 hamburger today. (Our apologies to Popeye's Whimpy.)

It has been suggested that consideration is a proxy for reliance, which is what the law is really testing for when determining whether to enforce a contract. In other words, the law wishes to concern itself with enforcement of promises that were sufficiently important that the parties relied upon them. Because reliance, especially negative reliance in the form of not pursuing other options, is hard to prove, in order to encourage reliance on contracts, the law dispenses with its proof and uses consideration (the bargained for exchange, which suggests that there will be reliance -- after all, what are you bargaining for if not for something to rely upon?) as the way to prove reliance by proxy. See E. Allan Farnsworth, CHANGING YOUR MIND: THE LAW OF REGRETTED DECISIONS (Yale 1998).

2. **Does it matter whether the 500,000 drachmae had a market value of $25 (as Ms. Demotsis claimed) or $750 (as the trial court found)?**

Not really. Ms. Demotsis promised to pay $2,000 in exchange for 500,000 drachmae. So, she has to pay $2,000 now, whether the drachmae were worth $25 or $25,000 on the market.

3. Let's assume that (i) the 500,000 drachmae was worth only $25, (ii) the court accepts the R2d's position that nominal consideration will not make a contract enforceable, and (iii) $25 was such a small sum as to be nominal. **Would these assumptions change the outcome in the case?**

These assumptions may change the outcome of the case. If the only consideration were $25, and $25 is nominal, then, under the Restatement, there *would not be an enforceable contract. However, in this case, it wasn't just $25, it was $25 in Greece in the middle of World War II to a person who was suffering severe financial hardship. The combination of these factors probably makes the $25 more valuable. But of course, this is taking issue with point number 3 of the hypothetical.*

◆ -- ◆

NOMINAL CONSIDERATION *(Self-explanatory)*

◆ -- ◆

Schnell v. Nell
Supreme Court of Indiana
17 Ind. 29 (1861)

Wife dies without property and thus her bequests in her will are unfunded.

In consideration of one cent, Husband promises to pay $600 over three years to those who would have been her heirs.

Not good enough. Consideration of $.01 for $600 will not support the contract. Court seems to say that grossly unequal money for money when both are in the same currency won't satisfy the requirement of consideration, but that grossly unequal money for land will.

What about past love and affection? No good. (Maybe for future love and affection and industriousness . . . court does not go there . . . love and companionship, maybe; someone always seems to want to discuss when it crosses the line to illegal contract of prostitution -- be prepared to defuse or explore that issue.)

What about in memory of? No consideration.

QUESTIONS

1. **Is this just an early case rejecting nominal consideration or is there more to it?**

The court is also rejecting, as consideration, the love a person has for his dead wife or his desire to satisfy her wishes, and the promise not to sue on a legally groundless claim. The court makes mention of three different purported considerations: the one cent paid by plaintiffs, the love he had for his wife, and the fact that his wife wanted the plaintiffs to have $200 [para. 8]. The court says that the love of his wife and her desires are not consideration, because they wouldn't be consideration even if she were alive [para. 9]. There is also the possibility that the promise of the plaintiffs to not sue defendant on any claim under his wife's will is consideration. However, the court says a valid consideration cannot be found in the fact of a compromise of a disputed claim, because the agreement itself says that the claim was without merit as the will was void [para. 9]. Since there's not even a

100

bona fide dispute it can't be consideration. The defendant was essentially promising to make a gift, in consideration of a penny, which the court says is nominal [para. 9].

2. Suppose that instead of promising to give the plaintiffs $600 for one cent, Schnell had agreed to sell them 40 acres of land for one cent. **Would the result have been different in 1861? Would it be different today?**

The court in 1861, embracing a formalist notion of consideration, may have found one cent consideration for 40 acres of land. The court takes issue with the exchange of one cent for six hundred dollars, the mere exchange of different sums of money in the same currency whose value is exactly fixed [para. 9]. The land may make such an exchange okay, though the court does seem to reject the idea of really nominal consideration, if it would make the contract unconscionable [para. 9]. Today, so long as the person receiving the penny REALLY wanted it in exchange for the land, there will likely be consideration, even though it's "nominal" in the sense of being small, because it's bargained for and thus is not "nominal" in the sense of being "in name only." (Restatement § 71(1)). This distinction about the different senses of the word "nominal" and which one is part of the consideration analysis seems to ring a bell with some students. It pays to tease it out of them.

3. In the next to last paragraph of the document, the plaintiffs agree to give up any claims they may have under the will. **Why isn't this consideration under R2d § 74(1)? Why isn't it consideration under § 74(2)? What do you suppose is the purpose of R2d § 74(2)?**

For the agreement to give up a claim to be valid consideration under Restatement § 74(1), the claim must be doubtful because of uncertainty about the facts or the law, or the people giving up the claim must believe that they do have a valid claim. In this case, the parties were not uncertain about the law or facts, and stated in the document that the will was void, illustrating that there was no belief on the part of the plaintiffs that they had a valid claim. (Note that this is a subjective belief standard.)

The purpose of R2d § 74(2) is to allow insurance companies to obtain valid releases without worrying about consideration.

Note on Illusory Promises. Watch the use of "shall" or "may." One is for duties (shall), the other for rights and options (may). "May" only is a problem in terms of finding consideration.

Note on Conditional Promises. A conditional promise is consideration if the condition is outside the control of the promisor. These are aleatory promises (i.e. gambling promises) and they underlie all insurance and derivative securities.

Note on Alternative promises. In exchange for X, I will do A or B, my option. Consideration? Yes, if *both* A and B, separately, would be consideration.

Conditional Promises where the condition is in the control of the promissor – really alternative promises. Phrase as alternative consideration and then use a nominal consideration analysis on each. If any are merely nominal, then consideration is wanting.

♦ – – ♦

PROBLEM 5-3

Term life insurance is the original form of life insurance. It is a temporary policy that builds no cash value and covers only a specific term or period of time. It is earned in exchange for a premium payment and, if the insured dies during the term, the death benefit will be paid to the beneficiary. **In a term life insurance policy, what is:**

(a) the promise made by the insurance company?

In a term life insurance policy the promise made by the insurance company is to pay a certain amount of money if the person with the policy dies within the term of the policy.

(b) the consideration for that promise?

The premium paid by the owner of the policy is the consideration for the insurance company's promise.

PROBLEM 5-4

A real estate developer who is building a project will often require the contractor who is doing the actual building to purchase a "completion bond." (Actually, it is usually the lender who is financing the project who requires the bond in order to ensure that the building will be completed so that, if the lender later forecloses, they are not foreclosing on a half-completed building. But to avoid making the problem unnecessarily complex, let's keep the lender out of it for now.) The terms of the bond provide that if the contractor does not finish the project, the bonding company will (at the bonding company's expense) hire another contractor to complete the project. **If the bond is a bilateral contract in which the contractor agrees to pay the bonding company a fee (called the "premium"), what is the consideration for the contractor's promise? What is the consideration for the bonding company's promise?**

The consideration for the contractor's promise is the bonding company's promise (the bond) to hire another person to complete the building if the contractor doesn't complete the project. The consideration for the bonding company's promise is the contractor's promise to pay the premium.

PROBLEM 5-5

In the natural gas industry, "take-or-pay" contracts are common. A gas producer and a pipeline company will enter into a contract under the terms of which the gas producer will promise to sell the pipeline gas at a price of X dollars per million cubic feet of gas. The pipeline company will promise to either (a) take the gas and pay for it *or* (b) pay a cancellation fee of Y dollars. **What is the consideration for the producer's promise to sell the gas?**

The consideration for the producer's promise is the pipeline's alternative promise to either take the gas and pay for it or pay the cancellation fee.

PROBLEM 5-6

Sherlock Holmes lets (rents) his lodgings at 221B Baker Street from Mrs. Hudson at a rent of 4£ per month. For many years, Holmes has taken the lodgings on a month-to-month basis, but recently Mrs. Hudson became your client, and you advised her to put Holmes on an annual lease. Holmes insisted that the lease contain a provision allowing him to vacate the premises at any time and have no further obligation for paying any further rent upon the payment of a "cancellation fee." Against your advice, this clause was included in the lease.

Mrs. Hudson has just discovered the secret behind Holmes' high energy level and she has told you in no uncertain terms that you have to find a way to "get that dope fiend out of my house." After reviewing the lease, you discover that you neglected to include a provision that would allow Mrs. Hudson to evict Holmes on the basis of his pharmacological predilections. **Can she avoid the lease on the basis that there is no consideration:**

(a) if the cancellation fee is 10£?

Holmes promises to either abide by the terms of his lease or pay a 10£ cancellation fee in exchange for Mrs. Hudson allowing him to live on Baker Street. Because either of these promises would provide consideration on its own (as long as Mrs. Hudson bargained for it), there is consideration, and Mrs. Hudson cannot avoid the lease.

(b) if the cancellation fee is sixpence?

A cancellation fee of 6 p seems more unreasonable, and is probably nominal. Unless Mrs. Hudson bargained for the 6 p, which seems unlikely, there is no consideration for the promise that Holmes has made to pay a cancellation fee. Because this alternative promise does not provide consideration, there is no consideration for the lease, and it can be avoided.

◆ -- ◆

MORE ON CONDITIONAL PROMISES *(Self-explanatory)*

◆ - - ◆

PROBLEM 5-7

Gourmet Cheeses, LLC sells expensive cheeses by mail. To keep its customers happy, it is always looking for new cheeses. It discovered a small family-owned dairy and cheese factory in Iowa that produced a wonderful sharp cheddar. The factory had been in business for more than one hundred years. Gourmet Cheeses entered into an agreement with the owners of the factory. Under the terms of the agreement, the factory would sell, and Gourmet would purchase, all of the cheese produced by the factory over the next three years at a price specified in the contract. After Gourmet entered into the agreement, it discovered that its customers would not pay Gourmet's premium prices for cheese produced in Iowa. They seemed to think that it could only be good cheddar if it was produced a few miles away in Wisconsin.

Gourmet is now arguing that the agreement is not enforceable because the factory's promise is an illusory promise. The factory can avoid its obligations under the contract by going out of the cheese business for three years. Evaluate that argument.

The factory has essentially made two alternative promises: 1. Sell all of its cheese to Gourmet, or 2. make no cheese. Under a nominal consideration analysis, the alternative promise of the factory to not make any cheese is a substantial one, not one made "in name only." It is a small, family-owned factory engaged in the business of making cheese, and the promise to not make any cheese would almost certainly cause severe problems for it. It would not be avoiding its obligations under the contract, but actually fulfilling them, if it stopped making cheese for three years.

Kuney explains this to students -- or leads them to conclude for themselves -- that if the potentially illusory promise would be a "big deal" for the obligor, then it is consideration. Shutting down for 3 years would be a "big deal" to the dairy and cheese factory. The "Big Deal" test seems to stick in their minds. It is really just the obverse of the test for nominal consideration.

PROBLEM 5-8

Real estate developer is contracting to purchase parcels of land for a shopping center. Worried that he may not be able to get enough tenants, however, he expressly conditions each of his contracts to purchase on getting leases that he finds are satisfactory to him in his sole discretion within 120 days. When, before 120 days are up, one of her sellers changes her mind and tells him that she is not selling, he sues.

The seller defends the suit based upon an illusory consideration theory. She argues that all she got in return for her agreement to sell was Developer's illusory promise, one which he could get out of merely by claiming that the leases obtained were not satisfactory or by not making any effort to get leases in the first place.

Who should win?

The developer has promised to purchase property with the condition of obtaining a lease that he finds satisfactory within 120 days. He actually has no obligation to find a lease and purchase the property.

However, he has a 120-day time limit. He can't tie the property up forever, just for 120 days. This seems a lot like an option contract. The developer is contracting for the right to purchase the land at a set price within a certain time period. If the offer is in writing, signed by the offeror, recites a purported consideration and proposes an exchange on fair terms within a reasonable time, then it is a valid option contract. (R2d § 87(1)(a)). Alternatively, it is a conditional sales contract and, subject to any implied duty of good faith and fair dealing (See Chapter 25), the contract is enforceable as written.

See Mattei v. Hopper, 51 Cal. 2d 119 (1958).

This is a good time to make sure that students understand that buyers always want free options to tie up property while they satisfy other contingencies. Sellers should avoid granting free options or putting the property under a cancellable contract as there will be few alternative buyers while the property is tied up. Once an asset is in play, sellers should strive to keep it in play until a definitive, binding deal is reached.

♦ -- ♦

Kuney likes to get all of the next 4 cases up on the board. Then he discusses them together, aiming for integrated rather than serial case analysis.

♦ -- ♦

Wood v. Lucy, Lady Duff-Gordon
Court of Appeals of New York
222 N.Y. 88, 118 N.E. 214 (1917)

IMPLIED PROMISE FOUND.

Lucy is a designer and contracts with a distributor, giving him the exclusive right to distribute products and to license others to market them.

She makes unauthorized side deals and sales (through Sears, Roebuck, actually). She argues that the contract fails for lack of consideration as he has not actually promised to do anything.

Facts are not just absolute. Beyond ultimate facts and facts that carry a legal conclusion, there is advocacy in delivery, slant, communication: we call it spin today.

NOTES AND QUESTIONS

1. There appears to be more than a little misogyny or anti-British sentiment or both underlying Cardozo's opinion in the *Lady Duff-Gordon* case. Consider whether views like these may have had an effect on the outcome of the case.

One view is this is an example of the patriarchy keepin' the women down. Note how the court is adopting a rule that favors the male, commercial interests at the expense of the female and her budding commercial interests and her intellectual property. Alternative interpretations are also possible.

◆ -- ◆

Additional Question (Teacher's Manual Only)

1. At the beginning of this chapter, there was a hypothetical in which a lobbyist tells a congressperson whose vote she wants: "I'll contribute $500,000 to your campaign." **Why wouldn't the court imply a return promise in the same way Cardozo did in *Wood v. Lucy, Lady Duff-Gordon*?**

In Wood, *a promise is implied because the defendant gave the plaintiff an exclusive right to sell her designs. When the plaintiff accepted that right, he assumed duties [para. 3], including the obligation to pay defendant half of all profits, and giving monthly accounting reports [para. 4].*

Because of these factors, Cardozo concluded that a promise to use reasonable efforts to bring in revenue existed [para. 4]. In the congressperson hypothetical, the congressperson isn't promising to do anything at all. The lobbyist hopes that the congressperson will vote a certain way, which is why the lobbyist is donating the money, but the congressperson isn't taking on any exclusive right or any duties from which a promise could be implied. Also, Cardozo says that "We are not to suppose that one party was to be placed at the mercy of another." In Wood, *if there had been no return promise, the defendant's livelihood would have been entirely subject to the plaintiff's good graces. No such disparity is thought (or said to be thought) to exist in the congressperson hypothetical, so it seems unlikely that a court would want to imply a promise for that reason.*

◆ -- ◆

Karl N. Llewellyn A Lecture on Appellate Advocacy

◆ -- ◆

106

Frishman v. Canadian Imperial Bank of Commerce
United States Court of Appeals, District of Columbia Circuit
407 F.2d 299, 132 U.S. App. D.C. 169 (1968)

Loan was supposed to have 4 guarantors. One (Frishman) didn't sign at the time the loan was made. Later, his guaranty was sent in. The bank asked him to verify that it really was his signature and he said that he was only guaranteeing ten per cent and that only for a year. Bank said that was not acceptable, and he verified the guaranty. Later there was a $12,000 overdraft.

Bank sued Frishman for the $185,000 loan balance plus the $12,000 overdraft. Court says he's responsible for the overdraft only. No consideration for the original loan guaranty. Forbearance is not enough because he didn't bargain for it.

NO IMPLIED PROMISE FOUND.

Bank Loan, requires credit support – security (explain) and personal guaranties (explain). Loan has future advances clause (explain).

Four guaranties required, one not given until after the loan funded. Company fails and bank sues on guaranty vs. fourth guarantor.

Trial Court: 12k future advance judgment, but no recovery on the initial funding the rest, as there was no consideration for the guaranty.

Ct. of Appeals: Affirms. No consideration.

Bank argues forbearance. Court requires an actual forbearance and evidence of same in the record. None found. Bank argues for presumption of forbearance, court rejects because, among other things, there are practical problems – did the bank give up its call rights? We don't think so.

NOTES AND QUESTIONS

1. The courts' language is sometimes a little misleading. Sometimes they merely say "forbearance," when what they really mean to say is "bargained for forbearance." Like a promise or a performance, a forbearance is consideration only if it is *bargained for.*

2. Suppose that as soon as Mr. Frishman signed the guaranty, the bank had made demand that the borrower pay the loan, saying "we just wanted to try to get Frishman on the hook before we pulled the plug on you." **In a suit by Abel Construction Co. against the bank, do you think the court would say that the bank had made no implicit promise to forbear?**

The Bank has not made an implicit promise to forbear. The Bank claims that it has made a contract with Frishman, supported by the consideration of it forbearing from calling the loan. There is no evidence that this forbearance was

107

bargained for, so it cannot be consideration. If it were consideration, the Bank would have contracted away the right to call the loan at its discretion, making an implicit promise to forbear, and leaving it unclear when the Bank could call the loan. (para. 13). Because there is no consideration, however, there is no contract between Frishman and the Bank, only between the Company and the Bank. The Bank has not contracted away its right to call the loan whenever it wants, and therefore, has made no implicit promise to forbear.

3. Note how, as described in paragraph 1, the bank sought confirmation of Mr. Frishman's signature on the guaranty. This is a good idea. Make sure no one can claim their signature was forged. It's more common than you think for business people to forge signatures of their associates. Sometimes they do it with no thought of defrauding anyone. They figure the person would sign anyway and it's easier to forge the signature than to wait until the person gets back from a trip. Other times it's real fraud. Martha Stewart's colleague Sam Waksal was sentenced to five years in prison for securities fraud. Part of what he pled guilty to was forging a banker's signature on a letter stating he still owned stock when he had actually sold it. In the Parmalat scandal in Italy, the perps forged a letter from Bank of America saying that one of Parmalat's subsidiaries had a billion dollars on deposit. The accountants accepted the letter, apparently without verifying its accuracy and legitimacy with the bank.

4. If you had been representing the bank, how would you have documented the deal to make it clear that the guaranty was supported by consideration?

In the documents that were sent to Frishman to sign, the bank could have pointed out an event of default, like the lack of the Frishman guaranty, and offered to forbear from calling the loan for 30 days if Frishman would execute and return the guaranty.

♦ - - ♦

Palmer v. Dehn
Court of Appeals of Tennessee
29 Tenn. App. 597, 198 S.W.2d 827 (1946)

IMPLIED CONSIDERATION FOUND.

Palmer: Business Owner
Dehn: Mehanic/Victim and employee of out of state defendant.

Bus driver loses two fingers while working on a belt with manufacturer's rep. present. On the way to the hospital, rep. tells the victim that he "will see you are compensated for your finger."

Majority Opinion: There was a contract based upon forbearance in bringing suit on his chose in action (note how he waited until about a week before the statute of limitations ran – it being one year in TN). Minority: You must be kidding. This should be a mere tort suit.

What is going on here? Well, the negligence suit was barred or substantially weaker due to contributory negligence. Maybe the jury and court had sympathy for the victim and the court is engaging in result-oriented jurisprudence. Just speculating. But the important point is how one gets there in the reasoned opinion.

♦ -- ♦

Whitten v. Greeley-Shaw
Supreme Judicial Court of Maine
520 A.2d 1307 (1987)

NO IMPLIED CONSIDERATION FOUND.

Massachusetts contractor and Maine Mistress payoff and dump case.

The mistress is the defendant in the foreclosure action and she claims she never read the mortgage papers. Contrary evidence on this point, but she had the opportunity to look and if she did not, that was her own fault. (It doesn't help her that she did not bring up this claim prior to the foreclosure action.)

This, the court says, is a one way agreement. The defendant promises to pay her $500 per month, make major repairs to her home, pay for medical needs, take one trip and supply one piece of jewelry a year, and visit and phone at stated intervals. The only item that could be consideration is the statement that she will not call him at home without prior approval.

The court hangs its hat on the lack of bargaining and finds lack of consideration.

But, wasn't the real consideration outside the document? Wasn't it the promise that she would not raise hell with his friends and his wife on the trip when he signed it? Could this decision be an example of the patriarchy defending one of its own? Was it the blackmail-like atmosphere?

NOTES AND QUESTIONS

1. The *Hamer* court said that giving up a legal right can be consideration. **Did Ms. Greeley-Shaw have a legal right to call Mr. Whitten without prior permission?**

Defendant did have the legal right to call Plaintiff without permission. The problem here is that, at least according to the court, Plaintiff didn't ask Defendant to refrain from calling him. In Hamer, *the uncle asked his nephew to not smoke, drink, etc., which indicated that the abstention from sin was bargained for, and the consideration could support the contract.*

2. In the roofing case, we saw that the customer was deemed to have made the offer even though she just signed a form the roofing company stuck in front of

her. **Is that a valid analogy? If so, how does it affect the court's reasoning?**

Plaintiff signed a document prepared by Defendant in the same way that the roofing customer signed the form prepared by the roofing company. Plaintiff was offering to give Defendant various things, as the roofing customer was offering to hire the roofing company. The court's reasoning is sound, however. In the roofing case, the customer wanted the roof work to be done, and the company wanted payment. In Whitten, *Defendant wanted $500 a month, etc., but Plaintiff didn't want her to not call him. (He probably did want her to stop calling, but he didn't want it in exchange for the things he agreed to give.)*

3. **Wasn't the real consideration for his signing an implicit agreement that she would not cause a disturbance and embarrass him in front of his wife and friends?**

This could be consideration, but there are a couple of problems. First, Defendant doesn't have the legal right to harass someone, at least at some level. So, Defendant giving up something she doesn't have the right to do can't be consideration. Also, Defendant never promised to not embarrass Plaintiff in front of his wife, and even if she did, she didn't promise to not embarrass the Plaintiff as consideration for the written document. "She demanded I see her or she would come up and raise hell . . . ." The Defendant's promise to forbear from "raising hell" was in exchange for the Plaintiff's "seeing her," NOT his giving her the many items listed in the document she later wrote.

4. Of the last four cases, there have been two in which the court was willing to imply a return promise and two in which it was not. In each of the cases, try to identify the factors that influenced the court to imply or not imply a return promise.

In Wood, *the court pointed to the duties that the plaintiff assumed when he accepted the exclusive right to sell defendant's designs, and found an implied promise. In* Frishman, *the critical factor was that the "consideration" of forbearing from calling the loan was not bargained for, so there was no implied promise to forbear. In* Palmer, *the court found an implied promise to exist because there was a benefit and detriment that were sufficient consideration. In* Whitten, *the court found that because the promise to not call was not bargained for, it was not consideration.*

5. The statement in the previous question might not be entirely correct. **Is it clear that the *Palmer v. Dehn* court was implying a return promise, or is there another way to read the opinion?**

The court in Palmer *states that the jury could reasonably infer that there was sufficient consideration because there was a benefit to one party and a detriment to the other [para. 7]. They ignore the problem that the implied promise was that the Plaintiff would not sue, and the lawsuit could only have occurred if the Plaintiff sued. So, he didn't give up his right to sue after all.*

♦ -- ♦

IMPLIED PROMISE OF CONSIDERATION *(Self-explanatory)*

♦ -- ♦

Kirksey v. Kirksey
Supreme Court of Alabama
8 Ala. 131 (1845)

Facts: Plaintiff was defendant's brother's wife. After plaintiff's husband died, the defendant wrote her a letter saying that if she would like to abandon her current place of residence and live with him, he will provide her with a place to live until her children grow up. The plaintiff abandoned her place of residence and moved in with the defendant. After 2 years, the defendant asked her to move out.

Issue: Was the promise of the defendant to the plaintiff enforceable?

Holding: No. **Rationale:** The promise on the part of the defendant was mere gratuity and was not an enforceable promise; although the writing judge claims to disagree. Is the writing judge being honest about his position, or is he telling a "white lie" as he couches his opinion as the one the other judges would not accept? What do you think? They may say "watch what I say, not what I do," but watching what they do is so, so much more informative.

Far from being a merely family-oriented man, the defendant appears to have invited the plaintiff down to live on and claim homestead rights to a parcel adjacent to his own. When the law changed and he no longer needed her for this purpose, he asked her to move out. Funny how none of that made it into the opinion.

♦ -- ♦

PROBLEM 5-9

Frank hears that his brother Jesse has been shot dead. He writes Jesse's widow and states that if she moves to the state where he lives, he will give her a tract of land and a home to live in until the children are grown. He says he wants her to move "so that my nieces and nephews will be close by. I am getting old and lonely." After she has been there two years, he kicks her off the property. **Can she stay until the kids are grown?**

The letter is worded in a way that illustrates something the promisor is bargaining for. Because he is old and lonely, Frank wants his nieces and nephews to be close by. In exchange for them being near their uncle, Frank will provide a home for them. The nieces and nephews being close by seems a more substantial consideration than the "I want you and the children to do well" statement that the court called a mere gratuity in Kirksey. *Still, it is only a little bit different, and could easily be found by a court to be insufficient to form a contract.*

PROBLEM 5-10

The president of a company writes the following letter to a retired employee:

Dear Frank:

Because you worked so hard for the company for so many years, the Board of Directors has authorized me to grant you a pension of Two Thousand Dollars ($2000) per month commencing immediately. Thank you for your faithful service.

Sincerely yours,

ACME MANUFACTURING CORP.

John Acme
President

After Frank has been retired for three years, Acme Manufacturing Corp., now presided over by John's successor, Tom, ceases to pay the pension.

Can Frank recover future pension payments?

No. Frank isn't doing anything in return for the $2,000 each month. Though the letter says that it's for all the hard work Frank did, he's already done the work and been paid for it. There is no consideration flowing from Frank to Acme. Because there is no consideration, there is not an enforceable contract, and Frank cannot recover future pension payments.

PROBLEM 5-11

A wealthy man sees a homeless person freezing in the cold on the street. He says, "If you'll walk over to that store over there with me, I'll buy you a coat." **Is there consideration for his promise?**

At first glance, it doesn't seem that there's consideration flowing from the homeless person to the wealthy man. However, if the wealthy man had arthritis and needed help to get to the store, or if the street was a very dangerous one and the wealthy man wanted a little extra protection, the homeless man escorting him to the store might be consideration. The trick here is that the "consideration" (going to the store) is actually a necessary step in obtaining the desired benefit (the coat). This is, of course, "Williston's Tramp."

112

PROBLEM 5-12

A grandfather promises to pay his granddaughter $100,000 saying: "None of my grandchildren work, and I am making sure that you don't have to." **Is there consideration for his promise?**

There doesn't seem to be consideration in this situation. The grandfather isn't asking his granddaughter to do anything in return. He's making sure that she doesn't HAVE to work, but he isn't making her promise not to work, or quit her job, or anything like that. There's no consideration flowing from the granddaughter to the grandfather.

PROBLEM 5-13

Suppose the grandfather in the previous problem had said: "It's a matter of pride with me that none of my grandchildren work. I'll give you $100,000 so you can quit your job." **Is there consideration?**

These circumstances give more indication of what the grandfather wants to bargain for. He's giving his granddaughter money so she can quit her job, because he doesn't want his grandchildren to work. Unfortunately, he's not doing a good job of actually bargaining for that.

He's not requiring her to quit her job – he's making it so she CAN quit her job. Since she's not required to do anything, there is still no consideration flowing from the granddaughter to the grandfather. In this situation, the court would be more willing to infer an implied promise to stop working by the granddaughter if she accepted the money, but it still seems unlikely.

♦ -- ♦

NOTE ABOUT SEALS *(Self-explanatory)*

♦ -- ♦

Lawyering Skills Problem

You are visiting an old friend, Max, when Max's nephew Shelby stops by with good news. Shelby has been accepted to Cal Tech, his undergraduate institution of choice, where he hopes to major in Physics. Unfortunately, he did not receive a very generous scholarship offer, but Shelby tells Max that, if he can maintain a 3.6 or better GPA in his freshman year, he should be able to obtain a better scholarship package for his sophomore year.

Max tells Shelby how proud he is of him for being accepted to the school and notes that he expects to come into a little money at the close of the quarter, when a company that formerly characterized its equity as a "growth stock" will begin paying a dividend. Max says he would like to contribute to Shelby's college fund with that money. Shelby is very appreciative.

Max says, "let's make this binding, in case I get hit by a bus before the end of the quarter" (Max has always had a somber streak to his humor). He takes some note paper and writes:

For value received, I, Max Faber, promise to pay my nephew, Shelby Lynn, $5,000 on or before July 30, 2011.

He signs his name to the paper and starts to give it to Max, but stops and hands it to you, asking if he has done it right. You ask him, what is the 'value received'? He says he doesn't know, but that phrase has been at the start of every promissory note he has ever seen. You explain that consideration doesn't work that way, and that if there isn't any, it won't be enforceable. He offers you the note pad and a pen and says, "You do it for me – I want it to be enforceable."

Can you oblige Max?

CHAPTER 6

QUASI-CONTRACTS

— ♦ —

Cotnam v. Wisdom
Supreme Court of Arkansas
83 Ark. 601 (1907)

Facts: The deceased was thrown from a street car and he hit his head on the curve and was unconscious. The plaintiffs, two physicians, performed surgery on the deceased while he was unconscious, but the plaintiffs were unable to save his life. The defendant, administrator of the deceased, did not pay the plaintiffs for their services because the defendant argued that since the deceased was unconscious, no contract was made between the deceased and the plaintiffs. Value of estate was $18,500. Decedent was bachelor, so estate would go to collateral relatives if not to the doctor.

Procedure: The jury verdict for the plaintiffs.

Issues:

1. Can the plaintiffs recover for their professional services that they rendered to the deceased? (Yes.)

2. Should the jury consider the benefit to the plaintiff (he died)? (No. It is not a contingency quasi contract, just a quasi contract. Focus on value of services rendered. Court states it wouldn't be fair to the doctor to have to prove the value to the patient of the operation, because it's known that operations don't always work, but doesn't really explain this reasoning.)

Rationale: The plaintiffs can recover under a well accepted legal fiction of *implied contract* (aka *quasi contract, constructive contract*).

In *Sceva v. True*, the court stated: "an insane person, an idiot, or a person utterly bereft of all sense and reason by the sudden stroke of an accident or disease may be held liable, in assumpsit, for necessaries furnished to him in good faith while in that unfortunate and helpless condition."

As far as the second issue is concerned, the jury could consider the means of the patient if there was an actual contract involved, but in the current legal fiction, such evidence should not be considered. And there are side issues about whether or not you can let in the fact that the intestate estate would pass to nephews and nieces, etc.

Court states it was error to admit testimony as to value of estate. That would be OK for an implied-in-fact contract because physicians scale their services based on ability to pay. But here the only inquiry is to the value of the services. Here it is implied in law.

Reversed and remanded. On those evidentiary grounds. Not harmless error.

Tom Growney Equipment, Inc. v. Ansley
Court of Appeals of New Mexico
119 N.M. 110 (1994)

Ansley (Owner) sold backhoe to Edwards. Edwards took it to Growney for repairs. Growney repaired it and released it to Edwards for his note. The note was uncollectible, and Growney sued Ansley. Court says quantum meruit not available because it would impair the owner's right to free choice.

"Quantum meruit" comes from Latin, meaning "as much as he deserves."

Owner sells backhoe to Edwards on credit, takes security interest but does not perfect it. Edwards takes it to the repairer for fixing. Repair shop takes a note for the work and releases the backhoe to Edwards. Edwards defaults on both obligations and the Owner repossesses. Repairer seeks to recover in restitution for the work performed.

It is critical to diagram the parties' relationship on the board and it is a great time to pre-introduce students to those wonderful creatures of commercial law, the security interest and the possessory lien. Just a quick reference to the cages at the zoo that contain these creatures, then back down the contracts row of cages and various forms of consideration or consideration substitutes.

Held: No UNJUST enrichment in these circumstances. (Remember: if there was recovery it would be measured by the benefit received—not cost, not price.)

Owner did not ask for the repairs. Perhaps not so much focus on enrichment as on unjust? Repair shop could have retained the backhoe under mechanics lien laws – but it chose to release it on unsecured credit terms. So, not unjust. They took a risk and lost.

NOTES AND QUESTIONS

1. The court is being disingenuous when it refers throughout the opinion to Ansley as "Owner." UCC § 2-401(2) makes it very clear that Ansley was not the owner of the backhoe during the period after he sold it and before he repossessed it. He's just the holder of a lien. By using this terminology, the court makes it seem that there is only one way the case could have come out.

2. These two cases cannot begin to give you a complete understanding of the complex area of restitution and quasi-contracts. They do, however, give you a

basic idea of what the principles and issues are. The concept is explored a bit further in later chapters.

♦ - - ♦

PROBLEM 6-1

Lawyer leaves the office early because it's a nice fall day. When she arrives at her home she finds a man she does not know cleaning the leaves out of her gutters. She is about to ask him what he's doing when she realizes that he works for the yard service her next-door neighbor uses. Apparently the gutter cleaner is new and mistook her house for the house where he was supposed to do the work. Lawyer doesn't like the neighbor or his lawn service. She's had a number of unpleasant conversations with them about the loud leaf blowers the service uses. So she decides to keep quiet and get a free gutter-cleaning to make up for all the times her peace and quiet have been ruined by the leaf blowers.

When the lawn service realizes its mistake, it sends her a bill. **Does she have to pay it?**

Under the rule in Ansley, *it is against public policy to require a person to pay for services he did not want, know about, or ask for. If the services have resulted in unjust enrichment, however, the beneficiary may have to pay for them. In this case, the portion of the services that were rendered before Lawyer arrived home were not wanted, known about, or asked for. Lawyer should not have to pay for those services. However, Lawyer didn't inform the worker of his mistake, and she was unjustly enriched as a result. Lawyer, perhaps, should have to pay for the portion of the services rendered after she realized the mistake. It may not be possible to separate the fees for the service like this. In that case, whether the Lawyer has to pay may depend on which is the greater injustice: her enrichment or the yard service's detriment.*

Lawyering Skills Problem

You are an associate general counsel of a nationwide automobile rental firm in 1984. The General Counsel has recently heard of and read the New Mexico Court of Appeals opinion in *Tom Growney Equipment v. Ansley*, and has become quite concerned. Specifically, the company often rents its cars to travelers at airports who need them for short trips to various cities and other locations. Often, if the renter has a problem with the car and is late or fears he or she will be late to the airport, the renter will abandon the car, leaving the keys inside, take a cab to the airport, and call the company after arriving at the renter's destination, so that the company can pick the car up and close out the billing to the traveler's company. This is, not unsurprisingly, particularly common with lawyers traveling into a locale for a hearing or a meeting and then attempting to jet away quickly to return to their home offices.

The General Counsel's concern is this: What if the renter has work done on the car while he has it but does not pay for the work done or, worse, simply leaves the car in the shop where the work was done? What if the car is picked up and repaired or stored gratuitously by a stranger after being abandoned by the renter? What if it is illegally parked or left in a hotel parking lot and towed and then stored or repaired by the towing company? How can the company be absolutely certain that such a shop would not have a colorable claim for quasi-contractual recovery (quantum meruit or quantum valebat)? The General Counsel has asked you to come up with some suggestions to help prevent such a claim or, if such a claim is brought, ensuring that it can be dismissed early on in the trial court, perhaps through a motion to dismiss for failure to state a claim upon which relief can be granted or judgment on the pleadings, or, if needed, a motion for summary judgment. There is no way that she wants to have to take a case like this (the little, local, helpful garage vs. the big, national, impersonal rent-a-car company) to trial.

What do you suggest?

Various techniques are usually suggested, most involving notice. Signs on the dash or back window and in the engine compartment are most common. Contents of notice? Identify company as owner. Disclaim any right to repair or store for a fee without contacting X phone number for instructions and express, written consent, etc.

CHAPTER 7

PRE-EXISTING DUTY AND PAST CONSIDERATION

— ◆ —

A.   The Pre-Existing Duty Rule

Alaska Packers' Ass'n v. Domenico
Ninth Circuit Court of Appeals
117 F.99 (1902)

A little context. Lots of labor unrest at that time, 1890 to 1920 esp. – Wobblies, Goons, the alleged frame up and conviction by kangaroo court of Joe Hill in Utah, etc. The establishment was very concerned with labor unrest as tensions rose worldwide—opposition groups in Russia and other European countries were forming and the Russian Revolutions of March and October 1917 were, perhaps, the culminating event of all the activity.

Plaintiff fishermen/seamen sign on for $50 plus 2 cents per salmon. Then sign articles (shipping papers – where the company deposits pay with the shipping commissioner – neat system to try and prevent disputes and to shift the risk of shipping company bankruptcy and non-payment of wages off of the sailors) at $60 plus 2 cents per salmon.

When they get to Alaska, the plaintiffs claim the nets were bad and go on strike, asking for a new contract at $100 plus 2 cents per salmon. Although the local manager says he does not have the authority, he signs the contract.

They get back to San Francisco and some settle out for $60 through negotiations and mediation by the commissioner – but some sue to recover under the $100 contract.

Trial Court: For the plaintiffs, even though it did not buy the excuse for the strike (the bad nets) as that would make no sense (so the court says, – has it not heard of negligence and agency problems?), there the company and the workers interests were perfectly aligned. Trial court uses a waiver of prior contract and breach theory (sort of a settlement) to uphold the new contract.

9th Cir: Reverse. A clearer case of pre-existing duty there cannot be. Avoids the "hold up" problem. Reviews the authorities.

◆ -- ◆

Tired of the condescending attitude of big city wine stewards, a tourist shoots the sommelier in a fancy French restaurant. The Wine Stewards Guild posts a reward of 100,000 francs for the arrest of the perpetrator. A police department detective catches the perp and obtains a confession from him.

(a) What does this problem have to do with the principles covered in the *Alaska Packers* case?

The detective already has a duty to find criminals, as it is his job. The fishermen in Alaska Packers already had a duty to fish. Both the reward for the detective and the new contract terms for the fishermen were not supported by consideration because the detective and the fishermen had pre-existing duties to perform.

(b) Is the detective entitled to the reward?

The reward offer has the elements of a unilateral contract that can be accepted only by a performance. However, because there is no consideration supporting the reward as pertains to the detective, the detective is not entitled to the reward as a matter of contract law.

(c) Would it matter that the crime occurred in a precinct other than the detective's and that the detective did the entire investigation during off-duty hours?

The detective does not have a pre-existing duty to investigate crimes that occur outside his precinct. Nor does he have a duty to detect when he's off duty. The reward may be enforceable under those circumstances. However, it seems other issues may arise if the detective interferes with another precinct's investigation.

◆ -- ◆

NOTES AND QUESTIONS

Only note the digression about Cal. Civ. Code section 1542. It is pretty self-explanatory.

Two competing policies are at work in the California Civil Code. On the one hand, there is the need to protect people from the consequences of them underestimating the extent of their injuries. On the other hand, there is the need to protect the finality of settlements and contracts. The Civil Code attempts to balance these two by taking the presumption that the injured party is not signing away any future or unknown claims. The injured party has a statutory protection that cannot be waived with a standard contract clause. It then places the burden on the other party to draft a document that specifically waives that protection. The injured party, by expressly agreeing to waive this statutory right, is then doubly aware of the potential consequences of signing away any future claims for unknown injuries. This reinforces both of the competing policies. The injured person is warned not once, but twice, that he may be doing something with grave consequences. At the same time, this reiteration protects the finality of the settlement because there is little chance that a contract in which an injured party properly waived his rights under the California Civil Code will be able to sustain a cause of action for future injuries.

As the note suggests, this is analogous to the Miranda *warning adopted by the Supreme Court to accommodate the competing policies of fostering the right against self-incrimination and the practical needs of the justice system to obtain confessions.*

Angel v. Murray
Supreme Court of Rhode Island
113 R.I. 482, 322 A.2d 630 (1974)

Maher was getting $137,000 a year for picking up all the garbage. Asked for and got additional $10,000 a year. At the time of contracting, the parties had anticipated an increase of 20-25 dwelling units a year and there was an increase of 400 units. (The facts don't tell us what period this increase was over, but the contract was a five-year contract signed in 1964 and the first increase was asked for in 1968.)

Challenged by taxpayer watchdog group on two grounds, one administrative and we ignore that one, the other on the ground that, since this was a unilateral increase in price with no other terms changing, there was no consideration.

Trial Court: For the taxpayer watchdog group. Violations of administrative process (not our issue) and lack of consideration on account of the pre-existing duty rule.

This Court: Reverse. Dismisses the administrative issue and turns to the preexisting duty rule. Modification of a contract is itself a contract and must be supported by consideration.

> — Discusses its own *Rose* case in which it held that a bald agreement with a creditor to repay less than the full amount of a debt was not supported by consideration; and

> — Discusses the minority rule (Mass.) that there is consideration for a promise to perform what one is legally obligated to do because the new promise is given in place of the action for damages (sort of a release theory); and

> — Notes that the primary purpose of the pre-existing duty rule is to prevent the holdup game; and

– Notes the exception – courts are reluctant to apply the preexisting duty rule when a party to a contract encounters unanticipated difficulties and the other party, not influenced by coercion or duress, voluntarily agrees to pay additional compensation for work already required to be performed under the contract. This the modern trend, reflected in the Restatement (Second) § 89; and

– Notes that the UCC does away with the pre-existing duty rule with regard to sales of goods under 2-209(1) (but there is still a duty of good faith, and thus duress will not work).

◆ - - ◆

PROBLEM 7-2

Susan Acme, President of Acme Manufacturing Company, received a call from Rolf Nadir of Nadir Supply.

"Susan, old friend, how's it going?"

"OK, Rolf. You OK? How are the kids?"

"The kids are fine, Susan, but I got bad news for you. The price of plastic has gone through the roof. I've got to raise the price 50% on that lot you just ordered."

"No way, Rolf. We've got a contract."

"Susan, I could sell that stuff to somebody else for twice what your contract calls for. The only reason I'm only raising the price 50% is that you've been such a good customer. My dad tells me stories about the way your orders saved the company when the bank was threatening to foreclose."

"We've got a contract, Rolf. I'll sue. I mean it."

"You wouldn't really do that. There's not enough money involved. Besides my lawyer would string this thing out for years, and everybody in the industry would find out you sue your old friends."

"Tell you what, Rolf, since we go back such a long time, I'll up the price 25%. Send me a confirming memorandum."

"Done."

Shortly after this conversation took place, Ms. Acme was hit by a bus and killed. The company is now run by her son Jeremy, who never liked Mr. Nadir. Jeremy has asked you whether he can avoid the price increase his mother agreed to, sue Nadir, recover damages, and, if possible, wipe that company out of business. Consult UCC § 2-209(1) and advise him.

There is no consideration supporting the decision of the parties to raise the price of the lot. However, under UCC § 2-209(1), "An agreement modifying a contract within this Article needs no consideration to be binding." The modification must meet the good faith test, however. UCC § 1-203 and 1-201(19) (defense of good faith). To avoid the contract, Jeremy would have to show that Rolf was extorting a modification without legitimate commercial reason. For example, if Rolf lied about the price of plastic increasing, or if the price of plastic increased, but not so much as to justify a 50% increase in Susan's price, there might not be a legitimate commercial reason for the modification. (This is a place to discuss the ethical rules governing lawyer negotiations: no affirmative misrepresentations but puffing is okay, and statements about value are puffing.)

On the other hand, if Rolf was telling the truth, Jeremy may be the one who is seeking to modify the contract in bad faith. He wants to avoid the price increase, maybe because it will save Acme money, or maybe because he never liked Rolf. Jeremy knows of the terms of the modified contract, but doesn't want to perform under those terms, and doesn't have a legitimate commercial reason for it. This does not meet the good faith test as described in the comment to UCC § 2-209.

NOTES

1. One of the most important skills you'll need as a lawyer is the ability to look beyond superficial characterizations of deals and see what, in terms of legal principles, is actually going on. That was what Enron was all about. The company had a lot of ducks. Its lawyers dressed them up like chickens, and the accountants, even though they heard them quack, let Enron carry them on their financial statements as chickens. The rest, as they say, is history. Arthur Anderson, once one of the most prestigious accounting firms in the world, died in disgrace (even though it was partially vindicated on appeal too late to save the firm). *See generally* Enron: Corporate Fiascos and Legal Implications (Foundation Press 2004).

2. In one case involving Enron's mischaracterization of a deal, J.P. Morgan Chase & Company announced that it had reached a settlement that had cost it approximately a half billion dollars. Eleven insurance companies had guaranteed Morgan against losses on $965 million in sales transactions that Morgan had entered into with an Enron subsidiary. When Enron collapsed, the insurance companies took the position that they were not liable because the transactions that had been represented to them as sales transactions were actually loans. Insurance companies are prohibited by law from guaranteeing loans. The litigation was settled with the insurance companies agreeing to pay 65% of the claim and Morgan agreeing to buy $85 million in worthless bonds from the insurance companies. Bill Lerach, at the time the nation's premier plaintiff's securities litigator who later agreed to plead guilty to a felony count of conspiracy with a sentence of one to two years in federal prison and forfeiture of $7.75 million, said that the settlement would be useful in cases on behalf of Enron shareholders who claim they were misled by Enron's lawyers and accountants who, in turn, had mischaracterized the loans. "The evidence that came out is very

favorable to our case," Lerach said. "It shows clearly that they were disguised loans and it shows clearly that J. P. Morgan characterized them as disguised loans at the top levels of the company. Of course we will use that evidence."

Later, J. P. Morgan and Citicorp agreed to pay almost $300 million dollars in fines and penalties on account of these transactions. The regulators who forced the settlement alleged that the bankers knew that these transactions were really loans but allowed them to be set up to look like sales in order to make Enron's sales look greater than they actually were and to make their debts appear less.

♦ - - ♦

PROBLEM 7-3

Maria Santos operated a lawn maintenance company. When she noticed that the lawn at the Plebeian Yacht Club was not being maintained, she wrote a letter to the board of directors offering to enter into a contract to mow and fertilize the club's lawn for $2,000 a year. In response, the chair of the board (who is authorized to act for the club in all respects) wrote her as follows:

Dear Ms Santos:

> We are unable to accept your offer to enter into a maintenance contract because we are a new club and are trying to make sailing affordable to the masses. We would, however, like to engage your services to cut our grass. If you will cut the grass on our property when, in your professional judgment, it requires cutting, we will pay you $75 per cutting. In determining when our grass needs cutting, please remember that we are a group of working people. We are not Augusta National Country Club.

Sincerely,

PLEBEIAN YACHT CLUB
Joe
Joseph S. Pack
President

As soon as her schedule permitted, Ms. Santos went to the club, cut the grass, and submitted a bill, which was paid. This arrangement went on happily for several months until Ms. Santos' mower threw up a piece of stone which damaged a member's car. The member and the board of directors demanded that Ms. Santos pay for repairs to the car, and Ms. Santos refused, saying that the accident was unavoidable on her part because the club, which was too poor to pave its parking lot, had surfaced the lot with coarse crushed stone, much of which had, one way or another, gotten into the lawn. It was therefore impossible to avoid occasionally throwing up pieces of stone while mowing.

The club responded by writing Ms. Santos the following letter:

Dear Ms. Santos:

Because we have been unable to resolve our disagreement otherwise, we are now informing you that in the future you will be liable for any damage caused by objects thrown up by your mowers, regardless of who is at fault. By continuing to mow, you agree that you will reimburse any club member or guest whose person or property is damaged by an object thrown by any of your mowers.

Sincerely,

PLEBEIAN YACHT
CLUB
/s/
Joseph S. Pack
President

The next time Ms. Santos mowed, her mower threw a stone which damaged a member's new car. Ms. Santos' lawyer has said she is not liable because (1) silence is not acceptance of the offer to modify the parties' contract and (2) there was no consideration for the modification. Explain whether Ms. Santos is or is not CONTRACTUALLY liable.

Silence is generally not an acceptance. However, under R2d § 69(1)(c), where it is reasonable that the offeree should notify the offeror if he does not intend to accept, silence may be an acceptance. Here, the letter to Ms. Santos stated that if she mowed the lawn again, she would be agreeing to reimburse for property damage. This makes it reasonable that she should have notified Plebian Yacht Club that she did not intend to accept, but was merely fulfilling her duties under the previous contract. The problem remains, however, that Ms. Santos wasn't silent or inactive as required under the R2d. She performed the action of mowing the lawn, which could be reasonably interpreted by Plebian as manifesting an asset to the terms of the bargain. [We think the second analysis is better. It's a unilateral contract. If it's bilateral they can't change without her agreement. Mowing isn't agreement because she's not bound to mow again.]

There was no consideration for the modification. Under the UCC, there does not need to be consideration, but that only applies to the sale of goods, not services like lawn-mowing. R2d § 89(a) takes the approach that a modification is binding if it is fair and equitable in view of circumstances not anticipated by the parties when the contract was made. To satisfy this, it would have to be shown that requiring Ms. Santos to pay for damage caused by thrown rocks is fair in view of the circumstances, and that neither party anticipated that rocks from the gravel lot might be thrown and cause property damage. If this cannot be shown, then Ms. Santos is not contractually liable.

There is another way of looking at the problem. The contract between Ms. Santos and Plebian could be seen as not one contract, but a series of contracts. The initial letter written by Plebian states that if Ms. Santos will cut the grass when it requires cutting, Plebian will pay $75 per cutting. This may indicate that there is a sort of open, standing offer made by Plebian that Ms. Santos may accept by cutting the grass every time it needs it. Each individual cutting would form the basis of a separate contract. When Plebian sent Ms. Santos the letter, it changed the terms of the offer. When Ms. Santos mowed the lawn after receiving this letter, she indicated her acceptance of these terms. Therefore, she is contractually liable for the damage to the car.

B.   THE PROBLEM OF PAST CONSIDERATION

Mills v. Wyman
Supreme Judicial Court of Massachusetts .
20 Mass. (3 Pick.) 207 (1825)

Action brought to recover against father for care given to adult son who took sick upon return from a voyage. Father had, after the care had been given, promised, in writing, to pay for services rendered. Suit brought to collect.

Trial court: No. No consideration.

Appeals court: Affirmed. No consideration. Moral obligation based upon past acts cannot be consideration. The exception for obligations that the law will not enforce (debt already discharged in bankruptcy or barred by the statute of limitations) is justified as, once the protections of the law are essentially waived by the promisor, we have consideration in the underlying transaction. (Nice legal fiction.)

♦ -- ♦

Webb v. McGowin
Court of Civil Appeals of Alabama
27 Ala. App. 82, 68 So. 196 (1935)

Plaintiff saves the life of McGowin and is permanently disabled as a result, and McGowin promises to pay him $15 per week for life as a consequence. Performs right up through life, then estate stops payments.

Trial court: No consideration. Nonsuit.

This court: Reversed (!!). Court twists precedents around and finds this to be like payment to a Dr. that saves your life when you don't know you are dying. Lots of gymnastics to get there. Sympathetic result, sure; but is this how the law should work?

If there is time, cover value of life in economic terms – babies are negative worth due to near period expenses and long delayed earning

126

potential; educated males in their 30s to 50s are most valuable, as it is their peak earning period, there appears to still be a gender-based wage gap, rearing expenses have already been paid, and the old age maintenance and repair bills haven't started yet; time value of money and discounted cash flow method.

The concurrence is better and more intellectually honest: We are bending the law to do substantial justice.

NOTES AND QUESTIONS

1. McGowin lived approximately eight and a half years after Webb saved his life, during which he was the president of the W. T. Smith Lumber Company in Chapman, Alabama. He led that company's expansion and diversification as old timber stands were depleted. He was also active in wildlife conservation.

2. Note that it was not Mr. McGowin who was trying to eliminate the need to pay Webb, the man who saved his life. By the time of the lawsuit, McGowin was dead. It is the executors of his estate, his sons, who are under a duty to the estate's beneficiaries and creditors to object to questionable claims. Note also that it is likely that they were the primary beneficiaries of the estate. Executors and other fiduciaries, like escrow agents, often will seek a declaratory judgment as to the validity of a claim, joining all the other parties in interest, before paying it in order to have the protection of a court order if the payment is questioned in a later lawsuit. It is useful to remember this in practice; a letter of objection to an executor, trustee, or escrow agent prior to a distribution will often cause that party to "freeze" until the parties in interest settle their differences or an insulating "comfort" order is obtained from a court of competent jurisdiction.

3. R2d § 86 deals with the situation presented by the cases above. **How would each of them have been resolved under R2d § 86?**

R2d § 86 states that a promise in recognition of a previous benefit is binding to the extent necessary to prevent injustice. It is not binding if the benefit was conferred as a gift or the promisor was not unjustly enriched, or to the extent that the value is disproportionate to the benefit.

Mills. No recovery. The Good Samaritan took care of a sick and dying young man. Though the young man eventually died, his father promised to pay the Good Samaritan back for the care provided. The father later decided he didn't want to pay after all. This is similar to the Cotnam v. Wisdom case in which the doctor rendered emergency aid to the unconscious man who later died. The court found that an implied contract in that case demanded that the doctor be paid for his services. An implied contract could be found in Mills *as well. Though the Good Samaritan did not render emergency aid, end-of-life comfort and care was provided that has a monetary value. The father would have to pay if he inherited his son's debts. Still, the benefit was not conferred on the father, but on the young man. This means that the promisor has not been unjustly enriched, and the promise is not binding under the Restatement.*

Webb. *Recovery. In a noble sacrifice, a man puts his own life in danger to prevent serious injury to another. In the process, the man is permanently crippled. In appreciation, the lucky, uninjured man promises to pay the man $15 every two weeks. Injustice may be prevented by continuing the payments, which binds the promisee unless any of the exceptions are present. The promisor has been unjustly enriched. He received the benefit of not being injured or killed at the expense of the man's own injuries. The value of the promise is not disproportionate to its benefit. In exchange for saving his life, the uninjured man promised to take good monetary care of his savior, providing for him since he was no longer able to work. One would hope that the man's lawyer would develop the facts appropriately; left to its own devices a jury could conclude it was a selfless act (gift).*

4. What differences are there between the rule of R2d § 86 and the rule articulated in *Webb v. McGowin?*

In Webb, *"Where the promisee cares for, improves, and preserves the property of the promisor, though done without his request, it is sufficient consideration for the promisor's subsequent agreement to pay for the services, because of the material benefit received." The R2d does not call this benefit a consideration. It merely provides that a promise to repay for a previous benefit is binding as justice requires (binding to the extent necessary to prevent injustice; not binding where the promisor has not been unjustly enriched; not binding to the extent that the value is disproportionate to the benefit). Also, the Restatement distinguishes previous benefits that were intended as gifts, stating that promises to repay gifts are not binding. The rule in* Webb *makes no allowances for gifts.*

Summation: So, here we have three basic rules, which are partially contradictory:

1. **Traditional Rule:** Past consideration will not support a current promise, period. There is the bankruptcy/SoL exception that posits a waiver of protection of the law and recognition of the prior consideration on both sides of the deal.

2. **Webb v. McGowin:** Moral obligation can be a substitute for consideration, even if it was structured as a gift.

3. **Restatement § 86.** Promise enforceable to the extent necessary to prevent injustice and unjust enrichment. This is different from a consideration substitute. It is an independent cause of action. Gifts are exempted as are situations where the promisor has not unjustly enriched or the value is disproportionate to the benefit it conferred.

♦ -- ♦

When the Malibu mansion of billionaire art collector J. Gaul Petty burned, J. Gaul rushed outside screaming "Somebody save my Van Goghs!" Kato, J. Gaul's permanent houseguest and "human pet," rushed into the mansion and attempted to save the paintings. Unfortunately, he was unsuccessful. He was beaten back by the flames and all the paintings were destroyed. When J. Gaul saw that Kato had suffered burns on his face, he told him: "Don't worry. I'll have your face fixed by the world's best plastic surgeon, and I'll have her give you a facelift while she's at it."

Shortly thereafter, J. Gaul and Kato had a falling-out and J. Gaul has come to you to see if he has to pay for Kato's plastic surgery. The scars from the burns aren't very noticeable, but Kato's jowls are really sagging. He really wants that facelift. "The world's best plastic surgeon" (the parties have stipulated as to who was meant by this) has quoted a price of $50,000 for the surgery. Kato's medical insurance will pay the first $1,200. For fixing the scars alone, the price would be $6,000.

How much should J. Gaul have to pay? *Under the R2d, J. Gaul's promise is binding to the extent necessary to prevent injustice. This promise is not binding if the promisor has not been unjustly enriched. Here, Kato rushed into a fire in the attempt to save J. Gaul's paintings. Was J. Gaul was unjustly enriched by an unsuccessful attempt to save his art? J. Gaul certainly has received no monetary benefit from this. The only possible benefit that he could have received would be a peace of mind or satisfaction in knowing that Kato at least tried to get his paintings out. If this peace of mind is worth $50,000 to J. Gaul, so as to satisfy the requirement that the value of the promise not be disproportionate to the benefit, it may be a binding promise. If it's a binding promise, then J. Gaul has to pay for the surgery. This seems unlikely. J. Gaul didn't really gain any sort of unjust enrichment. As such, R2d § 86(2)(a) indicates that the promise is not binding and J. Gaul wouldn't have to pay anything [could give Kato $6,000 to fix scars using language in § 86 "to the extent necessary. . ." or "value disproportionate"].*

Lawyering Skills Problem

Accord & Satisfaction vs. Novation

When one modifies a contract and one or both parties are released from their obligations under the original contract, the parties that are released are said to have received a "novation."

This stands in contrast to what is known as an "accord and satisfaction" in which the parties enter into a new contract, but the old contract remains in force (perhaps with an extension of time to delay the need for performance) until the new or modified contract is performed. The "accord" is the new or modified agreement. The "satisfaction" is the performance of the accord, and the satisfaction novates the original agreement (or releases the parties from their obligations under the original agreement).

So, for example, if A owes B $500 in six months, but knows she will have difficulty paying it, she may propose paying B $200 in three weeks in exchange for forgiveness of the balance ($300). This could be structured as either an accord and be satisfaction or a modification. What does it matter? Well, if it was an accord and satisfaction and she fails to make the $200 payment in a timely manner the accord will fail and the original obligation to pay the $500 in (now) five months will remain. If it was a modification, she will only owe B $200.

Recall the situation in *Peterson v. Patberg*. Was the modification at issue a modification with a novation or an accord and satisfaction, or either of these things? If you were the creditor in that transaction trying to structure the modification agreement from the outset, which type of modification would you prefer? What if you were the debtor? Why?

CHAPTER 8

PROMISSORY ESTOPPEL

— ◆ —

Note the relative recency of the development of this doctrine and its two interpretations, one as a "consideration substitute," the other as a separate cause of action.

Ricketts v. Scothorn
Supreme Court of Nebraska
57 Neb. 51, 77 N.W. 365 (1898)

I promise to pay Katie $2,000 on demand, at 6% interest. None of my other grandchildren work and neither should she.

In reliance on the note, she says, she quit her job. Subsequently, she got another job (and her grandfather did not care or object, in fact, he helped her).

Grandpa dies and executor stops paying claiming lack of consideration. *(Pause a while on the executor's status and discuss the motivations that affect behavior of fiducuaries.)*

Trial court finds for Katie.

Appellate court **affirms** in a strained opinion. No consideration found [para. 5]; the church/school exception [para. 6], which is based on a strained concept of reliance [para. 7]; equitable estoppel – *(is there any difference between equitable estoppel, although strained, and estoppel in pais? No, not really).* Bottom line: **Detrimental reliance** is enough to cause enforcement of this promise.

NOTES AND QUESTIONS

Equitable estoppel is a principle that holds that where a person makes a representation which another relies upon, the person making the representation cannot deny the truth of the fact represented. For instance, A tells B that C is A's agent for the purposes of making a contract to sell A's car. When B makes a contract with C, A cannot claim that he, A, is not bound because he never really appointed C as his agent. **How did the *Ricketts* court expand this doctrine?**

The doctrine of equitable estoppel applies to a party's conduct. The court in Ricketts expanded this theory to apply to a party's promise. The grandfather in Ricketts didn't make a representation to his granddaughter. He made a promise to her. Under equitable estoppel, if the other party relies on that representation to his own detriment, the representing party may not later claim that the representation is false. In Ricketts, the court expanded this doctrine to apply if a party has made a promise on which the other party has relied to his own detriment. The promising party may not later claim that he didn't mean it.

♦ -- ♦

Feinberg v. Pfeiffer Co.
Court of Appeals of Missouri
322 S.W.2d 163 (1959)

Ms. Feinberg is awarded a $200/month pension upon retirement. She later retires, allegedly in reliance, in part, on same. Change in control – nasty little·son-in-law cancels the payments. (Please emphasize that the world is a nasty place and the doctrine you can rely upon is "what have you done for me recently/today?") People are not to be trusted; if they can get away with it or think they can, they will try. Part of the job of a lawyer is to make sure that the "other side" does not think it can get away with it.

Trial Court: For the plaintiff.

Court of appeals: Affirmed.

She is in bad health – TC let that creep into opinion – ct. app. says not enough to be prejudicial.

Evidence of reliance? Sure, there is enough. Ct. app. goes to record and quotes extensively. *(Why do people bring these appeals? Why do lawyers file them? Can't be criticized for trying and losing, can be for not trying. Sad, but true, especially for the courts that must process them.)*

What is the legal reasoning for the recovery? Continued work post-promise and pre-retirement. No. Evidence will not support.

Change of position – retirement in reliance. YES, YES, YES [paras 11, 15].

Promissory Estoppel as defined in the original Restatement's § 90 [para. 15]. Court says PE = Consideration (i.e. a consideration substitute) – you will hear this, but perhaps the better view is that it is an alternate route to recovery. Understand the distinction.

♦ -- ♦

PROBLEM 8-1

You are planning to file a lawsuit to enforce a promise made to your client. Because you expect the defendant will claim there was no consideration, you want to allege that the promise is enforceable under promissory estoppel. **If the jurisdiction applies R2d § 90(1), what elements or factors do you have to plead and prove?**

To support the allegation that the promise is enforceable under the doctrine of promissory estoppel, you must first prove that the alleged promisor made a promise. Then, you must prove that the promisor should have reasonably expected to induce an action (or forbearance) by the promisee. You must also prove that the promise did in fact induce that action. Finally, you must show that injustice can only be avoided by enforcing the promise.

Put up the overheads – first the raw R2d section, then the 'elementized' one, show the elements and the intentional use of the vague standards, ***then ask:*** How do you protect yourself from promissory estoppel?   AN OFFER IS NOT MEANT TO BE A PROMISE UNTIL IT IS ACCEPTED!   Explore and be explicit.

♦ -- ♦

Salsbury v. Northwestern Bell Telephone Co.
Supreme Court of Iowa
221 N.W.2d 609 (1974)

Charitable subscription to start a college that failed.   Salsbury was participating in efforts to start a college.   He was the chair of the board of trustees.   A professional fund raiser (Peter Bruno) negotiated a subscription from the phone company.   Instead of a pledge card, which had been held not to be an enforceable contract in a prior case, the phone company sends its own letter stating its pledge.

Now, here is the thing, Salsbury guaranties the debt when the debt is flipped to a "supplier" of credit who sells the pledge to American Acceptance Corp. When the pledge is not paid, Salsbury pays off the debt and becomes subrogated to the position of the creditor and sues to collect upon the debt/pledge. (Cover guaranty and subrogation. This is the students' first exposure to these important and all too commonly neglected concepts.)

Bottom line: Court goes with Restatement 2d Contracts § 90(2). How does it get there? Looks over the other cases, finds the cross-consideration rationale disingenuous, Promissory Estoppel inapplicable as no reliance, and adopts R2d position as simple public policy.

INTELLECTUAL HONESTY IS GREAT, ISN'T IT?

NOTES AND QUESTIONS

1. In paragraph 10, the court states that promissory estoppel is an alternative to the consideration requirement in a contract action.   This is one approach, in which promissory estoppel is considered to be a consideration substitute.   Another approach is to treat promissory estoppel as an entirely independent action with its own elements that must be pleaded and proven and not as a "contract" action.   **Is this a distinction with a difference? Why would it matter?**

133

If promissory estoppel is a consideration substitute, then all other contract doctrine and rules, including statutes of limitations, damages limitations, etc. automatically apply. If it is a separate cause of action, this is not necessarily so.

♦ - - ♦

W.R. Grace & Co. v. Taco Tico Acquisition Corp.
Court of Appeals of Georgia
454 S.E.2d 789 (1995)

Del Taco was partly owned by Grace and had some public shareholders.

Taco Tico was negotiating to acquire Del Taco. As part of the deal, Grace was going to get warrants that would allow it to control Taco Tico.

The parties entered into a non-binding letter of intent for a deal which provided:

> Taco Tico would lease Del Taco's properties for 15 years with option to purchase Grace's stock at end.

> The agreement was contingent on parties' investigations of each other's financial condition.

The agreement has very well-drafted clause saying there is no legal obligation. An example of very careful, broad drafting of the type that's sometimes criticized by academics.

> Notwithstanding the foregoing ... **or any other past, present or future written or oral indications of assent or indications of results of negotiation or agreement to some or all matters then under negotiation,** it is agreed that no party to the proposed transaction **(and no person or entity related to any such party)** will be under any legal obligation with respect to the proposed transaction or any similar transaction, and no offer, commitment, estoppel, undertaking or obligation of any nature whatsoever shall be **implied in fact, law or equity,** unless and until a formal agreement providing for the transaction containing in detailed legal form terms, conditions, representations and warranties (secured by an appropriate escrow) has been executed and delivered by all parties intended to be bound. This paragraph sets forth the entire understanding and agreement of the parties **(and all related persons and entities)** with regard to the subject matter of this paragraph and supersedes all prior and contemporaneous agreements, arrangements and understandings related thereto. This paragraph may be amended, modified, superseded or canceled only by a written instrument which **specifically states that it**

134

amends this paragraph, executed by an authorized officer of each entity to be bound thereby.

At the same time, the parties executed a management agreement where the parties agreed that TT would manage DT's operations for $10 a month while they were completing the acquisition. Separate management agreement with a $10 per month stated rate of payment (**what is this about?** Consideration. But they wanted to make sure the stores were under management; so, make this agreement binding but not the other one).

Parties broke off the deal.

TT sues for a number of things including quantum meruit and promissory estoppel–it won on those two.

Court of Appeals states that the trial court should have rendered a directed verdict for DT and Grace on the promissory estoppel claim because the agreement specifically said it couldn't be relied on.

Couldn't recover for quantum meruit because they had an express contract.

What is Taco Tico trying to recover for? DT and Grace backing out of the agreement or at least not doing the deal.

What happened in the trial court? DT defeats all claims except promissory estoppel (PE) and quantum meruit (QM).

Can you formulate their PE argument? Put elementized R2d § 90 on the overhead and have them link up facts.

The agreement has a great "no legal obligation" clause. **Take a look at it.** Three parts: (1) no legal obligation/non-binding, (2) integration clause for the paragraph, and (3) a no-oral-modification clause. **This is a very broad, carefully drafted clause of a sort that is often criticized by academics but is the stock in trade of experienced corporate attorneys.**

Court of Appeals: Should have been a directed verdict (**what is that?** Standard in paragraph 7. DV proper if there is no conflict of the evidence on any material issue and the evidence introduced demands a certain verdict) on the PE claim because of the express disclaimer and on the QM claim because there can be no QM when you have an express contract.

NOTES

The next case illustrates the failure of promissory estoppel to expand the protections available even to loyal employees that are hired on an "at will" basis, by far the most common method of employment.

◆ -- ◆

Loghry v. Unicover Corp.
Supreme Court of Wyoming
927 P.2d 706 (1996)

Loghry developed a concept for her employer. It appeared that her boss had disclosed the concept to a competitor.

A VP of sister corporation launched an investigation and asked Loghry to turn over her files.

She said she was afraid she would lose her job if she did, and he assured her she wouldn't. Her employer then fired her for "lack of loyalty."

Disclaimer signed at hiring:

> My employment and compensation can be terminated, with or without cause, and with or without notice, at any time, at the option of either the Company or me. I understand that no employee, manager, or other agent of the Company other than the President of the Company, has any authority to enter into any agreement for employment for any specified period of time, or to make any agreement contrary to the foregoing. Any amendment to the foregoing must be in writing and signed by the President.

Employee handbook says:

> Your employment and compensation may be terminated, with or without cause, and with or without notice, at any time by the Company in its sole discretion. There are no promises, express or implied, for continued employment, and no one except the Board of Directors of the Company is authorized to waive or modify these conditions of employment.

Employee loses in trial court and came up to the Wyoming Supreme court once before where the court affirmed the finding that the employee handbook did not make her anything but an at will employee. She tries again on theories of **promissory estoppel**, breach of the covenant of good faith and fair dealing (tort), and seeking punitive damages. **Loses in the trial court.**

This appeal:

(1) Employee at will and promissory estoppel has not been recognized as an exception to that doctrine (**Can you see why?** The exception would swallow the rule).

(2) Even if we think that there is a PE exception, there would not be any reliance, as she would still be an at-will employee and they could fire her at any time for no reason or any reason at all.

(3) Then the court finds that there is no injustice because she could always be fired at any time, thus no damages, thus she hasn't lost anything.

Better reason is that because of the disclaimers it was unreasonable of her to rely on the VP from the sister corporation – You need the pres. or the board of *your* employer – take them literally, and the board would have to approve and the president would have to sign.

"Trust but verify" - Ronald Reagan.

Note that promissory estoppel is not very useful in commercial transactions – all too true, although it is hard to tell when we get so many settlements in cases that, therefore, don't make it to trial, much less to written opinions, so it still may contribute to the process.

From David v. Synder, *Go Out and Look: The Challenge and Promise of Empirical Scholarship in Contract Law*, 80 TUL. L. REV. 1009 (2006):

FIGURE 1

Table 1.3

Win Rate of Promissory Estoppel Claims on the Merits—Trial Courts

	Plaintiff Wins		Plaintiff Loses		
	N	(%)	N	(%)	Total
Promissory Estoppel Claims[2]	6	(5.45)	104	(94.55)	110
Comparison: Win Rates for Contract Claims in Federal Court Cases[3]	14,308	(54.77)	11,818	(45.23)	26,126

---

[2] These state trial court and federal district court claims from the data were successful or failed on the merits, as defined *supra*.

[3] These data are derived from a "database of about 3.7 million federal district court civil cases terminated over the last 17 fiscal years. The data were gathered by the Administrative Office of the

Table 2.1
Win Rates of Promissory Estoppel Claims by Subject Matter—Outcome of Cases
Decided on the Merits

Subject Matter of Dispute	PE claim succeeded on the merits		Total
	N	(%)	
Employment	6	(4.23)	142
Construction	2	(22.22)	9
Sale of Real Property	1	(10.00)	10

♦ -- ♦

NOTE

♦ -- ♦

Lawyering Skills Problem

Look, again, at R2d § 90(1), and determine what elements or factors need to be proven in order to state a claim under it. When your clients are engaging in negotiations and making offers, how can you advise them so they are protected from claims of promissory estoppel before the negotiation of the contract is complete?

Specific disclaimers. Make it clear that your discussions are not promises to be relied upon, that no deal exists until it is fully documented, etc. And remember that an offer is not a promise that can be relied upon until it is accepted.

United States Courts, assembled by the Federal Judicial Center, and disseminated by the Inter-university Consortium for Political and Social Research." Quoting from the Internet at http://teddy.law.cornell.edu:8090/questcv2.htm (visited Feb. 3, 1998) (on file with the *Columbia Law Review*) where the data is available. The plaintiff win rate reported in this Table is for all types of contract cases terminated in federal district courts during fiscal years 1990-1994 (July 1, 1989 through September 30, 1994) for which the method of disposition was a pre-trial motion, jury verdict, directed verdict, or non-jury trial. Cases that were disposed of by default judgment or consent judgment are not included.

CHAPTER 9

MISUNDERSTANDING AND MISTAKE

— ♦ —

Raffles v. Wichelhaus
Court of Exchequer
2 Hurl. & C. 906 (1864)

Two ships named Peerless.

Demurrer to an answer.

"To arrive ex "Peerless" from Bombay". Defendant claims he meant the Peerless sailing in October, plaintiff meant the Peerless sailing in December.

Held: Latent ambiguity, let in parol evidence (explain briefly), shows mutual mistake as to subject matter, so no contract.

NOTES AND QUESTIONS

1. What was the argument for the plaintiff? For the defendant?

The plaintiff's argument was that, because the contract did not specify when the cotton would arrive, it didn't matter on which ship the cotton arrived, so long as it arrived on a ship called "Peerless." Furthermore, since the contract appears to be complete on its face, the defendant cannot introduce parol evidence to contradict it [para. 4].

The defendant argued that because each party meant a different "Peerless," the parties were not agreeing to the same thing, and neither could have known that the other meant something else. Additionally, the defendant should be allowed to introduce parol evidence because there was a latent ambiguity due to the two ships named "Peerless" [para. 5].

2. What was the holding of the court?

The court held that the defense had made a valid answer. There seemed to be evidence that supported the conclusion that there was a misunderstanding, which should be determined by the jury (or finder of fact). Also, because of the latent ambiguity in the contract, the parol evidence should be allowed [para. 5, 6].

3. As noted in the introduction to this chapter, R2d § 20 captures the modern version of the misunderstanding doctrine, structured to cover the situation where neither party knows of the misunderstanding, both do, or only one does.

4. The case that follows is another of the classics. It presented more of a challenge for the judges who were trying to avoid creating any new doctrine for dealing with a mistake of fact—something different from a simple misunderstanding. The case involves the sale of a cow, and both parties were definitely referring to the same cow, but because they both were under a misapprehension as to its breeding capabilities (at least as the majority of the court viewed the facts), the majority wanted to avoid finding that a contract had been formed. Watch the clever way they do it.

◆ - - ◆

Sherwood v. Walker
Supreme Court of Michigan
66 Mich. 568 (1887)

Facts: Walker contracted to sell Sherwood a cow. The price suggested that both parties thought the cow was barren. If the cow is barren, its only worth its value in meat. But the cow turned out to be pregnant, and it is worth a whole lot more as a breeder. After the contract had been signed, and the calf had been discovered, the defendant tried to back out of the contract.

The plaintiff sued for replevin. The trial court ruled that the sale must proceed and found for the plaintiff. The defendant appealed.

Issue: Can the defendant rescind the contract on the basis that the parties didn't know the cow was fertile when they entered into the contract?

Rule: A contract may be rescinded if it was made in reliance upon a mutual mistake of fact.

Analysis: Majority says there was mutual mistake. The two sides didn't really know what they were making a contract about. The dissent says that the evidence tends to show that the plaintiff (buyer) knew what was going on even though the defendant didn't.

Conclusion: The contract is declared void for mutual mistake.

NOTES AND QUESTIONS

1. **Mutual mistake? Or a skilled (or lucky) guess and investment by Mr. Sherwood? Did the majority or the dissent get it right?**

The dissent may be right in this case. In paragraph 6, the majority states "That where a horse is bought under the belief that he is sound, and both vendor and vendee honestly believe him to be sound, the purchaser must stand by his bargain, and pay the full price..." In this case, it seems that there was no evidence, nor does the defendant claim, that the plaintiff secretly knew that Rose the 2d of Aberlone was not barren. Following the horse example, a purchaser would be forced to go through with a sale even after it became clear that the horse was not as good as the parties originally thought. If this is true, then justice requires that the SELLER should be forced to go through with a sale even after it became clear that the horse (or cow) was not as BAD as the parties originally thought.

In support of the majority's argument, because the ability of a cow to breed is so important, it is an issue that goes to the substance of the cow. A cow that can breed is a substantially different animal than a cow that cannot. If the parties are mistaken about the ability of a cow to breed, then the contract may be avoided on the basis of mutual mistake.

2. Rose 2d of Aberlone is a good illustration of business valuation. If she was only "a beef creature" [para. 7] to be sold essentially as scrap or for liquidation, she was worth approximately $80. If she could breed and produce milk, she was worth "at least $750." *(Id.)* What explains the $670 differential? The answer is the net present value of the income that Rose could generate over her useful life. In other words, after subtracting the cost of her care, feeding, and housing, she was expected to produce a series of cash flows with a discounted present value of $750 as a breeder but only $80 if she was to go to immediate slaughter. Business assets like Rose, an apartment building, a copyright-protected song, patented process, or a newly-minted associate attorney are viewed, for business purposes, as things that will produce a stream of positive and negative cash flows that, when discounted, their net present value determines their value. Objective as that sounds, valuation is difficult. One must accurately forecast not only the revenues and their timing—in Rose's case, the cash from slaughter or the sales of milk and calves—but also the operating costs—here, Rose's care, feeding, and housing—as well as the appropriate discount rate or required rate of return (to perform the discounting of future dollars into present value dollars). Changing any of these variables changes the indicated value.

3. Notice the final five words of paragraph 6 in *Sherwood v. Walker*: "unless there was a warranty." A warranty is a statement of fact about the subject matter of a contract in which the warranting party states the condition of the subject matter. If the condition of the subject matter is later proved to be different than as stated, the party in whose favor the warranty runs may seek damages from the warranting party for breach of warranty. Warranties are used in contracts to allocate risk between the parties. They are essentially what are colloquially known as guarantees" for, say, a mattress or vacuum cleaner. (Legal guaranties like the one at issue in the *Frishman* case in Chapter 5, are different and are never spelled with the double "e" at the end.)

4. Plaintiff Sherwood was a gentleman farmer who made his living as president of the Plymouth National Bank at the time of the lawsuit. Later, he would be appointed to be Michigan's first State Commissioner of Banking.

5. The defendants are the same Hiram Walker & Sons that make alcoholic beverages. Anticipating prohibition in the United States, Mr. Walker built his distillery on the Canadian side of the Detroit River. He proved prescient, if not

about 60 years early, in his anticipation. Attempting to stigmatize him, his competitors secured the passage of a law requiring alcoholic beverage manufacturers to label their product with their country of origin. He managed to turn this tactic in his favor through an advertising campaign for the Canadian Club brand of whiskey that hinted Canadian whiskey was superior to its United States counterpart.

6. After this appeal, on remand a circuit court jury sided with Sherwood. No further appeal was taken and Walker lost Rose. She went on to have five additional calves. She had previously calved in 1883, but not in 1884 or 1885, the two years prior to the events involved in *Sherwood v. Walker*.

♦ -- ♦

PROBLEM 9-1

It is 1890. You are a lawyer in Michigan. You are representing a party in a case on appeal to the Michigan Supreme Court, which recently decided *Sherwood v. Walker*. The case involves the sale of a mine. At the time the contract of sale was made, both parties believed that there was sufficient commercial grade iron ore in the mine to make the mine worth the contract price. When it was discovered that there was substantially less ore than the parties thought, the buyer tried to back out. At trial, the court issued the following "Findings of Fact":

1. The mine contains iron ore, but it does not contain sufficient ore to be commercially viable.

2. Because the mine does contain iron ore, it is NOT different in substance from what the parties bargained for.

3. Both parties bargained for a mine that contained sufficient commercial grade iron ore to make the mine worth the contract price.

4. The buyer would not have entered into the contract if it had known the true facts.

You are bound by the above findings of fact, which the Supreme Court will accept as true. Never mind the fact that some of these "findings of fact" might more properly be categorized as conclusions of law, which the court could decide de novo on appeal. The Court has indicated it will not go into that issue.

Assume that the only reported decision relevant to the case is *Sherwood v. Walker*. Locate, in that case:

(a) the language most favorable to the buyer.

The mine is not different in substance from what the parties bargained for. Still, the buyer may be able to avoid the sale. The language most favorable to the buyer appears at the end of paragraph 5, that a party may avoid a sale if his assent was founded on "some collateral fact materially inducing the bargain." The buyer may argue that the presence of iron ore in a sufficient quantity to be commercially viable was a collateral fact which materially induced the bargain.

(b) the language most favorable to the seller.

Because the mine is not different in substance from what the parties bargained for, the seller only needs to point to paragraph 6, which states that "If it be only a difference in some quality or accident, even though the mistake may have been the actuating motive to the purchaser or seller, or both of them, yet the contract remains binding."

♦ -- ♦

Wood v. Boynton
Supreme Court of Wisconsin
64 Wis. 265, 25 N.W. 42 (1885)

Uncut diamond sold for $1. No showing of fraud on the part of jeweler.

The diamond in the *Boynton* case was later called the Eagle Diamond (named after the city in which it was found). Boynton, after buying the diamond, went to Chicago to get it appraised. He was told that it was 16.25 carats and was worth $700. So, Boynton went to New York and sold it to Tiffany's. JP Morgan then bought it, and put it in the American Museum for Natural History where it sat in the same case with the Star Sapphire of India and de Long Ruby. It stayed there until it was stolen in 1964 by Murphy the Surph in what was the biggest jewel heist in the history of the United States.

Note the legal formalism of analysis re: when title passed and whether it can be rescinded [para. 4].

Two grounds for rescission: (1) fraud, and (2) mutual mistake made by vendor in delivering the article sold – a mistake in fact as to the identity of the thing sold with the thing delivered upon the sale. Neither prevails.

♦ -- ♦

The following excerpt from http://jewelry-blog.internetstones.com/sri-lanka-gemstones/star-of-india provides some additional background on the diamond in question:

The biggest jewel heist in the history of America

The thieves had planned the robbery in advance and had come to know that security was lax or virtually non-existent. They visited the American Museum of Natural History during usual open hours and entered a second floor bathroom and left the window open. Later that night they climbed in through this window and entered the Hall of Gems. They discovered that the "Star of India" sapphire was the only gemstone that was protected by an alarm, but the battery for the alarm was dead. Their task was made easy. They collected up to 22 gemstones that were on display, including the renowned "Star of India" and left through the same window through which they gained access. The total value of the gems stolen was estimated to be $400,000.

Four of the gemstones stolen were so famous that disposing of them in America would have been a very difficult task. The 16.25-carat Eagle diamond was discovered accidentally in Eagle, Wisconsin in 1876 by Charles Wood when he was a digging a well. Charles believed the rough stone to be a cheap topaz and just put it aside, but preserved it instead of throwing it away. After some years when the Wood family was in financial difficulties Charles' wife Clarissa sold the stone for $1.00 to Samuel B. Boynton of Milwaukee. Boynton took the stone to Chicago for testing and appraisal, when it was revealed that the stone was actually a diamond worth about $700. Later Boynton sold the diamond to Tiffany's of New York City, for $850, where it remained until J. P. Morgan purchased it at the beginning of the 20th century, and presented it to the American Museum of Natural History.

Within 48 hours of the crime police aided by information from confidential sources arrested two men in New York and two in Miami. Among those arrested was Jack Murphy a legendary surfer and beach boy, and Allan Kuhn, the notorious and wealthy gangster who introduced Jack Murphy to a life of crime, and had his own yacht, a 50-knot speed boat and a cadillac convertible. The Star of India and most of the other gems were recovered from a locker in a Miami bus station. The DeLong Star Ruby was recovered after the payment of $25,000 as ransom, when it was dropped at a designated site, a phone booth in Florida. However, the Eagle diamond was never recovered.

Jack Murphy and his accomplices were given a three-year prison sentence for their part in the sensational crime, which subsequently became the theme of a thrilling Hollywood movie "Murph the Surph," starring Robert Conrad, released in 1975.

Jack Murphy was born in Los Angeles, California, but his parents later moved to Pennsylvania. The young Murphy was an all-round brilliant student who not only excelled in his studies but also in sporting and other extra-curricular activities. He was the perfect model among children, whom parents usually dream of being blessed with. Surfing became his passion and in 1963 he bragged the title of the State's top surfer, winning the National Hurricane Surfing Championship on two occasions. But his greatest and most amazing achievement was being selected to play for the Pittsburgh Symphony Orchestra at the age of 15 years. His other achievements in his long and colorful carrier included concert violinist, tennis pro, movie stunt man, and high-tower circus diver.

From an early life Murphy showed a tendency and a satisfaction in taking part in daring acts, which subsequently helps to explain the daring life style which he chose to live. Unfortunately, his talents in executing the daring was not harnessed in a constructive direction for his own benefit and the benefit of the society in which he lived. Instead he came under the dominating influence of the wealthy and notorious gangster Allan Kuhn, who was also a swimming instructor. Kuhn introduced him to a life of crime, with all the thrills and dangers associated with it, which was most appropriate to his temperament. Murphy took to a criminal life as a duck would take to water.

His first breakthrough in his chosen career came when he was co-opted by Allan Kuhn for the infamous robbery at the American Museum of Natural History, in New York, which became the biggest jewel heist in American History. The 21-months he spent in jail after this robbery had hardened him as a professional criminal, and he was now prepared for more daring criminal acts. Next came the robbery in 1968, when Murphy and two of his partners broke into the Miami beach mansion of Mrs. Olive Wofford. They held a pistol to her head and threatened to pour boiling water over her eight year old niece if she refused to co-operate in opening the safe. However Murphy and his gang were tracked down by the police, which also involved a high powered car chase in which Murphy was the getaway driver. From daring robberies to murder was a simple step, and Murphy was then found to be involved in a double murder known infamously as the Whiskey Creek Murders, in which two Californian women secretaries were shot, bludgeoned to death, and dumped in the creek, near Hollywood, in Florida, in 1967. The apparent motivation for the murder was said to be a dispute over half a million dollars worth of securities stolen from a Los Angeles brokerage firm. Murphy was sentenced to life imprisonment in 1969, after being found guilty of first degree murder. In 1970, Murphy received a second life sentence for his role in the Olive Wofford assault and robbery case.

After spending nearly 19 years in prison, Murphy was finally paroled in 1986, for exemplary behavior and showing remorse for his previous crimes. While in prison he was converted to [become] a born-again Christian, and assisted the prison's chaplain, and was also involved in counseling young offenders. Murphy has today totally dedicated his life to the service of God, and serves as an evangelist style preacher visiting prisons, and helping to re-habilitate other offenders through religion.

◆ -- ◆

PROBLEM 9-2

Buyer and Seller entered into a contract for the purchase and sale of a quantity of apples. Both Buyer and Seller believed that the apples had little value because they were being stored in a Latin American city that had been surrounded by a rebel army and would rot before the siege was lifted. As a result, the apples were sold for a small fraction of their market price. Unknown to either party, at the time the contract was entered into, the local government had already routed the rebels, and the Seller's agents were in the process of arranging shipment of the apples to the United States.

(a) How would this case be analyzed under the rule of *Sherwood v. Walker?*

The analysis of this situation under Sherwood *depends on whether the presence of the rebel army goes to the substance of the apples, or whether its presence is just an accidental property of the apples. If the army's presence is a substantial quality of the apples, then there is no contract because the parties were mistaken about the substance of the apples at the time the contract was made. If it was just an accidental property of the apples, then there is a contract, and the apples must be delivered at the price in the contract.*

(b) How would this case be analyzed under R2d § 152?

Under Restatement § 152, the central issue is whether the assumption that the rebel army was still around the city had a material effect on the contract. If it is, then the contract is voidable by the seller (the adversely affected party) unless he bears the risk of the mistake under § 154. It may be argued that the seller bore the risk of the mistake under Restatement § 154(b), because he had only limited knowledge with respect to the facts to which the mistake relates but treated his limited knowledge as sufficient.

(c) How would this case be analyzed under UNIDROIT articles 3.4 and 3.5?

Under UNIDROIT, the contract may be avoided if it can be shown that a reasonable person would not have concluded the contract on those terms. Since both parties were mistaken about the same facts, the requirements of UNIDROIT article 3.5(1)(a) are met. However, UNIDROIT article 3.5(2)(b) may apply if the seller assumed the risk of the mistake. If this is the case, then the contract may not be avoided.

(d) Would the result be the same if, at the time the contract was made, the city was still surrounded with no expectation that the siege would be lifted, but shortly after the contract was made the government forces launched a bold and totally unexpected offensive which lifted the siege?

146

If the city was still surrounded at the time the contract was made, then neither party was mistaken about the facts at the time the contract was entered. Mistake may only be used to void a contract if at least one party was mistaken about the facts at the time the contract was made. It doesn't matter if the situation changes after the contract is entered.

NOTES AND QUESTIONS *(Largely self-explanatory)*

1. *The Modern Law of Mistake and Formation of Contract.*

Restatement § 20 – Misunderstanding – bottom line: No Mutual Assent if neither knows – but if one does, then will be charged with it. Close to fraudulent inducement.

Restatement §§ 151 through 154. Put them up and go over them.

151 – Easy definition – A mistake is a belief that is not in accord with the facts.

152 – Mistake by Both	**153** – Mistake by *One*
Basic assumption	Basic Assumption
Material Effect	Material Effect
Then voidable, unless	Then voidable, unless
assumption of the risk.	assumption of risk, IF:
	(a) E n f o r c e m e n t Unconscionable, or
	(b) other party had reason to know *(not "knows")* or caused it.

Discuss Allocation of Risk – that is what contracting is all about. Representations, Warranties, Covenants, and Indemnities.

2. *Discuss fixed price and cost-plus and contingency contracts.*

4. *The ALCOA/Greenspan case* (mutual mistake in belief that Greenspan's formula would work.)

◆ - - ◆

Jaynes v. Louisville & Nashville R.R. Co.
United States District Court, Eastern District, Tennessee
560 F. Supp. 57 (1981)

Injured person settles claim for payment of $1,321. Then claims mutual mistake when injuries are worse than expected.

147

RR Co. seeks summary judgment. This trial court denies it. Material issues of fact (and are trying to keep it alive for a jury or to promote settlement, perhaps).

This language was pretty clear. *How could you make it really clear?*

Go the Cal. Civ. Code section 1452 route (Cal. Approach). Mirandizing the releasor.

Say it very clearly, several times, in bold.

How about saying he is getting more than we would otherwise give him to assume the risk?

How about having him say he was advised to seek legal counsel and had the opportunity?

NOTES AND QUESTIONS

2. Suppose a person with a broken leg signs a release in the reasonable belief that the leg will heal and that she will be able to walk normally. If, for reasons that she could not have anticipated, the leg does not heal properly and she can never walk again, the straightforward application of the mistake doctrine holds that she cannot avoid the release on the grounds of mistake. Her mistake is of a future, not a present, fact. **What is the rationale for this result?**

♦ -- ♦

Anderson Brothers Corp. v. O'Meara
United States Court of Appeals, Fifth Circuit
306 F.2d 672 (1962)

This case involves both mutual (trial court basis) and unilateral (appellate court basis) mistake.

O'Meara purchases a special slit dredge intending to conduct sweep dredging.

Tries to get out of the contract using mutual mistake.

Trial court tried to make it all go away by finding mutual mistake based upon two different mistakes, one made by each party and offsetting damages. Note how two different unilateral mistakes do not properly equal mutual mistake.

Court of appeals says, no, reverse, not mutual mistake. Any mistake here was unilateral and O'Meara did not exercise reasonable diligence, thus the contract is not voidable at his option. Basically a R2d approach.

Note how the R2d's use of "materiality" and "unconscionability" are intentional uses of vague terms to allow for a standard that is flexible.

NOTES AND QUESTIONS

People can't tell the future. Parties in a contract should not be expected to know everything that will happen as a result of their present conditions. This is why a contract can't be avoided based on a mistake about a future fact, even if both parties believed that something else would happen.

A party to a contract, before entering the contract, should take the time to consider the possible outcomes of the present situation and allocate the risk of these outcomes by adjusting the consideration or otherwise. This encourages people to be responsible, and provides some degree of certainty for the future. Representations, warranties, covenants, conditions, indemnities, and the like are used to allocate risk, including the risk of the unknown.

Lawyering Skills Problem

You are general counsel for an insurance company. The company's standard-form release to be signed by people whom the company has compensated for injuries allegedly caused by its insured reads:

> Releasor hereby releases, acquits, and forever discharges Releasee and any other persons and entities of and from any and all actions, causes of action, claims, demands, damages, costs, loss of services, expenses, and compensation on account of or in any way growing out of any and all known and unknown personal injuries resulting or to result from the accident that occurred on or about [date and time], at or about [location].

In spite of the language of the release, a number of courts have held that it does NOT release claims for injuries that the signer does not know she has when she signs the release and accepts the money, based on the doctrine of mistake.

You have been asked to re-write the release to make it more likely that courts will interpret it to release claims for injuries not known at the time the release is signed. Explain what you would do. Specific examples of how you would redraft it are preferred.

NOTE: Don't worry about the California Civil Code section discussed earlier. You will have local counsel draft a California-specific release. You will also, of course, have a law clerk do research to see if there are other states that have unusual requirements. But your job here is just to draft a basic release that will do the job in the ordinary run-of-the-mill state.

CHAPTER 10

MISREPRESENTATION AND FRAUD

— ♦ —

Halpert v. Rosenthal
Supreme Court of Rhode Island
107 R.I. 406, 267 A.2d 730 (1970)

Contract for the sale of a house. Defendant buyer didn't show for closing because termite inspection showed it had termites. Jury found for defendant.

Plaintiff appeals on ground there should have been directed verdict for plaintiff because no evidence misrepresentation was intentional or unqualified.

Court relies on the First Restatement and a lot of other authorities for the proposition that a contract is voidable for a material misrepresentation–even if innocent.

The plaintiff says her statements were qualified "to the best of her Knowledge." The court says that's not relevant because the question on appeal is whether the trial court should have directed a verdict for the plaintiff.

There was a merger clause, but the court says (not clearly) that the fraud exception to the parol evidence rule applies to innocent misrepresentations as well as to fraudulent ones.

Rule: Where one induces another to enter into a contract by means of a *material* misrepresentation, the other may rescind the contract (or recover damages). It does not matter if the representation was innocent or fraudulent.

What about a merger clause that would seem to "wipe out" noncontractual representations? Nope. Parol evidence exception for fraud or misrepresentation.

Note [para. 22] the discussion about unqualified statements being made at one's peril. *Does anyone not understand why prudent lawyers never answer a question in an unqualified manner? Get in the habit now. You are not laypersons anymore!*

♦ - - ♦

PROBLEM 10-1

Seller Corporation entered into a contract to sell one of its subsidiaries to Buyer Corporation. The contract contained a representation that all of the subsidiary's patents were valid. Before making the representation, Seller Corporation received assurances from its patent counsel that all of the patents were in fact valid. **If, before the time Buyer Corporation is to perform its** obligations under the contract (*i.e.*, to pay the purchase price and take title to the stock of the subsidiary), Buyer Corporation discovers that some of the patents are invalid, can it refuse to perform? *See* R2d § 164(1); UNIDROIT articles 3.5-3.8.

"If a party's manifestation of assent is induced by either a fraudulent or material misrepresentation by the other party upon which the recipient is justified in relying, the contract is voidable by the recipient." So, no fraud here; focus on materiality.

Was there a bring-down of representations and warranties at closing? Discuss use of bring-down certificates and then limitations.

PROBLEM 10-2

Seller entered into a contract to sell his small hotel to Buyer. In the course of the negotiations, Seller deliberately overstated the profits in his attempt to induce Buyer to purchase the business. In fact, Buyer was never concerned about the profits of the hotel. She was planning to tear it down and use the land as part of a major resort she was developing.

Buyer's plans have now fallen apart because she could not get the adjoining landowners to sell and therefore she could not put together a large enough parcel of land for her resort. **Can she use Seller's fraudulent misrepresentation to get out of the contract to buy his property?** *See* R2d § 164(1); UNIDROIT articles 3.5-3.8.

Same standard, but focus on fraud prong and materiality is immaterial. No inducement.

♦ -- ♦

Leasco Corp. v. Taussig
United States Court of Appeals, Second Circuit
473 F.2d 777 (1972)

Who can cut through all the details to sum up what went on in this case?

What are the key facts? There are a lot of facts, but only a few are actually key.

Leasco acquired Berger, Inc. Louis Berger Associates was a sub of Berger, Inc. Leasco hired Taussig as VP and Counsel of Berger, Inc. In that capacity, Taussig was involved in the efforts of Berger, Inc. to acquire the assets of MKE, which they took into a newly-formed subsidiary of Berger, Inc, called MKI.

Taussig became VP of MKI. Part of his job was to keep Leasco advised of financial condition of MKI.

Taussig bought MKI. Price was basically 5 times earnings. A million dollars for $200,000 in earnings, half of which had to go to MKE.

Before closing, Taussig learned that MKI had suffered an unexpected loss. Taussig refused to perform. Leasco sued and won in the trial court.

Timeline

Dec 70–Taussig officially stops working for MKI but keeps on working unofficially for Leasco.

· Late Dec 70–Jackson and Taussig discuss sale of MKI to Taussig. Estimated earnings of $200,000 for FY ending Sep 71.

Jan 71–engineers discover design problems. Apparently after 12 Feb 71 (not clear whether after 26 Feb when contract signed)–January earnings released showing profit.

Feb 71–MKI CFO learns of design problems.

26 Feb 71–contract signed.

12 Mar 71–Taussig learns of losses in Feb.

28 May 71–closing–Taussig refuses to close.

Taussig claims mistake. Court said he assumed that risk, but they also seem to be saying that the earnings weren't even a basic assumption–you can't even have an assumption about things that are so uncertain. Normally earnings would be a future event, but here the court and the parties seem to be focusing on current earnings. Court also says flat out that you can't void a contract for unilateral mistake.

Taussig also claims misrepresentation. He claims the January financial statement was a misrepresentation. Court says he didn't rely on it. He had all the info it was based on. It wasn't material. The warranties and reps section of the agreement disclaims all warranties and reps not included in the agreement.

♦ - - ♦

Danann Realty Corp. v. Harris
Court of Appeals of New York
5 N.Y. 2d 317, 184 N.Y.S. 2d 599, 157 N.E.2d 597 (1959)

Farnsworth calls it a "questionable decision." Contract for "the sale of a lease of a building." Plaintiff alleges it was induced to enter into the lease by representations as to the operating expenses of the building and the profits to be made from the investment. Supreme Court (NY) Special Term, granted motion to dismiss. Appellate Division reversed. This court reverses, reinstating grant of motion to dismiss.

Clause specifically says no representations made as to rents, expenses, or anything else. Court says this isn't a case of a "general and vague merger clause" but specific disclaimer. Relies on prior cases for proposition that where there's a specific disclaimer that's read and understood, you can't get around it by alleging fraud. The key language is in paragraph 15.

What is the alleged misrepresentation? Inflated profits and understated operating expenses.

The contract contains a "no reps and warranties other than what is in this piece of paper" clause. Characterized as "just boilerplate" in paragraph 22 – this is the kind of judicial statement that drives careful transactional attorneys and formalists absolutely crazy. The provision was specifically included and allocates risk per the contract's terms. Why demean this? Enforce it!

Held: No misrepresentation. The clause is specific (not a general merger clause) and works.

Dissent: Treat just like a general merger clause and read through it to get to allegations of fraud.

Why not just say that anybody who has been defrauded or thinks that they have been has a right to try and prove it in court? Doesn't that make people have confidence in the legal system rather than saying that folks can cheat if they have good lawyers that put the right language in their contracts?

NOTES AND QUESTIONS

Winning the war but losing the peace. And the peace, the end game, is where the action lies, in Microsoft's antitrust settlement, and in all settled litigation. Once it is already "over," paper it right or lose even though you "won."

So, all you hot litigator types – get some transactional skills – cowboys have a good time Saturday night, but they generally wake up hung over and poor, while the railroads, bankers, and saloon keepers and their trusted advisors clean up. Those transactional folks will grind you down and wear you out. Steady, transactional lawyer patience and perseverance is like water on a rock: it works, steadily, and carves a deep trench that can even be a thing of beauty – see, e.g., the Grand Canyon.

Go over the representation and warranty negotiation process, beginning with unqualified reps and then adding in baskets, materiality thresholds, and knowledge limitations.

(If desired a brief writing assignment can be assigned at this point in the course to reinforce the point of representations and warranties. Kuney uses ones taken from his book THE ELEMENTS OF CONTRACT DRAFTING *(2d ed., West 2006); there are many other good sources of such short exercises.)*

3. How are unilateral mistakes and innocent misrepresentations different?

First, misrepresentation requires a statement or representation (or an omission in certain circumstances) from one party to another; unilateral mistake does not. Second, focus on the remedy that is available: (a) mistake=no contract, (b) innocent misrepresentation= either rescission and restitution or enforce the contract and award damages.

Lawyering Skills Problem

If you want to eliminate – or at least dramatically reduce – the risk that a party to a contract will later be able to successfully assert a claim for misrepresentation or breach of warranty, what can you do in terms of drafting and design of the contract at issue? Are there any limits on this or these techniques? Should there be?

Disclaimers. "As is, where is, no representations and warranties" provisions. Carefully draft representations and warranties when they are necessary, using baskets, carve-outs, materiality thresholds, and other limiting techniques to keep them as narrow as possible. Limits are found in statutes and case law, mostly for consumer transactions.

CHAPTER 11

DURESS

— ♦ —

First, let's get the standards out and on the table. Use overhead.

Common Law Standard:

A threat of death or serious bodily harm that negates the threatened party's free will. *(RP, objective standard.)*

Professor Farnsworth Standard:

An improper threat that induces assent and is grave enough to justify assent. *(RP, objective standard).*

Restatement 2d Standard:

§ 174 – Physical Duress – physical compulsion duress negates consent.

§ 175 – Duress by Threat – Improper threat that induces assent and there was no reasonable alternative. *(Subjective standard!) (Note third party stuff in section 2.)*

Now, on to the cases.

♦ - - ♦

Austin Instrument, Inc. v. Loral Corp.
Court of Appeals of New York
29 N.Y. 2d 124, 324 N.Y.S. 2d 22, 272 N.E.2d 533 (1971)

Loral has a contract with the Navy for radar. Austin is the subcontractor on 23 of 40 precision gear components.

Loral gets a second Navy contract and Austin says it will stop production on the first contract unless (1) Loral pays extra on the first contract and (2) Loral gives Austin the subcontract for all 40 parts on the second contract.

Loral checks with everyone on its approved vendor list – nobody else can substitute in within time.

Loral writes set up letter to Austin making record of duress.

After performance, Loral tells Austin that it will seek recovery of the price increases.

July 65–Loral gets first contract.

Early 66–Loral begins deliveries on first contract.

May 66–Loral gets second contract.

July 15, 55–Loral tells Austin it won't get all the subcontracts.

July 16–Austin makes threat.

July 22–Loral gives in.

Austin files first (trying for first mover advantage – who can get to the teacher on the playground first to tell their side of the story) seeking $17k still due on the contract.

Loral sues seeking $22k for over charges.

Trial court for Austin as it found that Loral had not shown there was no reasonable alternative source. Appellate Court affirms.

The New York Court of Appeals reverses. **And it couches it as a matter of law – why?** (That is all an appellate court can properly rule upon.)

Why shouldn't Loral be required to talk to its customer and see if more time was available making it possible to use other sub? Might this be detrimental to Loral's reputation with the government?

Is there a sub-text here? Context matters. In what year is this taking place? 1965 to 1966.

Cuban Missile Crisis – 1962. The American intervention in Vietnam began in 1963 with the direct aim of stopping the South falling into communist hands. Kennedy is assassinated in 1963.

In August of 1963, Lyndon Johnson, who had taken over the American presidency in the wake of the assassination, ordered the first air strikes on North Vietnam.

Six months later, in March 1964, the 'Rolling Thunder' air campaign began. In this campaign alone more bombs were dropped on North Vietnam alone than were used in the whole of the Second World War. In the following five years (1965-1970) the two Vietnams received the equivalent of 22 tons of explosives for every square mile of territory, or 300lb for every man, woman, and child. 7 million tons of bombs and defoliants were dropped in total and 2.6 million Vietnamese were killed. The American deployment jumped from 23,300 in 1963 to 184,000 in 1966 and reached a peak of 542,000 in January 1969 under Richard Nixon's presidency.

The United States was at war – like a war on terror – and what are our societal attitudes toward war-time profiteering?

Why couldn't Loral just sue Austin for breach of contract when the first threat was made? Now, what would that solve? They needed the components. They had to keep working with Austin and accede to the demands, at least until the components were delivered.

NOTES

1. In paragraph 3 the court quotes from Loral's letter of July 22. Review that quoted language. This letter is a perfect example of good lawyering behind the scenes to create a self-serving factual record for later litigation. The letter, and the response it elicited, serves as evidence to prove the second main element of economic duress: no alternative source of supply and a need to accede to the wrongful demand.

2. One of the jobs of a lawyer handling a transaction is to shape the parties' relationship and create a record of events for later litigation should that relationship deteriorate. Not only is this useful when it comes to litigation, but being prepared to litigate can actually help avoid litigation: the other side may sense this preparedness and evaluate the weaknesses in its own position accordingly. Thus, as in rock climbing, counsel should mind the ascent and be forward looking while all the while creating a useful record and preparing to "fall correctly" if falling becomes necessary.

♦ - - ♦

Totem Marine Tug & Barge, Inc. v. Alyeska Pipeline Service Co.
Supreme Court of Alaska
584 P.2d 15 (1978)

Economic duress. Alyeska knocks down invoices of $300,000 or so down to $97,500 for prompt payment and a release (the invoices were presently due and owing and there does not seem to have been much of a bona fide dispute).

Then Totem sues and Alyeska moves for summary judgment based on its release. It wins at trial. This appeal follows and the Supreme Court of Alaska reverses – sends it back for trial.

Nice statement of the law in paragraphs 13 to 22; application of law to facts in paragraph 23. Why all the back story about the voyage to Alaska with the pipe and the difficulties (mostly caused, it seems, by Alyeska)? Certainly sets up the equities, doesn't it? The little tug boat that could. I think I can, I think I can, win a case for economic duress after all this heroic struggling. An example of the "theory of the case." Doctrines like duress provide a framework for storytelling, and able lawyers document or otherwise preserve facts that can be drawn upon later by a storyteller when it comes time to tell a persuasive story to a court or other decision-maker.

[Put up Restatement 2d standard on board and do problems 1 and 2 if there is time.]

NOTES AND QUESTIONS

1. The R2d §§ 175 and 176 state the modern law of duress, stripped of all the old common law baggage. Be sure to analyze these two cases under these rules. **Would the results be the same?**

If applying the R2d, a court is most likely to find that duress induced the contracts in both Loral and Totem.

Loral's assent was induced by Austin's improper threat. Loral had no reasonable alternative but to accept Austin's demands to meet its obligations to the government. This satisfies the requirements of R2d § 175(1). The threat is improper under R2d § 176(1)(d), because it is a breach of Austin's duty of good faith and fair dealing under its original contract with Loral. (GFFD is covered in chapter 25). Furthermore, the new contract also falls under R2d § 176(2)(b) requirements for an improper threat, as the resulting exchange is not on fair terms and the effectiveness of the threat inducing the assent is significantly increased by Austin's previous unfair dealing [para. 3].

Totem's assent was induced by Alyeska's improper threat. Totem had no other choice, outside of bankruptcy, but to consent to Alyeska's proposal. So long as bankruptcy is not a reasonable alternative, R2d § 175(1) is satisfied. This will depend on Totem proving that Alyeska threatened to withhold payment under the contract. This would be an improper threat under R2d § 176(1)(d), since the threat was a breach of Alyeska's duty of good faith and fair dealing under the contract with Totem.

2. The UNIDROIT principles cover duress in articles 3.9 (threat) and 3.10 (gross disparity). **How do these standards differ from those of the R2d?** Be sure to analyze these two cases under the principles, too.

It is likely that there is duress in each case under UNIDROIT.

Loral was led to conclude the contract by Austin's unjustified threat which left Loral with no reasonable alternative. The threat is unjustified because it is wrongful in itself to refuse to conclude an already existing contract (in most cases). This satisfies the threat requirement set forth in UNIDROIT article 3.9. Loral may avoid the contract.

Loral may also be able to prove a gross disparity under UNIDROIT article 3.10. Austin was unjustifiably given an excessive advantage under the contract. The factors for determining unjustifiably excessive advantage include whether the other party has taken unfair advantage of the party's dependence and the party's urgent needs. In this case, Loral was dependent upon Austin to provide the radar parts under the original contract, and urgently needed them. If this gross disparity can be proven, then Loral may avoid the contract.

Under UNIDROIT article 3.9, Totem may be able to prove that it was led to conclude the contract by Alyeska's unjustified threat to not pay, which was serious enough to leave Totem no reasonable alternative but to assent. In this case, Totem's choices were agreeing to the substantially lower settlement payment or bankruptcy. The threat is unjustified because the threat of refusing to pay under a contract is wrongful in itself (usually).

Totem may also be able to prove a gross disparity under UNIDROIT article 3.10. The settlement agreement between Totem and Alyeska gave Alyeska an excessive advantage. It took advantage of Totem's dire economic need to drastically underpay its portion of the original Contract.

The R2d speaks of improper threats and defines them in specific ways (a crime or tort, prior unfair dealing, etc.). UNIDROIT speaks of unjustified threats and defines them in general ways (wrongful in itself, wrongful as a means to a contract). In either case, a party shouldn't make a threat unless it has a good reason (one good enough to convince a third party that it's good) to do so. In fact, Kuney takes the position that naked threats (nudem threatnum) are never good to make, but that promises regarding consequences used in a threatening manner are perfectly acceptable and often very effective.

UNIDROIT deals in more detail with gross disparity, stating that a contract can be avoided if a party had an excessive advantage at the time of conclusion of the contract. It lists several factors to be considered, like the inexperience or urgent needs of the other party, when determining unfair advantage.

The R2d only deals with unfair advantage in certain specific instances, which are listed in § 176(2). There is the broad provision in § 176(2)(c), which allows avoidance if the resulting exchange is not on fair terms and what was threatened is a use of power for illegitimate ends.

Also, the R2d only addresses the disparity as it relates to a threat. UNIDROIT addresses the disparity itself.

UNIDROIT provides room for the court to amend the contract or terms of the contract to make it commercially reasonable when a party has an excessive advantage over the other. (3.10.) The R2d does not.

3. Could the *Alaska Packers* case from Chapter 7 (on pre-existing duty) have been decided as a duress case? If so, does that take away from the policy argument in favor of the pre-existing duty rule?

The manager who signed the modified contract for Alaska Packers did not have the authority to do so. Because the manager did not have the authority to represent it, Alaska Packers was not a party to the revised contract, so it could not have been forced to enter it under duress.

If Alaska Packers had been a party to the revised contract, the elements of duress are met under both the R2d and UNIDROIT. The workers' threat to stop working was improper because it was a breach under the existing contract, the duty of good faith and fair dealing (§ 176(1)(d)), and it left Alaska Packers no reasonable alternative but to manifest assent to the new demands (§ 175(1)). Duress thus exists under the R2d.

Similarly, the requirements of UNIDROIT article 3.9 are met as well. The workers make an unjustified threat which was so imminent as to leave Alaska Packers with no reasonable alternative.

Though this may overlap with the pre-existing duty rule especially in the classic "hold up" case, it does not take away from the policy argument in favor of the pre-existing duty rule. A contract fails its essential purpose if people cannot rely on it. We want to be able to depend on the contracts we enter. We protect this interest by not allowing people to benefit from breaching their contracts, and by putting those who have been wronged back to where they used to be. These concerns support the pre-existing duty rule.

The policy arguments in favor of avoiding contracts made under duress come from a different, but related, concern. A party must manifest willingness to enter a contract. If a party is under duress, it cannot manifest actual willingness. To protect people from being exploited and to prevent people taking advantage of others, we want to discourage contracts made when one of the parties was under duress. We can do this by allowing the party under duress to avoid the contract.

A duress analysis may overlap with the outcome under a pre-existing duty analysis when a previous contract exists. However, because the policy reasons behind each rule are so distinct, and because duress may exist when there is no prior contract, it's important to keep the defenses separate.

4. **If *Alaska Packers* and these economic duress cases were decided under the UCC (no pre-existing duty rule but the modification must be in good faith), is there any need for the defense of economic duress? Isn't lack of good faith a lesser, necessarily included standard within economic duress?**

A lack of good faith may often accompany the threats of economic harm that appeared in these cases. A lack of good faith may be more difficult to prove than economic duress. A party may illustrate its economic condition with bank statements and invoices and ledgers. A party may have a more difficult time trying to illustrate what the other party's intentions were when it made a modification. Also, does the party have to prove that the other acted in bad faith or simply acted not in good faith? And what is good faith? Save extended discussion for chapter 25.

PROBLEM 11-1

Mary Inventor developed a new program for screening e-mail to eliminate spam. She got a federally-guaranteed loan from Bank to market the program. Her marketing effort encountered considerable resistance at first, but early in 2010 it took and it began to look as if her product would be a major success. Unfortunately, the government guarantee expired in June 2010, and her loan came due at that time. Bank refused to renew the loan and demanded payment. Ms. Inventor tried a number of other lending institutions, but none of them was willing to lend her the money she needed to pay off the loan from Bank and to continue her marketing efforts because she had neither collateral nor a track record. The only person who would give her the money she needed was Shark, who demanded a 51% percent ownership interest in the business as compensation for the "risk" he was taking. Ms. Inventor reluctantly agreed to the deal Shark proposed. Now the business is doing well and Ms. Inventor has come to you to ask if you can help her "get back all that Shark has pressured me out of."

(a) Will the doctrine of duress help her case under the approach of the R2d? Under the UNIDROIT principles?

Duress may help Mary's case under UNIDROIT but probably not under the R2d. It seems her primary concern should have been to find a way to pay off the bank loan. If, by insisting that she get funding to pay the loan AND continue her marketing, she limited her opportunities, she may have caused her own duress.

To satisfy R2d § 175(1), Shark must have made a threat that induced Mary's assent. Shark has not made a threat in this case. Also, the threat must have left Mary with no reasonable alternative. There may have been a reasonable alternative in this case (Mary giving up on the marketing funding). It does not seem likely that the R2d requirements for duress have been met. (As an aside, a 51% interest in the company would be rather standard for a first round venture capital investment, which could be structured as debt in whole or in part).

Under UNIDROIT article 3.10, Mary may avoid the contract if she can show that, at the time of the conclusion of the contract, the contract unjustifiably gave Shark an excessive advantage. This may be possible, since Mary gave up more than half of her business. Factors to be considered in determining whether there is an excessive advantage include: urgent need, inexperience, and lack of bargaining skill. Mary arguably had urgent need, since the bank had just called in her loan. She was inexperienced, and probably lacked bargaining skill. This is the most favorable statute for Mary, but she has to prove excessive advantage on Shark's part and need and naivety on her part before she can recover.

The key fact is that nobody else would give her the money. If the deal has been exposed to "the market" and nobody was willing to give her more advantageous terms, it's hard to say Shark's deal is unfair.

(b) Does she have a claim against Bank or only against Shark?

The bank has not made an improper or unjustifiable threat. The bank has the right to call in the loan anytime after it's due. The bank has no duty to renew the loan. Even though many other banks may have renewed the loan, and it may have been commercially reasonable for them to do so, they didn't have to.

Note the manipulation of student perceptions based upon character names and emphasize the persuasive power of assigning names to people and things in the story. Shark's terms are standard or even lenient for venture capital deals. The price of using other people's money is giving up control.

PROBLEM 11-2

In 1917, the United States entered World War I. At that time German submarines were inflicting heavy losses on ships crossing the Atlantic. The need to get American troops and supplies to Europe made it imperative for the United States government to get a large number of ships built in the shortest possible time. The government approached the nation's largest shipbuilder and was told that the shipbuilder would build ships for the government only if it was compensated under a plan which provided (i) the shipbuilder was paid the cost of construction plus a percentage thereof as its profit, (ii) if the actual cost of construction of any ship was greater than the estimated cost, the government paid the actual cost plus the profit percentage based on the actual cost, (iii) if the actual cost was less than the estimated cost, the shipbuilder got its profit computed on the estimated cost plus it got half the difference between the actual cost and the estimated cost as a bonus for saving the government money, and (iv) the shipbuilder got to estimate the costs all by itself. The government agreed to the contract, and when the shipbuilder made a claim for its enormous profit, the government claimed the defense of duress.

How should the court decide the case under the approach of the R2d? Under the UNIDROIT principles?

Under the R2d § 175(1), no threat has been made, unless the implied threat to not make the ships unless the terms were agreed to counts, which does not seem likely. The government would have to prove that the threat was improper (most likely under § 176(2)(c)), and that the government had no reasonable alternative before it could void the contract.

There may be a sufficient threat under § 175(2), if the threat of attack by the Central Powers in World War I induced the government to enter the contract with the shipbuilder. The contract would be voidable by the government because the shipbuilder had reason to know of the government's duress.

UNIDROIT 3.9 probably does not apply because the shipbuilder has not made a threat to the government.

However, UNIDROIT 3.10(1) allows a contract or term to be avoided if it unjustifiably gave the other party an excessive advantage. The government could use the factors of urgent need to help prove this excessive advantage. Also, it would have to be shown that the terms of the contract were unfair.

Under UNIDROIT 3.10(2), the court may modify the terms of the contract to make the contract in accord with reasonable standards of fair dealing. The most disparate terms of the contract seem to be iii and iv, which allow the shipbuilder alone to estimate the price, and provide an incentive to overestimate that price. These terms could easily be removed and result in a more fair contract. (Also, ii could go, but it's not as bad as iii or iv.)

This problem is based upon the Bethlehem Steel case. Everybody now cites Frankfurter's dissent and forgets the court held there was no duress. Probably influenced by the fact WWII had already started. Illustrates how long litigation can drag out.

Lawyering Skills Problem

You are general counsel for an insurance company. The company's standard-form release to be signed by people whom the company has compensated for injuries allegedly caused by its insured reads:

> Releasor hereby releases, acquits, and forever discharges
> Releasee and any other persons and entities of and from any and
> all actions, causes of action, claims, demands, damages, costs, loss
> of services, expenses, and compensation on account of or in any way
> growing out of any and all known and unknown personal injuries
> resulting or to result from the accident that occurred on or about
> [date and time], at or about [location].

In spite of the language of the release, you are worried that there are some courts that might hold that it does NOT release claims for injuries, known or unknown, based on the doctrine of duress.

You have been asked to re-write the release to make it more likely that courts will enforce the release as written and reject any duress challenge to it. Explain what you would do. Specific examples of how you would redraft it are preferred.

NOTE: Don't worry about the California Civil Code section discussed earlier in the book. You will have local counsel draft a California-specific release. You will also, of course, have a law clerk do research to see if there are other states that have unusual requirements. But your job here is just to draft a basic release that will do the job in the ordinary run-of-the-mill state.

165

CHAPTER 12

UNCONSCIONABILITY

— ♦ —

We have looked at mistake and duress and now turn our attention to unconscionability. This is the next doctrine that we look at that is used to let parties out of a contract that is otherwise (offer, acceptance, and consideration) formed and enforceable.

Nobody has developed any good, hard rules for unconscionability. Most of what we have are some categories and some reasoning – the cases are all over the map, as we will see today.

What we have done is to *categorize* – which is the first step in the inquiry looking for the rules (think of 18th Century science – mostly gathering, categorizing, and labeling (and blowing things up in bell jars)). Only after that was done could folks come up with anything approaching "rules" to explain how all these cataloged things relate – a process that continues to this day.

There are two types of unconscionability: substantive and procedural. Substantive unconscionability focuses on the actual terms of the challenged contract. Procedural focuses on the manner in which the deal was struck and the contract entered into and, in this way, looks a lot like economic duress.

Perhaps more than any other doctrine in this text other than the duty of good faith and fair dealing, unconscionability demonstrates how law can be seen as a flexible framework within which the parties (counsel) tell a story to drive a result. The court does not "do whatever it wants" as first year law students often assert – it does what the record (the story composed by the parties or counsel based upon what facts the parties or counsel have documented or otherwise preserved) supports, and what it then concludes is the right result. There is a difference.

♦ -- ♦

Williams v. Walker-Thomas Furniture Co.
United States Court of Appeals, District of Columbia Circuit
350 F.2d 445, 121 U.S. App. D.C. 315 (1965)

Per J. Skelly Wright.

The transaction was nominally a lease.

Plaintiff is raising 7 children on $218 monthly welfare check.

She purchases stuff from Walker-Thomas, a ghetto rent-to-own outfit. Their documents spread payments over all purchases, leaving outstanding balances on all until all paid off, thus allowing repossession of every item ever purchased if she defaults. Structured as a capital lease. *(What is that?) Note that the court only uses the term "lease" once and otherwise calls it a "purchase."*

Contracts allowed them to repo anything she had bought as long as there was a balance outstanding on any of it. (Just like the Sears credit agreements of the late 1980's. *See* In re Hodges, 83 B.R. 25 (Bkrtcy., N.D. Cal. 1988)).

Court says unconscionability is the (1) absence of meaningful choice (2) together with terms unreasonably favorable to the other party [para. 8]. *"In many cases the meaningfulness of choice is negated by gross inequality of bargaining power."*

"In determining reasonableness or fairness, the primary concern must be with the terms of the contract considered in light of the circumstances existing when the contract was made" [para. 9]. (What kind of standard is that? Either a very flexible one or none at all, or both).

The dissent points out that the lower court was also appalled but said the matter was for the legislature. (What is the problem with that? Debtors and poor folk have no effective lobbyists.)

Wright says it is unconscionable, but because no findings were made as to unconscionability, he remands for findings.

The term "inequality of bargaining power" comes up in many discussions of inequality, like in the Walker case. **What did Judge Wright mean when he used this term?**

Wright seems to say that what is meant by inequality of bargaining power is that one party can't understand what is going on – see footnote 47 on page 313 – Others have used it to mean that the other party does not have bargaining strength to get concessions from the other party.

Well, if one party does not know what is going on, then what if we just explain it very carefully to the customer, maybe record it on video tape or DVD, and make sure that they have time to think it over and then use the same terms? *Does that work?* (Maybe.)

After the Walker decision, business lawyers were worried that courts were going to run around invalidating contracts willy nilly. This just has not happened. First, note the prevalence of payday lenders, pawn shops, car title loan places, and rent-to-own outfits. *Second, although the cases sound good when you read them, outside of the procedural unconscionability setting of a contract of adhesion (especially in the area of cell phone, cable, or internet service contracts and arbitration clauses), practically the only time that unconscionability is applied to defeat a contract is in the BIG Co. v. Little, Unsophisticated, Poor Individual setting.*

Note the evils of paying interest for non-income-producing or capital-appreciation producing goods.

◆ -- ◆

PROBLEM 12-1

You *Need* $3,000 Wheels!

Christy Chenney, a resident of a desert community in Southern California, lived four days with her car's plastic hubcaps. On day five, armed with three of her boyfriend's pay stubs, a bank statement and the names of references, the unemployed mother of three drove to a strip mall in the suburbs and outfitted her new used car with a set of gleaming, $57-a-week, rent-to-own chrome wheels. If she makes her payments on time for the next 52 weeks, every 11th payment will be forgiven. In the end, she will have paid $2,736 for a set of $1,800 wheels.

Nothing's worse than plastic hubcaps.

(1) Does Ms. Chenney have an unconscionability claim? Under her "rent-to-own" contract, she can stop payment at any time and have no obligation to pay anything more. She just has to give back the wheels. If she doesn't make all the payments, though, she loses all the money she's paid to date.

Under the guidelines set out in Williams [para. 8 & 9], to establish a claim of unconscionability, Christy will have to demonstrate an absence of meaningful choice on her part and contract terms that are unreasonably favorable to Rent-A-Wheel. In evaluating this, courts consider all the circumstances surrounding the transaction. Gross inequality in bargaining power, and the manner in which the contract was made may indicate unconscionability. In this problem, Christy was an unemployed mother of three desperately seeking chrome wheels. There may be inequality of bargaining power if Christy is unsophisticated and uneducated, and Rent-A-Wheel is large and experienced in wheel rent-to-own transactions. Christy would have to prove that this inequality was so gross as to give her no meaningful choice in entering the contract to support a claim of unconscionability. The manner in which the contract was made will also be considered. If Christy had the opportunity to fully understand the terms of the contract, and the obligations and risks she was assuming, it is unlikely that she can avoid the contract for unconscionability. However, if Rent-A-Wheel engaged in deceptive business practices, and hid terms which were very unfavorable to Christy in the fine print, this may indicate unconscionability. Traditionally, a party who entered a contract and was not fully aware of the terms was still held to those terms. This stacks the odds even more against finding unconscionability, even though the court in Williams carved out an exception for parties with little bargaining power. It does not seem likely that Christy can establish an unconscionable contract. The dissent in Williams states that what is a luxury to some may be an absolute necessity to others. Though this may be true, it is difficult to sympathize with the unemployed mother of three who signs up to pay $57 a week for a year for a set of wheels. Her car already had a set of wheels.

169

(2) Can you think of a way to use the fact that Rent-A-Wheel generously forgives every eleventh payment (providing the other payments are made in a timely manner) into an argument in favor of a finding of unconscionability?

The forgiving of every eleventh payment may indicate that the payments and the payment schedule were more favorable to Rent-A-Wheel than necessary. It shows that Rent-A-Wheel was getting more money than it actually needed to bargain for to make the contract profitable. If a company is trying to get more money than it truly needs to make a decent profit, it is probably to the disadvantage of the customer. If Rent-A-Wheel is taking advantage of the customer, this goes toward unconscionability.

But more pointedly, let's examine the provision critically as a late payment penalty that has been disguised and packaged as a "benefit" to the consumer – "we forgive every 11th payment if you pay on time." Put another way: you can lose $57 by paying a day late. Sounds like a penalty not a bonus. Think critically and don't elevate form over substance.

◆ -- ◆

Weaver v. American Oil Co.
Supreme Court of Indiana
257 Ind. 458, 276 N.E.2d 144 (1971)

Clause exculpated Amoco from liability to Weaver for their negligence at his station. Also required him to indemnify them against claims by others on account of their negligence at his station.

Amoco employee fixing gas pump sprayed gas on Weaver and his employee, causing them to be burned.

Intermediate appellate court held indemnifying clause valid and exculpatory clause invalid. Idea was that they could insure against their own liability. (Reason may not be in the opinion.) Clauses were in fine print.

Weaver had a year and a half of high school and no business experience. Wasn't asked to read the lease. It was just placed in front of him and he was told "sign."

So, when the employee or Weaver sues Amoco, *Weaver is contractually bound to cover any damages and attorneys' fees*!

The court below held that the indemnity clause was valid but the exculpatory clause was invalid (why? Against public policy to allow one to exculpate themselves for negligence – that would be like repealing most of the law of torts for them). But, note, most modern law allows it as long as it is not exculpatory for gross negligence.

Held: Unconscionable. Picks up where Frankfurter's dissent left off in Bethlehem Steel – "The law is not so primitive that it sanctions every injustice except brute force and downright fraud."

> *When a party can show that the contract, which is sought to be enforced, was in fact an unconscionable one, due to a prodigious amount of bargaining power on behalf of the stronger party, which is used to the stronger party's advantage and is unknown to the lesser party, causing a great hardship and risk on the lesser party, the contract provision, or the contract as a whole, if the provision is not separable, should not be enforceable on the grounds that the provision is against public policy. The party seeking to enforce such a contract has the burden of showing that the provisions were explained to the other party and came to his knowledge and there was in fact a real and voluntary meeting of the minds and not merely an objective meeting.*

Paragraph 11: Show prima facie case of unconscionability and the burden (of proof? of production? of persuasion? Something else?) shifts to the party seeking to enforce the contract – and they have to show a subjective meeting of the minds!

You can see why business lawyers worried about this loose cannon doctrine. (What is a loose cannon? Explain re: ships, heavy cannon, and broken ropes.) *But why would you want to take a case like this to trial? Oil Co. worker sprays franchisee with gasoline and lights him on fire, then Oil Co. claims victim needs to indemnify it? This is not a good story to tell.*

Dissent: He should have read the lease – if we don't require that, then we encourage savvy folk not to read. And these clauses have been upheld before – why are we reversing ourselves now? Weaver accepted the risk and now must live with it.

Why did the lower court think that the indemnity clause – which sounds like the worst one – was ok? Because he could insure against it. Can't insure against exculpation.

Why did Amoco include the indemnity clause? They are the deep pocket. Any plaintiff injured on the gas station premises will go after them to the hilt and largely leave Walker alone. It is not a bad transactional structure, but, as applied
. . . .

◆ -- ◆

Haines v. St. Charles Speedway, Inc.
United States Court of Appeals, Eighth Circuit
874 F.2d 572 (1989)

Plaintiff struck by his own race car in the midway. He had signed a release in order to enter the midway. He admitted not reading it – he had only a second or third grade reading ability. It is a good, broad, unambiguous release and waiver of liability.

"Contract of Adhesion" – Defined: "a form contract submitted by one party and accepted by the other on the basis of this or nothing. . . It is a transaction not negotiated by one which literally adheres for want of choice" [para. 9].

When this court finds a contract of adhesion, it then goes on to see if it is unconscionable under the particular circumstances – here it is not – the language alone makes it clear that it is significant (kind of circular. . .) [end of para. 7].

◆ - - ◆

Zapatha v. Dairy Mart, Inc.
Supreme Judicial Court of Massachusetts
381 Mass. 284, 408 N.E.2d 137 (1980)

Franchise termination provision – for cause or no cause at all. He renews, they want to change the form of the franchise agreement, he refuses, they terminate him.

There had been a signing ceremony for the franchise agreement; he said he understood every term but understood termination to be only for cause, the company encouraged him to see an attorney, he did not. The company also told him that the agreement was non-negotiable (i.e., a contract of adhesion).

Held: Reverse court below; no unconscionability.

First the court examines whether the UCC applies – it finds that the sale of goods is ancillary to the franchise, so UCC does not apply, really, but may be reflective of the general non-UCC law anyway. (This avoids the need to say that the UCC applies to franchise agreements, which would be a big change in Massachusetts law, but which still allows the court to use the UCC's unconscionability doctrine.)

Second, the court goes to the general law of Massachusetts and finds unconscionability by analogy. (Again, note this technique–adopt the principle from the UCC without having to hold that the whole UCC applies to franchise agreement.) The focus for this court is on the comment to UCC 2-302 and R2d § 234 [paras. 13 and 14].

The issue is one of law (get it out of the hands of a jury) [para. 13].

The test is to be conducted as of the time the contract was made (fatal here as he was advised to seek counsel) [para. 13].

The principle is one of prevention of oppression and unfair surprise . . . and not of disturbance of the allocation of risks because of superior bargaining power [para. 14].

Note on Economic Analysis

This is what contracting is all about: Allocation of risk.

What is risk? The possibility that things will not go as intended.

Are there different types of risks? Sure. Development risk, operating risk, bankruptcy risk, casualty risk, etc. Categorize and address or assume them. Ignore risk at your peril. Discuss.

◆ -- ◆

Note on Alternative Dispute Resolution

◆ -- ◆

Cooper v. MRM Investment Co.
United States District Court, Middle District of Tennessee
199 F. Supp. 2d 771 (2002)

Sexual harassment claim. Enforce arbitration clause that imposes some costs on the complainant?

Do not enforce if (1) contract of adhesion and (2) unconscionable under the circle of assent doctrine [para. 25].

Defendants motion denied; refuse to dismiss; refuse to compel arbitration.

◆ -- ◆

The Circle of Assent Doctrine: An Important Innovation in Contract Law

Robert M. Lloyd
Abstracted from 7 TRANSACTIONS: TENN. J. OF BUS. L. 237 (2006)
(Teacher's Manual Only)

The problem of the form contract, quickly reviewed and signed by a customer, which contains some sort of waiver or other bar to the customer's later claim or complaint in the "fine print."

Traditional rule: You signed it, you are presumed to have read it and you are stuck with it. This is subject to the escape valve of unconscionability, esp. in Little Guy vs. overreaching BigCo cases. (This all developed and worked well when standard form contracts were more unusual than they are today).

Tennessee's Innovation: The Circle of Assent Doctrine. A "party who signs a printed form furnished by the other party will be bound by the provisions in the form over which the parties actually bargained and such other provisions that are not unreasonable in view of the circumstances surrounding the transaction." *Parton v. Mark Pirtle Oldsmobile-Cadillac-Isuzu, Inc.*, 730 S.W. 2d 634 (Tenn. Ct. App. 1987) (exculpatory clause in printed form contract does not bar action for negligence in storage of vehicle during repair work in unlocked, unfenced yard from which it was stolen).

The focus of the doctrine is what have the parties actually assented to, and the answer is the terms they have bargained for and the not-unreasonable ones in the form. Based upon Karl Llewellyn's emphasis of "assent" as the basis of contract.

See also Harriman School District v. Southwestern Petroleum Corp., 757 S.W.2d 669 (Tenn. Ct. App. 1988) (warranty disclaimers on back of order from unenforceable) and others cited by the Transactions article.

What the Circle of Assent is Not:

- Not unconscionability, as the focus is not on fairness or bargaining power imbalances, but upon what the parties have actually agreed upon.

- Not a UCC conspicuousness test, which is mechanical in its application and can be satisfied by merely using large type or contrasting color or type. The circle of assent, being a totality of the circumstances doctrine, is more nuanced.

It is the closest, we think, to the "reasonable expectations doctrine" from insurance law: "The objectively reasonable expectations of applicants and intended beneficiaries regarding the terms of insurance contracts will be honored even though painstaking study of the policy provisions would have negated those expectations." (Doctrine applicable in at least 33 of the 50 states).

The Factors Considered:

1. Size and location of the provision,
2. Readability of the language,
3. Length of the document,
4. Whether the headings in the document have the effect of warning a party or misleading her,
5. Sophistication of the party,
6. Conditions at the time of assent (time to review, relaxed or rushed setting, etc.),
7. Substantive fairness of the provision, and whether the provision was expected or not.

Where may this show up in terms of deals and litigation?

Arbitration clauses. We are seeing a growing aggressive use of these provisions, and the challenges will continue to grow.

Rolling contracts. Like *Hill v. Gateway* and the in the box terms, bound unless you
return the computer within 30 days.

Unilateral Amendments. Credit cards, bank accounts, brokerage accounts, wireless communications contracts – unilateral amendment upon notice.

Where there is a mismatch between the salesperson's claims and the contract document. Businesses need to be able to integrate a contract with a merger clause, but sometimes contracts are oversold, and courts have, in some cases, had to break or bend the merger clause or the parol evidence rule to address the situation. The circle of assent provides a principled way of doing that, without breaking merger clauses, the parol evidence rule (which is what Traynor did in California), or launching unconscionability out of control.

◆ -- ◆

Starting in the 1980s, businesses began to embrace the concept of ADR because of its perceived speed and efficiency when compared to the over-crowded court dockets of the day. Business also benefitted from the secrecy of the proceedings and the outcomes as well as from often being repeat players before the same arbiters or arbitration organizations, which may have the effect of creating arbitral bias in the decision-making process. As in many things, what may have started out as a good thing got taken too far. Aggressive use of arbitration provisions has, in some cases, as a practical matter stripped consumers and others of their right to be heard and to seek redress. It has fallen to the courts to take the punch bowl away and tone down the arbitration party using UCC 2-207 and the doctrine of unconscionability.

In *Tillman v. Commercial Credit Loans, Inc.*, the North Carolina Supreme Court refused to enforce an arbitration clause for many of the same reasons. The provision was so lopsided that the court refused to sever the clause and instead invalidated the entire agreement. Tillman v. Commercial Credit Loans, Inc., 655 S.E.2d 362 (N.C. 2008). The following opinion illustrates the potential unfairness of arbitration clauses in an employment setting.

◆ -- ◆

WARNING: Don't Get Carried Away with Unconscionability *(Self-explanatory)*

Lawyering Skills Problem

You are general counsel for an insurance company. The company's standard-form release to be signed by people whom the company has compensated for injuries allegedly caused by its insured reads:

> Releasor hereby releases, acquits, and forever discharges Releasee and any other persons and entities of and from any and all actions, causes of action, claims, demands, damages, costs, loss of services, expenses, and compensation on account of or in any way growing out of any and all known and unknown personal injuries resulting or to result from the accident that occurred on or about [date and time], at or about [location].

> Releasor and Releasee agree to use confidential binding arbitration for any claims that arise between themselves, including disputes that involve third parties. In any arbitration, the prevailing rules of the American Arbitration Association and, to the extent not inconsistent with those rules, the prevailing rules of the Federal Arbitration Act will apply.

In spite of the language of the release, you are worried that there are some courts that might refuse to enforce the arbitration clause based on the doctrine of unconscionability.

You have been asked to re-write the release to make it more likely that courts will enforce the arbitration clause as written and reject any unconscionability challenge to it. Explain what you would do. Specific examples of how you would redraft it are preferred.

Various techniques can be used to address procedural unconscionability including conspicuous language, plain English, indications of choice, initialing by key provisions to indicate that the party read and understood them, etc. Substantive is harder—don't cut really unfair deals?

CHAPTER 13

THE STATUTE OF FRAUDS

— ♦ —

The statute of frauds is one of the classic law school doctrines that you have to cover, that is on the bar, and that, normally, presents little trouble in real life, since the doctrine is riddled with exceptions and the like. The British – who made it up in the first place – have even repealed it as it caused too much trouble and did not prevent fraud, really.

Historical background: once oral promises became enforceable in England, perjury and subornation of perjury became common. In 1677 Parliament enacted an Act for the Prevention of Fraud and Perjuries that required certain contracts to be evidenced by a writing. But this, in turn, led to frauds in denial of contracts! Squeezing a balloon only moves the air around (unless it pops!).

Put up Restatement (Second) of Contracts §§ 110 & 130. Go over them line by line. Note limitation to executory contracts.

Note: Keys are (1) memorandum or note (maybe not the full K or all of its terms), (2) signed, (3) by the party to be charged, and (4) categories covered:

(a) a promise to answer for the debt of another (suretyship, guaranty),

(b) contracts to transfer real property or instruments transferring real property,

(c) a promise that, by its terms, cannot be performed within one year,

(d) a promise in consideration of marriage, and

(e) a contract for the sale of goods (sometimes of over x amount, like $500).

NOTE

♦ - - ♦

Azevedo v. Minister
Supreme Court of Nevada
86 Nev. 576, 471 P.2d 661 (1970)

Azevedo is the buyer; Minister is the seller. Telephonic contract for the sale of hay. Escrow used to secure payment and buyer to send hay trucks to pick up.

Minister says agreement is for 1,500 tons; Azevedo says no quantity specified.

At the end of March, Minister loads only 2 of 4 trucks sent as the money in escrow has run out.

On January 21, Minister sent Azevedo an accounting showing approximately 16,600 bales left to be hauled (suggesting a quantity term to the oral agreement). On February 22 he sent another showing 14,000 bales to be hauled.

Whether they are both merchants could be a big issue – although I think they were – but they stipulated to that [para. 11], so UCC § 2-201(2) applies.

Held: These accountings are sufficient for purposes of 2-201(2). No timely objection, so they are binding. (Why is this case in court? *See footnote 10* – the price of hay has dropped since they made their contract and Azevedo wants a lower price.)

◆ -- ◆

PROBLEM 13-1

A young Hollywood star and the star's personal trainer enter into an oral contract under the terms of which the trainer will work for the star for the rest of his life. **Is this contract subject to the statute of frauds?**

The oral contract in this problem seems to be a contract of indefinite duration and is thus outside of the coverage of the statue of frauds. It does not give a specific time by which performance is to be completed. A contract of indefinite duration does not fall under the statute of frauds. It is not clear whether the "his" refers to the Hollywood star or the personal trainer. (Of course, if it were known that one of the parties was a woman, then there would not be any ambiguity.) However, it doesn't really matter whose life is at issue. The trainer can't work if he's dead, and the trainer can't train the star if the star is dead. So, the contract would end whenever one of the parties died. It does not change the indefinite duration of the contract.

Under the "theoretical possibility" approach, he could die tomorrow, in which case he would have completed his performance under the contract.

Note that if he had said "I will work for you for two years" that really means "I will work for you for two years or until I die, whichever period is shorter." But because he doesn't say so expressly, this different formulation makes it subject to the statute.

PROBLEM 13-2

A world renowned operatic tenor and an elderly opera fan enter into an oral contract under the terms of which the tenor will be paid $499 for performing at the fan's 80th birthday party. The fan is now 78 years old. **Is this contract subject to the statute of frauds?**

The UCC does not apply because this is a contract for the sale of a service, not for the sale of goods. Assuming that the fan is going to have his 80th birthday party in his (or very near his) 80th year, the contract in this case is to be performed more than one year in the future, if at all. Under Restatement § 110(1)(e), a contract that is not to be performed within one year will not be enforced unless there is a written memorandum. The contract is subject to the statute of frauds, and the contract does not meet the statute's requirements. In order to make the contract valid, the parties should sign a written memorandum of the agreement. Or, if the fan pays the $499, he will have completed his part of the contract, and the tenor will be held to complete his part of the contract under R2d § 130(2). (This reasoning would also apply to the fan if the tenor sings at the party. Remember, who is the party to be charged? The one refusing to perform.)

PROBLEM 13-3

Buyer and Seller enter into an oral contract for the sale of a vacant lot that Seller owns. Buyer sends Seller a signed letter that states:

This will confirm our agreement that you will sell to me and I will buy from you the lot at 123 Main Street, legally described as "Lot 99 in the Toxic Waste Subdivision, as per Map 44 recorded in the office of the Register of Deeds of Bigfoot County, California." The price will be $100,000 and all other terms will be as we have previously agreed.

Seller receives the letter but does not respond to it.

Can the contract be enforced against Seller? Can the contract be enforced against Buyer?

Land sale K, price specified, "all other terms as we have previously agreed." Can you use two or more writings? Sure. The SoF says nothing about "all in one writing."

The UCC does not apply because this is a contract for the sale of land. The contract is subject to R2d § 110(1)(d), which requires a written memorandum for the sale of an interest in land. The statute of frauds applies. Must the terms and conditions of the sale be stated in the written memorandum to satisfy the statute of frauds? Courts are split [para. 5]. In this case, there is a written memorandum, but it does not set out all the important terms of the transaction. Therefore, the

179

statute of frauds may not be satisfied and the contract will not be enforced. It cannot be enforced against either party.

Seller has not signed, so if it is enforced, it is only enforced against buyer.

PROBLEM 13-4

Buyer and Seller enter into an oral contract for the sale of a vacant lot that Seller owns. Buyer sends Seller a signed letter that states:

> This will confirm our agreement that you will sell to me and I will buy from you the lot at 123 Main Street, legally described as "Lot 99 in the Toxic Waste Subdivision, as per Map 44 recorded in the office of the Register of Deeds of Bigfoot County, California."

The letter goes on to spell out in detail all of the important terms of the transaction. Seller receives the letter but does not respond to it.

Can the contract be enforced against Seller? Can the contract be enforced against Buyer?

Can be enforced against Buyer, who sent it, but not against Seller, who did not. The lack of protest under UCC 2-201(2) does not work as this is a sale of land.

In this case, the important terms of the transaction are included in the memorandum. However, the memorandum was not signed by both parties, just the seller. The UCC holds a party to be bound if he fails to object to a written memorandum within 10 days. However, the UCC does not apply to the sale of real estate. It may be enforced against the buyer, because the buyer has signed the written document. It's probably not enforceable against the seller, because the seller has not signed anything.

PROBLEM 13-5

Farmer and Broker enter into an oral contract for the purchase and sale of 10,000 bushels of hops at a price of $3.00 per bushel. Broker sends Farmer a note that reads in full:

> This will confirm our agreement that you will sell me 10,000 bushels of hops at $2.75 a bushel.
>
> *Sleazy Q. Broker*

Farmer does not respond to the note. Farmer decides he doesn't want to deal with someone whose word can't be trusted, and he refuses to deliver the hops. Broker sues, and Farmer defends on the basis that the statute of frauds precludes enforcement of the contract. **Will this defense be successful?**

Depends upon whether the farmer is considered a merchant under the UCC. If so, then bound. If not, then not. He probably is a merchant.

The UCC applies to the sale of hops. Under UCC § 2-201(1), a written memorandum is required for all sales of goods in excess of $500. A party must have signed the document for the contract to be enforced against him. In this case, the farmer has not signed the confirmation memo, so he is not bound to it under subsection (1). However, if both parties are merchants, UCC § 2-201(2) applies. If the broker sent the confirmation within a reasonable time, the farmer had 10 days to send a written objection to the terms, or the confirmation would be held to satisfy subsection (1). Because the farmer failed to object within the 10 day time limit, the statute of frauds is not a valid defense to the broker's claim.

Let's not forget about UCC § 2-207, however. If the broker's memorandum is a non-conforming confirmation, then the $2.75 price does not come into the contract under the second sentence of § 2-207(2), assuming that price is material, which is generally the case in commodity contracts.

PROBLEM 13-6

Farmer and Broker enter into an oral contract for the purchase and sale of 10,000 bushels of hops at a price of $3.00 per bushel. Broker sends Farmer a note that reads in full:

This will confirm our agreement that you will sell me 10,000 bushels of hops at $2.75 a bushel.

Farmer mails the note back to Broker with the following annotation:
"The price was 3 bucks -- you jerk." /s/ Farmer

Farmer decides he doesn't want to deal with someone whose word can't be trusted, and he refuses to deliver the hops. Broker sues, and Farmer defends on the basis that the statute of frauds precludes enforcement of the contract. **Will this defense be successful?**

We leave that to you to figure out. UCC § 2-201(2) says the exception applies unless the recipient of the confirmation gives "written notice of objection to its contents... within 10 days after it is received." In the problem, the farmer has given "written notice" of his "objection" to the "contents" of the broker's confirmation. Doesn't it seem strange that something that qualifies as an appropriate "objection" under UCC § 2-201(2) would, at the same time, satisfy the statute of frauds so that the exception in UCC § 2-201(2) is no longer necessary.

The key here is that the writing from the party to be charged comes after the purported contract was formed, i.e. it is a UCC § 2-207 non-conforming confirming memorandum. Does this work? Posner held so in Monetti v. Anchor-Hocking. *What about an internal memorandum within the seller's organization? Why not?*

We think the statute is satisfied. You've got Farmer's signature on a memo listing the quantity and stating there's a contract. It's just a question of the price.

♦ -- ♦

Buckles Management LLC v. Investordigs, LLC
United States District Court, District of Colorado
July 20, 2010

Email can satisfy SoF, but must examine the facts in each case to see if it did. Same with signature requirement.

NOTE

♦ -- ♦

Lawyering Skills Problem

One law firm's computer system adds the following disclaimer on every email its lawyers send:

> This communication does not reflect an intention by the sender or the sender's client or principal to conduct a transaction or make any agreement by electronic means. Nothing contained in this message or in any attachment shall satisfy the requirements for a writing, and nothing contained herein shall constitute a contract or electronic signature under the Electronic Signatures in Global and National Commerce Act, any version of the Uniform Electronic Transactions Act or any other statute governing electronic transactions.

What do you do if you receive an e-mail from an attorney in this firm stating that she agrees to give you an additional 10 days to file an answer to her complaint? *Discuss. The question is intent. The statute of frauds does not apply to this agreement.*

expressly rejected Doliner and that case's standard for consistency, instead adopting a definition of "inconsistency" as "the absence of reasonable harmony in terms of the language and respective obligations of the parties."

Issue #1 – *Is there insufficient evidence of an oral or written contract at all as a matter of law?* Answer: *No.* UCC 2-204(1) (conduct evidencing a contract is enough). Enough to show the oral contract existed. Although it is true that, if the parties intended not to be bound prior to a writing being executed, then there would be no contract, that was not the case here (or at least not shown) [para. 10].

Issue #2 – *Does the parol evidence rule block introduction of evidence that the sale of scrap was conditioned on Pielet getting the scrap from a particular supplier?* Answer: *Yes.* UCC 2-202 does not permit terms that contradict the writing. This court rejects the Hunt court approach and uses a broader definition of "contradict" – *here an unconditional sale agreement would be converted into a conditional one, and that is a contradiction.* The court finds support in comment 3 to 2-202 providing that, if the additional terms are such that, if agreed upon, they would certainly have been included in the document in the view of the court, then the evidence must be kept out.

NOTES AND QUESTIONS

1. **Was there an integrated agreement (as the R2d uses that term) in this case? If so, what document or documents constituted the integrated agreement?**

The confirmatory memoranda were an "integrated agreement." They were "writings constituting a final expression of one or more terms of an agreement."

2. Suppose the writings had said nothing about who had to pay for the insurance on the shipment. **Should the court let in oral testimony to the effect that the parties had agreed that the seller would pay for the insurance?**

Yes, the court seems to assume that the merger clause in Luria's form was not effective. If, as the question assumes, there was nothing in the forms as to who pays for the insurance, an oral agreement as to that issue would be a "consistent additional term[]."

♦ - - ♦

Zell v. American Seating Co.
United States Court of Appeals, Second Circuit
138 F.2d 641 (1943)

This case is included not for any doctrine it teaches but as an example of the hostility that a vocal minority of judges have toward the parol evidence rule. It also introduces the students to Judge Frank and his extreme brand of realist jurisprudence.

Facts in plaintiff's affidavit in opposition to summary judgment: Just prior to America's entry into World War II, Plaintiff Zell agreed to act as agent to get defense contracts for defendant American Seating. The deal was that Zell would be paid $1,000 a month or an amount between 3% and 8% of the contract amounts (the exact percentage was left for later agreement).

The written document, however, said the compensation was to be $1,000 a month and "the company may, if it desires, pay you something in the nature of a bonus." The purpose was to avoid criticism of contingent fee contracts. The writing appeared on its face to be complete but, given the "real deal," was a deliberate non-integration.

The plaintiff got contracts worth $5,950,000 and sued for 3%: ($178,500).

Trial court gave summary judgment for the defendant.

Frank says this isn't a case where the deal was fraudulent or third parties relied on the writing.

What he's essentially saying (in Restatement (Second) terms) is that the agreement was NOT even partially integrated. They intended the oral agreement to be the deal and the writing was really just a cover-up. Since no integration, no parol evidence bar.

We don't spend much time on this case, but it does make a few interesting points. First, it is one of the few cases where the writing is not even a partially integrated agreement. Because it was just a sham, the parties did not intend it as a final expression of any of the terms of the agreement. Second, it shows the depths of the hostility that some judges bear for the parol evidence rule. For transactional lawyers, this means it's worth making the effort to have a merger clause that's as bulletproof as possible. For litigators, it means it's incredibly difficult to predict the outcome when parol evidence is involved. Finally, the case acquaints students with Judge Jerome Frank, one of the extremists of the Legal Realism movement.

Another obvious lesson from the case is that if you deal with crooks, you have to expect they'll try to cheat you, too. It's worth reminding students of this. They're soon going to be thrown into a business world they are not prepared for.

NOTES

1. Judge Jerome Frank, the author of this opinion, is considered to have been one of the most extreme followers of the Legal Realist school of jurisprudence. In an attempt to emphasize the importance of the judge's subjective impressions to the outcome of litigation, he once said that the outcome of cases could depend on what the judge ate for breakfast. This led critics to refer to Legal Realism as "gastronomic jurisprudence."

2. Learned Hand, considered one of the greatest American judges of all time, was on the panel that decided *Zell* and joined in the opinion. This fact should not be taken too seriously, however. When Hand was asked about Frank's long opinions, he reportedly said: "I see how [Frank] comes out and pay no attention to the shit." Laura Kalman, Legal Realism at Yale, 1927- 1960, 284 n.92 (1986), quoted in Paul Brickner, *Book Review,* 76 KY. L.J. 1077, 1082 (1988).

3. Judge Frank is also reputed to have said: "most lawsuits are won on a balance of the perjury." Quoted in S.G. Supply Co. v. Greenwood Int'l, 769 F. Supp. 1430, 1442 (N.D. Ill. 1991). Strange words from someone who wanted to abolish a rule designed to protect against perjured testimony.

Lawyering Skills Problem

Imagine that the parol evidence rule has been abolished. What would be the effect of this development? Specifically, if you were a lawyer documenting a deal, how would this affect your drafting, if at all?

If the parol evidence rule were abolished, one thought is that it would be necessary to invent it transactionally by broadening the standard merger clause with an express stipulation that the parties agree that no evidence of prior or contemporaneous communications, acts, or events would be admissible in any dispute between them regarding the contract.

Alternatively, a more civil law approach could be used, letting in such evidence broadly to allow the court to determine the true intent of the parties even if at variance with their written contract.

CHAPTER 15

INTERPRETATION OF CONTRACTS

— ♦ —

As the opening note of chapter 2 points out, there are a litany of canons of construction used to interpret contracts, and we will read about them as an aside in some of the cases. There is the doctrine of *contra preferentum*, or construing the document against the drafter, of *ejusdem generis*, where a list of specific sub categories will limit the interpretation of a general reference that could be more inclusive, etc. Llewellyn did a nice article showing that each has at least one contra canon and thus can be quoted back and forth ad infinitem. They are most useful for courts seeking to justify a result reached for other reasons. (So supply them but don't bank on them winning your case. . . .)

Kuney discusses the difference between vagueness and ambiguity at this point. Vagueness refers to a "fuzzy" standard in a contract while ambiguity refers to the potential for two or more different meanings. Generally, ambiguity is to be avoided at all costs in contracts, while vagueness has its place from time to time. This is covered in the practice pointer in this section of the casebook.

♦ - - ♦

Pacific Gas & Electric Co. v. G. W. Thomas Drayage & Rigging Co.
Supreme Court of California
69 Cal. 2d 33, 69 Cal. Rptr. 561, 442 P.2d 641 (1968)

Pacific Gas (plaintiff) hired Thomas Drayage (defendant) to replace the metal cover on one of its turbines. During the work, the cover fell on the turbine, causing $25,000 in damage. Pacific Gas's negligence claim was dismissed, but the trial court granted Pacific Gas judgment under an indemnity clause in the contract. The clause provided that Thomas would perform the work "at [its] own risk and expense" and "indemnify" Pacific Gas "against all loss, damage, expense and liability resulting from . . . injury to property, arising out of or in any way connected with the performance of this contract."

At trial Thomas sought to introduce evidence, including admissions by Pacific Gas personnel, that the indemnity clause was intended to indemnify Pacific Gas against loss resulting from damage to property owned by third parties, and not against damage to Pacific Gas's own property. The trial court excluded the evidence under the plain meaning rule, which states that where the meaning of a document appears to be plain on its face, extrinsic evidence cannot be used to give a different interpretation. Rejecting the plain meaning rule, Traynor goes overboard in arguing that language is elastic, saying such things as "A word . . . has no arbitrary and fixed meaning . . ." and "Although extrinsic evidence is not admissible to add to, detract from, or vary the terms of a written contract, these terms must first be determined before it can be decided whether or not extrinsic evidence is being offered for a prohibited purpose."

The result of the case, as subsequently fleshed out in California cases not presented in the materials, is a two step analysis for proffered parol evidence: (1) The evidence is provisionally admitted to determine whether or not the contract language is reasonably susceptible to the meaning for which the parol evidence is offered; (2) If so, the evidence comes in, if not, it is excluded [paras. 6, 11]. Note that this formal enunciation of the test may really be an expression of intellectual honesty reflecting what all or most judges actually do when applying the traditional parol evidence rules in cases like *Hunt & Luria Bros.* in the prior chapter. This issue can be explored with the students in terms of formalism vs. legal realism.

Trident Center v. Connecticut General Life Insurance Co.
United States Court of Appeals, Ninth Circuit
847 F.2d 564 (1988)

This case teaches a couple of good lessons in addition to making a point about contract interpretation.

In the early 1980s, inflation was out of control and real estate prices were climbing, particularly in Southern California. It seemed as if everyone who owned real estate was getting rich and everyone who didn't was seeing their wealth eaten away by inflation. At the height of the bubble, two large and respected law firms decided to cash in on the trend by joint venturing an office building. (Explain "joint venture" as, basically, a limited purpose partnership devoted to a single project. Defer more detailed discussion to after class or 2L Business Associations course.) They borrowed $56 million at 12¼ % interest to finance the project. That interest rate seems high today, but at the time it looked like a good deal. Because inflation had been so bad the last few years, this was the market rate of interest, and it appeared that rents would continue to rise so that the law firms could make their interest payments with a handsome profit to spare.

The trend didn't continue, though. Inflation came under control, rents stabilized and interest rates dropped dramatically. After a few years, the 12¼ per cent rate that looked like such a good deal before began to look really bad. The law firms began looking for a way around the "lock-in" clause that prevented them from refinancing the loan for the first 12 years of its term.

The clause stated that Trident (the joint venture) "shall not have the right to prepay the principal amount hereof in whole or in part before January 1996" [para. 7]. Trident, however, brought a declaratory judgment action, arguing that another provision providing for a 10% prepayment fee in the event the loan was prepaid on account of a default gave them an option to prepay at any time upon payment of the fee. The district court granted the lender's motion to dismiss and sanctioned Trident for filing a frivolous lawsuit [para. 5].

On appeal, Judge Kozinski "reject[ed] Trident's argument out of hand," saying that the language could not have been more clear [paras. 8-9]. (Subsequent paragraphs describe the event of default mechanism of the loan agreement. Describe function of these as an aside.) But then he went on to reverse the trial court, saying that as a federal court exercising diversity jurisdiction, it was bound to follow *Pacific Gas* and that *Pacific Gas* required the trial court to admit evidence of any proffered interpretation, however unreasonable. He then went on to ridicule *Pacific Gas* and say that it "chips away at the foundation of our legal system" [para. 17].

The opinion has been criticized because Kozinski failed to recognize the importance of the fact that the contract language in *Pacific Gas* may have been susceptible to the interpretation proposed, whereas in *Trident Center* it was not.

Trident made 2 arguments—(1) The contract is ambiguous. (2) Even if it's not ambiguous, they're entitled to present evidence of their interpretation.

Kozinski rejects "out of hand" the contention that it's ambiguous. He says it is not "reasonably susceptible" of their interpretation. Then he goes on to give *PG&E* a very broad reading, ignoring what Traynor said about "reasonably susceptible" and picking up on the theme that words don't have fixed meanings. He's really advocating a "plain" meaning rule.

NOTES

1. When Trident locked itself into a loan at an interest rate of 12 ¼ %, inflation seemed out of control and interest rates were rising faster than they had in anyone's memory. It seemed to everyone that they would go on rising. This may have been the reason that Trident agreed to what seems in hindsight to have been a very bad deal. One lesson to take from this case is that as a lawyer negotiating deals and drafting documents you need to think of the ways in which conditions might change and make sure your client, is protected if they do.

2. The California Supreme Court limited *Pacific Gas & Electric* in Dore v. Arnold Worldwide, Inc., 39 Cal. 4th 384, 46 Cal. Rptr. 3d 668, 139 P.3d 56 (2006). In the process of hiring an account executive, an ad agency wrote him a letter which provided in part:

> Brook, please know that as with all of our company employees, your employment with Arnold Communications, Inc. is at will. This simply means that Arnold Communications has the right to terminate your employment with Arnold Communications, Inc. at any time.

The agency required the executive to sign the letter. When he was terminated, the executive sued, alleging not only breach of contract, but also fraud and intentional infliction of emotional distress. His contract claim was that various oral representations, conduct, and documents had created an implied-in-fact contract that provided he would not be discharged except for cause.

195

The trial court granted summary judgment for the ad agency on the implied-in-fact contract claim. The Court of Appeal reversed, stating that the letter did not specifically state he could be terminated without cause. The California Supreme Court reversed the Court of Appeal. The majority opinion noted that under *Pacific Gas* extrinsic evidence may be admitted only if the language is susceptible of the meaning proffered. It said: "As a matter of simple logic, [the phrase 'at any time'] entails the notion of 'with or without cause.'"

Justice Baxter said in his concurring opinion that while the majority "to their credit" had chosen to apply *Pacific Gas* narrowly, it was susceptible to the broader interpretation given it in *Trident Center*. He quoted from that opinion and noted other criticisms of the opinion, including the later misgivings of Justice Mosk, who had joined in the *Pacific Gas* majority. Justice Baxter concluded that "it may be time for a fuller reconsideration of the meaning and scope of *Pacific Gas*."

◆ -- ◆

Frigaliment Importing v. B.N.S. International Sales
United States District Court for the Southern District of New York
190 F. Supp. 116 (1960)

The parties had two contracts for the sale of "US Frozen Chicken, Grade A, Government Inspected." The plaintiff buyer claimed that the defendant seller had breached the contract by shipping stewing chicken or "fowl" birds weighing 2 ½ to 3 pounds. The plaintiff claimed that there was a trade usage that "chicken" meant "young chicken." It introduced considerable evidence to this effect. At the end of paragraph 7, the court suggests that this evidence might have been sufficient to establish the trade usage if the defendant had not introduced considerable evidence to show that there was in fact no such trade usage. In the end, the case is one of the relatively few cases in the parol evidence field decided on the basis of the burden of proof. The presumption was that the word was used in the ordinary sense of the term, and it failed to prove that it was used in the narrower sense that it claimed.

The case is one for breach of warranty. This is a fine place, time permitting, to discuss what a warranty is, how it survives closing or delivery unless limited, and what sorts of remedies a breach will support (damages). Prelude to next chapter. Contrast to Representations.

Court looks at all the evidence and decides that it has to go with the ordinary meaning of the word because the evidence is not strong enough to rebut the presumption that it was used in the ordinary meaning.

NOTES AND QUESTIONS

3. The Supreme Court of Delaware has explained the principles governing contract interpretation as follows:

The principles governing contract interpretation are well settled. Contracts must be construed as a whole, to give effect to the intentions of the parties. Where the contract language is clear and unambiguous, the parties' intent is ascertained by giving the language its ordinary and usual meaning. Courts consider extrinsic evidence to interpret the agreement only if there is an ambiguity in the contract.

Northwestern Nat'l. Ins. Co. v. Esmark, Inc., 672 A.2d 41, 43 (Del. 1996).

The court must determine whether a contract is ambiguous by reviewing the entire contract. Pisano v. Delaware Solid Waste Auth., No. 05C-03-132-FSS, 2006 WL 3457686 (Del. Super. Ct. Nov. 30, 2006). "Ambiguity only exists when the contract's terms are 'reasonably or fairly susceptible of different interpretations' or if the terms may have more than one meaning." Id. (quoting Rhone-Poulenc Basic Chemicals Co. v. American Motorists, Ins. Co., 616 A.2d 1192, 1195 (Del. 1992)). The court will not create ambiguity where the ordinary meaning of the terms leaves no room for uncertainty. Id. (citing Rhoune, 616 A.2d at 1197). "If the language is clear and unequivocal, the parties are bound by its plain meaning." Id. (citing Emmons v. Hartford Underwriters Ins. Co., 697 A.2d 742, 745 (Del. 1997)).

5. A fairly recent California case may have significant effects on the way contract interpretation cases are decided. The court in *City of Hope v. Genentech* questioned the role juries should play in determining the validity of conflicting extrinsic evidence and how the resulting ambiguities should be construed. The court held that the jury could properly decide both issues or decide the evidence question alone and allow the judge to decide against whom the conflict should be interpreted. City of Hope National Medical Center v. Genentech, Inc., No. 129463, 2008 WL 1820916 (Cal. 2008). So drafters wishing to avoid jury interpretation of a contract may want to include boilerplate that provides for arbitration or judicial review of conflicting evidence. Also, a "mutual negotiation" clause may be wise in order to assert that ambiguities are not be construed against the drafter.

8. Judge Posner posits that the goals of a system of contract interpretation should be to minimize transaction costs. He divides these transaction costs into two types or stages of costs, drafting-stage costs and litigation stage costs. Faced with a gap in meaning caused by an omission or ambiguity in the parties drafting of the contract, he describes five approaches that the court might take, each with attendant costs and benefits:

1. Try to determine what the parties really meant; assume that they had covered the issue but failed to incorporate it into the contract.

2. Try to determine what resolution the parties would have agreed to if they had thought about the issue when negotiating the contract.

3.   Pick the economically efficient solution and assume that is what the parties
intended.

4.   Treat the matter as a toss-up and use some rule like "construe the contract against the drafter" to resolve the matter.

5.   Pretend that written agreements are always complete integrations and exclude all other evidence.

Richard A. Posner, *The Law and Economics of Contract Interpretation*, 83 TEX. L. REV. 1581 (2005). **Which approach do you think is superior? Why?** *Open-ended discussion.*

Lawyering Skills Problem

This is less of a problem than a story that illustrates how important punctuation can be to contract interpretation – and how a misplaced comma cost one company $2.13 million:

In 2002, Rogers Communications Inc. signed a contract with Aliant Inc., meaning to have entered into a long term agreement at a favorable rate. In 2005 they were surprised, therefore, when Aliant implemented a rate hike and were supported in this effort by the Canadian regulatory body with jurisdiction over the matter.

On page 7 of the contract a provision stated that the agreement "shall continue in force for a period of five years from the date it is made, and thereafter for successive five year terms, unless and until terminated by one year prior notice in writing by either party."

The problem, you see, is with the second comma in the quoted provision, which makes the contract terminable "at any time, without cause, upon one-year's written notice" in the words of the Canadian regulators. Without the second comma, the termination provision would apply only to successive terms, not to the original five-year term, which appears to be what the folks at Rogers Communication had in mind. But Aliant read the contract and sought to enforce its   literal   terms,   and   the   regulators   agreed.   *See* http://www.chaosscenario.com/main/2010/01/when-can-a-comma-cost-you-2-million.html.

The lesson is clear. Due to the parol evidence rule and the four corners rule, careful wording and punctuation in contracts is critical to transactional practice, and mistakes in these areas provide ample fodder for litigation over the interpretation of contracts.

CHAPTER 16

WARRANTY LIABILITY

— ✦ —

WARRANTIES *(Self-explanatory)*

✦ - - ✦

THE UCC APPROACH

Now starting with warranties—*now we see what contract the goods are supposed to conform with.*

If there's no promise—then the perfect tender rule doesn't mean anything.

Express warranties are covered by § 2-313:

- You don't have to say you warrant or even say anything.
- A mere description of the goods will do it.
- A warranty to conform to the description is implied.
- Showing somebody a sample or model is a warranty the goods will conform to that.

Two major questions for § 2-313:

(1) When is it an "affirmation of fact" (2-313(a)) and not just puffing? Cases are in conflict and often this will be decided on the basis of court's view of the equities.

(2) What do they mean by requiring it be part of the "basis of the bargain?" Knowledge of the warranty and reliance on the warranty. Generally a rebuttable presumption of reliance.

A couple more points:

- Warranties liability is strict liability in that if you make a warranty you're bound even though there was something you couldn't have known or controlled.
- Warranties are presumed to relate to the condition of the goods when delivered unless you say otherwise.

A. EXPRESS WARRANTY

Royal Business Machines v. Lorraine Corp.
United States Court of Appeals, Sixth Circuit
633 F.2d 34 (1980)

We lecture on this case and the next because they don't work well in a Q & A format.

Court says the decisive test is whether it's an assertion of a fact of which the buyer is ignorant or merely opinion or judgment on a matter of which the seller has no special knowledge and on which the buyer may be expected also to have an opinion and to exercise his judgment.

An express warranty requires:

(a)   An affirmation of fact or promise;

(b)   That relates to the goods at issue; and

(c)   Becomes a part of the basis of the bargain between the parties.

They're really asking: is it "fair to stick the seller with liability for this?" To answer this, the court looks to the following:

- "High quality"-It's the kind of puffing to be expected in every sales transaction.

- Frequency of repair was "very low" and would remain so—insufficient specificity.

- Replacement parts are readily available—doesn't relate to the goods themselves.

- Future cost of supplies—doesn't relate to the goods themselves.

- Will not cause fires—now, here is a warranty.

- Have been tested and are ready to be marketed—another warranty.

- Service calls would be required every 7,000-9,000 copies—another warranty.

What about the warranty that Booher will make a profit? Generally one doesn't find warranty in case like this; the Buyer should have its own opinion on profits that are likely. But in egregious cases they will, especially in franchise cases.

200

Here the appellate court finds that the district court made no finding that any of these purported warranties were the basis of the bargain.

Key lesson–pick out the elements of the statute and be sure you prove each one. The plaintiff's lawyers got $156,800 in attorney fees and couldn't do decent findings of fact. Explain how findings of fact are created by the lawyers for the court. In building a case, you are building a story, and that fact is very important in warranty cases. In theory, the defendant could have won on the basis that it hadn't been proved up.

With respect to cost of maintenance, on remand the District Court should determine at what point Booher's experience precluded his relying on the representations.

How did the court really go about determining if each statement was a warranty?

- Looked for analogous cases

- Two ways to reason:

  o Deductively from the rule – civil law.

  o Inductively from specific cases – common law.

Another thing the court says is that the same statement made with respect to the first copier and the last could be an express warranty with respect to one and not with respect to the other. How can that be? By focusing on the "basis of the bargain."

How do we determine whether it's part of the basis of the bargain?

Footnote 6 in the case says it's the basis of the bargain unless shown otherwise such as:

       (a)   The buyer didn't know about it,

       (b)   The buyer knew the statement was wrong, or

       (c)   It's clear that the buyer would have bought it anyway.

"It was the intention of the drafters of the UCC not to require a strong showing of reliance."

What about whether the warranty was different from what the seller thought? Note that the defect must exist when the goods are delivered, not afterwards due to abuse etc.

NOTES AND QUESTIONS

1. **How did the court justify its conclusion that no express warranty was created by the statements that the machines "were of high quality?" Are you convinced by this?** Suppose the seller had said, "This is Grade A merchandise." Suppose the seller had said, "These are Grade A eggs." **Would these statements create express warranties?**

Differentiate between puffery and slang terminology and use of a term of art or industry standard.

2. In Jones v. Kellner, 5 Ohio App. 3d 242, 36 UCC Rep. Serv. 784 (1982), a private party seller's oral statement that a used car was "in 'A-1' condition mechanically" was held to be an express warranty. In Chrysler-Plymouth City Inc. v. Guerrero, 620 S.W.2d 700 (Tex. Civ. App. 1981) the court held that the words "top quality" constituted an express warranty.

3. **How does the court reach the conclusion that the statement that replacement parts were readily available was not an express warranty?** *The statement did not relate to the goods.* **Would the court's reasoning support a conclusion that the statement, "replacement parts for this machine are readily available," is not an express warranty but "this is a machine for which replacement parts are readily available" is such a warranty?** *It would seem so.* **Regardless of how the statement was actually phrased, what do you suppose the seller was really trying to tell the buyer?** *The seller was saying that if you buy this product you won't have trouble getting replacement parts for it.*

4. **How does the court reach the conclusion that two identical statements could be made with respect to the first copier purchased and the last, and an express warranty would be created with respect to the first copier but not with respect to the last?**

Reliance wanes as experience grows.

5. **What does UCC § 2-313 mean when it says the affirmation or promise must become "part of the basis of the bargain?"** Under the old, now superceded Uniform Sales Act a statement could become an express warranty only "if the buyer purchases the goods relying thereon."

Reliance, which is generally presumed unless shown otherwise.

◆ - - ◆

Bayliner Marine Corp. v. Crow
Supreme Court of Virginia
509 S.E.2d 499 (1999)

Purchase of sport fishing boat. Complaint is that it is not fast enough to get out to sea for a full day of fishing. Sales person did not make representation, gave him prop matrixes that show a top speed of 30 mph, which had disclaimers and did not cover the prop size of his boat.

Note that the salesman gave the buyer the prop matrixes.

Prop matrixes had disclaimer that it was "for comparative purposes only." This presumably means only comparing props.

Express warranties alleged:

Prop matrix showed 30 mph

Court says that was a different boat with different weight and equipment

Court doesn't explain the letter that says the performance representations made at time of purchase were incorrect [Last sentence in 9th paragraph of opinion]. Bayliner wrote Crow a letter saying "the performance representations made at the time of purchase were incorrect." Were they admitting that the prop matrixes were wrong? Court seems to gloss over that.

Note that he asked about the speed and was shown the prop matrixes. We think the salesman knew he was relying on those even though, as the Appellate court notes, the matrixes were for different sized props.

The brochure's statement "delivers the kind of performance you need to get to the prime offshore fishing grounds" is pretty similar to "more maneuverable." Puffery.

Why didn't his lawyer strip the boat down and get 20x20 props and do some tests?

QUESTIONS

1. **If you were representing Bayliner, what additional language would you want to add to the prop matrixes to beef up the disclaimer?**

2. **Assuming that the disclaimer keeps the prop matrixes from being an express warranty by Bayliner, is it still possible to make a good argument that by giving the buyer the document, the dealer made a warranty?**

3. **Would there have been a breach of an express warranty if it were shown that when Bayliner did the tests upon which the prop matrixes were based, the boat had defective speed measuring equipment**

and was only making 25 mph rather than the 30 mph stated in the matrixes? Would Bayliner be liable? Would the dealer?

4. **How might Crow have been able to overcome the argument that the prop matrixes related to boats not configured the way his was?**

PROBLEM 16-1

Buyer went to Seller's used car lot looking for a car. She found one she liked and asked Seller: "How are the tires on this one?"

Seller replied: "It has good tires."

Buyer decided to take the car, and she and Seller signed a contract that was silent as to the subject of warranties.

A few days later, the right front tire, which had been defectively re-treaded, blew out while Buyer was on the Interstate. Buyer was injured and sued Seller, alleging breach of an express warranty. At trial Seller proved that he bought the tires from a reputable dealer who warranted to Seller that the tires were "better than new." Seller also proved that he had bought at least 200 tires from the same dealer and had never before had problems with them. The court found that the written contract was NOT a "fully integrated agreement."

Which is Seller's best defense? Why?

(1)   The written contract didn't say anything about the tires.

Incorrect. Not an integrated contract, so the sales pitch could be part of the basis of the bargain.

(2)   The buyer didn't rely on his statement.

Incorrect. The UCC does not require reliance. Being the "basis of the bargain" is enough. A statement of fact can be part of the basis of the bargain "without reliance, in that sense, warranties are creatures of strict liability."

(3)   The seller took all reasonable precautions to insure that the tires were in fact good tires.

Warranty liability is strict liability, so reasonable precautions have nothing to do with it.

(4)   The statement was "just puffing" rather than an affirmation of fact.

But isn't a statement that a car has good tires something that is an affirmation of fact rather than something that the buyer ought to have his own opinion about? This is, however, the best alternative among the answers given because the others are incorrect and this one is at least colorable.

Grower bought several bags of seeds, planning to grow his crop in the normal manner, using 600 pounds of fertilizer per acre. When he got home, he opened one of the bags and found inside a brochure that stated (among other things): "These are new and improved seeds. Because of advances in seed science, these seeds require only 300 pounds of fertilizer per acre, half the amount required with ordinary seeds." Grower followed the directions and used only 300 pounds of fertilizer. His crop failed. Surveying his neighbors, he discovered that those who believed the brochure and used only 300 pounds of fertilizer per acre also had crop failures, while those who ignored it and used 600 pounds had successful crops. Does Grower have a cause of action for breach of express warranty? *See* Official Comment 7 to UCC § 2-313.

As comment 7 indicates, the precise time when the statements are made is immaterial. If made after closing, the warranty "becomes a modification and need not be supported by consideration if it is otherwise reasonable and in order."

The real issue here is whether "instructions included" was part of the basis of the bargain. In a consumer transaction the case is a stronger one than with an experienced professional, but it can still be made.

B. IMPLIED WARRANTY OF MERCHANTABILITY

PROBLEM 16-3

Consumer buys a dozen eggs at the grocery store. When he gets them home, he discovers they are rotten.

(1)   Does he have a claim under UCC § 2-314? **If so, which of the specific tests in UCC § 2-314 does it fail to satisfy?**

At a minimum, § 2-314(a), (b) and (c).

(2)   **Does he have a claim under the Restatement of Torts?**

No. First, no physical harm. Also, not really defective in design, manufacture, or instructions.

PROBLEM 16-4

Sir Galahad bought a shield from Sir Mordred, a wandering knight who spends most of his time wandering from castle to castle, mooching off the local barons. In the course of his sales pitch, Mordred told Galahad: "this shield will never break."

The first time Galahad went into combat with the shield, it was shattered by a single blow of his adversary's sword, and Galahad was severely wounded.

Does Galahad have a claim for breach of express warranty, implied warranty of merchantability, neither, or both?

Express warranty

We believe so, although the matter is not free from doubt. This statement could be mere puffery in sales talk, but it seems sufficiently specific and reminds us of statement made to sell "Ginsu" knives.

Implied warranty of merchantability

No. Not a merchant in goods of that type

PROBLEM 16-5

Samantha purchased a used taxi with 212,000 miles on it from Executive's Taxi Company. Within two weeks after she purchased it, the transmission in the car failed, and Samantha had to spend $1,000 to have it repaired. Samantha sued and alleged a breach of the implied warranty of merchantability.

Can Executive Taxi Company prevail with the argument that no implied warranty of merchantability arose because it was not "a merchant with respect to goods of that kind?" *See* UCC § 2-104.

We would go with "maybe" on this question. Depending upon how Terry's Taxi Co. operates, it may or may not be an entity that "holds itself out as having knowledge or skill particular to the . . . goods involved in the transaction." UCC § 2-104(1).

It certainly looks bad for the seller when a car breaks down in such a serious way so soon after the sale. That indicates there was probably something wrong with the car at the time it was sold. On the other hand, the car had 212,000 miles on it. The standard for merchantability is often expressed in terms of reasonable expectations of the buyer. One can certainly make a good argument that a buyer should reasonably expect that a car with that many miles on it will have some major problems. On the third hand, if the car was one of those models made especially for service as taxis, it ought to hold up better than that.

So we think this could go either way.

Whether Jerry can recover may depend on how often Terry has sold used taxis in the past and on the caselaw in the jurisdiction in which the sale took place. The caselaw on the question of whether section 2-314 applies to a person who sells goods as an adjunct to his primary business is not entirely consistent. Here is a sample of some of the more interesting cases.

Some of the reported cases have held that a person is a "merchant with respect to goods of that kind" only if he "in a professional status sells the particular kind of goods giving rise to the warranty." Siemen v. Alden, 341 N.E. 2d 713, 714 (Ill. Ct. App. 1975) (holding that a sawmill operator's sale of a surplus saw did not give rise to a warranty of merchantability). One interesting case is Rock Creek Ginger Ale Co. v. Thermice Corporation, 352 F. Supp. 522 (D.D.C. 1971). A brewer of beer sold excess carbon dioxide produced in the process of brewing beer to a distributor, who in turn sold some of it to a bottler of ginger ale. When the ginger ale bottler got a load of carbon dioxide which smelled like rotten eggs (another witness said it smelled like "a dirty bar rag") and ruined a substantial amount of ginger ale, the bottler sued the distributor. The distributor in turn sued the brewer. The court held that there was no warranty of merchantability in the sale because the brewer was not a merchant of CO2. This was in spite of the fact that the brewer had sold more than 20 tank truck loads (714,000 pounds) of CO2 to the distributor over a period of more than six months.

Ashley Square Ltd. v. Contractors Supply of Orlando, 532 So. 2d 710 (Fla. Dist. Ct. App. 1988) addressed the question of how broadly "of that kind" should be read. A contractor had tried to purchase a special type of stucco from the manufacturer. The manufacturer refused to sell to the contractor directly and told him to buy it through the manufacturer's local distributor. The distributor ordered some of the stucco for the contractor, and when it was not paid for, filed a materialman's lien against the property where it was used. The property owner counterclaimed, alleging that the stucco was defective. This distributor claimed that it was not a merchant with respect to that kind of stucco because it had never sold it before. The court held that there was a warranty of merchantability. The holding seems clearly to be correct, although there is broad language in the opinion that would seem to say that the warranty arises any time the seller is a merchant. What the court really seems to be saying, though, is that a seller who holds itself out as a building supply business is a merchant for all types of building supplies, not just those it sells on a regular basis.

In a case that may have been influenced by the judges' sympathies, the Massachusetts Bay Transportation Authority ("MBTA") was held to be a merchant when it sold eight of its trolley cars for scrap. The plaintiff's brother died as a result of his exposure to PVC fumes while cutting the cars with an acetylene torch. The court relied on the fact that they sold most of its used cars for scrap and that it was "experienced and knowledgeable" with respect to trolley cars. The court specifically rejected the rule, adopted by other courts, that the warranty does not arise where the sale is merely "incidental" to the primary business of the seller. Ferrigamo v. Massachusetts Bay Transportation Authority, 395 Mass. 581 (Mass. 1985). The court noted, however, that the result would be different if the sale were merely an "isolated transaction."

Another Massachusetts case held that a person in the business of selling automotive supplies and parts and making automotive repairs created an implied warranty of merchantability when he sold a pickup truck. The court said that "his occupation involves a level of knowledge and skill sufficient to invoke the applicability of [section 2-314]." Fay v. O'Connell, 12 U.C.C. Rep. Serv. 2d 987 (Mass. Dist. Ct., App. Div. 1990).

♦ -- ♦

The court now considers whether (the trial court properly concluded) Bayliner breached an implied warranty of merchantability, and determines that Bayliner did not breach.

No evidence to support that the boat was generally not merchantable as an offshore fishing boat, even though it did not go as fast as Crow would like.

To be merchantable, the goods must be such as would "pass without objection in the trade" and as "are fit for the ordinary purposes for which such goods are used." [UCC] § 2-314(2)(a),(c). Crow presented no evidence of the standard of merchantability in the offshore fishing boat trade or that a significant portion of the fishing boat buying public would object to buying a boat with such speed capability.

[Please refer back to the facts of the case earlier in this chapter. – Eds.]

[1] We next consider whether the evidence supports the trial court's conclusion that Bayliner breached an implied warranty of merchantability. Crow asserts that because his boat was not capable of achieving a maximum speed of 30 miles per hour, it was not fit for its ordinary purpose as an offshore sport fishing boat. Bayliner contends in response that, although the boat did not meet the needs of this particular sport fisherman, there was no evidence from which the trial court could conclude that the boat generally was not merchantable as an offshore fishing boat. We agree with Bayliner's argument.

[2] [UCC §] 2-314 provides that, in all contracts for the sale of goods by a merchant, a warranty is implied that the goods will be merchantable. To be merchantable, the goods must be such as would "pass without objection in the trade" and as "are fit for the ordinary purposes for which such goods are used." [UCC] § 2-314(2)(a),(c). The first phrase concerns whether a "significant segment of the buying public" would object to buying the goods, while the second phrase concerns whether the goods are "reasonably capable of performing their ordinary functions." *Federal Signal Corp. v. Safety Factors, Inc., 125 Wash.* 2d 413, 886 P.2d 172, 180 (Wash. 1994). In order to prove that a product is not merchantable, the complaining party must first establish the standard of merchantability in the trade. Bayliner correctly notes that the record contains no evidence of the standard of merchantability in the offshore fishing boat trade. Nor does the record contain any evidence supporting a conclusion that a significant portion of the boat-buying public would object to purchasing an offshore fishing boat with the speed capability of the 3486 Trophy Convertible.

[3] Crow, nevertheless, relies on his own testimony that the boat's speed was inadequate for his intended use, and Atherton's opinion testimony that the boat took "a long time" to reach certain fishing grounds in the Gulf Stream off the coast of Virginia. However, this evidence did not address the standard of

merchantability in the trade or whether Crow's boat failed to meet that standard. Thus, we hold that Crow failed to prove that the boat would not "pass without objection in the trade" as required by Code § 8.2-314(2)(a).

◆ -- ◆

Adams v. American Cyanamid Co.
Nebraska Court of Appeals
498 N.W.2d 577 (1992)

- Here the court examines a more limited ordinary use: Controlling weeds in beans.

- The Court reverses judgment on strict products liability but affirms on merchantability.

- Note they decided that strict liability in tort didn't apply because Prowl was not unreasonably dangerous because the loss wasn't sudden (see the note following the case).

NOTE

In case you're wondering how the court held that a product that killed a farmer's crop was not "unreasonably dangerous," the definition, as the quote from the *Rahmig* case shows, requires "physical harm." While the court doesn't define that term, it has often been limited in a products liability context to mean damage caused by a sudden traumatic event rather than by a gradual process as would be the case with an herbicide of this type.

◆ -- ◆

General Motors Corp. v. Brewer
Supreme Court of Texas
966 S.W.2d 56 (1998)

- The automatic passive seatbelts were so cumbersome you couldn't really use them as passive restraints. You had to put them on every time you got in.

- Court says there is no fact issue—the court says "the product merely fails to fulfill the precise expectations of the consumer."

- But what about the fact that they may be so bad they don't "pass without objection in the trade under the contract description." 2-314(2)(a).

- Suppose GM had been trying to reject the belts under the perfect tender rule when the manufacturer delivered them?

- The Court didn't look at the Suminski point.

- A key fact is that this is a class action and a lot of judges don't like class actions.

◆ -- ◆

Suminski v. Maine Appliance Warehouse, Inc.
Supreme Court of Maine
602 A.2d 1173 (1992)

- Note that the store manager had never heard of the implied warranty of merchantability. I'm not surprised—as I said, it's almost always disclaimed.

- Court doesn't look at the merchantability of the switch. It looks at the merchantability of the TV as a whole.

- Why was the proof inadequate as to the merchantability of the TV? Would it have been adequate if the TV had done that from the beginning?

NOTES AND QUESTIONS

1. In each of the preceding cases, think of how the court characterized the product and its intended use. **Was there an alternative way of characterizing these things that might have changed the outcome of the case, or alternatively, one that might have made the decision even easier?**

2. The characterization of the product's intended use was outcome determinative in Daniell v. Ford Motor Co., 581 F. Supp. 728 (D.N.M. 1984). Connie Daniell felt "overburdened," so she attempted to commit suicide by locking herself in the trunk of her Ford LTD. At some point after she incarcerated herself, she changed her mind and discovered that she couldn't get out. Nine days later, she did get out. The opinion doesn't say how. She sued Ford, alleging, among other things, breach of the implied warranty of merchantability. The court said "the usual and ordinary purpose of an automobile trunk is to transport and store goods, including the automobile's spare tire. Plaintiff's use of the trunk was highly extraordinary, and there is no evidence that the trunk was not fit for the ordinary purpose for which it was intended." *Id.* at 731. The court also rejected the plaintiff's claim that Ford had breached a duty to warn her of the danger, saying: "the potential efficacy of any warning, given the plaintiff's use of the automobile trunk compartment for a deliberate suicide attempt, is questionable." *Id.*

C. IMPLIED WARRANTY OF FITNESS FOR A PARTICULAR PURPOSE

Lewis v. Mobil Oil Corp.
United States Court of Appeals for the Eighth Circuit
438 F.2d 500 (1971)

In November 1964, Lewis finished conversion of his sawmill to hydraulic equipment using used equipment purchased from another operator.

The prior owner had used Cities Service oil but Lewis had been a customer of Mobil for many years and wanted to continue using Mobil oil. The Mobil dealer said he didn't know the proper oil for the system but would find out. The only information the owner gave the dealer was that the mill was operated by a gear-type pump. Dealer didn't ask for more. Apparently the dealer contacted a Mobil representative for recommendation, though the court says "this is not entirely clear." Dealer sold Lewis Ambrex 810–a straight mineral oil without additives.

Trouble with the oil started immediately. After 6 months, the system broke down and a new "system" was installed. During the next two years, six new pumps were installed. After two years, Lewis changed to a different type of pump. He continued to use Ambrex and that pump broke down after three weeks. At this point he was visited by reps of the pump company and Mobil. This was the first visit of a Mobil representative. They recommended a different type of oil which contained a defoamant. After he changed to that, Lewis operated for 2½ years without a problem.

At trial, jury awards Lewis $39,500 for breach of warranty. This court affirms breach but reverses and remands on lost profit damages for new damages hearing.

Was there a breach of the implied warranty of *merchantability*?

No. But the court says there was "some proof" it was not "fit for the ordinary purposes for which such goods are used, which could mean the goods fail to pass under § 2-314(2)(c)."

Was there a breach of the implied warranty of fitness for a particular purpose?

Yes.

What was the ordinary purpose?

As a lubricant.

What was the particular purpose?

Use in <u>his</u> hydraulic system.

How does Mobil have reason to know of this particular purpose?

He went to his Mobil dealer.

How could they have discovered this purpose?

He told them of it.

Do they have a duty to send an engineer to the sawmill?

If that was what was required to "furnish suitable goods," they had to do it or tell them they could choose a product for him.

Do they have a duty to send an engineer or disclaim the warranty?

Court notes that the question is whether Mobil had reason to know the particular purpose but assumes they had an absolute duty to discover abnormalities in the system.

Suppose 99 out of 100 would work okay with Ambrex. Do they have a duty to make sure that he doesn't have the 1 in 100?

Court says so.

*Court makes a lot turn on the language. It seems to say that Mobil might win if he had said he wanted "oil that was okay for **a** gear type pump" but lose if he said "I want it for **my** pump."*

Arguably breach of express warranty:

Plaintiff says Rowe said he would find out the proper oil

◆ -- ◆

Interesting case—not in text.

Kobeckis v. Budzko, [pre-UCC] 225 A.2d 418 (Me. Supreme Ct. 1967)
Plaintiff purchased pork infected with tricinosis.
Said it was for sausage.
Customary for Polish sausage makers to taste it raw.
Should have known he was Polish because of his name.
Court said defendants weren't responsible for picking that up and trial courts dismissed the case. Appellate Court affirms.

You take your chances.

Bayliner Marine Corp. v. Crow
Supreme Court of Virginia
509 S.E.2d 499 (1999)

[Please refer back to the facts of the case earlier in this chapter. – Eds.]

To establish an implied warranty of fitness for a particular purpose for which the goods were required, buyer must prove that he made known to the seller the particular purpose for which the goods were required.

Evidence fails to support the trial court's ruling that Bayliner breached an implied warranty of fitness for a particular purpose.

QUESTIONS

1. **What is the court's stated reason for holding there was no breach of the implied warranty of fitness for a particular purpose?**

"Although Crow informed Atherton he intended to use the boat for offshore fishing and discussed the boat's speed in this context, these facts do not establish that Atherton knew on the date of sale that a boat incapable of traveling at 30 miles per hour was unacceptable to Crow."

Basic idea is that the buyer didn't come in and say "I need a boat that will do 30 miles an hour." Of course if he puts it this way and you tell him it's what he needs, it looks like an express warranty.

2. Suppose that Crow had come to Atherton and said "I need a boat for offshore fishing. It'll be based in the Tidewater." Atherton said "I think the Bayliner 3486 is just what you need."

(a) **Would that create an express warranty?**

We think Atherton's statement could be considered puffing.

(b) **Would it create an implied warranty of fitness for a particular purpose?**

Still have to show Atherton knew Crow was relying on [Atherton's] skill and judgment to select . . . suitable goods.

Arguably not because Crowe was the one checking on the speed. When Crowe asked about the speed and Atherton said he didn't know, that probably prevented any implied warranty that dealt with speed.

(c) **If there was created a warranty of fitness for a particular purpose, was it breached?**

Still have to show the boat wasn't suitable for offshore fishing.

As originally shown or as fitted out?

Does Atherton now have a duty to tell him that he's slowing it down too much?

This would be a good case for an implied warranty of fitness for a particular purpose IF THE SALESMAN HAD TRIED TO COVER UP HIS IGNORANCE.

Good lesson in being willing to admit you don't know.

♦ - - ♦

PROBLEM 16-6

Gwen developed a fever and red spots on her face. Art went to Merlin, described Gwen's symptoms, and asked Merlin to prepare a potion to cure her. Merlin told him, "For five shillings I can give you a potion that will fix her right up." Art paid the five shillings and Merlin mixed up a batch of his world-renowned chicken pox potion. Gwen took the potion but remained sick for two weeks until a wandering monk called at the castle and said a blessing over her. At that point, she began to get better. Subsequently, it was determined that Gwen had measles, rather than chicken pox.

Art has sought your advice as court solicitor. First, he wants to know if there has been a breach of the implied warranty of fitness for a particular purpose. **What do you tell him?**

If you said that Merlin breached the implied warranty of fitness for a particular purpose, we replied: But the potion that Merlin gave Arthur was an excellent potion that would have cured the chickenpox. You can take that on faith. Considering what other feats Merlin had performed, he could easily have prepared a potion to cure measles, if only Arthur had told him that was what he needed. Is Merlin responsible for diagnosing the illness, too? After all, he's not an internist. He's only a magician.

If you said that Merlin did not breach, what is the basis for your contention that there was no breach of the warranty of fitness for a particular purpose. After all, Merlin knew Art was purchasing a potion for the purpose of curing Gwen. He knew Art was depending on him to furnish a potion that would do the trick, and he sold the potion. Hasn't he met all the requirements of UCC § 2-315?

PROBLEM 16-7

Now let us look at the same question in Problem 16-6 from the standpoint of express warranty.

CHAPTER 17

DEFENSES TO WARRANTY LIABILITY

— ♦ —

Read 2-316(2). It says you can modify or exclude the warranty of merchantability. To do so, one must:

1. Mention "Merchantability," and

2. If the disclaimer is in a writing, it must be "conspicuous." Conspicuous is not in the definitional cross-references to UCC § 2-316 but *is* defined in 1-201(b)(10) as "A term [or clause is conspicuous when it is so written] that a reasonable person against whom it is to operate ought to have noticed it...."

3. One may also disclaim or modify the warranty of fitness for a particular purpose in writing if the disclaimer is conspicuous. Look at definition and discuss it.

UCC § 2-316(3) lists other ways of excluding warranties which overrides UCC § 2-316(2):

(a) Use of commonly used expressions:
"As-Is"
"with all faults"
"other language which in common understanding ..." (Don't count on it).

(b) Inspection or refusal to inspect waives defects to the extent inspection ought to have disclosed them.

(c) Course of performance   1-303(a)   2-208
Course of dealing   1-303(b)   1-205
Usage of trade   1-303(c)   1-205

Make sure the class understands those terms.

One way sellers limit their warranty liability is by limiting or excluding the warranty itself. These are called *disclaimers*.

Another way is not to limit what warranties arise but to limit what obligations exist if they are breached. This is really more common. We won't say the stuff we're selling you isn't any good. We'll just say that if it isn't, all you're entitled to is the return of your money or a replacement. UCC § 2-719(a)—read it. These are called exclusionary clauses, which is a little misleading.

Note that these provisions are in different parts of Article 2. Disclaimers are in Part 3--"General Obligation and Construction of Contract," while exclusionary clauses are in Part 7--"Remedies."

◆ -- ◆

PROBLEM 17-1

Read carefully UCC § 2-316(2) & (3).

(1)   **Is it possible to have an oral disclaimer of the warranty of fitness for a particular purpose? What about merchantability?**

No.

(2)   **Is the warranty of merchantability excluded by the statement: "There are no warranties which extend beyond the description on the face hereof?"**

Under UCC § 2-316(2) this would disclaim a warranty of fitness for a particular purpose; but as to the warranty of merchantability, doesn't mention merchantability, but could test with UCC § 2-316(3)(a) as § 2-316(3) opens with the words "notwithstanding subsection (2)."

As you read the case that follows, look for the differences between disclaimers and exclusionary clauses.

◆ -- ◆

Schroeder v. Fageol Motors
Supreme Court of Washington
544 P.2d 20 (1975)

Trucker purchased used truck. Had 94,000 miles left on the factory warranty. Broke down. Cummins Engine Co. repaired it under the engine warranty, but it never functioned properly. Trial court gave $8,000 for repair bills and $12,000 for lost profits. The "Owner Book" given to him with the truck had an exclusion of consequential damages that wasn't conspicuous.

Court says issue is whether exclusion of consequential, addressed by UCC 2-719, must be conspicuous and decides it doesn't have to be. The UCC § 2-719(3) standard is unconscionability—look at conspicuousness and presence in negotiations through that lens. Reverse and remand so that can be accomplished.

Court then discusses whether the clause is unconscionable. Discusses procedural and substantive unconscionability and says the case has to go back to the trial court to decide whether the exclusion of consequential damages is unconscionable in this context.

WHAT DID THE LOWER COURTS DO WRONG IN SCHROEDER? According to the Supreme Court of Washington, they applied the standards of UCC § 2-316, properly applicable to disclaimers, to exclusionary clauses, which are covered by § 2-719(3).

NOTES AND QUESTIONS

1. **What is the difference between a disclaimer and an exclusionary clause?**

2. Most commentators agree that Article 2 treats disclaimers and exclusionary clauses as two different animals. Disclaimers are governed by § UCC § 2-316, which is in Part 3 of Article 2, the same part that governs the creation of warranties. **(Do you see how the organization of the article can be important to its interpretation?)** Exclusionary clauses are governed by UCC § 2-719, which is in Part 7, the remedies part. **But does this result necessarily follow from the language of the particular sections?** Consider an exclusionary clause that prevents the buyer from obtaining any real recovery for a breach of the implied warranty of merchantability. **Isn't it within the express language of UCC § 2-316(2)?** *See* UCC § 2-316(4) and comment 2. **How much weight should be given this comment?**

We see a conflict between (2) and (4). Comment (2) resolves it in favor of (4). Without comment (2) and (4) we would read modifying remedies to be modifying the warranty.

PROBLEM 17-2

A manufacturer's standard form agreement for a farm tractor provides:

Manufacturer's sole obligation with respect to the warranties arising out of the sale of this vehicle is limited to the repair of the vehicle and the replacement of defective parts for a period of 24 months from the date of purchase. In no event shall Manufacturer be liable for any consequential loss or damage of any nature arising from any cause whatsoever.

Is this clause subject to the requirements of UCC § 2-316(2)? Is this clause prima facie unconscionable under UCC § 2-719(3)? If so, is it substantive or procedural unconscionability?

This clause is only exclusionary and is thus governed by § 2-719(3).

Here, argue this is like consumer goods, and even then it is only prima facie unconscionable.

It is not consumer goods, it's a farm tractor.

*Does the Article 9 definition of consumer goods apply? §9-102(23). Article 2
does not have a definition of "consumer goods."*

See 2-103(3), which specifically adopts the Article 9 definition.

*If it did, would this clause be substantively or procedurally
unconscionable?*
> *Substantive--if clear and not hidden.*
> *Procedural--Would person understand that their estate can't recover
> if it rolls over and kills them?*

PROBLEM 17-3

Unbeknownst to her wicked step-sisters, Cinderella has been running an
Internet auction site from her dismal quarters in the basement. As a result,
when the Prince's ball was announced, she had more than enough ready cash to
buy a coach and six horses to pull it. She went to Honest Earls Used Coaches and
picked out a coach and six horses to pull it. The sales contract she signed
provided in large red letters:

> IN THE EVENT THAT THE GOODS SOLD SHALL
> PROVE DEFECTIVE OR OTHERWISE FAIL TO CONFORM TO
> THE CONTRACT, BUYER'S SOLE REMEDY SHALL BE THE
> REFUND OF THE PURCHASE PRICE PAID. IT IS EXPRESSLY
> UNDERSTOOD THAT THIS IS IN LIEU OF ALL OTHER
> REMEDIES AND THAT IN NO EVENT SHALL SELLER BE
> LIABLE FOR CONSEQUENTIAL DAMAGES.

Cindy took the coach to the ball and the Prince was entranced by her
charms. Sometime after midnight (it's not clear exactly when; they had both
consumed considerable champagne) the Prince escorted Cindy back to her coach,
dropping subtle hints about marriage and not-so-subtle hints that they should
take a ride together in the country. When they got to the spot where the coach
was parked, however, they discovered that the coach had turned into a pumpkin
and the horses into mice.

Cindy has, of course, sued Honest Earl. She is seeking damages for the
humiliation she suffered and also for the loss of the chance to become wife of the
ruler of the principality. (It was a small principality, but it had considerable
mineral resources). Honest Earl has asked for a ruling that even if Cindy prevails
on her argument that the coach and horses were unmerchantable (something
Earl is not yet willing to concede) the most Cindy would be entitled to recover is
the amount she paid for the coach and horses.

How should the court rule on this motion?

*Can you make the argument that it's prima facie unconscionable because it
would preclude recovery if she had been injured?*

This is the strongest UCC § 2-719(3) analysis: Consumer goods, thus prima facie unconscionable. Can it be defended? If the clause is struck, what can she recover (with certainty)? Contract claims?

PROBLEM 17-4

A clause in a contract for the sale of a used car provides, "This vehicle is not warranted in any way." The clause is in small print on the back of the form, but the seller specifically draws the buyer's attention to the clause. **Is it adequate to exclude the implied warranty of merchantability?** *See* Harriman School Dist. v. Southwestern Petroleum, 757 S.W.2d 669 (Tenn. 1988), and Hull-Dobbs, Inc. v. Mallicoat, 57 Tenn. App. 100, 415 S.W.2d 344 (1966).

THREE ISSUES

1. *Is the language adequate under 2-316(3)(a)?*

WHAT WOULD YOU THINK?

Don't depend on anything other than the two examples given in the statute.

Court have gone both ways on "in lieu of all other warranties, express or implied" or (b) "buyer accepts the goods in their present condition"

Tennessee case - <u>Hull-Dobbs, Inc. v. Mallicoat</u>, 57 Tenn. 100, 415 S.W.2d 344 (1966) "accepted in its present condition" was not sufficient to disclaim express warranties.

2. *Is there a conspicuousness requirement?*

Why should something that specifically mentions merchantability have to be conspicuous and "as is" not?

Isn't it a principle of statutory construction that the legislature clearly knew how to say "conspicuous?"

Article 2A, the new article covering leases, specifically adds a conspicuousness requirement in its equivalent of 2-316(3). New Article 2 requires it only in "consumer contracts"–a defined term that means a contract between a consumer and a merchant.

The majority of cases require conspicuousness. TN follows the majority. Harriman School District v. Southwestern Petroleum, 757 S.W.2d 669. The lawyer who lost the case in the Supreme Court was in this class the first time Lloyd taught it. Lloyd went back and reduced his grade retroactively.

3. *Is conspicuousness satisfied by pointing it out?*

Some cases say so. White & Summer say no. Their point is that one should be able to make the determination from the documents themselves and not have to rely upon the parties testimony.

◆ -- ◆

Jaskey Finance & Leasing v. Display Data Corp.
United States District Court, Eastern District of Pennsylvania
564 F. Supp. 160 (1983)

Defendant moves to dismiss Plaintiff's claims for breach of express warranties, warranties of fitness, and for negligent design of a computer system.

Plaintiffs bought a 32K computer from Defendant, and they were dissatisfied with the computer's operation. The sale involved two contracts: one for the sale of the equipment, programming and installation services and another for maintenance of the computer system.

The bottom of the front side of both contracts says: "Terms and Conditions on Reverse Side Are Part of This Contract." Both parties signed immediately under that. The reverse side of the contract is titled "Terms and Conditions" and contains two paragraphs that are relevant to the case. The first said:

> (a) Seller warrants that it will provide maintenance service for Purchaser according to the terms and conditions of the separate maintenance contract executed by and between the parties.
> (b) For a period of one (1) year after the program is delivered, Seller will make every reasonable effort to remedy or correct any errors in the program which are brought to the attention of the Seller.
> (c) EXCEPT AS SPECIFICALLY PROVIDED HEREIN, THERE ARE NO WARRANTIES, EXPRESS OR IMPLIED, WHICH EXTEND BEYOND THE DESCRIPTION ON THE FACE OR REVERSE SIDE HEREOF.
> (d) IN NO EVENT SHALL SELLER BE LIABLE TO PURCHASER FOR LOSS OF PROFITS OR OTHER ECONOMIC LOSS, INCLUDING SPECIAL, CONSEQUENTIAL OR OTHER SIMILAR DAMAGES ARISING OUT OF ANY CLAIMED BREACH BY SELLER OF ITS OBLIGATIONS THEREUNDER.

The second relevant paragraph says, "This contract contains the entire agreement between the parties, and shall be binding upon both parties and their respective heirs, successors and/or assigns."

The Maintenance Contract further states: "EXCEPT AS SPECIFICALLY PROVIDED HEREIN, THERE ARE NO WARRANTIES, EXPRESS OR IMPLIED, WHICH EXTEND BEYOND THE DESCRIPTION CONTAINED HEREIN."

Plaintiffs claim Defendant warranted a lot of things, but neither contract reflects that; and the contract plainly says it "contains the entire agreement between the parties."

The Court dismisses Plaintiff's claims.

Court doesn't seem to dispute that the express warranties were made. How does it justify not sticking them with them? Disclaimers coupled with an integration clause.

Isn't this just boilerplate? What do we mean by boilerplate? Discuss.

What do you do?

They've told you all these wonderful things about the computer?

Then they give you the K to sign?

PROBLEM 17-5

Mr. and Ms. Bear went to Grimm Bros. Discount Furniture to buy a chair for their cub. Mr. Bear saw an official NFL-sponsored child's chair with the logo of his favorite team (the Chicago Bears) on it. He told Ms. Bear "now Teddy can pull up his chair next to my recliner when the ball games come on and we can engage in some male bonding." Ms. Bear was not so impressed. She expressed concern that one of Papa Bear's buddies might have a little too much to drink one night and sit in the kid's chair.

"Not to worry," said the sales associate, "this chair will hold an adult. It's not nearly as flimsy as it looks. It's made of new space-age particle board."

Based on the sales associate's assurance, Ms. Bear reluctantly agreed to the purchase of the chair. Mr. and Ms. Bear signed a sales contract that said in large red letters just above the signature line:

EXCEPT AS EXPRESSLY SET FORTH IN THIS CONTRACT, THIS PRODUCT IS SOLD WITHOUT ANY WARRANTIES, EXPRESS OR IMPLIED.

A few days later, the Bear family returned from an outing and discovered that an intruder had sat in the child's NFL-endorsed chair and broken it while eating porridge. The chair was made of ordinary particle board, and, while it was quite satisfactory for use by a small child, there was no way it would support an adult or even a young golden-haired woman.

Has there been a breach of an express warranty?

"No"- If you said that there has been no breach of the express warranty: But section 2-316(1) says that where an express warranty and a disclaimer are

inconsistent, the express warranty prevails. It's true that section 2-316(1) makes an exception for the parol evidence rule, but suppose the sales contract wasn't a fully integrated agreement (after all, it didn't have a merger clause), then couldn't the warranty then be given effect?

No. If the contract is not fully integrated, CONSISTENT prior oral terms may be given effect. But an express warranty is inconsistent with a statement that says very clearly there are no express warranties.

"Yes"- If you said that there has been a breach of an express warranty: But what about the disclaimer in the contract that very clearly and conspicuously states that there are no express warranties? Doesn't the parol evidence rule provide that the signed document renders inoperative any inconsistent oral terms? See UCC § 2-316(1).

In consumer cases, courts generally find a way to give effect to warranties like this.

What to do to make an enforceable disclaimer for an unsympathetic seller: Have customer initial next to the disclaimer.

Put on board the readings of 2-719(2) and the effects on consequential damages exclusions. Don't forget consumer protection act–deceptive trade practices act. We post the relevant sections to our course website.

PROBLEM 17-6

Ms. Muffett, a dairy products broker, entered into a contract with In The Dell Farms, Inc. The contract calls for In The Dell Farms, Inc. to deliver "one thousand gallons of USDA Number 1 curds and whey." The contract contained a clause which conspicuously provided:

> SELLER DISCLAIMS ALL WARRANTIES, EXPRESS AND IMPLIED, INCLUDING WITHOUT LIMITATION ALL WARRANTIES OF MERCHANTABILITY OR FITNESS.

In The Dell Farms, Inc. delivered 1000 gallons of USDA Number 2 curds and whey. Number 2 curds and whey are less valuable than Number 1 curds and whey.

Does Ms. Muffett have a breach of warranty claim? *See* UCC §§ 2-313(1) and 2-316(1).

She has no warranty of merchantability or fitness liability, as that is conspicuously disclaimed. What about the express specifications that are in the contract. Are these disclaimed as well? Or, can we characterize the specifications as part of a covenant to deliver the specified goods and claim that failure to perform the covenant is a material breach of contract, and seek recory for breach of covenant not breach of warranty? Discuss canons of construction and contradictory clauses.

She can, however, reject the goods or, if accepted, revoke acceptance if she meets the standard.

PROBLEM 17-7

Your client sold one of his customers a drill bit for oil drilling. (These bits are expensive. Howard Hughes was as rich as he was because his father had founded Hughes Tool Company, which made bits like the one in question). The bit broke the first time the customer tried to use it, and the customer immediately brought it back and demanded the return of his money. Your client, being a typical oil patch good old boy, told the customer exactly what he could do with the broken drill bit.

Not surprisingly, the customer sued, alleging breach of the implied warranty of merchantability. You asked the client what documentation there was for the sale, and he showed you his standard invoice. It contained no warranties, no disclaimers, and no exclusionary clauses. When you asked why these terms were not in the document, he told you that everybody in the oil business knew that when you buy a drill bit you get an "Oklahoma warranty." You overcame your reluctance to admit your ignorance, and you asked what an "Oklahoma warranty" was. He explained with some condescension that "if it breaks, you got two bits instead of one. You don't whine about it. You just buy another one from somebody else." Your investigation indicates that this is in fact the way things are done in the oil patch.

What is the effect, if any, of the fine tradition that is the "Oklahoma Warranty" if the buyer doesn't take his medicine but instead hires a big-city lawyer and sues? *See* UCC § 2-316(3)(c).

The point of this question is to focus on the effects of course of dealing, usage of trade, or course of performance. Here, it does not appear that the parties have dealt with one another previously, so only usage of trade could create the limitation of the warranty.

◆ - - ◆

Bishop Logging Co. v. John Deere Indus. Equip. Co.
South Carolina Court of Appeals
455 S.E. 2d 183 (1995)

Bishop Logging purchased equipment from John Deere for use in swamps. Sales price was $600,000.

Warranty provided that Deere would repair or replace the equipment during the warranty period and did not warrant the suitability of the equipment.

It was part of the deal, however, that the standard warranty would apply in spite of the unusual use that was to be made of the equipment.

Deere agreed to do this because it saw the possibility of additional sales to other users if this worked out. In some sense, Bishop was really doing product testing for Deere.

Express disclaimer of merchantability and fitness and exclusion of consequential damages.

Deere made over $100,000 in warranty repairs, but the equipment was still down so much that Bishop lost about $600,000 in profits over three years.

Court says the warranty failed of it essential purpose under UCC § 2-719(2).

So it held that Bishop was entitled to damages based on value of equipment, i.e., the difference between what it was worth and what it would be worth if it worked like it was supposed to.

But they want consequential damages.

2 ideas of 2-719(2)

Does 2-719(2) wipe out the consequential damage limitation?

Cases are split. Some turn on whether it's in a separate provision.

Could you say, "Buyer may not recover any consequential damages, including those caused by failure to repair or replace." We think you could. On the other hand, buyers might not agree to it, or it might be unconscionable.

This court says that the consequential damage limitation falls with the rest. The argument is that it was agreed to on the assumption the seller would be able to repair the equipment.

In fact, it probably wasn't carefully thought out by the parties in advance. Deere people probably didn't realize that they were practically guaranteeing the success of this operation—at least to the extent that it depended on the equipment working in the swamp.

What could they have done? How about preparing a document that clearly spelled out their responsibilities—How many hours, how many repairs. But that might have thrown the deal off track.

This was really an experiment and the court made Deere the guarantor of the experiment.

Why didn't Deere document it better? Our guess is that the sales people never consulted the legal people.

What do you do in this case if you're the house counsel for a company in Deere's position?

One possibility is to keep sticking your nose into deals and watch for these things

Problem is that the business people will hide things from you and even get you fired–businesses are about producing and selling the product, not about covering themselves legally.

Better to have a good relationship with the business people so they will come to you and consult you before they do something with adverse legal consequences. The trick is to find out their business objective and then to design a transaction that achieves it and is legal and enforceable.

Don't kill their deals

Easier said than done – Enron

Don't slow them down

Also easier said than done–You miss a lot of dinners with your family that way– a lot of golf games – a lot of watching the Final Four.

Another possibility in this case–Deere really knew what it was doing. It took a calculated risk and this one didn't pan out–Maybe the next one will.

◆ -- ◆

PROBLEM 17-8

Trucker purchased a truck with a warranty which read as follows:

Manufacturer warrants to the owner each part of this vehicle to be free under normal use and service from defects in material and workmanship for a period of 12 months from the date of original retail delivery or first use.

Manufacturer's obligation under this warranty shall be limited to the repair of the vehicle and the replacement of defective parts.

The warranties herein expressed are **IN LIEU OF** any other express or implied warranty, including without limitation any implied **WARRANTY** of **MERCHANTABILITY** or **FITNESS**, and of any other obligation on the part of Manufacturer or Dealer. In no event shall Manufacturer or Dealer be liable for any consequential loss or damage of any nature arising from any cause whatsoever.

The contract also called for Trucker to pay for the truck in monthly installments over a period of three years.

During the first year, the truck was in Dealer's shop for a total of 60 days to remedy a variety of problems, some major and some minor. Trucker loses $300 in profits every day the truck was in the shop. At the end of the year, seeing his warranty coverage coming to an end and his mechanical problems not coming to an end, Trucker stopped making payments and returned the truck to Dealer. **Is Trucker liable for the loan balance?** *See* § 2-608(2). **Is Dealer liable for consequential damages?** *See* § 2-719(2).

See § 2-608(2). *UCC* § 2-608(2) provides that revocation of acceptance must occur within a reasonable time of discovering the non-conformity that substantially impairs the truck's value to him and before there has been a substantial change in the condition of the goods not caused by the defects. Here, it appears he has waited too long—too many miles have been put on the truck.*

Is Dealer liable for consequential damages?

See § 2-719(2). *UCC* § 2-719(2) provides that remedies can be exclusive if the contract so provides, and this one does. One way would be to find that it failed of its essential purpose under § 2-719(2).*

♦ -- ♦

Van Den Broeke v. Bellanca Aircraft Corp.
United States Court of Appeals, Fifth Circuit
576 F.2d 582 (1978)

Could he really have believed he was going to get a plane without disclaimers?

Don't you look at the warranty when you buy a car or a computer? (Ha!)

Court finds warranty delivered with plane that contained the disclaimers was post-contracting and thus not part of the contract. Since the plane cost more than $500, the UCC Statute of Frauds applied and you would need a signed writing incorporating the disclaimers in order to modify the contract. The warranty card mailed in did not satisfy this requirement. Reverse trial court.

Contrast with *Hill v. Gateway*, in which Easterbrook delays the moment of contracting from the order date to post-delivery to allow "in the box" terms to be effective.

What's fair or unfair about it?

♦ -- ♦

Eastern Air Lines, Inc. v. McDonnell Douglas Corp.
United States Court of Appeals, Fifth Circuit
532 F.2d 957 (1976)

Eddie Rickenbacker retired in 1963– a year before the order was placed–at 73 and an alcoholic. He was too cheap and old-fashioned to buy jets. He thought they were a fad. (J.P. Morgan thought the auto was a fad.) Stayed on the board and interfered so much his successor took to drink as well.

Here we've got a huge case--$25 MM in damages--4 and 1/2 months of trial--and they've got to go back and do it over because of a "technicality."

Contract for McDonnell Douglas to supply 90 passenger jets to Eastern on a specific time-table. On average, each of the 90 late planes was delivered 80 days after the date specified in the contract.

Anybody who could read a calendar knew they were late.
There was even an Eastern engineer in the Douglas plant.
Letter from Eastern says delays "have been expensive to Eastern." Not an effective UCC § 2-607 notice of breach.
Alot of conversations.

But also some indications that Eastern had no plans to sue.

What did Eastern's attorneys do wrong here? *No formal UCC § 2-607(3) notice of breach within reasonable post-acceptance time period. Definite notice would bring things to a head.* <u>*You are in breach*</u>. *More than what is required is better than less!*

The UCC § 2-607(3) notice is not just about informing the other side about a non-conforming tender. It is also about communicating that the buyer considers the seller to be in breach (rather than waiving the non-conformity). This is also supported by the same policies that support statutes of limitation: no prosecution of state claims, allow discovery while evidence is fresh, clear the air and move on.

Can you seriously believe that Douglas didn't know there was a problem?
So what should they have done? So why didn't they? Hadn't they taken Commercial Law in law school? Nobody in the whole legal department?

The opinion is long--in fact we only gave you about half of it. We could have edited it down more, but it would have lost some of its flavor--the court talks about all the things that went back and forth between the parties and still says that as a matter of law we can't say that the notice requirement was met.

Toward the end, the court indicates it was bothered by the fact that Eastern may have misled McDonnell Douglas by indicating it believed the excuse and entering into other contracts without seeking to negotiate the damage claim.

Eastern failed to make a decent factual record that would later support a claim of breach.

But that's not really the issue—the issue is when a person knows there's a problem, do they have to give formal notice? The court says yes.

NOTES AND QUESTIONS

1. **What should Eastern's attorney have done? Will her malpractice policy cover her for $25 million or should she see the credit union about a loan?**

Formal notice of breach within the reasonable post-acceptance time period under 2-607(3).

2. **What is the lesson from this case?**

The lesson is that when you have a statutory requirement, you follow it formally and precisely—you don't count on substantial compliance.

♦ -- ♦

PROBLEM 17-9

Homer purchased a new sports car from Dealer. While he was driving a curving mountain road, wondering why it wasn't as much fun as the television commercials made it seem, the car's steering failed. Both Homer and the car were damaged in the resulting crash. Homer filed suit against Dealer alleging breach of the warranty of merchantability. Upon receipt of the summons and complaint, Dealer forwarded a copy to Manufacturer (from whom Dealer had purchased the car) along with a letter that read in full as follows:

July 21, 2010

Manufacturer
99-1/2 Jitney Blvd.
Detroit, Michigan 48100

Gentlemen:

Enclosed is a copy of a summons and complaint served upon us in connection with an allegedly defective automobile that you manufactured. Demand is hereby made that you appear in and defend in this action on behalf of my dealership.

Very truly yours,
/s/ Dealer

Having better things to do, Manufacturer ignored the letter. The case was tried and judgment was entered against Dealer. The jury found as facts (1) the steering mechanism in the car was defective, and (2) this defect had caused the injury. Dealer then filed a separate action against Manufacturer for breach of the implied warranty of merchantability.

In the Dealer-Manufacturer litigation, will Manufacturer be able to argue successfully that under § 2-607(5) it is not bound by the prior jury's determinations that the steering mechanism was defective and that that defect caused the accident? Why or why not? *See* Bendix-Westinghouse Automotive Air Brake Co. v. Swan Rubber Co., 55 Cal. App. 3d 256 (1976).

UCC § 2-607(5): Where buyer sued for breach of warranty from one that he sold to, and his seller is answerable (saying, warranty of merchantability), then he can give written notice to his seller and the opportunity to come in and defend. If this notice is given and the seller does not participate in the litigation, he will be bound by any findings of fact on issues common to both litigations.

Why sue Dealer and not Manufacturer?

1. *Perhaps there are jurisdiction problems.*

2. *The manufacturer is likely to be able to put up a good defense.*

3. *The plaintiff may not know about the person who really caused the problem.*

The idea of § 2-607(5) is to prevent the dealer from getting whipsawed.

Here, the notice is insufficient to trigger § 2-607(5) in that it does not explicitly state that manufacturer can be bound by findings of facts common to both actions.

Remember the lesson from the Eastern Airlines case—don't count on substantial compliance.

Don't try to make a notice that reads nice and smooth like it was an English paper or an article from People magazine. Follow the statutory language as closely as possible. We would even cite the statute.

NOTE

In Uniroval, Inc. v. Chambers Gasket and Manufacturing Co., 380 N.E.2d 571 (Ind. App. 1978), the court explained the purpose of the "vouching-in" procedure:

> The common-law right of a defendant to "vouch-in" a person liable over to him was set forth in the leading case of Littleton v. Richardson 34 N.H. 179, 66 Am. Dec. 759, 760 (1856):

[W]hen a person is responsible over to another, either by operation of law or by express contract . . . and he is duly notified of the pendency of the suit, and requested to take upon him the defense of it, he is no longer regarded as a stranger, because he has the right to appear and defend the action, and has the same means and advantages of contravening the claim as if he was the real and nominal party upon the record. In every such case, if due notice is given to such person, the judgment, if obtained without fraud or collusion . . . will be conclusive against him, whether he has appeared or not . . . .

"Voucher to warranty" has deep roots in common-law emanating from England. (*See* Comment, 29 ARK. L. REV. 486 (1976)). Its application in America has flourished. In 1963, the General Assembly saw fit to codify the practice as it relates to the law of sales concerning "middlemen" by enacting § 2-607: [The court then quoted § 2-607(5).] Vouching-in is a "simple and expedient way for defendants who have a right over against another to avoid the necessity of relitigating the issues of liability to the plaintiff in the first suit." IB Moore's Federal Practice 0.405[9]. It has the unique advantage of not requiring personal service of process. *Id.*

♦ -- ♦

PROBLEM 17-10

On July 8, 2007, Aerostar Aircraft purchased an aircraft engine from Oceanic Engines. The engine sat in Aerostar's warehouse until 2009, when it was installed in a new airplane. The airplane was sold to Dealer, and it sat on Dealer's lot until August 15, 2011, when it was sold to Purchaser. The first time Purchaser flew the plane, the engine failed. Purchaser made a crash landing in a cornfield. He was uninjured but the aircraft suffered extensive damage. So did the cornfield. It was determined that the cause of the crash was Oceanic's failure to install a cotter key on a crucial nut. The cotter key is required by Federal Aviation Regulations, and because it was not installed the nut came loose in flight. **Is Purchaser's UCC § 2-314 claim against Oceanic barred by UCC § 2-725?**

Oceanic (2007) > Aerostar Aircraft (2009) > Dealer (2011) > Purchaser (crash)

UCC § 2-725 provides for a 4 year statute of limitations from the time of claim accrual. This can be reduced by agreement to not less than one year. Under (2), the cause of action accrues when the breach occurs and a breach of warranty occurs when tender of delivery is made, regardless of when the aggrieved party knew it or not. This is different from the tort product liability rule which is an accrues-upon-discovery rule.

When does the warranty of merchantability under § 2-314 start to run?

When does the breach occur? Tender of delivery. So Oceanic, the manufacturer, is not a viable defendant, but Aerostar Aircraft and Dealer are.

♦ -- ♦

Poppenheimer v. Bluff City Motor Homes
Tennessee Court of Appeals
658 S.W.2d 106 (1983)

[The court summarized the complex procedural history of the case. When you cut through all of the details, it amounts to this: the suit is barred by the statute of limitations if the statute began to run when tender of delivery was made on June 25, 1973.]

Court says this is not a warranty that extends to future performance OF THE GOODS. All they promised was that the product was free from defects when delivered. Thus, the statute of limitations begins to run as of the date of delivery.

GMC MOTOR HOME NEW VEHICLE WARRANTY

> **What is Warranted and for How Long?** GMC truck (GMC Truck & Coach Division, General Motors Corporation) warrants to the owner of each GMC Motor Home (hereinafter called "Motor Home") that for a period of 12 months or 12,000 miles, whichever first occurs, it will repair any defective or malfunctioning part of the Motor Home -- except tires and tubes which are warranted separately by the tire manufacturer. This warranty covers only repairs made necessary due to defects in material or workmanship.

Lots of cases involving bricks on buildings. After 10 years the bricks start falling apart. Obviously, a brick that starts to fall apart after 10 years is defective unless there's some outside cause. But courts say: "Tough luck. The statute is 4 years." One may, however, proceed in tort for a defective product or building defect, which is usually deemed to accrue when the victim knew or should have known. But tort is no good for purely economic damages.

♦ -- ♦

PROBLEM 17-11

On March 1, 2005, Purchaser purchased a set of tires with a warranty that provides:

"Manufacturer warrants that these tires will perform satisfactorily in normal service for a period of five years or until 50,000 miles have been driven on them, whichever comes first."

There were no disclaimers, exclusionary clauses, or other provisions concerning warranties in the sales contract.

(1) On September 1, 2009, the right front tire blew out causing a minor accident resulting in $4,000 worth of damage to Purchaser's Mercedes. Purchaser replaced the right front tire, and the other three tires logged their 50,000th mile on December 1, 2009. Purchaser has sued, alleging a breach of the implied warranty of merchantability. **Is his claim barred by § 2-725?** (Read the question carefully.)

It's more than 4 years from tender of delivery

But the express five-year warranty extends to future performance and thus would accrue upon the blowout.

But—the question asked about merchantability, so the answer is "yes, the claim for breach of the implied warranty of merchantability is barred by the statute of limitations, but the express five-year warranty course of action is not."

(2) Suppose that on June 1, 2007, when the tires had been driven 55,000 miles a blowout occurred, causing a serious accident. The tires still had plenty of tread left, and the cause of the accident was determined to be a manufacturing defect. **Could Purchaser assert a breach of warranty claim? If so, when would the statute run?**

No claim under the express warranty, but still one under the implied warranty of merchantability. Statute runs March 1, 2009—four years from date of purchase.

♦ -- ♦

USING OTHER LAW TO CIRCUMVENT WARRANTY DEFENSES

♦ -- ♦

PROBLEM 17-12

(1) Manufacturer purchased a furnace from Furnace Co. and had it installed in its factory. The sale contract provided: "In no event shall Furnace Co. be liable for consequential loss or damage arising from any cause whatsoever." The following January, a small but vital part in the furnace malfunctioned and the furnace stopped heating. Manufacturer was forced to close its plant for two weeks until a replacement part could be found. **Can Manufacturer recover for the profits lost while the furnace was down?**

No. The contract bars consequential contract damages and tort law will not cover pure economic loss.

(2) **What would be the result in Part (1) if the furnace exploded and destroyed Manufacturer's computer system and the destruction of the computer system was the reason for the shutdown?**

Clear property damage case.

Consequential damage exclusion is purely contract, so recovery in tort should be allowed under section 18 of the Restatement (Third) of Torts, which says that waivers, disclaimers, limitations, and the like do not bar or reduce product liability claims against sellers. But see Restatement (Third) of Torts § 21, cmt. f (seeming to suggest that R3d does not take a position on such contractual provisions).

(3) **What would be the answer in Part (1) if the furnace exploded but did not damage anything other than the furnace itself?**

Violent injury to the property itself. Cases are split on whether it's property damage.

♦ -- ♦

Instructors may wish to discuss or assign reading on the applicable state's consumer protection act at this point.

♦ -- ♦

Morris v. Mack's Used Cars
Supreme Court of Tennessee
824 S.W.2d 538 (1992)

Disclaimers permitted by UCC § 2-316 may limit or modify liability otherwise imposed by the code, but do not defeat separate causes of action for unfair or deceptive acts or practices under the Consumer Protection Act.

Lawyering Skills Problem

In 1992, Penny King purchased a used 1977 model Ranch-Aire aerobatic airplane (one that is specially-designed for loops, rolls, and other air show-type maneuvers) from Uncle Sky's Aircraft Sales, a dealer in new and used aircraft. Penny operates a small flying school, just herself and two or three part-time instructors. The part-time instructors turn over regularly as they get airline jobs (or give up trying to get airline jobs, as the case may be). At any given time Penny would own two or three aircraft. Typically, she would keep an eye out for good deals in used aircraft and when she saw a good deal, she would buy the plane, use it for a couple of years and sell it when something better came along.

235

As an aviation professional, Penny knew that an aircraft that has been damaged (ever) is much less valuable than one that has never been damaged. Therefore, Penny required that the bill of sale she received from Uncle Sky provide "subject aircraft has never been damaged."

Similarly, Penny knew that aircraft are subject to *airworthiness directives*. The Federal Aviation Administration from time to time issues airworthiness directives when it discovers unsafe design features in a particular type of airplane. (E.g., it recently issued one when it was discovered that the rudder in the Boeing 737 sometimes goes in the direction opposite to the direction the pilot commands.) These are like automobile recall notices, but with a couple of major differences—the *owner* (not the manufacturer) of the aircraft has to pay for the work done on the aircraft and it is **illegal** to fly the aircraft if the airworthiness directive has not been complied with. To make sure that there weren't any airworthiness directives that had been issued with respect to the Ranch-Aire and not already incorporated into her airplane, Penny made sure that the bill of sale she got from Uncle Sky provided "all airworthiness directives pertaining to this aircraft have been complied with."

In 1998, Penny decided it was time to sell the old Ranch-Aire. Penny's middle-aged body no longer took kindly to the g-forces generated by beginners incompetently attempting barrel rolls. Penny placed the following ad in an aviation magazine:

> 1977 Ranch-Aire. Fun aerobatic airplane. New radios. Never damaged. All airworthiness directives complied with. Call 423.573.0489.

Mike Grey saw the ad. He called Penny and told her he had seen the ad. She gave him a demonstration flight, and he decided he had to have the aircraft. They entered into a contract where he agreed to buy the aircraft subject to the express condition precedent that "Buyer shall be satisfied with the results of an inspection of the aircraft and its log books performed by a Federal Aviation Administration-licensed aircraft mechanic."

The contract was one page long and was prepared by Penny. The last line in contract, in ordinary type, directly above the signature line, read simply: "no warranties."

After signing the contract, Mike hired a mechanic to inspect the aircraft and its log books. The inspection of the log books was important because federal regulations require that a log book be maintained for every aircraft and that all damage to the aircraft and all repairs to the aircraft be recorded in the log books, which are always transferred along with an airplane.

Prior to signing the contract for the purchase of the aircraft, Mike glanced at the log book, but he did not review it thoroughly because he intended to have his mechanic, who knew better what to look for, take a very close look at it.

236

The mechanic inspected the aircraft and its log book, and told Mike that there appeared to be nothing wrong with either. Mike thereupon paid for the airplane and took possession of it.

Two years later, Mike went to sell the plane to buy a plane that was newer and more powerful. When his buyer had the plane inspected, her mechanic found two major problems with the plane. First, he found that the airplane had in fact been damaged some years earlier, before Penny bought the plane. The damage had been repaired so that it was not detectable even by the most careful inspection of the plane, but the repairs were logged in the log book, and a careful reading of the log book by Penny, Mike, or the mechanics who inspected the airplane when Penny and Mike made their purchases would have revealed the damage. Unfortunately, none of these folks read the log book that carefully, and in spite of the quality of the repair, the fact that the aircraft had suffered this damage reduced its value. Also, the buyer's mechanic discovered there was an airworthiness directive that had been issued three years before Penny bought the plane. The airworthiness directive required adding a stiffener to the wing to reduce metal fatigue in the wing. It would cost $2,000 to comply with the airworthiness directive, and the fact that the airplane had flown so many years without the stiffener meant that the wing had suffered more than the usual amount of metal fatigue and this further detracted from the value of the plane.

Mike's mechanic could not have determined that there was an airworthiness directive that had not been complied with solely by looking at the log book, but a careful mechanic making an inspection such as this would have obtained a list of airworthiness directives applying to this particular model of aircraft and checked against the log book, where each repair made to comply with an airworthiness directive is logged, to make sure that every one of them had been complied with. Instead, Mike mechanic relied on entries made by Penny's mechanic when he did his annual inspections of the aircraft. At each annual inspection, Penny's mechanic had written in the log book: "All airworthiness directives complied with." When he made this notation he did not actually check that all the airworthiness directives ever issued against the plane had been complied with. Instead, he went back to the similar entry made at the last annual inspection and then just checked to make sure no airworthiness directives had come out since that date or if one had, it had been complied with. A very careful mechanic would have obtained a list of all the airworthiness directives ever issued against this model and checked that compliance with them had been logged in the log book before he made this notation the first time, but Penny's mechanic had not done this. Instead he relied on the entry made by the previous owner's mechanic and only looked for airworthiness directives issued since that entry. The previous owner's mechanic had done the same thing. He had relied on the entries made by the mechanic before him. An earlier mechanic had overlooked an airworthiness directive, and nobody had picked it up.

The discovery of these defects means that Mike won't be able to sell the plane except at a much reduced price. He has come to you to see if he has any breach of warranty claims against Penny. Please advise him.

One idea—2-317—logs conflict with the statement in the ad about never being damaged.

What warranty would be controlling?

How far back does the chain of liability go?

CHAPTER 18

PRINCIPLES OF CONTRACT DAMAGES

— ♦ —

1. Specific Performance is the exception to the rule and is generally only ordered when money damages are not adequate to give the prevailing party the benefit of its bargain.

2. Compensatory Damages generally seek to give the prevailing party *the amount of money that would place the non-breaching party in as good a monetary position as she would have been had the contract been performed* (this is the benefit of her bargain). They are not based on a punishment theory.

3. There are other remedies available, generally by the choice of the plaintiff, including rescission and restitution (cancel the contract and get money and property back).

What can be done in contracting? Provide for damages for delay— liquidated damages (not penalties). Include incentive clauses and bonding requirements. There are no perfect solutions. But you can plan . . .

That is a preview of what we will be examining in this and subsequent chapters.

♦ - - ♦

Menzel v. List
Court of Appeals of New York
24 N.Y. 2d 91, 298 N.Y.S. 2d 979, 246 N.E.2d 742 (1969)

1932 – Menzels purchase Chagall painting for $150.

1940 – Menzels flee the Nazis invasion of Belgium. Nazis take picture and leave receipt.

1955 – Perls (N.Y. Art Gallery) buy the painting from Parisian art gallery
        for $2,800 with
no questions asked.

1955 – later – Perls sell painting to List for $4,000.

1968 or so– Menzel sues List and List impleads Perls on a breach of implied warranty of title claim. Judgment for Menzel and List. List to give painting to Menzels or pay them $22,500 (present value of painting at time of suit), and judgment for List against Perls in the amount of $22,500 (plus costs).

Appellate division reduces amount awarded to List to $4,000, the purchase price List had paid, plus interest. Basically a "here is your money back" award.

This court reverses and reinstates the $22,500 judgment. The $4,000 plus interest would be in the nature of restitution and rescission, not benefit of the bargain or, more specifically here, "the loss directly and naturally resulting, in the ordinary course of events, from the breach of warranty."

What's the issue here? Court says it in so many words in paragraph 5. Under the formula in the Restatement, the "loss in value" is $22,500. The Menzels bought a painting, and if the contract had been performed, they would have had a $22,500 painting.

The damage remedy for breach of a warranty is: the value of the goods or services as warranted less the value of the goods or services as received.

♦ -- ♦

United States Naval Institute v. Charter Communications
United States Court of Appeals, Second Circuit
936 F.2d 692 (1991)

Trial court awards $35,000 as loss of profits by plaintiff plus $7,700 as profits defendant made from breach.

Court says defendant's profits shouldn't be included.

Plaintiff (USNI) sought review of the amount of damages awarded in its favor by the United States District Court for the Southern District of New York in breach of contract and copyright infringement actions and defendants sought review of judgment and award to plaintiff.

The court reviewed the copyright infringement claim and determined that according to the agreement between the parties, defendants became the owner of the right to publish the paperback book, therefore, its publication could not constitute copyright infringement (thus, no award of profits for the infringement).

However, defendants were in breach of contract, and the court determined that plaintiff was entitled to money damages measured by UNSI's lost profits due to early publication of the paperback edition. The court held that as to the quantification of that loss, it was within the district court's discretion as finder of fact to examine plaintiff's sales. The court determined it was not error to lay the normal uncertainty in such hypotheses at the door of the wrongdoer who altered the proper course of events, instead at the door of the injured party. (*Hard back sales were declining, but, really, soft back sales depressed them further, so use the last month's hardback figures and assume that the same number of hard backs would have sold, but for the availability of a soft back*).

Note how the clearly erroneous standard all but immunizes the district court on a finding of fact. The court could have used the first half of September sales to estimate the second half rather than using the August sales to estimate all of September as both methods are plausible. In a "push" situation, defer to the district court under a clearly erroneous standard. Would the result be the same if the standard was abuse of discretion? *(Probably)*.

◆ -- ◆

DAMAGES PROBLEMS
(Teacher's Manual Only)

Damage calculations produce more anxiety than anything else we teach in this course. Many of our students (and even a few of our faculty colleagues) freely admit that they are uncomfortable with numbers and even rudimentary mathematics. As a result, many contracts teachers avoid the subject altogether, preferring just to cover the basic principles with a series of cases.

We believe, however, that a person doesn't really understand the damages principles unless they can work the numbers. It's only by putting numbers to them that a person really understands what these abstract concepts mean.

We teach our students two methods of calculating damages in non-UCC cases. One follows the formula in the Restatement; the other looks at the position the non-breaching party is in after the breach and compares it to the position she would have been in if the contract had been performed. This is just an application of the principle that the purpose of contract damages is to put the non-breaching party in the position she would have been in if the contract had been performed.

We have a pair of interactive tutorials that we require students to complete before we discuss damage calculations in class. We find that this saves a lot of class time, and the students generally enjoy the tutorials. They are available at:

http://www.law.utk.edu/ccel/transactions-journal.shtml.

Scroll to the bottom of the page and follow the links provided. We hope to create additional tutorials in the future and make them available here as well.

◆ -- ◆

REMEDIES UNDER THE R2d AND THE COMMON LAW OF CONTRACTS

(Self-explanatory)

♦ -- ♦

PROBLEM 18-1

Remodeler and Homeowner enter into a contract for the remodeling of Homeowner's kitchen with a price of $10,000. Before Homeowner pays anything or Remodeler does any work, Homeowner breaches. At trial, Remodeler is able to prove that if she had been allowed to perform the contract, she could have done it for $8,000. **How much is Remodeler entitled to in damages?** *Answer: $2,000.*

This is a simple illustration of the benefit-of-the-bargain principle. Remodeler would have made a $2,000 profit, so that is her damage recovery. At this point, we deflect any questions about whether the $8,000 includes the value of Remodeler's time and the like and encourage the students to accept the fact that the cost to perform is $8,000. This is seldom a problem. Most of the time the class is happy to have an easy problem, so they seldom raise the issue.

Even though the answer is intuitively obvious, we go through both calculation methods. This makes sure everybody understands the process before we go on to the more difficult problems. In fact, there are usually some people who can't apply the Restatement method, even though they know what the answer is.

Restatement Method: The "loss in value" is $10,000; the "other loss" is 0; and the "cost avoided" is $8,000. There will always be students who want to know why the loss in value isn't $2,000. (If they don't ask the question, we do.) We point out that the loss in value is the value of all the performances that the non-breaching party would have received if the contract had been performed but did not receive because of the breach. It's not just the net or the profit that was lost.

Comparison Method: If the contract had been performed, Remodeler would have had a profit of $2,000. After the breach, Remodeler is even with the board. So it will take $2,000 to move her from the position she is in to the position she would have been in if the contract had been performed.

PROBLEM 18-2

Roofer and Owner enter into a contract for the roofing of Owner's building for a price of $6,000. Owner makes a $500 down payment and then breaches. At trial Roofer is able to show that if he had performed the contract it would have cost him $5,200. **How much is Roofer entitled to recover?** *Answer: $300.*

Restatement Method: The loss in value is $5,500, the amount remaining to be paid under the contract. One thing we use this problem for is to illustrate the point that the "loss in value" is only that part of the consideration that has not been received. There is no "other loss," and the "cost avoided" is $5,200.

Comparison Method: If the contract had been performed, Roofer would have been $800 ahead. As it is, he has the down payment and is $500 ahead. So it will take $300 to put him in the position that performance would have.

PROBLEM 18-3

Painter and Farmer enter into a contract for the painting of Farmer's barn for a price of $800. Farmer makes no down payment. After Painter has spent $75 on the job, Farmer breaches. At trial, Painter is able to show that if he had been allowed to finish the job, it would have cost him a total of $700 (i.e., the $75 spent to date plus an additional $625). **How much is Painter entitled to recover?** *Answer: $175.*

Restatement Method: The loss in value is $800. There is no other loss, and the cost avoided is $625. Students often want to know (so we raise it even if they don't) why the $75 Painter spent on the job isn't an "other loss." After all, he spent the money and now he's not getting paid for the job. So isn't that an "other loss?" There are two explanations for this, and we try to make sure students understand both.

The first explanation is that the Restatement says that the element in question is "other loss caused by the breach." The $75 Painter spent is not a loss caused by the breach. It's money he would have spent anyway. To put it very starkly: it's not a loss caused by the breach; it's a loss caused by entering into the contract in the first place. That's the mechanical explanation, and for some students, that's what they need at this point.

The second explanation is more conceptual. As his "loss in value," Painter is going to recover the full contract price, the same amount he would have received if the contract had been fully performed. If there had been no breach and he had performed, he would have spent the $75 and a whole lot more in order to become entitled to that contract price. So giving him his $75 back in addition to giving him the full contract price would put him in a much better position than he would be in if the contract had been fully performed.

Comparison Method: If the contract had been performed, Painter would have had a profit of $100. As matters now stand, he is going to suffer a loss of $75. So to put him in the position he would have been in if the contract had been performed, the court will need to give him $175.

PROBLEM 18-4

Slumlord and Electrician enter into a contract for the re-wiring of Slumlord's building for a price of $6,000. After Electrician has spent $4,000 on the job and Slumlord has made $3,000 in progress payments to Electrician, Slumlord breaches. At trial Electrician is able to show that if he had been allowed to complete the job, it would have cost him an additional $800 (in addition to the $4,000 spent to date) to complete the job. **How much is Electrician entitled to recover?** *Answer: $2,200.*

We explain to our students that this problem is entirely theoretical. No slumlord would spend $6,000 to have his building re-wired. If the student housing near your campus is like that near ours, your students will understand.

Restatement Method: The "loss in value" is the $3,000 remaining to be paid under the contract. There is no "other loss." The "cost avoided" is $800.

Comparison Method: If the contract had been performed, Electrician would have made a profit of $1,200. As it is now, he has spent $4,000 and has been paid $3,000. He therefore is $1,000 behind. To put him in the position he would have been in if the contract had been fully performed will take $2,200.

PROBLEM 18-5

Bank and Programmer enter into a contract under the terms of which Programmer agrees to re-program Bank's computer to alert management to any hacking attempts for a price of $3,000. Before Bank has paid Programmer any money and before Programmer has done any work or incurred any expenses, Programmer realizes that the job is a lot bigger than she thought. She tells Bank to forget about it. (This is a breach of the contract.) Bank contacts a number of programmers and finds that the best price any of them will give is $20,000, so Bank has its computer re-programmed at a cost of 20 grand. **How much is Bank entitled to recover from Programmer?** *Answer: $17,000.*

Restatement Method: This is the first problem where students have to put a value on a non-monetary performance. It bothers some of those who don't have some background in economics. The market says that the value of the job is $20,000, so that's the "loss in value." There's no "other loss." The "cost avoided" is the $3,000 Bank didn't have to pay Programmer.

Comparison Method: There are a couple of different ways of looking at it. One is to say that if the contract had been performed, Bank would have had its computer programmed and would have paid out $3,000. As it now stands, Bank has had its computer programmed, but it has paid $20,000. Alternatively, it can be analyzed as Bank would have had a beneficial bargain worth $17,000 (a $20,000 job for $3,000). They lost that because of the breach. To make them whole, the court needs to give them $17,000. This causes anxiety for a couple of reasons. Some students have a hard time grasping the idea that the value of the performance is different from the contract price. To them we point out that this is the essence of the benefit of the bargain. Others are bothered by the fact that Bank is being rewarded for making such a "sharp" bargain.

244

PROBLEM 18-6

Promoter and Singer enter into a contract under the terms of which Singer will perform at Promoter's concert for a fee of $10,000. Before Singer has been paid any money, Singer breaches the contract. In order to get a comparable entertainer as a replacement for Singer, Promoter has to pay $15,000. He also incurs $3,000 in additional transportation costs in order to get the replacement entertainer to the concert on time. **How much is Promoter entitled to recover from Singer?**

Answer: $8,000.

Restatement Method: There are a couple of ways to approach it. You can assume that the value of Singer's performance is the $10,000 contract price or you can assume that the value is the $15,000 it cost to get a replacement. If the value of the performance was $10,000, then $10,000 is the "loss in value." There are then two elements to the "other loss:" the extra $5,000 he had to pay to get a "comparable" performer (presumably he had to pay extra because of the short notice) and the $3,000 in additional transportation expenses. If we look at it from the point of view that the performance was $15,000 and Promoter was getting a good deal by getting Singer's services for $10,000, then the "loss in value" is $15,000 and the "other loss" is $3,000. Either way, the "cost avoided" is the $10,000 that would have been paid Singer if she performed.

Most students understand both of these analyses, even if they prefer one over the other. But the students who want a mechanical approach are bothered by the fact that there are two ways of looking at it. We try to reassure them by telling them that if they learn both the Restatement method and the comparison method, they will find that where the Restatement method is tricky, the comparison method is usually pretty straightforward and vice versa.

Comparison Method: If the contract had been performed, Promoter would have had the performance and would have paid $10,000. As it now stands, he's had his performance, but he's had to pay $18,000. So he needs $8,000 to put him in the position performance would have.

PROBLEM 18-7

Power Company and Construction Company enter into a contract under the terms of which Construction Company agrees to build a power plant for a cost of $100 million. Before any money has been paid or any work has been done, Construction Company discovers that because of rising labor and materials costs, it will cost Construction Company $125 million to build the plant. Construction Company breaches the contract. Power Company hires another company to build the plant at a cost of $110 million. **How much is Power Company entitled to recover from Construction Company?**

Answer: $10 Million.

Restatement Method: The "loss in value" is $110 million. Because Power Company could purchase the job in the market for $110 million, that seems the best value we can place on the performance. This illustrates a problem with the Restatement method. It requires us to place a monetary value on a performance, often using the cost of a replacement performance as the standard. But in other contexts we have to emphasize that the fair market value of the property or services in question is not necessarily the same as the cover price or resale price. See, e.g., Problems 18-8 and 18-9. We explain this by telling students that for purposes of the problems, unless there is an indication to the contrary, they can assume that the cover/resale price reflects the fair market value. We have tried to word the problems in such a way that it is clear that the cover/resale is at the fair market value.

We tell students that in practice they want to have the best possible proof (consistent with the economics of the case) of the fair market value of the property or performance involved. In non-UCC cases, some courts have been quite willing to accept the cover/resale price as the measure of damages and others have not.

The "cost avoided" is the $100 million that would have been paid Construction Company if it hadn't breached, and there is no "other loss."

Comparison Method: This is another situation in which most people find the comparison method a lot easier to apply. If the contract had been performed, Power Company would have had its plant and would have paid $100 million. As it now stands, Power Company has its plant but has had to pay $110 million. So it will take $10 million to put Power Company in the position it would have been in if the contract had been performed.

PROBLEM 18-8

You are representing the plaintiff in a breach of contract case. Your client, a builder, entered into a contract to sell for $300,000 a home he had recently completed. The buyer defaulted. Your client sold the home some time later for $250,000. On cross-examination of your client by the lawyer for the defaulting buyer, the following exchange occurred:

Q: Are you a good judge of the value of a home?

A: Yes, I am.

Q: Do you normally try to sell your homes for more than they're worth?

A: I try to sell my homes for a fair price.

Q: Fair market value?

A: Yeah.

What is the defendant's lawyer going to argue in her summation? What would you ask on re-direct to minimize its effect?

The plaintiff has admitted that he sells his homes for fair market value. If the contract price and the fair market value (at the time the deed was to be delivered) are the same, he is entitled to no damages. The $50,000 difference between the fair market value and the resale price would have to be attributable to a change in the market or to his reselling at a price below the market price. The best argument (and one that is often supported by the facts) is that the contract price was the fair market value at the time the contract was made, but buyer backed out because prices dropped between the time he entered into the contract and the time he was to close. Because the seller's damages are computed on the value at the time title was to pass (not at the time the contract was made), he would still be entitled to damages under this theory.

It's of course quite possible that the buyer just made a bad deal, but that theory is likely to play badly in front of a jury.

◆ -- ◆

REMEDIES UNDER THE UCC

Read UCC Section 2-706 and the accompanying comments and Section 2-708(1). Then apply all that good stuff to the problems that follow.

Read 2-706 and go over all the special little terms, including all those noted in the book.

◆ -- ◆

PROBLEM 18-9

Heinz operates a nightclub, Studio 57, in downtown Pittsburgh. When the bloom goes off the business, he decides to switch to welding as a career, and he enters into a contract to sell the furniture and sound system to French for $12,000. French breaches the contract and Heinz gives the proper notice (§ 2-706(3)) and resells the goods to English in a commercially reasonable manner for $8,000. At trial, French shows that at the time and place for tender (*i.e.*, when and where Heinz was to turn over the goods) the market price for such goods was $10,000.

This problem illustrates the UCC's approach, which allows the buyer who covers or the seller who resells to avoid the expense of having to prove fair market value and instead use the cover/resale price to determine damages. We point out, however, that in practice it's dangerous to rely solely on the resale/cover price. If the plaintiff fails to prove the market price and the court finds that the resale or cover did not meet the statutory requirements, the plaintiff will get no recovery.

Contract price = $12,000; Foreclosure price = $8,000; "True" fair market value $10,000.

(a) If the court finds that notice was proper and the resale was "commercially reasonable," what are Heinz's damages?

Answer: $4,000. § 2-706 (resale).

(b) If the court finds that the sale was not commercially reasonable, what are Heinz's damages?

Answer: $2,000. § 2-708 (improper resale so 2-706 doesn't apply).

(c) If the court finds that notice was not given, what are Heinz's damages?

Answer: $2,000. § 2-708 (improper resale so 2-706 doesn't apply).

(d) How can the sale be commercially reasonable if it's at less than the going market price?

We explain that for this type of analysis, there are basically two types of goods: those that have a readily-ascertainable market value and those that don't. The goods in the problem don't have a readily ascertainable market value, and for goods like that, what the UCC is really saying is that the price they bring in a commercially reasonable resale is a better indication of their true market value than a price arrived at through a battle of the appraisers.

We explain how a high-stakes battle of appraisers often works: Both sides might hire three appraisers as "consultants." The seller would hire appraisers known to give low-value appraisals, and these appraisers would know (without being told) that they were expected to come in with the lowest value possible consistent with what their ethics and self-respect demanded. The same would be true on the buyer's side, except that the buyer's side would be looking for high valuations. When the lawyers got their appraisals, the seller's lawyer would name the appraiser who came in the lowest as his expert witness and the buyer's lawyer would name the one who came in the highest as hers. The other four appraisals would be labeled "CONFIDENTIAL– ATTORNEY WORK PRODUCT" and would be filed away, never to see the light of day. The result would be that the court would be presented with two wildly divergent appraisals, neither of which would be of much use in determining the true market value of the goods.

Students enjoy it when we tell them that real estate appraisers append to their signatures the initials M.A.I., which stands for Member of the American Institute of Real Estate Appraisers, but lawyers joke that it means their appraisal was "Made as Instructed."

(e) If Heinz decides to keep the goods, what are his damages? *$2k.*

PROBLEM 18-10

Petty runs the local Chevrolet dealership. Except for the cost of the cars he sells, all his costs are fixed, i.e., they remain the same regardless of whether he sells one car or one hundred. (Remember these problems are referred to as "hypotheticals.") Foyt comes in and orders a new 'Vette for $55,000, which is the market price. It costs Petty $53,000 to purchase the car from GM. *So, Petty expected to make a $2,000 profit.* A few days later Foyt repudiates. But within the hour, Oldfield comes in and orders a new 'Vette for $55,000. Instead of canceling the order for Foyt's car, Petty just sells that car to Oldfield. **In an action for damages against Foyt, what is Petty entitled to recover under 2-706? Assuming (everyone seems to) that "market price" means retail market price, what are Petty's damages under 2- 708(1)?** Section 1-106 says the UCC remedies should put the aggrieved party in as good a position as if the other party had performed the contract. **Does either of these measures of damages do this?** For a suggested method of analysis, read *VERY CAREFULLY* UCC § 2-708(2) and Comment 2 following it. The case that follows should also be helpful.

This problem illustrates the reason we have section 2-708(2) and lost volume seller damages. The resale price is the same as the contract price, so there are no damages under section 2-706. Similarly, the market price and the contract price are the same, so there are no damages under section 2-708(1).

♦ -- ♦

Locks v. Wade
New Jersey Superior Court, Appellate Division
36 N.J. Super. 128, 114 A.2d 875 (1955)

Lease of jukebox—Lessor was to get $20 a week minimum

Court gives $840 for two year lease

$2,040 is $20/week for 2 years

Less $500 for the cost of installation and furnishing records and $700 for depreciation

Defendant compares it to a house being rented and says he's entitled to credit for the rents that would have been received.

Note that the $20 was the minimum on some sort of revenue-sharing payment stream arrangement. Apparently the court found the actual profits too speculative.

Juke Box lease breached. Full minimum contract price awarded. Defendant claims that since juke box rented to another, no damages (wants to treat like a lease of real property where another tenant is immediately found). Realty is finite (at least in most cases). This undermines the "lost volume seller" assumptions that are applicable here to this lease of fungible personal property.

Trial court awards lost profit (contract price less cost of performing). On appeal, court considers whether lessor mitigation by rental to another should result in decrease in damages. Held: No, lost volume seller. Affirm the trial court.

Good context to think about this business model, a form of equipment leasing, really a cash flow generation and bundling business. Explain industry context.

Affirm, lost volume damages – why is the rule different for real property? The "unlimited supply of identical product" requirement is not met.

◆ -- ◆

NOTES AND QUESTIONS

People like the plaintiff in the above case have been referred to as "lost volume sellers." This means that when the buyer defaults, they aren't just faced with the prospect of re-selling the goods at a lower price; they lose all the profit they would have made on the sale. That is the reason sections 2-706 and 2-708(1) don't give them adequate compensation, and they must be compensated under 2-708(2).

◆ -- ◆

PROBLEM 18-11

Dealer sells new Volvos for $30,000 each. It costs Dealer $25,000 to purchase each vehicle and prepare it for sale. The market price for new Volvos of this type is $30,000. Lawyer enters into a contract to purchase a new Volvo for $30,000. Lawyer breaches, and Dealer sells the car to Accountant in a commercially reasonable manner after giving Lawyer the proper notice. The sale to Accountant is for $30,000. **What are Dealer's damages?** (P.S., Volvo will supply Dealer with as many of these cars as he needs to fill his orders.)

Answer: $5,000. Lost volume seller.

If Lawyer hadn't breached, Dealer would have made two sales, earning a profit of $5,000 on each. Because of the breach, he's only made one sale and one $5,000 profit.

PROBLEM 18-12

Dealer sells antique cars. Dealer enters into a contract to sell a 1903 Oldsmobile (the kind with a tiller instead of a steering wheel) to Collector for $110,000. The market price for such a car is $110,000. Dealer purchased the car three months ago from Sucker for $80,000. Collector breaches the contract. Dealer sells the car to Enthusiast for $110,000 after giving Collector proper notice. The sale is made in a commercially reasonable manner. **What are Dealer's damages?** (P.S., there are no other 1903 Oldsmobile available on the market.)

Answer: $0. Not a lost volume seller.

Dealer is not a lost volume seller in this case, so his damages are determined under sections 2-706 and 2-708(1). (Or, to put it more precisely, he can't use 2-708(2) because the measure of damages in 2-708(1) is adequate "to put the seller in as good a position as performance would have done.") Because the contract price, the market price and the resale price are all the same, Dealer is not entitled to damages under either 2-706 or 2-708(1) (except for any incidental damages not mentioned in the problem). This is as it should be, because after the resale Dealer was in the same position he would have been in if Enthusiast had performed.

PROBLEM 18-13

Dealer sells new motorbikes for $400 each. Dealer can get an unlimited supply of motorbikes for $300 each. Professor agrees to buy a new motorbike from Dealer for $375. (We professors are tough negotiators.) The fair market value of the motorbike is $400. Professor defaults and, after giving the proper notice, Dealer sells the motorbike in a commercially reasonable manner for $400. **What are Dealer's damages?**

Answer: $75

If Professor had performed, Dealer would have made a profit of $75 on the first sale and a second profit of $100 on the second sale. As it is, all Dealer has made is the profit of $100.

PROBLEM 18-14

Dealer sells new Econoboxes for $8,000 each. Dealer can get an unlimited supply of Econoboxes for $7,000 each. Civil Servant agrees to buy an Econobox from Dealer for $8,500. Civil Servant defaults. **What are Dealer's damages?**

Answer: $1,500

Lost volume seller. If the contract had been performed, Dealer would have made a profit of $1,500. As it now stands, he has no profit.

PROBLEM 18-15

Dealer sells new Maseratis for $150,000 each. Dealer can get an unlimited supply of these examples of fine Italian craftsmanship for $140,000 each.

Developer agrees to buy a Maserati for $150,000 and makes a $5,000 down payment. Developer defaults. **What are Dealer's damages?**

Answer: $5,000

If the contract had been performed, Dealer would have been ahead by $10,000; he has already been paid $5,000, leaving $5,000 in damages.

Read UCC Sections 2-712 and 2-713 and the accompanying comments and apply them to the next problem.

PROBLEM 18-16

Farmer contracts to deliver 5,000 bushels of wheat to Elevator Co. on September 5 at a price of $2.00 a bushel. On September 15, when the market price is $4.00 a bushel, Farmer fails to show up. It takes Elevator Co. until September 18 to get in contact with Farmer, who doesn't admit until September 21 that he is not going to deliver. It then takes until September 22 to make a substitute contract. On September 21 and 22, the market price for wheat is $4.50 a bushel, and Elevator Co. purchases wheat from another grower at $4.50 a bushel in substitution for the wheat Farmer failed to deliver.

(a) **What can Elevator Co. recover as damages?**

Elevator Co. can recover $2.50 a bushel (a total of $12,500). The facts indicate that Elevator Co. acted without unreasonable delay when it "learned of the breach" on September 21, and nothing indicates it was not acting in good faith, so under section 2-712, it is entitled to the difference between the contract price and the cover price.

If you think that they "learned of the breach" on September 15, then damages would be $2.00 a bushel (a total of $10,000).

(b) Suppose that Elevator Co. had chosen not to buy any wheat in substitution for the wheat it was supposed to get from Farmer. **What would its damages be then?**

Under the pre-revision version of 2-713, which is still widely applicable as revised Article 2 has not been adopted in most jurisdictions, we would argue that Elevator Co. can recover $2.50 a bushel because September 21 was when it "learned of the breach." Others have argued that Farmer was in breach on the 15th when the price was $4.00 and Elevator Co. knew of it then, so the damages are $2.00 a bushel (total of $10,000). Revised section 2-713 removes this uncertainty and says that the time for measuring the damages is the time for tender, although this revised version has not been adapted widely.

Additional Damage Problems
(Teacher's Manual Only)

PROBLEM 1

Landscaper agreed to maintain the grounds around Law Firm's building for the season for a price of $5,000. It would have cost Landscaper $4,000 to perform his obligations under the contract. If Law Firm breached the contract before Landscaper did any work and before any money changed hands, **how much is Landscaper entitled to receive in damages?** *$1,000.*

PROBLEM 2

Plant Service agreed to maintain the plants in Accountant's office for a year for a price of $3,000. It would have cost Plant Service $2,500 to perform this service. If Plant Service breached the contract and the best price Accountant could get for replacement services was $3,300, **how much is Accountant entitled to recover in damages?** *$300.*

PROBLEM 3

Painter painted a bridge for the state highway department. The total price was $50,000. It cost Painter $45,000 to do the job. After Painter had completed the entire job and the state had paid her $45,000, the state wrongfully refused to make the last payment. **How much is Painter entitled to receive in damages?** *$5,000.*

PROBLEM 4

Builder agreed to build a store for Retailer for a price of $3,000,000. It would cost Builder $2,700,000 to do the whole project. After Builder had spent $1,200,000 and been paid $1,000,000, Retailer breached the contract. **How much is Builder entitled to in damages?** *$500.*

PROBLEM 5

Contractor agreed to build a garage for homeowner for $10,000. It would have cost Contractor $8,000 to complete the job. After Contractor had spent $5,000 and Homeowner had paid Contractor $4,000, they got into a dispute. Contractor refused to do any more work. Homeowner hired someone else to complete the project. The best price she could get was $11,000.

(a) **If Homeowner is the one in breach, how much is Contractor entitled to recover as damages?** *$3,000.*

(b) **If Contractor is the one in breach, how much is Homeowner entitled to recover as damages?** *$5,000.*

PROBLEM 6

Buyer and Seller agreed to a sale of a certain quantity of scrap metal for a price of $80 a ton. The parties got into a dispute and each accused the other of breaching the contract. Seller resold the metal for $76 a ton, and Buyer purchased substitute metal for $85 a ton. At the time the contract was to be performed, the market price for such metal was $82 a ton.

(a) **What damages is Seller entitled to if the court finds that Buyer was in breach and that Seller gave proper notice and resold the metal in a commercially-reasonable manner?** *$4 per ton.*

(b) **What damages is Seller entitled to if the court finds that Buyer was in breach and that Seller *did not* resell the metal in a commercially-reasonable manner?** *None.*

(c) **What damages is Buyer entitled to recover if the court finds that Seller was in breach and Buyer's purchase of substitute metal was a reasonable purchase in substitution, made in good faith, and without unreasonable delay?** *$5 per ton.*

(d) **What damages is Buyer entitled to recover if the court finds that Seller was in breach and Buyer's purchase of substitute metal was *not* a reasonable purchase in substitution, made in good faith, and without unreasonable delay?** *$2 per ton.*

CHAPTER 19

LIMITATIONS ON CONTRACT DAMAGES

— ♦ —

A. FORESEEABILITY

Hadley v. Baxendale
Court of Exchequer
9 Ex. 341 (1854)

Facts: The plaintiff's mill crank shaft broke. It was the only one they had, and without it they could not run their mill. They contracted with the defendant to send it to the engineers. The delivery was delayed, and the plaintiff sued for lost profits. The jury awarded lost profit damages of 25£. The defendant appealed.

Issue: Is the plaintiff entitled to damages for lost profits (which this court sees as consequential, not direct damages)?

Rule: The defendant will only be held liable for the plaintiff's losses if they are generally foreseeable or if the plaintiff tells the defendant about any special circumstances in advance.

Analysis: The court makes an argument that from the evidence that a client wants to ship a broken item fast, it does not necessarily follow that they are necessarily going to lose profits if it is not delivered on time. The court goes through a series of hypotheticals showing that there are other circumstances under which the plaintiff could have sought out the transaction they did, so that the defendant need not have assumed the situation was as dire as it was.

The court further argues that if special circumstances exist, special provisions can be made in the contract by both parties voluntarily to impose extra damages if there is a breach. The court doesn't wish to take that power away from the parties.

Conclusion: The court finds that lost profits should *not* have been awarded at trial; therefore, the court orders a new trial with a statement of the jury instructions to be used.

NOTES AND QUESTIONS

The foreseeability limitation of *Hadley v. Baxendale* is found in section 351 of the R2d and article 7.4.4 of the UNIDROIT Principles. One is phrased in the negative, the other in the positive. **Apart from this, is the standard that is expressed the same? Is there a difference in meaning caused by stating the standard in the positive or the negative?**

◆ -- ◆

Marquette Cement Manufacturing v. Louisville & Nashville R.R.
United States District Court, Eastern District, Tennessee
281 F. Supp. 944 (1967)

Applying the *Hadley v. Baxendale* standard.   Air-entrained cement misdelivered.

Note the attempt to get a negligence cause of action through – why? Probably the potential for punitive damages as well as to gain the benefit of the eggshell plaintiff rule (no forseeability requirement for negligence damages, just the proximate cause limitation).

Hadley v. Baxendale applied and the plaintiff gets to recover the value of the cement and the shipping price but not the costs to remove and fix the damaged installations.

[Factual aside: One of the greatest advances in concrete technology was the development of air-entrained concrete in the late 1930s.   Today, air entrainment is recommended for nearly all concretes, principally to improve resistance to freezing when exposed to water and de-icing chemicals. However, there are other important benefits of entrained air in both freshly mixed and hardened concrete.   Air-entrained concrete contains billions of microscopic air cells. These relieve internal pressure on the concrete by providing tiny chambers for the expansion of water when it freezes.

Air-entrained concrete is produced through the use of air-entraining portland cement, or by introducing air-entraining admixtures under careful engineering supervision as the concrete is mixed on the job. The amount of entrained air is usually between 5 percent and 8 percent of the volume of the concrete, but may be varied as required by special conditions. The use of air-entraining agents results in concrete that is highly resistant to severe frost action and cycles of wetting and drying or freezing and thawing and has a high degree of workability and durability.

See www.cement.org/basics/concretebasics_airentrained.asp (last visited January 30, 2006).]

◆ -- ◆

Stroh Brewery v. Grand Trunk Western R.R.
United States District Court, Eastern District Michigan
513 F. Supp. 827 (1981)

RR delivers wrong grain to Stroh's. Stroh's could have checked – they had the car number and could have checked – negligence.

Two claims for breach – (1) wrongful delivery of Rickel car and shipment of the Stroh car (damages sought – out of pocket costs, cost of the contaminated Rahr malt, cost of removing it from brewery, cost of bulk barley delivered, less amount received for scrap malt/barley mixture); and (2) failure to deliver the Rickle car to Rickle. Damages for both are $19,198.99.

Standard applied? The *Marquette* standard (*Hadley v. Baxendale*).

Negligence by Stroh disregarded. Defendant had even more notice than in *Marquette*. So award Stroh the whole $19,198.99.

Do you see how the same standard is applied and then we analogize and reason to the prior application of the standard, not the standard itself? Are the courts in these three cases being consistent? Defend the affirmative and the negative positions on this question.

♦ - - ♦

Additional Discussion Point
(Teacher's Manual Only)

Kuney varies the facts of *Marquette* and *Strohs* by positing a shipper that mixes up two freight cars filled with grain. One car is filled with grain headed to mill where it will be ground into flour and introduced into the food supply in the form of bread for school lunch programs. The other has been sprayed with rat poison and is bound for a manufacturer of rat traps. Thus, substitute sick and dead children for damaged concrete and machinery when determining where to draw the "reasonably foreseeable" line. Usually students notice the similarity of this determination after working through the two cases and this hypo to the "proximate cause" test from *Palsgraf* that they have studied in Torts. If not, Kuney forces the issue by comparing and contrasting the two doctrines. This also allows students to analyze whether they are reaching the result that they do through a formalist chain of reasoning or a more result-oriented, legal realist approach.

♦ - - ♦

Linc Equipment Services v. Signal Medical Services
United States Court of Appeals, Seventh Circuit
319 F.3d 288 (2003)

MRI (Magnetic Resonance Imaging) lease.

Linc — lease —> Signal Medical — sublease —> hospital.

Signal Medical to return MRI in good condition at end of year. In fact, its sublessee returns it in damaged condition to the tune of $130,000 and 10 months worth of repairs.

Linc sues Signal and the trucker; Linc's insurance company intervenes and makes third party subrogation claim against Signal (it paid Linc, so it gets Linc's rights by subrogation; make sure to explain subrogation clearly as this is often neglected in law school but arises often in practice).

Trial Judge thought it was a question of whether the lost income was a consequential damage or not, and that this depended upon whether the parties "expressly contemplated" them under Illinois law. They did not.

Easterbrook reverses.

First, as to consequential damages question, the standard is reasonably *foreseeable – Hadley v. Baxendale –* not expressly *contemplated* (although those are synonymous to Easterbrook).

Second, to Easterbrook these are not consequential damages at all. These are direct outcome damages of the broken promise and do not depend upon the details of Linc's business or any idiosyncratic way that Linc would deploy the MRI.

Look at discussion of the market [para. 5] and value. Discuss Net Present Value, Valuation, and Capitalization Rates.

See value discussion and Easterbrook's contention that the damages are not LOST rents but DELAYED rents. Value that.

◆ - - ◆

PROBLEM 19-1

Precision Sound, Inc. ("Seller") enters into a contract to sell an item of recording equipment to Solid Gold Recording Studios ("Buyer"). *A few days later,* Seller learns that Buyer needs this piece of equipment in order to fulfill its obligations under a major contract. Seller had no reason to foresee this at the time the contract was made. Shortly after learning this fact, Seller's general manager places the order for the equipment with the manufacturer. He makes a mistake in filling out the order form, and the manufacturer ships the wrong equipment. By the time the mistake has been rectified, the time for Seller to deliver the equipment to Buyer has passed and Buyer has lost the big contract. **Can Buyer recover damages resulting from the loss of the contract? What is the policy behind this result?**

Buyer can't recover damages for loss of the contract. The policy is to make the breaching party liable only for the damages that it could foresee at the time it entered into the contract. The theory is that a party should be able to evaluate its potential loss from a breach at the time it enters into the contract so that it can make its decision whether to enter into the contract and set its price with that risk in mind. Knowing and voluntary assumption or allocation of risk is at the heart of the standard.

Making a record is important in defeating the limitation of foreseeability. Discuss use of parol evidence to determine foreseeability (is this "to prove the terms of the agreement?") and the use of factual recitals in the contract to memorialize discussions to avoid the issue. This is a good area for testing the two concepts and the ability of the students to distinguish the issues covered in this and the last 3 chapters.

B. CERTAINTY

Chicago Coliseum Club v. Dempsey
Court of Appeals of Illinois
265 Ill. App. 542 (1932)

Dempsey breaches his contract via anticipatory repudiation. The issues in the case are all about what damages are allowable, and the answer is "not much." Court divides damages sought into 4 categories and finds as follows:

1. Loss of profits which would have been derived by the plaintiff in the event of holding the boxing match? *Nope – purely speculative in this sort of venture [para. 13]. (It doesn't help that in its earlier action for an injunction that damages were incapable of "commensuration"). Today we might be more accepting of expert testimony.*

2. Expenses incurred prior to signing the contract with Dempsey? *Nope. Not the result of the breach of the subsequent contract with Dempsey.*

3. Expenses incurred in attempting to restrain Dempsey from boxing in other matches? *Nope. No attorneys' fee clause, so American rule applies, each side bears its own attorneys' fees.*

4. Expenses incurred after the signing of the agreement and before the breach? *Yep, a teeny little bit. If there were special expenses incurred yes, but not the general costs of running the business, salaries, and the like.*

What!!! A blatant breach and minimal damages? The arrogant boxer needs to be punished! No, not the goal of contract law. What is the answer to this problem? Draft contracts with teeth. What sorts of things might you put in this contract to give it teeth?

Attorneys' fee provision, and draft it broadly.

Liquidated damages (more on that later).

Consent to jurisdiction, venue, and accelerated equitable remedies in court. Consent to an injunction.

NOTES AND QUESTIONS

3. The certainty limitation is found in section 352 of the R2d and article 7.4.3 of the UNIDROIT principles. They are phrased differently. **What are the substantive differences? Which is likely to lead to greater recovery by the non-breaching party?** *Question not in Casebook: Would the* Dempsey *case have come out differently under the UNIDROIT Principles?*

♦ - - ♦

Ericson v. Playgirl
Court of Appeal of California
73 Cal. App. 3d 850, 140 Cal. Rptr. 921 (1977)

Photo does not get on the cover of the Best of Playgirl. The problem is not the breach (it was an admitted mistake), but the damages. There is no market for the cover of this magazine. (Talk about opportunity for product placement). Trial court took Advertising Manager of TV Guide's testimony that the cover would be worth about $50,000 and divided it into 4ths, awarding $12,500.

Reduced damages to $300 nominal damages (by statute) and affirm. The original award was too speculative and uncertain.

♦ - - ♦

Fera v. Village Plaza Inc.
Supreme Court of Michigan
396 Mich. 639, 242 N.W.2d 372 (1976)

Book & Bottle Shop.

Do the facts, and discuss percentage rent, deed in lieu of foreclosure, atournment and non-disturbance agreements.

Issue is the claim for anticipated lost profits of a business that did not open (landlord leased out to another by mistake after taking the property in a deed in lieu of foreclosure transaction and the attendant mix ups).

Trial court awarded $200,000 in lost profits.

Ct. Of Appeals – reverses (holds that lost profits are per se too speculative if the store doesn't open, leaving them with the differential between market rent and lease rent for term of the lease).

Supreme Court of Michigan – Reverses. If there is a reasonable basis on which to estimate profits, of course they can be awarded. (Opens the door for expert testimony. Time permitting, discuss that, valuation, comparables, net present value of expected profits, experts as hired guns and the like).

Would this be in addition to the rent differential remedy? NO. That would be double counting.

Dissent: Agrees on law, just not factual analysis. Finds the assignment of liquor license issue to inject substantial uncertainty. Would allow lost profits for the book side of the business but not the bottle side.

Comment – The cases discussed in *Fera* illustrates a pattern that often occurs in legal reasoning. A rule in general (no damages if uncertain) is repeatedly applied to a specific set of facts (claim for lost profits) and leads to a result (claim denied) and that set of opinions is then later interpreted to mean that the result is always required for that specific set of facts. So, the rule becomes "lost profit claims are disallowed." We will see this again in specific performance and the "unique nature" of land. Caution students to avoid mistaking the proxy for the true rule and to dig back to first principles, then apply those principles to the facts at hand. That is, unless the proxy for the rule supports your client.

C. AVOIDABILITY

Restatement (Second) Section 350 reads as follows:

Avoidability as a Limitation on Damages

> (1) Except as stated in Subsection (2), damages are not recoverable for loss that the injured party could have avoided without undue risk, burden, or humiliation.

> (2) The injured party is not precluded from recovery by the rule stated in subsection (1) to the extent that he has made reasonable but unsuccessful efforts to avoid loss.

◆ -- ◆

In re Worldcom, Inc.
United States Bankruptcy Court, S.D. New York
361 B.R. 675 (2007)

Objection to Jordan's breach of contract claim in the Worldcom bankruptcy. Objection based on 11 U.S.C. § 502(b)(7)'s cap for employment contracts—overruled as he was an independent contractor—and failure to mitigate—sustained.

◆ - - ◆

PROBLEM 19-2

In 1994, the owner of a lot in East Flatbush, Brooklyn, New York, enters into a lease of the lot to a nationally recognized owner-operator and franchisor of Mexican-themed fast food outlets. The fast food company had inquired about purchasing the property, but the owner was adamant that the property was not for sale, although he would enter into a 99-year lease. The lot owner, delighted to have a long term lease of the property with a financially well-heeled, class "A" tenant, gave notice to the prior tenant – a used car lot – that its lease would not be renewed at the end of the term in 60 days. The used car lot owner, therefore, vacated the lot at the end of the term, relocating a couple of blocks away.

Then, apparently for the first time, the fast food company discovered that there was crime in New York City that might adversely affect the operation of the restaurant. In fact, the local Crime Prevention Officer for the precinct informed the fast food company that the area experienced excessive drug trafficking, violence, and firearm use, and the proposed restaurant would likely be robbed frequently. Seeking to back out of the long term lease, the fast food company contacts the lot owner, tells him that it no longer wishes to lease the property, and that it will provide the lot owner with a substitute tenant, a shell corporation with no assets except for a franchise agreement from another grade "B" Mexican fast food franchisor.

(a) Under the duty to mitigate, must the lot owner accept the substitute tenant? *The answer depends upon the responses to sub-parts (b) and (c) below, which are included to focus the students on the issue and are not really for separate discussion. The problem is also an introduction to notions of assignment and novation in the context of mitigation.*

(b) Does it matter whether or not the grade "B" substitute tenant sublets the lot from the nationally recognized owner-operator and franchisor of Mexican-themed fast food outlets? *Yes. In that case, the real tenant is the nationally recognized owner-operator and franchisor of Mexican-themed fast food outlets, not the grade "B" tenant. Unless the nationally recognized owner-operator and franchisor of Mexican-themed fast food outlets would be dependent upon the rent flow stream from the subtenant (unlikely), then the lot owner's risk has not materially changed.*

(c) Does it matter whether the nationally recognized owner-operator and franchisor *of* **Mexican-themed fast food outlets is proposing to assign the long term lease to the substitute tenant and receive a novation (what is that?) from the lot owner?** *Yes. In that case, the lot owner's risk is materially changing and there is no duty to accept this substitute tenant under the duty to reasonably mitigate.*

(d) Does it matter whether or not the rent specified in the lease is a particular sum or has a percentage of sales component? *Yes. If the substitute tenant's sales are likely to be less than the original tenant's, this proves an additional ground for the landlord to claim that the proposed mitigation is unreasonable.*

This problem is based upon Kahn v. Taco Bell, No. 92 Civ. 6304, 1994 U.S. Dist. LEXIS 7069, 1994 WL 240343 (S.D.N.Y. 1994).

PROBLEM 19-3

The County Highway Department enters into a contract with Builder for the construction of a bridge for $250,000. The bridge is to be built on a new highway which will connect the airport and a prosperous suburb. When Builder has expended $175,000 and has received $125,000 in progress payments, the county, in breach of the contract, announces that it is not going to build the highway and tells Builder to stop work. Builder expends another $35,000 and completes the bridge at a total cost of $210,000. Since the highway is not built, the county now has a bridge out in the middle of a cotton field. Builder sues for $125,000. **How much is she entitled to?**

Answer: $90,000

This problem is based on Rockingham County v. Luten Bridge Co., *35 F.2d 301 (4th Cir. 1929). The proposition on which it's based seems so obvious that it wasn't worth making the students read a case. Instead, the problem gives a chance for a quick review of damage calculations, something a lot of students can use at this point.*

We tell students that the way to deal with losses that the nonbreaching party could have avoided without undue risk, expense, or humiliation is to just assume they never occurred. In this case, we just assume Builder stopped work when she was told to.

Restatement Method: The loss in value is $125,000 (the $250,000 contract price less the $125,000 paid to date). There is no "other loss." The "cost avoided" is $35,000, the cost Builder would have avoided if she had stopped when told to. Thus, damages are $90,000.

Comparison Method: If the bridge had been completed according to the contract, Builder would have had a profit of $40,000. If she had stopped when she *was told, she would have been behind by $50,000 ($175,000 expended less $125,000 in progress payments). So if she had stopped when told, it would have taken $90,000 to put her in the position she would have been in if the contract had been performed.*

♦ - - ♦

NOTES AND QUESTIONS

1. The traditional rule in Anglo-American law is that physical pain and suffering or emotional distress damages are not recoverable as damages under a breach of contract theory. Read R2d sections 352 and 353, which generally embody this rule. Compare UNIDROIT article 7.4.2. **Which do you think is the better rule?** *Why?*

2. Parties may include waivers of consequential and incidental damages in their contracts in order to allocate the risk of non-performance. For example, a contract could provide:

> In no event will either party be liable for loss of profits or any special, incidental, or consequential damages, regardless of their cause, amount, or severity, and regardless of whether either party has or should have knowledge of the potential for such damages or whether they were reasonably foreseeable at the time of contracting or otherwise.

Note how the clause is drafted precisely around *Hadley v. Baxendale*, excluding "incidental, or consequential damages" as well as "reasonably foreseeable" damages, and also goes beyond those standards so as to narrowly circumscribe the damages that can be awarded due to breach.

Could a similar provision relieve the parties of a duty to mitigate? Should such a provision be enforced? If enforceable, how would you draft the provision?

Transactional lawyers are incorporating case law into their contracts constantly, adjusting the language to embrace or draft around language that has been blessed or damned by the courts. This is a different, continuous form of legal research than that often practiced by litigators, who generally have the comparative luxury of waiting until after the dispute has arisen to do their research. The transactional lawyer should be focused on proactive drafting to shape and control the relationship of the parties at its conception, during the relationship's life, and its ultimate demise. Litigation, all too often, is focused on reactive drafting and advocacy over the remains of a relationship that is dead or needs to be put out of its misery.

CHAPTER 20

OTHER MEASURES OF RECOVERY AND A REVIEW OF DAMAGES

— ♦ —

We don't spend a lot of time on damages based on the reliance interest or the restitutionary interest. In spite of all the law review articles written about these theories, they aren't very important in practice. What the plaintiff wants in a breach of contract case is the expectation interest. (There are, of course some notable exceptions. See, e.g., Westfed Holdings, Inc. v. United States, 55 Fed. Cl. 544 (2002) (plaintiff who put capital into a failed thrift on promise of a government agency awarded $300 million in reliance damages)).

A. THE RELIANCE INTEREST

[Restatement (Second) of Contracts § 349 – put up on board.]

♦ - - ♦

Security Stove & Manufacturing v. American Railways Express
Court of Appeals of Missouri
227 Mo. App. 175, 51 S.W.2d 572 (1932)

Shipper v. Transporter dispute.

Lost profits expectation damages would be too speculative. Award expenses. Paragraph 17 features the black letter law.

So, award reliance damages: (1) express and freight charges, (2) personal railway fares, (3) hotel charges, (4) time of the president out there (how is this measured?), (5) wages for other employees, and (6) rental of the trade show booth, for a total of $801.51. (The equivalent of approximately $12,600 in 2010 dollars using the CPI or $10,700 using the GDP deflator).

Note, in paragraph 18 how the court awards reliance damages that were incurred before the contract was entered into. Can that be right? What about notice and forseability problems and the principle of knowing assumption of risk?

B. THE RESTITUTIONARY INTEREST

Southern Painting Company of Tennessee v. United States, *ex rel.* Silver
United States Court of Appeals, Tenth Circuit
222 F.2d 431 (1955)

Breach by contractor found and judgment of $13,000 entered for Sub. ($13,000 in 1955 dollars is the equivalent of approximately $104,000 in 2010 dollars using the CPI and $85,000 using the GDP deflator). But the contract was $10,000 plus fair share of profit, total, and he had already been paid $7,000, leaving a balance of $3,000 plus share of profit.

Note the paragraph 5 discussion of the "who breached first" debate. This foreshadows later material on materiality of breach and the like.

He chooses to proceed in quantum meruit and recovers value of services. Note that this ability to choose to sue in quantum meruit is one that may be exercised by the non-breaching party. Breachers' damages are capped at the contract price.

◆ - - ◆

PROBLEM 20-1

Buyer and Seller enter into a contract for the sale of a house for $100,000. Seller breaches after Buyer has made a $10,000 down payment. The house is worth $100,000. **How much is Buyer entitled to recover? Is Buyer's recovery based on a restitutionary or a reliance theory? Do we care?**

This problem is just to set things up for the next one. Buyer can recover $10,000 under either a restitutionary or a reliance theory. Because his recovery is the same under either, it doesn't matter which he uses. Restitution $10,000 down payment.

PROBLEM 20-2

Same facts as the immediately preceding problem except that the proof shows conclusively that the house was worth $95,000. **How much is Buyer entitled to recover?** *See* Restatement (Second) § 349.

Under a reliance theory, Buyer is entitled to recover only $5,000 because the Restatement formulation of the rule requires deduction of any loss that the nonbreaching party would have suffered if the contract had been performed, provided that the breaching party can prove the loss with reasonable certainty. There isn't much case law on this point, and we expect that it's going to be pretty hard for a breaching party to prove the theoretical loss with the necessary certainty.

Under a restitutionary theory, Buyer may recover the $10,000 down payment.

C. REVIEW OF DAMAGES

PROBLEM 20-3

Owner puts her house on the market, asking $180,000 for it. Buyer offers $150,000 for the house. Owner accepts the offer, and they enter into a contract for the purchase and sale of the house at a price of $150,000. In connection with the sale, Owner becomes obligated to pay Broker a commission of $9,000. This commission is not refundable in the event of Buyer's breach. Buyer does in fact breach the contract. Seller pays Broker the commission. Evidence at trial shows that at the time title to the house was to be transferred, the fair market value of the house was $140,000. (And Owner in fact re-sells the house for that price, paying no brokerage commission.) **How much is Owner entitled to receive as damages?**

Answer: $10,000

We added the asking price just to start making students aware that in real world damages cases there are going to be a lot of irrelevant numbers and they have to start learning to separate the relevant from the irrelevant.

Restatement Method: The "loss in value" is $150,000, the purchase price not received. There is no "other loss." The brokerage commission is not an "other loss . . caused by the breach." It was an expense incurred because the contract was entered into, not because it was breached. The $140,000 is the "cost avoided." The plaintiff has avoided the cost of transferring property worth $140,000.

Comparison Method: If the contract had been performed, Owner would have had $141,000 and no house. As it is, he is out $9,000 in cash and has a house worth $140,000. So we can say his position is that he has a net of $131,000. To put him in the position that performance would have, we have to give him $10,000. Alternatively, we can say that if the contract had been performed he would have been $1,000 ahead because he would have sold a $140,000 house for $150,000 (a "profit," if you will, of $10,000), but he would have had to pay a commission of $9,000. As it stands, he is $9,000 behind because he had to pay the commission even though the deal didn't go through. As a result, it will take $10,000 to put him in the position that performance would have.

PROBLEM 20-4

Owner puts her house on the market, asking $180,000 for it. Buyer offers $150,000 for the house. Owner accepts the offer, and they enter into a contract for the purchase and sale of the house at a price of $150,000. In connection with the sale, Owner becomes obligated to pay Broker a commission of $9,000. This commission, however, is payable only in the event Buyer completes the sale and pays Owner the purchase price. Buyer breaches the contract. Seller does not pay Broker the commission. Evidence at trial shows that at the time title to the house was to be transferred, the fair market value of the house was $140,000.

(And Owner in fact re-sells the house for that price, paying no brokerage commission.) **How much is Owner entitled to receive as damages?**

Answer: $1,000

Restatement Method: The "loss in value" is again $150,000 and again there is no "other loss." The brokerage commission is now a "cost avoided," so the total recovery is now $1,000.

Comparison Method: If the contract had been performed, Owner would have had $141,000 and no house. As it is, he has a house worth $140,000 and has no change in his cash position. To put him in the position that performance would have, we have to give him $1,000. Alternatively, we can say that if the contract had been performed he would have been $1,000 ahead because he would have sold a $140,000 house for $150,000 (a "profit," if you will, of $10,000), but he would have had to pay a commission of $9,000. As it stands, he is even. He still has the house and has incurred no expenses. As a result, it will take $1,000 to put him in the position that performance would have placed him in.

PROBLEM 20-5

Owner puts her house on the market, asking $180,000 for it. Buyer offers $150,000 for the house. Owner accepts the offer, and they enter into a contract for the purchase and sale of the house at a price of $150,000. The contract between Owner and Broker provides that if the sale is completed and Buyer pays Owner the purchase price, Owner will pay Broker a commission of $9,000. This contract further provides (as is the custom in many parts of the country) that if Buyer breaches, Owner only has to pay broker half the commission ($4,500). Buyer does in fact breach the contract. Seller pays Broker the $4,500. Evidence at trial shows that at the time title to the house was to be transferred, the fair market value of the house was $140,000. (And Owner in fact re-sells the house for that price, paying no brokerage commission.) **How much is Owner entitled to receive as damages?**

Answer: $5,500

Restatement Method: The "loss in value" is again $150,000 and there no "other loss." The $4,500 Owner didn't have to pay Broker is the "cost avoided," so the total recovery is now $5,500. Comparison Method: If the contract had been performed, Owner would have had $141,000 and no house. As it is, he has a house worth $140,000 and he has paid $4,500 in commission (so we can say he has $135,500). To put him in the position that performance would have, we have to give him $5,500. Alternatively, we can say that if the contract had been performed he would have been $1,000 ahead because he would have sold a $140,000 house for $150,000 (a "profit," if you will, of $10,000), but he would have had to pay a commission of $9,000. As it stands, he is behind by $4,500. He still has the house, but he's paid a commission of $4,500. As a result, it will take $5,500 to put him in the position that performance would have.

268

PROBLEM 20-6

Developer enters into a contract with Paver for the paving of Developer's parking lot for a price of $25,000. Developer breaches the contract at a time when Paver has spent $12,000 on the job and received a total of $10,000 in progress payments. If Paver had to finish the job, it would have cost her a total of $19,000 (the $12,000 she has already spent plus an additional $7,000). The fair market value of the work Paver has done to date is $11,000. **How much is Paver entitled to receive in damages?**

Answer: $8,000

Restatement Method: The "loss in value" is $15,000 (the $25,000 contract price less the $10,000 paid to date). There is no "other loss." The "cost avoided" is $7,000.

Comparison Method: If the contract had been performed, Paver would have made a profit of $6,000. As it stands, she is $2,000 behind.

PROBLEM 20-7

Landlord and Painter enter into a contract under the terms of which Painter will paint Landlord's building for a price of $10,000. (Painter intends to do all the labor himself. No employees or subcontractors will be involved.) Landlord pays Painter a down payment of $2,000, and Painter spends $1,500 of it to purchase all the paint necessary for the job. Before Painter starts work, Underbid contacts Landlord and offers to do the job for $7,000. Landlord takes her up on it and tells Painter to forget the gig. Painter attempts to return the paint and is told it cannot be returned because it is a custom color. Then he attempts to dispose of the paint and is told that he has to pay a $50 fee to have it disposed of in an environmentally-responsible manner. Painter's brother-in-law offers to sneak the paint into the landfill at night in exchange for a $7.29 six pack of Sam Adams, but Painter, perhaps because he has been inhaling too many fumes, declines the offer and pays the $50. Painter is unable to find any other work to do during the six weeks he had set aside to do Landlord's job, so he takes his family to Disney World. The cost of the trip is $3,800.

How much is Painter entitled to receive in damages?

Answer: $8,050

Restatement Method: The "loss in value" is the $8,000 Painter did not receive because of the breach. The "other loss" is the $50 it cost to dispose of the paint in a responsible manner. There is no cost avoided. So Painter's recovery is $8,050.

Comparison Method: If the contract had been performed, Painter would have made a profit of $8,500. After the breach, Painter is ahead by $450 ($2,000 *down payment less the $1,500 spent on paint and less the $50 spent to dispose of the paint.)*

If Painter could have found other jobs during the time that he would have been painting Landlord's building, he would have had to take the jobs and deduct the money he was able to make because of Landlord's breach. Under the Restatement method, we'd have to shoehorn it in under "cost avoided," saying that the money he was able to earn selling his time in the market establishes with a reasonable degree of certainty the value of the time he saved. In the problem, Painter got full payment for the job and got to spend time with his family, while if Landlord hadn't breached, Painter would have been out in the hot sun breathing paint fumes. Here's how we justify that: The cost avoided, like any other element of damages, has to be proven with reasonable certainty. Because it's impossible to put a dollar value on having free time (some people would prefer to be working), we don't include any value for it in doing our calculations. It's only fair that a nonbreaching party can benefit from this rule, because in most cases it's the breaching party that benefits from the certainty requirement, as when the nonbreaching party is unable to recover for the hassle, inconvenience, and mental anguish caused by a breach.

Shouldn't the $50 for disposal be disallowed? After all, there would have been no "undue, risk, burden or humiliation" involved in letting the brother-in-law put the paint in the landfill. We tell students that because the language is from the Restatement, not a statute, it's clear that it's the spirit of the rule, not its literal language that controls. It should be pretty clear there's no duty to break the law to mitigate damages. But suppose a lawyer in such a situation were faced with a judge who was inclined to follow literally such language (maybe because it was in an opinion of a higher court). Then we would say that it was risky to break the law, and burdensome and humiliating to have it on your conscience.

What about the trip to Disneyland? That can probably be disposed of by saying that it wasn't foreseeable. But suppose Painter had said before the contract was formed, "It's a good thing I'm getting this job, because if I didn't I'd have to take my family to Disneyland. I can't afford to, but the kids' shrink says that if I sit around the house and don't take them to Disneyland, they'll be scarred for life." It might be an interesting exam question, or a fun way to kill some time in class. It's pretty clear to us what the answer is, but articulating a good rationale would be an interesting exercise?

PROBLEM 20-8

When Trader made a killing in the stock market, she bought herself an airplane at a cost of $300,000. Recently, the market has been even better to her, so she decided to buy a new plane. She hired Broker to sell the airplane for her and agreed to pay Broker a commission of $20,000 in connection with the sale. The contract between Trader and Broker required Trader to pay the commission only if a buyer located by Broker actually completed the sale and Trader was paid for the plane. After several months of advertising and dozens of long-distance calls to potential buyers (all at Broker's expense), Broker found Buyer, who entered into a contract to purchase the plane for $180,000.

After entering into the contract, Buyer realized that the fair market value of the plane was only $150,000. He thereupon informed Trader that he would not honor his contract. Tired of fooling around, Trader hired Auctioneer to sell the plane at a public auction. Buyer was given notice of the sale and the plane was sold at auction for $135,000. Auctioneer was paid a fee of $2,000, and Broker never got his $20,000 because the buyer he found (Buyer) never completed the deal.

Trader sued Buyer for breach of contract. At trial, there were two major issues: (1) Was the sale by auction made in good faith and in a commercially reasonable manner? (2) What was the market price of the airplane at the time and place for tender? On the latter issue, Broker, testifying for Trader, testified that the market price was $130,000. Buyer's lawyer hired two appraisers. Highball said the airplane was worth $200,000. Lowball said the airplane was worth $140,000. Buyer's lawyer paid Lowball his fee, stamped his report "Confidential--Attorney Work Product" and stuffed it in the file, never to see the light of day again. She hired Highball to testify at trial. The judge found as a fact that the market price of the airplane at the time and place for tender was $155,000.

> **(a) How much should Trader recover in damages if the court finds that the sale was conducted in good faith and in a commercially reasonable manner?**

Answer: $27,000.

Section 2-706 provides that where the resale is made in good faith and in a commercially reasonable manner, the seller may recover the difference between the resale price (here $135,000) and the contract price ($180,000) together with incidental damages ($2,000 for Auctioneer) less expenses saved in consequence of the breach (the $20,000 fee to broker).

We don't go at length into the question of whether a sale can be commercially reasonable if it brings a price far less than the fair market value. Our explanation for contracts students (and at least one of us thinks it takes care of the issue in all contexts) is that if the sale is conducted in a commercially-reasonable manner, the sale price obtained is the market price. Any market price determined by a court on the basis of appraiser testimony is only an estimate of what a commercially-reasonable sale would bring. (This reasoning does not apply, of course, in the case of fungible commodities for which there is an established market price.)

> **(b) How much should Trader recover in damages if the court finds that the sale was NOT conducted in a commercially reasonable manner? (Consider this. If the sale is not commercially**

reasonable, should Trader be able to claim the $2,000 auctioneer's fee as an element of incidental damages?)

The fact that the sale was not made in a commercially reasonable manner does not preclude Trader from recovering under section 2-708(1). It only keeps him from recovering under section 2-706. There is no counterpart to the absolute bar rule applied in some circumstances under Article 9. Under 2-708(1), he can get the difference between the market price ($155,000) and the unpaid contract price ($180,000) together with incidental damages but less expenses saved in consequence of the buyer's breach (the $20,000 commission not paid).

We think that the $2,000 paid to the auctioneer shouldn't be recovered. After all, Trader wouldn't have recovered it if he had just kept the plane. Moreover, the sale was commercially unreasonable, and expenses incurred in unreasonable attempts to mitigate damages generally aren't recoverable. Nevertheless, the few courts that have addressed the issue have allowed plaintiffs to recover expenses incurred in commercially unreasonable resales. None of the opinions has offered any rationale for doing so.

♦ - - ♦

D. PROBLEMS TO REVIEW ON YOUR OWN

Answers for these problems in the text are on the pages following the problems. Here we have paired them for your ease of reference.

1. Seller and Buyer enter into a contract for the sale of Seller's house to Buyer at a price of $100,000. No real estate commissions or other expenses are involved in the sale. Buyer breaches and the court determines that the fair market value of the house is $92,000. **How much can Seller recover in damages?**

Problem 1: $8,000

Loss in value is $100,000. Cost avoided is $92,000.

If the contract had been performed, Seller would have $100,000 in cash. Now she has a $92,000 house. The difference is $8,000.

2. Sailor and Contractor enter into a contract under the terms of which Contractor is to build a boathouse on Sailor's property for a price of $5,000. Contractor breaches before any work has been done or any money has been paid. Sailor discovers that it will cost her $6,500 to have the work done by another contractor. **How much is Sailor entitled to recover as damages?**

Problem 2: $1,500

Loss in value is $6,500. Cost avoided is $5,000.

272

If the contract had been performed, she would have had a boathouse and been out $5,000. Now she has the boathouse but it will cost her $6,500. She needs to get $1,500 to get where she would have been.

3. Sailor and Contractor enter into a contract under the terms of which Contractor is to build a boathouse on Sailor's property for a price of $15,000. Contractor breaches before any work has been done, but after Sailor has paid Contractor an initial payment of $5,000. Sailor discovers that it will cost her $19,000 to have the work done by another contractor. **How much is Sailor entitled to recover as damages?**

Problem 3: $9,000

Loss in value is $19,000. Cost avoided is $10,000. (That is the amount owing on the contract that she would have had to pay if it hadn't been breached.)

If the contract had been performed, she would have had a boathouse and been out $15,000. Now she has the boathouse but is out $24,000 ($5,000 to Contractor and $19,000 to the person who actually built the boathouse).

4. Sailor and Contractor enter into a contract under the terms of which Contractor is to build a boathouse on Sailor's property for a price of $8,000. Sailor repudiates before any work has been done or any money has been paid. Contractor proves that it would have cost her $6,000 to build the boathouse. **How much is Contractor entitled to recover as damages?**

Problem 4: $2,000

Loss in value is $8,000. Cost avoided is $6,000.

If the contract had been performed, she would have made $2,000. As it is now, she has nothing.

5. Sailor and Contractor enter into a contract under the terms of which Contractor is to build a boathouse on Sailor's property for a price of $12,000. Sailor repudiates before any work has been done, but after Sailor has paid Contractor $3,000 as a deposit. It is established that it would have cost Contractor $10,000 to build the boathouse. **How much is Contractor entitled to recover as damages?**

Problem 5: $0. We'll discuss in a later chapter whether or not she might have to give something back.

Loss in value is $9,000. Cost avoided is $10,000.

If the contract had been performed, she would have made $2,000. As it is, she has $3,000.

6. Grower and Broker enter into a contract under the terms of which it is agreed that Broker will purchase Grower's wheat crop for a price of $3.00 per bushel. At the time and place for delivery, the market price for wheat is $3.25 per bushel. Broker waits for Grower to show up with her wheat. When Grower fails to show up, Broker investigates and determines that Grower has sold her crop elsewhere. Without unreasonable delay, Broker purchases some wheat to replace the wheat she had expected to get from Grower, but by the time she can act the price has gone up and she has to pay $3.40 per bushel. **How much (per bushel) is she entitled to recover in damages?**

Problem 6: 40 cents a bushel

Section 2-712 allows the non-breaching buyer to recover the difference between the cost of cover ($3.40—she can get the higher price because she purchased "without unreasonable delay") and the contract price ($3.00) together with incidental or consequential damages (there weren't any) but less expenses saved in consequence of the breach (there weren't any).

7. Grower and Broker enter into a contract under the terms of which it is agreed that Broker will purchase Grower's wheat crop for a price of $3.00 per bushel. At the time and place for delivery, the market price for wheat is $3.25 per bushel. Broker waits for Grower to show up with her wheat. When Grower fails to show up, Broker investigates and determines that Grower has sold her crop elsewhere. Broker gets so fed up she decides to quit the wheat business and become a beach bum. **How much (per bushel) is she entitled to recover in damages?**

Problem 7: 25 cents a bushel

Section 2-713 allows the buyer who has not covered to recover the difference between the market price ($3.25) and the contract price ($3.00) together with incidental and consequential damages (none) less expenses saved (none).

8. Dealer agrees to buy Collector's Expressionist painting for $2 million. Dealer repudiates the contract. Collector re-sells the painting in good faith and in a commercially reasonable manner to another art gallery for $1.5 million and sues Dealer for breach of contract. At trial it is determined that the fair market value of the painting was $1.8 million dollars. **How much is Collector entitled to recover as damages?**

Problem 8: $500,000

Section 2-706 allows the non-breaching seller to recover the difference between the resale price ($1,500,000) and the contract price ($2,000,000) together with incidental damages (none) less expenses saved (none).

9. Dealer agrees to buy Collector's Expressionist painting for $2 million. Dealer repudiates the contract. The fair market value of the painting at the time it was to be delivered is $1.8 million, but Collector decides she no longer wants to

sell the painting, so she keeps it. **How much is Collector entitled to recover as damages?**

Problem 9: $200,000

If the non-breaching seller does not re-sell, section 2-708(1) gives her as damages the difference between the market price ($2,000,000) and the unpaid contract price ($1,800,000) together with incidental damages (none) less expenses saved (none).

10. Wholesaler and Grocery Store enter into a contract under the terms of which Grocery Store agrees to buy a ton of apples from Wholesaler for $1,000. Wholesaler can get as many apples as it wants for $900 a ton. Grocery Store breaches its contract with Wholesaler, and Wholesaler in good faith and in a commercially reasonable manner re-sells the apples it had planned to sell to Grocery Store to Kroger for $975 a ton. **How much is Wholesaler entitled to recover in damages?**

Problem 10: $100 a ton

Because Wholesaler can get as many apples as it can sell, it is a "lost volume seller" and is entitled to the profit it would have made on the contract that was breached.

11. Farmer and Broker enter into a contract under the terms of which Broker agrees to buy Farmer's entire apple crop for $1,000 a ton. It costs Farmer $900 a ton to grow the apples. Broker breaches its contract with Farmer, and Farmer in good faith and in a commercially reasonable manner re-sells the apples she had planned to sell to Broker to Health Food Store for $975 at ton, giving proper notice, of course. **How much is Farmer entitled to recover in damages?**

Problem 11: $25 a ton

Because Farmer has a limited supply of apples, her damages are determined by section 2-706, which gives her the difference between the resale price and the contract price.

CHAPTER 21

LIQUIDATED DAMAGES

— ♦ —

Damages agreed upon at time of contracting.

Historical prejudice against them because they resembled a penal bond (penalty-based performance bond) and encroached on judicial discretion.

Generally favored these days even if the language about them is somewhat stingy. The standards are somewhat interesting as they plainly are an attempt to identify the factors that make such a clause "fair" or "efficient," which is very much an "in the eye of the beholder" concept.

Concerns regarding unequal bargaining power—shades of the penal bond remain.

Drafting hints:

Don't make it more profitable for a party to have a breach than performance (i.e., don't draft a clause that puts the non-breacher in a better position in the case of breach than in the case of performance).

Do try and have the liquidated damage provision provide variable damages depending on the severity and duration of the breach.

♦ - - ♦

Diffley v. Royal Papers, Inc.
Court of Appeals of Missouri
948 S.W.2d 244 (1997)

Collective Bargaining Agreement and Trust Agreement for pension plan. Pension plan trustees issue memorandum providing for late fee of 10% of total contributions due for the month if they are late in submitting payments and reports. (How can they do this by memorandum, what does that mean? Discuss delegation to third party of rule making powers in a contract).

Late fee if 15 days late, and reports and payments due 15 days after the end of the month being reported – total of 30 days, then late.

September payment, due October 30, not received until November 9. October payment, due November 30, not received until December 6.

Rule from paragraph 6: Liquidated Damage Clauses are Enforceable, while penalty clauses are invalid. A penalty clause specifies a punishment for default. Liquidated damages are a measure of compensation that the parties agree at the time of contracting will represent damages and (1) the amount fixed as damages is reasonable as a forecast of the harm caused by the breach, and (2) the harm must be of a kind difficult to accurately estimate at the time of contracting.

Here the court finds it is a penalty because:

(1) Parties called it a late penalty (bad drafting); and

(2) it bears no relationship to the harm (loss of market interest); and

(3) the harm is easily estimatable (again, market interest).

NOTES AND QUESTIONS

1. In the quoted portion of the Trustees' Memorandum, the language used is a "late *penalty* of ten percent (10%)." This was an unfortunate and spectacularly uninformed choice of words due to the case law regarding unenforceable penalties discussed in the introduction to this chapter. A well drafted contract will say the sum is payable "as liquidated damages and not as a penalty." Although courts are supposed to look through the form of the transaction and base their decision on substance, using words that the other side can turn against you is never wise.

2. In paragraph 7, the court states: "The provision must be fixed on the basis of compensation, otherwise it is construed as a penalty clause designed primarily to compel performance." The court seems to be saying that the fact that the clause is intended to compel performance makes it an unenforceable penalty. Watch how the next opinion treats that issue.

♦ - - ♦

DJ Manufacturing v. United States
United States Court of Appeals, Federal Circuit
86 F.3d 1130 (1996)

Upholds liquidated damage clause of 1/15 of one percent of the contract price for each day of delay. Contract was for supply of combat field packs for Operation Desert Storm. Amounts to a penalty of $663,266.92 out of $8,493,828 contract price (That is 8% – how did you calculate it? Show division. Students should get in the habit of automatically calculating percentage relationships between numbers.).

Motion for SJ by government. The court holds that claimant bears burden of showing that the clause is unenforceable (presumption of enforceability).

What evidence did the claimant bring? Affidavit of claimant's president that says the damages clause "does not seem related to any specific need with respect to the item in question. . . [and] seems to be a standard rate used in many solicitations."

Not enough.

Test: harm from breach difficult to estimate and the amount is a reasonable forecast of the harm. Here, pretty clear it is hard to estimate.

Reasonable forecast – focus on the amount itself, not the individual making the forecast or the method of forecast – so standard form is just fine.

Incentive to perform ok but penalty not ok. How to tell the difference? Argue the facts. Here, does it matter that the United States was the plaintiff and underlying events involve military supplies during a time of war? What about the forum—the Federal Circuit—reviewing court of claims?

NOTES AND QUESTIONS

1. In paragraph 6 of the opinion the circuit court states (with apparent approval) the rule that the trial court applied. Read carefully R2d § 356. **How does the Restatement rule differ from the rule the trial court applied?** *Open discussion - overhead helps.*

2. **Why have rules such as these? Why not allow freedom of contract where the parties can agree to whatever damage provisions they want?** *Open discussion.*

3. A Federal Communications Commission decision synthesized and summarized the law of liquidated damages as follows:

> When parties enter into a contract, the law allows them to apportion risk through the establishment of a liquidated damages clause. A liquidated damage clause will be enforced as long as the amount stipulated for is not so extravagant, or disproportionate to the amount of property loss, as to show that compensation was not the object aimed at or to imply fraud, mistake, circumvention, or oppression. With that narrow exception, there is no sound reason why persons competent and free to contract may not agree upon this subject as fully as upon any other, or why their agreement, when fairly and understandingly entered into with a view to just compensation for the anticipated loss, should not be enforced.

In re BDPCS, Inc., 15 F.C.C.R. 17590, 17610 (2000) (footnotes and internal citations omitted).

◆ - - ◆

Vanderbilt University v. Dinardo
United States District Court, Middle District, Tennessee
974 F. Supp. 638 (1997)

Head coach quits Vandy and goes to LSU. Liquidated Damages clause that he will pay them his base salary for the period remaining on his contract.

Note that in paragraph 4, the court mislabels the parties. Vanderbilt is the plaintiff and Dinardo is the defendant, as properly stated in paragraph 2. Some students find this reassuring; others confusing.

Test: Whether the amount stipulated was reasonable in relation to the amount of damages that could be expected to result from the breach.

Held: This was. Totes up all the salaries and potential losses.

NOTES AND QUESTIONS

1. Review section 8 of DiNardo's contract. **What is the point of the first sentence?** *It is an internal recital, a statement of agreed facts that can be useful in supporting enforcement of the liquidated damages clause in later litigation.* **Doesn't the next sentence contain the operative language of the parties' agreement?** *Yes, but background and context and a finding of unforseeability.*

2. In paragraph 6 of the opinion, the court notes that the language of section 8 was "modified at the request of" DiNardo. **What is the point, if any, of this?**

It was negotiated. Not a contract of adhesion. UCC 2-718(1) – up on board – is this the same standard as the Restatement?

♦ - - ♦

Monsanto v. McFarling
United States Court of Appeals, Federal Circuit
363 F.3d 1336 (2004)

Farmer saves seed from prior crop in violation of Monsanto's Technology Agreement signed when he purchased the seed.

District court grants summary judgment as to the issue of breach and enforces the liquidated damages clause, which it finds enforceable under Missouri law. The liquidated damages clause called for payment of "120 times the applicable Technology Fee" of $6.50 per bag of seed.

Court of appeals affirms on all points except enforcement of liquidated damages and reverses for a determination of actual damages. Anti-one-size-fits-all rule. Damages were not, at time of contracting, a reasonable estimate of harm.

NOTE

♦ -- ♦

PROBLEM 21-1

Read carefully UCC §§ 2-719(1)(a) and 2-719(3) and Restatement (Second) § 356. **Which of the following clauses limiting remedies would be upheld?**

(a) The contract for the sale of a burglar alarm provides that damages for the failure of the burglar alarm are limited to $100. The alarm fails to function and $50,000 worth of jewelry and antiques are stolen from the buyer's home.

(b) The contract for the sale of photographic film provides that if the film is defective, the buyer's remedies are limited to a return of the purchase price. The film is defective and the buyer is left without any pictures of her wedding, the first ever wedding on the summit of Mount Everest.

(c) The contract for the delivery of an overnight package provides that if the package is not delivered on time, the shipper's only remedy is the return of her money. The package fails to arrive on time, a billion dollar corporate merger is delayed, and the lawyer who sent the package goes from being on the fast track for partnership to looking for a job.

In all of these situations, courts have upheld liquidated damages clauses that provide for relatively nominal amounts as liquidated damages. The theory is that to do otherwise would be in effect to require the seller or service provider to bundle an insurance policy with the goods or services being sold. The UCC and R2 sections cited all support this result.

PROBLEM 21-2

Reconsider the *Diffley* case. **If you had been representing the Teamsters, what could you have done to give your liquidated damages provision a good shot at being enforceable while still making it a strong incentive for employers to get their money in on time?**

The most obvious thing is to say that the sum is payable "as liquidated damages and not as a penalty." Beyond that, the trustees' lawyer should ask why it's important to have the payments made on time. Presumably, there are two reasons: late payments result in increased administrative costs and the pension fund is losing the investment return on the money from the time it was to be paid until it is actually received. The clause should state this and say that the parties have agreed that a reasonable estimate of the additional administrative costs is X dollars for each payment that is late and a reasonable estimate of the investment loss is Y percent of the amount in arrears per day (or week or year) and that they have agreed that this amount will be payable as liquidated damages. Also consider using a variable late charge based on prime or other reference rate of interest plus a spread to mimic potential investment returns in equity markets, e.g. LIBOR plus 500 basis points.

PROBLEM 21-3

A general contractor had a contract to build an office building. The general contract provided that if completion of the building was delayed, the general contractor would pay liquidated damages of $1,000 a day. The lowest bid on the electrical work was from a new and rather small company. The general contractor told the electrical contractor he would like to give them the job, but he could not take the risk that the sub would be late in completing the electrical work and throw the whole project off schedule. The electrical sub therefore suggested that the electrical subcontract provide for liquidated damages of $2,000 per day. The head of the electrical sub stated that the reason for this provision was "to show that we have confidence we can perform." At the time the parties entered into the subcontract, they both knew that each day of delay in the completion of the electrical work would result in no more than one day's delay in the completion of the entire project, and there was a substantial likelihood that the delay in the completion of the entire project would be even less.

As it turned out, the electrical work was completed 30 days late. The project was completed 21 days late, and if the electrical work had been completed on time, the project still would have been 15 days late.

How much is the general contractor entitled to recover as damages?

The general contractor would probably be entitled only to $6,000 in damages. This is the amount of the loss ($21,000 in liquidated damages he had to pay on his contract 21 days @ $1,000) that was caused by the sub's default. The liquidated damages clause would probably be invalidated because the parties knew at the time they entered into the subcontract that the actual damages would be less than the amount specified as liquidated damages. The fact that the sub suggested the liquidated damages provision would be helpful to the general contractor, but it is not likely that it would be decisive if the transaction were structured as suggested in the problem. The next problems suggest ways of structuring the transaction that might give the general contractor a better chance.

This problem is based on a hypothetical posed by Judge Richard Posner. Judge Posner used the hypothetical to argue that liberalizing even further the rules regarding liquidated damages would help people in the position of the subcontractor who might want to agree to large liquidated damages so as to get work that might otherwise be available only to well-established businesses.

PROBLEM 21-4

A law professor and law book publisher entered into a contract under the terms of which the professor would revise a chapter in the publisher's treatise on contract damages. The contract provided that the professor's fee would be $600 if the manuscript were delivered by March 1, $450 if it were delivered by April 15, and $200 if it were delivered at any time thereafter.

Is there a problem with this provision?

These are the facts of an actual contract signed by one of the authors. We've seen a number of similar provisions in publishers' contracts. In substance they're liquidated damages clauses disguised as consideration clauses, but in this area, courts seem quite willing to elevate form over substance, so we think there's a good chance it would be upheld. If any of you have ever talked to the publishers about these clauses, we'd be interested in hearing about it. (gkuney@utk.edu)

We talk about form vs. substance here and in the next two problems because we think students can't hear enough about it in their first year of law school. It gives them a big leg up for a number of advanced business courses.

PROBLEM 21-5

Mark Dove, a law student, entered into an employment contract with Rose Acre Farms, a large agri-business concern. Under the terms of the contract, Mr. Dove would work for Rose Acre Farms for ten weeks during the summer for the sum of $7,500. The contract provided that if a certain construction project on which Mr. Dove was to be working in a supervisory capacity was not completed on time OR if Mr. Dove was late for work even one time, Mr. Dove would pay "as liquidated damages and not as a penalty," the sum of $5,000.

Is the liquidated damages provision enforceable?

Consideration $7,500 subject to liquidated damages of $5,000. The facts of these problems are based (slightly simplified) on those of Dove v. Rose Acre Farms, *the lead-off case in Chapter 23 (Express Conditions). Dove's contract characterized the $5,000 as a bonus subject to a condition precedent, and if his counsel ever tried to argue that it was just disguised liquidated damages, the court didn't bother to mention that in its opinion. We're fairly confident, however, that if it had been structured as in Problem 19-5, Dove would have had no problem in collecting the full $7,500.*

PROBLEM 21-6

Mark Dove, a law student, entered into an employment contract with Rose Acre Farms, a large agri-business concern. Under the terms of the contract, Mr. Dove would work for Rose Acre Farms for ten weeks during the summer for the sum of $2,500. The contract provided that if a certain construction project on which Mr. Dove was to be working in a supervisory capacity was not completed on time and if Mr. Dove was not late for work even one time, Mr. Dove would receive a bonus of $5,000.

Mr. Dove was late for work one morning because his car wouldn't start. (He planned to use the bonus to buy a new one). Because he was late, he didn't get the bonus and he sued to recover it. **Should he win?**

Consideration $2,500 with "bonus" for timely performance of $5,000. The facts of these problems are based (slightly simplified) on those of Dove v. Rose Acre Farms, the lead-off case in Chapter 23 (Express Conditions). Dove's contract characterized the $5,000 as a bonus subject to a condition precedent, and if his counsel ever tried to argue that it was just disguised liquidated damages, the court didn't bother to mention that in its opinion.

PROBLEM 21-7

Your client has agreed to pay liquidated damages of $200,000 if it fails to perform its part of a contract. It wants to be sure it is not required to pay more. **What provisions would you put into the contract to make sure its exposure is limited to $200,000?**

As the immediately preceding note indicates, the liquidated damages clause should provide that the liquidated damages are the other party's exclusive remedy. As the Loveday opinion indicates, this may not be necessary in all jurisdictions, but why take the chance?

PROBLEM 21-8

When Trista Rehn was chosen to be the bachelorette on the reality-based television program of that name, she was required to sign a contract of 17 single-spaced pages. One clause provided:

F.   **Liquidated Damages:** I agree that any breach or violation by me of any of the terms or provisions of this Agreement shall result in substantial damages and injury to Producer and/or the Network, the precise amount of which would be extremely difficult or impracticable to determine. Accordingly, Producer and I have made a reasonable endeavor to estimate a fair compensation for potential losses and damages to Producer and/or the Network which would result from any breach by me of any material term of this Agreement, including, but not limited to paragraph IV D. [paragraph IV D. provides that she assumes the risk of all the dangers and hazards she will encounter on the show, including the risk of pregnancy and sexually-transmitted diseases – as we'll see in the next two chapters, it's not clear how one would breach a clause like this; possibly she could do it by suing on account of damage from one of the risks she assumed] and, therefore, I further agree that, in addition to the remedies set forth hereinabove, I will also be obligated to pay, and I agree to pay to Producer and/or the Network, the sum of Five Million Dollars ($5,000,000) as a reasonable and fair amount of liquidated damages to compensate

Producer and/or the Network for any loss or damage resulting from each breach by me of the terms hereof. I further agree that such sum bears a reasonable and proximate relationship to the actual damages which Producer and/or the Network will or may suffer from each breach by me.

This clause was separately initialed by Ms. Rehn, as were most other significant clauses in the contract. There were a total of 35 provisions in the contract to be initialed by Ms. Rehn. Among the provisions, the breach of which would trigger the liquidated damages clause, were:

> Paragraph I A. requiring her to appear on news shows, talk shows etc. "when and where designated by Producer in its sole discretion."

> Paragraph II A. requiring her to refrain from taking photographs during the period of the show's taping without the permission of the producer.

> Paragraph VI B. requiring her to refrain from using the series name in any publicity except as provided in the agreement.

> Paragraph VI A. requiring her to refrain from taking refuge in any place where the series cameras cannot photograph her.

> Paragraph VI C. requiring her to refrain from wearing any apparel with a nationally recognized logo unless it has been provided by the producer and further requiring her to "abide by . . . all U.S. laws and all applicable local laws."

This is a fun problem. The entire contract is available at http://www.thesmokinggun.com/documents/celebrity/bachelorettes-arranged-marriage. This site often has outrageous celebrity contracts posted.

Having a party separately initial one or two provisions in a contract is a good way to increase the likelihood that those provisions will be enforced. But each additional provision that is initialed detracts from the force of the initialing. And what about the uninitialed provisions? Where you make someone initial every clause, it makes the contract look like it's a one-sided, unnegotiated contract.

(1) **If Ms. Rehn were arrested for speeding while wearing her Mickey Mouse wristwatch, could the producer get a judgment for five million? (Or could they get ten million?** [She has breached two provisions.])

This points out one of the many problems with the liquidated damages clause in the problem. Every violation, no matter how trivial, results in a five million dollar penalty.

(2)   If Ms. Rehn breached the contract in a way that caused the producer damage that was serious but not provable with reasonable certainty, how would you argue that Ms. Rehn is not liable for the five million?

The liquidated damages clause should be unenforceable. As noted above, it fails to distinguish between trivial and serious breaches, it doesn't really attempt to estimate the producer's losses in the event of a breach, and it clearly is included primarily for its in terrorum *effect.*

(3)   What is the intended effect of the provision that states "Producer and I have made a reasonable endeavor to estimate a fair compensation for potential losses and damages . . .?" Can you think of an unintended effect it may have?

Because it's pretty clear she and the producer didn't actually try to estimate the damages, this casts doubt upon the accuracy of the other recitals in the contract. It also raises questions as to whether she read and understood the contract.

◆ - - ◆

Bear Sterns Gov. Securities, Inc. v. Dow Corning Corp.
United States Court of Appeals for the Sixth Circuit
419 F.3d 543 (2005)

Facts are fairly straightforward. Dow-Corning Breast Implant litigation. Settlement discussions lead to structured settlement with installment payments over time. Plaintiffs are concerned about late payment or default and propose a no-credit-for-prior-payments default clause. Dow-Corning finds this unacceptable and suggests a "penalty" of $100 per day, per plaintiff.

The plaintiffs agree but insist on calling the $100 a "liquidated damages" provision.

Plaintiffs sell their settlement agreement contract rights to Bear Sterns, Dow-Corning goes into bankruptcy. Ultimately, Dow emerges under a 100-cents-on-the-dollar plan, and Bear Sterns claims the liquidated damages amount.

Held: Penalty, unenforceable.

Couple of thing to emphasize:

1. None of the parties are the original parties to the settlement agreement, Dow-Corning is a reorganized debtor & Bear Sterns is an investor that bought the settlements. Discuss purchase and sale of structured settlements.

2. Discuss whether the identity of the real parties in interest did or should affect the court's analysis.

3. Other than context, those points, and the drafting evidentiary record, this case is included for its basic overview and review of liquidated damages law.

CHAPTER 22

SPECIFIC PERFORMANCE

— ♦ —

Centex Homes Corp. v. Boag
Superior Court of New Jersey, Chancery Division
128 N.J. Super. 385, 320 A.2d 194 (1974)

Specific performance for the *vendor* in a New Jersey condo sale? No. What is a condominium? Explain.

Seller is looking for specific performance of contract to purchase condo. The vendor's claim is that, since this is a real estate contract, and real estate is unique, money damages are per se inadequate, and SP would issue for the vendee (would they really, under the rule of this case?), so mutuality demands that they lie for this vendor too.

Court explains (not fully) why specific performance is available to purchaser. It continues by explaining that the reason it was given to sellers was mutuality of remedy and that's now a dead doctrine in New Jersey.

The test is not uniqueness or whether the subject matter is real estate, but whether an adequate remedy can be had at law. *Liquidated damages clause says they can keep the deposit, so that's all they get.*

This opinion demonstrates the error of letting the result of a rule or standard that is repeated in a common fact pattern evolve into a rule or standard itself. We start with "no adequate remedy at law," and apply that to "land," which is deemed "unique," meeting the test of no adequate remedy, and this becomes the rule of "specific performance is available for all contracts for the sale of land." Peel back the skin and find the actual rule and apply that to the facts at hand.

A condo has no real unique quality (explore this just a bit—is that really true?). What do you think about the liquidated damage provision – does it meet the restatement standard? (We don't think so.)

NOTES AND QUESTIONS

3. In the case discussed in paragraph 3, was the court elevating form over substance? Can you think of a good reason why the court might be justified in elevating form over substance in that situation?

The court was elevating form over substance. The dissenting opinion in that case pointed it out. A co-op is functionally very similar—practically identical—to a condominium. As discussed in Note 2, the reason one form is used instead of the other is primarily a matter of local custom. They both do the same thing. In that case, however, the majority probably felt it was justified in elevating form over substance. If it hadn't the developer would have had a windfall of 10% of the purchase price.

♦ - - ♦

Van Wagner Advertising v. S & M Enterprises
Court of Appeals of New York
67 N.Y. 2d 186, 501 N.Y.S.2d 628, 492 N.E.2d 756 (1986)

Michaels leased Van Wagner space on a building for a billboard.

Michaels sold the building to S&M, which was going to tear it down and develop the site. S&M, and S&M purports to terminate the lease per section 1.05:

> Notwithstanding anything contained in the foregoing provisions to the contrary, Lessor (or its successor) may terminate and cancel this lease on not less than 60 days prior written notice in the event and only in the event of:

> (A) a bona fide sale of the building to a third party unrelated to Lessor.

Let's examine this for ambiguity – is the right of termination that of only the seller, or the purchaser too (before purchaser becomes a seller)? What do you think? Let in the parol evidence. Trial Court – for Van Wagner, there was a breach. Note how appellate court affirms this based upon the interpretation of the contract as a factual matter – thus insulating this from review [para. 9].

What about whether or not to award specific performance? Well, it is not awarded as a matter of course. Uniqueness is not the magic element – the key for this court is how likely is a judicial valuation to be incorrect [para. 14]? The more uncertain is the valuation, the more appropriate is specific performance. This is the law and economics spin on when damages at law are inadequate.

We can project damages into the future for this sort of commercial injury. So damages are sufficient and adequate. Review, again, was "abuse of discretion" [para. 11].

Finally, imposition of an equitable remedy should not itself work an inequity. . .

Trial court refused specific performance on basis that it would result in disproportionate harm.

App. Div. affirmed; this court affirms but remands on damage issues.

NOTES AND QUESTIONS

Suppose the trial court had granted specific performance. **What do you suppose the parties would have done?** *"Buy the injunction." Up to you if you have the time or interest to discuss the economic efficiency argument of letting the parties bargain themselves out of their dispute.* Note that this may also be covered in Property or Torts in discussions of nuisance. **Can you see how, if damages are difficult to award because of valuation, awarding specific performance may force the parties to reveal their true, subjective valuations? Wouldn't this argue for routine awards of specific performance? Or are there competing considerations?** *Judicial efficiency and difficulties of supervising performance.*

♦ - - ♦

Walgreen Co. v. Sara Creek Property Co.
United States Court of Appeals for the Seventh Circuit
966 F.2d 273 (1992)

Appeal of permanent injunction specifically enforcing a "no other drug store in this shopping center" clause in a lease. Appellate court affirms, but rules that enforcement is not automatic, damages are the norm [para. 9]. Only when monetary damages are inadequate should specific performance be ordered [paras. 6-9].

This may be a good time to discuss the proper role, if there is one, of an appellate court. Judge Posner goes out of his way to present a lengthy "law and economics" framework for considering this and related issues. Arguably, much of that is dicta. But powerful dicta. This discussion is useful in a world where students (and lawyers) increasingly research issues by looking for "magic words" with "a search engine" and give little thought to subjects like precedential weight and what is or is not dicta. The explanation of the economic efficiency of injunctive relief and the concept of forcing the parties to negotiate to buy and sell the injunction—a form of solanonic justice.

Note the preliminary injunction standard. Explicitly lay out the four prong test for a preliminary injunction or temporary restraining or protective order:

> (1) Likelihood of Success on the Merits,
> (2) Irreparable Harm otherwise,
> (3) Balancing of the Equities, and
> (4) Public Interest considerations.

This is something every (business) lawyer should know by heart and be able to access instinctively.

♦ - - ♦

Campbell Soup Co. v. Wentz
United States Court of Appeals, Third Circuit
172 F.2d 80 (1948)

Carrot supply contract, bump in market price, farmer breaches and sells through straw purchaser. Campbell seeks injunction to prevent.

Wentzes agreed to sell Campbell all their carrots for $23 - $30 per ton, with prices varying by month.

In Jan. 1948, the contract price was $30 and the market price was $90 a ton. Wentzes said they would not deliver Campbell any more carrots. They sold the carrots to Lojeski, and he sold about half of them to Campbell.

Trial Court: Money damages adequate.

Appellate court: Affirm, but for different reason. The contract is too tough, too unconscionable taken as a whole and equity must hold its nose and withhold equitable relief. *See also* R2d § 364, esp. § 364(1)(a). What do you think?

◆ - - ◆

Lumley v. Wagner
Lord Chancellor's Court
1 De. GM & G. 604, 42 Eng. Rep. 687 (1852)

Johanna Wagner contracts to sing for Her Majesty's Theater and nowhere else during the contract term. Then she breaches to take another engagement.

Theater owner seeks injunction preventing her from singing for another. Faces the defense that equity should not issue an injunction unless it will grant complete relief as well as the rule that positive injunctions will not be granted for personal services contracts.

Court: No, we will enjoin her and maybe this will prod her to sing at HMT.

NOTES AND QUESTIONS

Remedies in Reality. *Discussion of Ms. Rehn's rights and duties under "The Unattached Female" Contract.*

Lawyering Skills Problem

Suppose that you want to draft a contract so as to make it more likely that a court will specifically enforce an agreement. What sort of provisions would you draft in light of the case law on the subject? Remember, the key is to read the cases to see what the courts were looking for in order to grant specific performance and then to draft into that standard and out of or around any prohibitions on the remedy.

Stipulations regarding inadequacy of monetary damages if contract is breached. Stipulation to choice of law, choice of jurisdiction to an injunction-friendly, hometown tribunal, consent to injunctive relief on shortened time, etc.

CHAPTER 23

EXPRESS CONDITIONS

— ◆ —

R2d § 224 (put up on board).

A condition is an event, not certain to occur, which must occur, unless its non-occurrence is excused, before performance under a contract becomes due. (Kuney dislikes this definition as it defines out conditions subsequent, which the R2d deals with under discharge, which is sometimes unnecessarily confusing to students.)

A CONDITION is an event not certain to occur, which must occur or be excused before a duty arises (or that, when it occurs, cancels, or modifies a duty). All conditions are subsequent to the contract – that is not the distinction.

CONDITIONS PRECEDENT are conditions that, when they happen, create a duty.

CONDITIONS SUBSEQUENT are conditions that, when they happen, cancel or modify a duty.

A REPRESENTATION is a statement of presently existing fact made to induce another party to rely upon the statement and take action based on that reliance, like entering into a contract or closing a transaction. Remedies for "breach" of a representation, or misrepresentation, are rescission and restitution for damages.

A WARRANTY is a statement made about certain facts under which the warranting party promises that those facts will be as stated. The remedies for breach of warranty are damages, generally the difference in value between the thing or service as warranted and as delivered. Warranties can be express (stated by the parties) or implied (from conduct or as a matter of law).

A COVENANT is a promise to act or not act in the future. It is an individual promise in a contract.

The ramifications and remedies for breach or inaccuracy or non-occurrence of each of these provisions are different. It is critical to use the right provision for the right task or your contract will not work as intended.

Note also that careful drafting can disguise a liquidated damages clause as a condition precedent or subsequent and perform other alchemy to elevate form over substance.

Here you can display and discuss, in broken down fashion (exploded to explicitly separate elements and factors), R2d §§ 224, 227,229, and then build a three column chart of the cases, from *Dove* to *Battista* listing the date of the decision, the case name, and the outcome in terms of condition enforced, construed as covenant, or waived. This facilitates a discussion of Condition vs. Covenant; Substantial vs. Specific Performance; Material Covenant vs. Collateral Matter; Form over Substance; Formalism vs. Realism. Try to get away from each case and look at the whole group. From a practical, deal structuring perspective, this is some of the best meat of the entire course. A mastery of conditions allows an attorney to carefully plot the unfolding, development, and demise of the parties' relationship.

◆ - - ◆

Dove v. Rose Acre Farms
Court of Appeals of Indiana
434 N.E.2d 931(1982)

Rose Acre Farms has a bonus program, lots of different ones, all with common feature – to earn a bonus employees must not miss work or be tardy at all, for any reason whatsoever.

Dove on construction team, bonus of $6,000 if work 5 full days each week for 12 weeks, later amended to 10 weeks for Dove so that he could go to law school. In the last week, he gets strep (on the second to last day it looks like). Fever of 104. He is told he can sleep at work and it will count, but he leaves to get medical attention.

He seeks the bonus. Trial court rules against him on the basis of failure to satisfy the condition precedent. He points to all kinds of over-performance on his part and argues that substantial compliance should be the rule.

Affirmed.

He was knowledgeable (why is this important? No unfair surprise, thus no unconscionability claim here).

The condition was central to the contract and not a collateral matter. (What does this matter? Defeats his argument that there was substantial compliance – this condition was at the heart of the deal.)

Is the court rejecting substantial compliance as the standard and holding that strict compliance is necessary?

Or could substantial performance still be the standard?

The Court does not really tell us, does it?

What about Restatement (Second) of Contracts § 229?

"To the extent that the non-occurrence of a condition would cause disproportionate forfeiture, a court may excuse the non-occurrence of that condition unless its occurrence was a material part of the agreed exchange."

Would this standard lead to the same or a different result for Mr. Dove? (Probably the same result based upon materiality as interpreted by the court.)

NOTES AND QUESTIONS

1. Lest you have the impression that Rose Acre Farms is a small operation run by quirky Farmer Rust and that this sort of thing would never happen in a commercial operation, think again. Rose Acre Farms, Inc. began as a single-layer hen farm with 1,800 hens, and today is a highly integrated table egg production system with multiple eight-layer hen farms and millions of hens. It is one of the largest egg producers in the United States. *See* Rose Acre Farms v. United States, 55 Fed. Cl. 643, 647 (2003).

2. Take a look at R2d § 229. **Does that section suggest that the court should or could have reached a different result?**

♦ - - ♦

Howard v. Federal Crop Insurance Corp.
United States Court of Appeals, Fourth Circuit
540 F.2d 695 (1976)

Tobacco farmers, crop loss due to storm, they disk under their fields before the claims adjuster can get there.

Condition and Covenant or merely a Covenant is the issue.

Put up the provision on the board.

When in doubt, construe a possible condition as a mere covenant to avoid forfeiture.

No magic language, but it sure can help. Here in 5(b) they say condition, and in 5(f) they are silent.

Puzzle through the Restatement illustrations (at least one of us thinks they make sense but see what the students think). R2d section would be 227. Still confusing.

NOTES AND QUESTIONS

1. This case illustrates an important principle of drafting: Never use different phrases to convey the same meaning. If you make even the smallest change, it may (in fact, it should) be interpreted as an indication you mean something different than what you meant when you used similar language in another part of the document.

2. An article on the front page of the *The Wall Street Journal* on May 5, 2003, entitled *Abuses Plague Crop Insurance*, discussed the problem of fraud in the federal crop insurance program. A headline said the "system is proving easy to fool." It described one farmer alleged to have defrauded the government out of at least $4 million.

3. Redraft paragraph 5(f) to make sure the government doesn't have to pay if a farmer destroys the tobacco stalks.

Here the key is to make it an express condition linked to a consequence of failure to be satisfied and making it a material part of the contract.

♦ - - ♦

In the context of the home sale discussion, present the deal time line from the introduction on the board and discuss what is going on at each stage.

♦ - - ♦

ON TRANSACTIONAL PRACTICE
(Discussion of typical residential real estate sales and bigger deals).

♦ - - ♦

Appeal of Edwin J. Schoettle Co.
Supreme Court of Pennsylvania
390 Pa. 365, 134 A.2d 908 (1957)

Sale of stock of company for $2,100,000 of which amount $187,863.60 is reserved into an escrow to cover claims that are within an indemnity agreement.

What is indemnity? New concept to add to the terms. What is an escrow? New concept to add to the terms.

Claim against indemnity escrow for overvaluation of company. Plaintiff claimed $69,998.42 and was awarded $3,182.88 (error in computing taxes due and rent).

Date of contract: 9/17/54

Clauses at issue:

5(g) – Material Adverse Change (MAC) representation and warranty.

9(a) – Financial condition at closing no less favorable than as shown on financials dated June 30, 1954 and warranted to be true [para. 5(e)]. Labeled a condition.

9(b) – Rep and warranty bring down at closing. Labeled a condition.

9(c) – Performance of all agreements and conditions by closing. Labeled a condition.

10(d) – Indemnification from misrepresentation, breach of warranty, nonfulfillment of any agreement (does not mention condition).

15. – Survival of reps, warranties, and covenants after closing.

Buyer position: 9(a) is a warranty of financial condition and it was breached, so pay us from the indemnity.

Seller position: No, 9(a) is a condition, and you waived it by closing.

At arbitration, evidence of negotiations is introduced – see how you are creating a record for litigation when you are documenting a deal. And you don't know if it will be admitted or not, in whole or in part. So be careful. And be thinking.

But, since the language of the contract is clear and unambiguous and it is an integrated agreement, exclude the extrinsic evidence, says the court.

Note how the condition mechanism works for the closing – once all the conditions have been met, the closing can occur. Alternatively, they can be waived, excused, or estopped away. Once they are gone, they are gone, and you must recover, if at all, under the reps and warranties that survive, here a more limited MAC that only covers out of the ordinary course performance.

The argument in paragraph 11 that the buyer says you can't know the financial condition on the date of closing, so you must be making a warranty or a representation is good, but doesn't fly when one labels the provision a condition, at least for this court.

Closing waived the condition.

NOTES AND QUESTIONS

1. Suppose a provision in the construction contract in question had read: "The obligation of the general contractor to make payment to the subcontractor for any work is subject to the condition precedent that the general contractor shall have received payment for such work from the owner or the owner's agent."

If the owner declared bankruptcy and did not pay the general contractor, would the general contractor have to pay the subcontractor? *See* Gulf Construction Co. v. Self, 676 S.W.2d 624 (1984) *(risk of non-payment by the owner on a construction contract was not shifted from the contractor to the subcontractor unless there was a clear, unequivocal and expressed agreement between the subcontractor and the contractor to that effect).* **If you're not sure, how would you draft the provision to make sure it did? Or is that possible?**

2. The conditions we've seen so far had to occur before a contract came into being or a duty became effective. These are called conditions precedent (pronounced "pre SEED n't"). They are by far the most common type of condition. But there is a second type of condition called a *condition subsequent*. If a condition subsequent occurs, a duty that is already in effect is discharged or modified. *(The R2d treats conditions subsequent as a form of discharge of duty, an alternative analysis that is preferred by some; it also unduly confuses some students by introducing what seems like a whole new subject matter . . .).* The case that follows illustrates this.

♦ - - ♦

Gray v. Gardner
Supreme Court of Massachusetts
17 Mass. 188 (1821)

Contingent promissory note to pay additional sum if no more sperm oil delivered to local market between 4/1 and 10/1 this year than last year. I.E., that is the condition. Based upon vessels "arrived" – here, a vessel with more oil got "to the Nantucket Roads" but not "at" Nantucket or New Bedford" – held, condition, burden on the defendants, not met – not at anchor, not moored at dock. Strict compliance required, the condition was not in the power of defendants to control, it appears.

♦ - - ♦

Inman v. Clyde Hall Drilling Co., Inc.
Supreme Court of Alaska
369 P.2d 498 (1962)

Derrickman sues for wrongful discharge (firing w/o cause).

Employment contract had a *notice of claim requirement* – provide notice of claim within 30 days of events giving rise to the claim and then wait six months before filing suit. *Clause says this is a condition precedent to any recovery.*

He just goes ahead and sues. (Later says that he thought the suit would be the notice – this doesn't fly under the contract language, but he could have thought it if he was a stereotypical derrickman—or maybe via conversations with counsel—discuss ethics and suborning purgery).

Held: Dismissal was proper. Freedom of contract will not be disturbed unless there are constitutional or legislative prohibitions [para. 3] or there is inequity and injustice that rises to the level of unconscionability [para. 4], which this court views as an unfair and unreasonable standard [para. 5].

His misreading and lame after-the-fact notice argument is not compelling to this court.

So, what is the outcome for him? Pretty drastic – he lost his claim entirely.

Alaska, 1962, who are we going to side with, if we are engaged in result-oriented jurisprudence? Oil or oil men?

◆ - - ◆

Clark v. West
Court of Appeals of New York
193 N.Y. 349, 86 N. E. 1. (1908)

Clark contracts to write books for West Publishing for $2 per page plus an additional $4 per page if he will "totally abstain from the use of intoxicating liquors."

He delivers, but he also drinks.

Held: The drinking ban is a condition precedent that can be waived.
It may have been waived (send back for trial). So the motion to dismiss for failure to state a claim must be reversed.

The defendant (West) claimed that the non-drinking provisions were part of the consideration and therefore could not be waived except by a new agreement supported by additional consideration.

The plaintiff (Clark) claimed it was a condition precedent that could be waived without a formal agreement or new consideration.

The court holds that West could have insisted upon literal performance, but if an express waiver was made, as alleged, then strict performance not required.

Note that the court holds open the right to sue for damages for the breached condition (even if waived?) -- a little odd -- but what would those damages be, anyway?

Definition of Waiver: A voluntary and intentional relinquishment of a known right.

301

Waiver – a sub-species of equitable estoppel? "Sure" – a party may be precluded by acts or conduct from asserting a right to the detriment of another party who, entitled to rely on such conduct, has acted upon it. Or, "no"– but closely related, as waiver does not, strictly speaking, require reliance (but practically speaking it often does). The two terms are often conflated in the cases–be specific and choose the right one – the one that you mean.

NOTES AND QUESTIONS

1. In the fall of 1899, about four months before he entered into the contract in question, Mr. Clark was dismissed from his position as a law professor at Washington & Lee University, a position he had only had for a month or two. The university president explained that Professor Clark was "addicted to drinking beyond what would be proper in a college professor." *It is doubtful that a university president today would be so forthright. Rather, Clark would probably be said to be resigning to "spend more time with his family."*

2. In the next case, the difficulty of administering contracts, conditions, and waivers of conditions in practice is illustrated. The best laid contracts and plans can easily go awry.

◆ - - ◆

Burger King v. Family Dining, Inc.
United States District Court, Eastern District, Pennsylvania
426 F. Supp. 485 (1977)

Master franchisee of Burger King (friend of founder). Exclusive territory and schedule to build and operate 10 BK restaurants in 10 years. That schedule is the condition at issue.

Delay and difficulty and BK had previously granted waivers. As it becomes a big company, it gets less personal with the master franchisee, but still grants waiver until, suddenly, it insists upon strict performance, declares a forfeiture and termination of the exclusive territorial agreement [para. 21]. "The abrupt manner in which Burger King's position was communicated to Family Dining, under the circumstances, was not straightforward."

Paragraph 28, ". . . after one party by conduct indicates that literal performance will not be required, he cannot without notice and a reasonable time begin demanding literal performance."

(Here, Kuney asks "Why doesn't the parol evidence rule block the evidence?" A: We are not talking about prior or contemporaneous agreements. <u>Simple</u>. But the question can wake students up.)

Practical Lesson: Manage your and your clients' affairs strictly and do not rely upon personal relationships for comfort. People move on.

NOTES AND QUESTIONS

1. What was the condition involved in this case and what was the duty which arose or ceased if the condition occurred?

Opening restaurants on schedule; failure to do so would cause loss of exclusivity .

2. Suppose that in May, 1973, when the letter quoted in paragraph 19 was being written, you had been asked to give legal advice to Burger King. **What would you have told them to do with Mr. Ferris?**

Be more definite. If you are going to declare a default and exercise remedies, do it. No point in issuing ambiguous letters and notices. Be straightforward and clear. You are building a record for later litigation.

♦ -- ♦

Note—Teacher's Manual Only: Tennessee Code Annotated § 47-50-112(c), proposed and backed by proactive financial institutions faced with the problem of purported waivers of provisions in loan documents, provides:

> *If any. . . security agreement, note, deed of trust, or other contract contains a provision to the effect that no waiver of any terms or provisions thereof shall be valid unless such waiver is in writing, no court shall give effect to any such waiver unless it is in writing.*

The authors have not surveyed other states to determine how many have taken a similar approach, but believe that it is increasingly common. Knowledge of local law is important. When doing deals outside of one's home jurisdiction, consulting competent, local counsel is invaluable.

♦ -- ♦

Cantrell-Waind & Associates v. Guillaume Motorsports, Inc.
Court of Appeals of Arkansas
62 Ark. App. 66, 968 S.W.2d 72 (1998)

Lease with option to buy real property, if option exercised within first 24 months, then 10% of the monthly rental payments discount is applicable to the purchase price of $295,000 and the credit decreases by 2% per year. For a commission to be payable, sale must close in first 24 months, and then it is a $15,200 commission.

Take a look at that arrangement and understand it. It is likely that there was no other payment made to the leasing broker, or at least it was a small payment.

Within the 24 months, tenant decides to exercise option to buy. Seller approaches tenant/buyer and offers to credit him with ½ the commission avoided if they delay closing beyond 24 months. Tenant/buyer declines.

Bank loan (financing contingency) satisfied within 24 month period.

"Can we schedule closing?" says title company. "Yes," says the seller, "but I will be out of town until month 25 [not really!]. No, we can't use a power of attorney."

Sale closes 14 days into month 25 – no commission paid.

Trial Court – no duty to close within period, and commission was thus clearly avoidable.

Court of Appeals: Reversed. The term is a condition precedent. A party has an implied obligation not to do anything that would prevent, hinder, or delay performance or occurrence [para. 15] – to do so will excuse the condition [paras. 12-16].

So, remand for a determination as to whether a triable issue of fact remains.

And, if you want summary judgment, you have to move for it! [para. 19].

◆ - - ◆

Western Hills, Oregon, Ltd. v. Pfau
Supreme Court of Oregon
265 Or. 137, 508 P.2d 201 (1973)

Contract to purchase land subject to a condition. "Closing of transaction is subject to [the] ability of purchasers to negotiate with City of McMinnville as to a planned development satisfactory to both first and second parties within 90 days from [contract] date. A reasonable extension not to exceed 6 months to be granted if necessary."

6 months out, they inform seller that they are not going forward and do not have the approval of a planned unit development – but they abandoned the process themselves! They claim that sewers are too expensive (but they knew this going in, so it can't be argued to support abandonment).

When an agreement contains a condition that is under the control of a party, that party must make a reasonable effort to satisfy the condition (they can't just abandon).

Further, when there is a condition that something be obtained or performed to the satisfaction of a party, there are two types of provisions: (1) those that involve taste, fancy, or personal judgment – for these good faith is all

304

that is required, and (2) those that involve utility, fitness, or value, which can be, measured against some objective criteria – for these ,a rule of reasonableness applies.

Lesson for contract preparation: Your client's approvals and conditions should be subjective and fit category (1) and you should insist that the other side have category (2) conditions or, better yet, completely objective standards by which to measure performance. But, as in *Burger King v. Family Dining*, course of conduct and risk of undue forfeiture can undermine even this structure.

♦ - - ♦

Laurel Race Course, Inc. v. Regal Construction
Court of Appeals of Maryland
274 Md. 142, 333 A.2d 319 (1975)

Laurel is developing its race course.

Regal Construction contracts to do it.

Watkins was the engineering firm.

Laurel is not happy with final project and refuses to pay the final bill.

The work was to be done in strict accordance with the bid specs and under the direction of the engineer.

Watkins, engineer, established as Laurel's agent with power to inspect, reject, interpret specs and resolve disputes.

Laurel could withhold payments for failure to fix defects and retainage was set at 10% until final completion.

Guarantee (really a warranty) of all construction against defective materials, equipment, and workmanship for 12 months.

Making a faster, all weather track, with new substrate and drainage tiles. Watkins recommends not paying full bill as defects are present – big rocks are coming up, the amount of clay is excessive, and the drain tiles have not been laid to grade and mortared.

The issue here is whether the actual failure of Regal to procure Regal's certificate for payment is a condition precedent to liability under the written contract.

The general rule is that *absent fraud or bad faith*, where payments under a contract are due only when the certificate of an architect or engineer is issued, production of the certificate becomes a condition precedent to liability of the owner [paras. 19, 20]. There are also the *waiver and estoppel exceptions*.

The court's decision does not overrule the parties' dispute mechanism. Note the limits of the holding – at some point the refusal to issue the certificate becomes bad faith or fraudulent, so the court can overrule it.

◆ - - ◆

Summing Up Express Conditions:

A CONDITION is an event not certain to occur, which must occur or be excused before a duty arises (or that, when it occurs, cancels or modifies a duty). All conditions are subsequent to the contract – that is not the distinction.

CONDITIONS PRECEDENT are conditions that, when they happen, create a duty.

CONDITIONS SUBSEQUENT are conditions that, when they happen, cancel or modify a duty.

Dove v. Rose Acre Farms, Inc., He was knowledgeable (why is this important? No unfair surprise, thus no unconscionability claim here). The condition was central to the contract and not a collateral matter. (What does this matter? Defeats his argument that there was substantial compliance – this condition was at the heart of the deal.) Condition not met, no duty to pay arises.

Restatement (Second) of Contracts § 229. [a] To the extent that the non-occurrence of a condition would cause disproportionate forfeiture, [b] a court may excuse the non-occurrence of that condition [c] unless its occurrence was a material part of the agreed exchange (i.e., the party had assumed the risk).

Howard v. Federal Crop Insurance Corp., When in doubt, construe a possible condition as a covenant to avoid forfeiture. There is no such thing as magic language, but the right language sure can help.

Carter v. Schoettle Co., Note how the condition mechanism works for the closing – once all the conditions have been met, the closing can occur. Alternatively, they can be waived, excused, or estopped away. Once they are gone, they are gone, and you must recover, if at all, under the reps and warranties that survive, here a more limited MAC that only covers out of the ordinary course of performance.

Gray v. Gardner, Based upon vessels "arrived" – here, vessel with more got to the Nantucket Roads but not at Nantucket or New Bedford – held: condition, burden on the defendants, not met – not at anchor, not moored at dock. Strict compliance required, condition not in power of defendants to control, it appears.

Inman v. Clyde Hall Drilling Co., Notice of Claims provision. Strictly construed. This is common.

Clark v. West, Application of R2d § 229. Excuse condition of not drinking. Or was this a waiver by West?

Battista, Waiver by conduct. Of a no waiver clause.

Cantrell- Waind & Associates v. Guillaume Motorsports, Inc., A party has an implied obligation not to do anything that would prevent, hinder, or delay performance or occurrence – to do so will excuse the condition.

Burger King v. Family Dining, ". . . after one party by conduct indicates that literal performance will not be required, he cannot without notice and a reasonable time begin demanding literal performance."

Western Hills, Oregon, Ltd. v. Pfau, When an agreement contains a condition that is under the control of a party, that party must make a reasonable effort to satisfy the condition (they can't just abandon).

Further, when there is a condition that something be obtained or performed to the satisfaction of a party, there are two types of provisions: (1) those that involve taste, fancy, or personal judgment – for these good faith is all that is required, and (2) those that involve utility, fitness, or value, which can be measured against some objective criteria – for these a rule of reasonableness applies.

Lesson for contract preparation: Your client's approvals and conditions should be subjective and fit category (1) and you should insist that the other side have category (2) conditions or, better yet, completely objective standards by which to measure performance.

Laurel Race Course, Inc. v. Regal Construction, The general rule is that absent fraud or bad faith, where payments under a contract are due only when the certificate of an architect or engineer is issued, production of the certificate becomes a condition precedent to liability of the owner. There are also the waiver and estoppel exceptions.

Next, we are off to constructive conditions. Good time to crystallize your thinking about express conditions as it is the foundation of this next subject.

NOTES AND QUESTIONS

1. The litany continues: Time or another term is of the essence; Nonseverability; No amendment or waiver by conduct; All amendments and waivers must be in writing; Recitations that both parties have been represented by counsel, or at least had the opportunity to consult with counsel, have read the agreement and understand it. All these provisions are attempts by the parties to avoid having a court later refuse to enforce a condition by finding that is was waived by conduct, was unconscionable, would otherwise lead to a forfeiture, and

the like. A determined court can generally find some way to excuse a failed condition should it choose to do so, and can often do so in a ruling that is so fact-based that it is largely immune on appeal, at least if counsel has done her job and presented the judge with an adequate record to protect the ruling . **(Why are fact-based decisions more immune on appeal than purely legal determinations?** Consider the applicable standards of review.)

Counsel can best guard against this result by: (a) drafting the consequences of failure of a condition explicitly into the same provision, not just leaving it to the default and remedy provisions of the agreement, (b) employing good boilerplate to attempt to document the parties' intention that all the terms of the document be strictly construed, and (c) explicitly stating the reason that the condition was included and that it was a fundamental inducement for one or more of the parties to enter into the transaction. This is not foolproof, but it is a good start.

Clients, further, should be guided through the process of documenting waivers of conditions so that each waiver is as limited as possible and so that client conduct does not undo the results that would otherwise be obtained through careful drafting and contracting. The best lawyerly solution or structure can be undone by a client's subsequent actions, so designing a legal structure that is usable by the client is critical to its success.

2. When reviewing or analyzing conditions, focus on what is likely to occur if the condition is not met. Does the client have an appropriate course of action— or cause of action—to pursue under the terms of the contract. If not, one should be provided. Also, consider whether this test is met for the opposing party. **If not, is it better for your client if this remains the case? Or is it better to attempt to fix the potential problem and fill the void?** Answers to these last questions will vary enormously depending on the circumstances.

Lawyering Skills Problem

Your client is a trade organization of building contractors. You have been hired to draft a standard-form contract that contractors and their customers will use on building projects that are too small to make it economical for both of the parties to hire a lawyer to negotiate and draft on their behalf. The contract is to be between the owner and the contractor and is to cover such things as when various phases of the work are to be completed and when progress payments are to be made. The standard form contract has to be fairly evenhanded (i.e., it can't give the contractor an unfair advantage) because the people the contractors will be dealing with are sophisticated enough that they will not sign a one-sided contract. Explain how you would use express conditions to limit the risks to which the parties are exposed.

CONSTRUCTIVE CONDITIONS

— ◆ —

Kingston v. Preston
Court of King's Bench
2 Doug. 689 (1773)

Sale of a business upon retirement. Covenant servant arrangement for a year to learn the business, and then partners to take over silk merchant's trade, paying 250£ per month until the stock has been reduced to 4,000£. All this is after the partners have furnished sufficient security. When the time comes, the old man refuses to go, citing insufficient security.

Held: These covenants are dependent, one upon the other, and the furnishing of security is an implied condition precedent to the duty to turn over the business.

There are three types of covenants:

(1) Mutual and independent covenants – no implied condition, where a breach gives rise to a claim for damages but not cessation of performance.

(2) Conditional, dependent covenants – implied condition, where a breach gives rise to a claim for damages and cessation of performance.

(3) Mutual, simultaneous covenants – tender is sufficient and if there is no counter tender, then claim for damages and cessation of performance.

Constructive conditions are implied when the parties fail to specify that covenants are conditions of counter-covenants.

Restatement 2d § 234 – put on overhead.

Restatement 2d § 234(1) says – if mutual, simultaneous interpretation possible, use that (unless provided otherwise).

Restatement 2d § 234(2) says – if one performance takes time, then that performance is due first (unless provided otherwise).

NOTES AND QUESTIONS

Prior to *Kingston v. Preston*, English law presented the following anomalous situation: Suppose Builder and Owner entered into a contract whereby Builder promised to build a house on Owner's land and Owner agreed to pay Builder 100£. Builder then, instead of building the house, went off and got drunk (a not uncommon occurrence). When Builder sobered up he could go to a solicitor and have a suit filed against Owner, alleging that Owner had breached his promise to pay the 100£. If Owner had failed to put an express condition in the contract, making his promise to pay the money conditional upon the building actually being built, Builder would have a good cause of action. (Owner would of course have a cause of action against Builder, but he would have to get a lawyer and go through the hassle of a lawsuit. Even then he might not be able to prove that the building would have been worth 100£, so he might have come out on the short end.)

After *Kingston v. Preston*, the courts began imposing constructive conditions where the parties neglected to put express conditions in their contracts. Constructive conditions are generally conditions that the other party perform her obligations under the contract, or at least that she be ready, willing, and able to do so (called "tender" of performance). For example, suppose Seller and Buyer contract for the purchase and sale of a car. Seller being ready, willing, and able to deliver the car is a constructive condition to Buyer's obligation to pay the money. Likewise, Buyer being ready, willing, and able to deliver the money is a constructive condition to Seller's obligation to deliver the car. Thus if Seller fails to deliver the car, Buyer not only has an action for breach of contract, she is also relieved of her obligation to pay the money. Seller's delivery of the car is a constructive condition to Buyer's obligation to pay the money and Buyer's payment of the money is a constructive condition to Seller's obligation to deliver the car.

Where it is possible for the parties' performances to be rendered simultaneously, they are to be rendered simultaneously unless the language or the circumstances indicate to the contrary. *See* R2d § 234(1). Thus in our example of the delivery of the car, the presumption would be that the car would be delivered at the same time the full purchase price is paid. But the contract could provide that the buyer has to make a deposit ahead of time or that she is to be given extra time in which to pay all or part of the purchase price.

Sometimes one of the performances takes place over time. For instance, it takes time to build a house. The rule here is that, unless the parties intend otherwise, where one performance takes time, that performance is required before the other party's performance is due. *See* R2d § 234(2). It has been said that the theory behind the development of this rule is that the performance that takes time is usually some sort of labor (like building a house) whereas the performance that can be rendered instantaneously is usually paying money, and the people that had money were more dependable than those that did the work. In other words, the builder might take the money, get drunk, and never build the house. There may have been some truth in that, especially in England in the eighteenth and nineteenth centuries, where the rule developed. Nevertheless, some will seize upon the explanation that the judges in those days came from the monied class, and they were simply looking out for their own.

The rule isn't as harsh as it seems. Builders can and do protect themselves by requiring the owner to make "progress payments" as the construction proceeds. (Well-drafted agreements make these payments express conditions to the duty of the builder to do any further work.) So the rule requiring the person whose performance will take time to complete to fully perform before being paid anything is only a default rule. It only applies if the parties don't provide differently in their agreement.

The two cases that follow illustrate one important difference between constructive conditions and express conditions. As we saw in *Dove v. Rose Acre Farms*, express conditions have to be performed precisely and to the letter, unless they are excused. Constructive conditions, however, only have to be "substantially performed."

♦ - - ♦

Jacob & Youngs, Inc. v. Kent
Court of Appeals of New York
230 N.Y. 239, 129 N.E. 889 (1921)

The "Reading Pipe case." (In which Cardozo sanctions different than promised work and substantial performance). Contract specifies Reading (Pa.) Pipe, but not all Reading Pipe used. As a result, architect's final certificate was refused and final payment was not made.

Paragraph 4 - "The courts never say that one who makes a contract fills the measure of his duty by less than full performance. They do say, however, that an omission, both trivial and innocent, will sometimes be atoned for by allowance of the resulting damage, and will not always be the breach of a condition to be followed by a forfeiture.

Some promises are so plainly independent that they can never by fair construction be conditions of one another. Others are so plainly dependent that they must always be conditions. Others, though dependent and thus conditions when there is a departure in point of substance, will be viewed as independent and collateral when the departure is insignificant" [para 4].

Note that strict compliance is possible – but the requirement must be very clear. Thus the evolution of the "_____ is of the essence" clause. But better drafting would be to tie the condition to the performance and use events of default, declarations of default, and specific remedies. Explain.

So, the owner's damages are the delta of FMV of what was promised and what was delivered (which could be nothing at all as is probably the case here). This is the basic breach of warranty damage calculation. Is this an example of a disproportionate harm limitation on consequential damages? Do you think there should be one?

Dissent – willful neglect here. Demand strict performance. Probably more "genuine" here. It may have been a mere whim, but do it that way if the contract says so.

Note the motion for reargument – what had the owner's attorneys argued in an attempt to break the 4:3 majority? Contract was pretty specific!!! Note that all judges concur.

NOTES AND QUESTIONS

1. Assume that the specification of "Reading Pipe" was part of a very detailed set of specifications and procedures for building the custom home at issue. Assume further that these specifications and procedures had been dickered over and negotiated as part of the contract. **In light of these assumptions, do you think the majority or the dissent got it right? Why or why not?**

2. Justice Cardozo, author of the opinion in the *Lucy, Lady Duff Gordon* case, was willing to imply a "reasonable efforts to perform" term into that contract. **Is that consistent with his willingness to excuse strict compliance with the detailed provisions in their contract and its specifications in this case?**

3. **What could Mr. Kent, a successful New York lawyer, have done to ensure that he got Reading Pipe and that his other specifications were followed?**

4. **How can you contract for perfect performance? Would a clause providing that (a) the contractor's strict performance of the contract with regard to each and every covenant and specification was at the heart of the contract, (b) strict performance was an express condition precedent to owner's duty to pay, and (c) failure of the contractor to perform strictly in accordance with the contract terms was intended by the parties to result in a forfeiture of the contractor's right to payment work?** *Consider* R2d § 229. **Is there no way to require perfect performance?**

5. **What is the downside, if any, of including a condition that may, at least in hindsight, appear over-reaching? Is it just that the court may blue line (cross out) that one provision?**

◆ -- ◆

Suit by owner to set aside mechanic's lien and suit by builder to foreclose it out. (What is a mechanic's lien? What does it mean to foreclose it out? Explain. Most students have difficulty conceptualizing liens.)

Allegations that the contractor did not perform the contract is a good and workmanlike manner and that defendant did not substantially perform.

What was at issue – yellow streaks in roof, not of a uniform color. It would need to be completely replaced to be fixed.

Paragraph 12 – the concept of material breach is introduced. A material breach is one that goes to the root of the matter and will excuse performance on the other side of the contract (here, payment). Sometimes this is analyzed as the doctrine of substantial performance (i.e., no material breach).

Paragraph 14 – hard to tell what a material breach is or what is substantial performance.

Was this to be a contract to install a roof? Or a roof of uniform color? Trial court found the latter, and there is evidence to support that finding, so not a mistake of law – thus affirm. Again, note the operation of the standard of review.

♦ - - ♦

NOTES

If a party has not substantially performed, we say that they have committed a *material breach*. It follows from the concept of constructive conditions that if one party has committed a material breach, the other party has no further duty to perform until the breach has been remedied. There are no precise standards for determining whether a party has committed a material breach. Read R2d § 241, which lists five "circumstances" that are "significant" in determining whether there has been a material breach. This list of factors should not be considered exhaustive. In determining whether there has been a material breach (or a failure to substantially perform, which is basically the same thing), a court should consider any factor that bears on the question of whether the non-breaching party should be excused from her duty to perform (and, as the next case shows, allowed to walk away from the contract) or whether she should be required to perform and be left with only a claim for damages on account of the breach.

♦ - - ♦

Jafari v. Wally Findlay Galleries
United States District Court, Southern District, New York
741 F. Supp. 64 (1990)

Does the UCC apply to the sale of a painting when one of the parties is not a merchant? YES. Dispell the notion that the UCC only applies to merchants.

Jafari was a surgeon that wanted to buy a Dali. But he wants a certificate of authenticity or other assurances (discuss Dali forgeries and what good an expert opinion would do).

They make a deal: Jafari to pay by certified check by 2/16/88. But he doesn't, so DiLorenzo does not ship.

On March 11, painting reoffered to Jafari, who wants still more authentication. On March 24, another expert vouches for the painting, and DiLorenzo asks for payment of the $210,000. But Jafari did not have the check with him – says come to Philadelphia and let's talk it over.

DiLorenzo does not go, sells it instead to Renee Fotouhi, who sells it at an art auction to Jafari for $330,000 (Ha!).

Court assumes there was a contract as of Jan. 26, when the first expert authenticated the painting and the purchase price was agreed to. The contract did not specify a delivery date –thus imply a reasonable time under UCC 2-309. DiLorenzo is repeatedly tendering, it is Jafari who is not, even as late as March 25.

Failure to tender is a material breach and non-substantial performance of the contract, excusing counter performance. No recovery for Jafari. He wasted $120,000 and a lot of people's time!

Note 2, following the case, is about the difficulties of telling just when a breach becomes material or performance is not substantially complete. One never wants to terminate one's own performance under the contract too soon and become the breacher! Thus, again, drafting with events of default and remedies is the way to go. Discuss.

NOTES AND QUESTIONS

1. The court oversimplifies a little bit when it says that a *material breach* discharges the non-breaching party's further obligations to perform. A material breach only suspends the non-breaching party's obligation to perform. That is, the non-breaching party doesn't have to do anything now, but she may have to perform later if the breaching party cures the default. A *total breach* discharges the non-breaching party's obligation to perform and gives rise to a damage claim for breach of the whole contract. R2d § 242 sets forth the factors to be taken into account in determining whether a breach is a total breach. As with a material

breach, the test is flexible and open-ended. In trying to determine whether there has been a total breach, consider any fact that bears on the question whether it is fair to require the non-breaching party to give the breaching party more time before declaring the contract is at an end and taking steps to mitigate his damages.

2. Determining whether there has been a total breach is one of the toughest decisions you will have to make as a practicing lawyer. There will be times when your client is incurring losses it may never be able to recover (either because of problems of proof or because the breaching party may go bankrupt), but if the client terminates the contract too soon, the client will be the one committing the total breach and the one held liable. That was the problem Mr. DiLorenzo faced. If the court had decided he should have let Jafari jerk him around a little more before he pulled the plug, DiLorenzo would have been liable for damages.

◆ - - ◆

Carter v. Sherburne Corp.
Supreme Court of Vermont
132 Vt. 88, 315 A.2d 870 (1974)

Road construction contracts – developer claims breach, contractor claims compliance (substantial completion). Trial court finds for contractor. This court affirms.

When time is of the essence, timely performance is a constructive condition of the other party's duty, usually the duty to pay. But time is not of the essence in a building or construction contract in the absence of an express condition saying that it is. Paragraph 7: Delays are attributable to the defendant. Here, no time is of the essence clause.

NOTES AND QUESTIONS

A newspaper cartoon showed a woman answering her doorbell. It was winter and there was snow on the ground, but the boy at the door said "Trick or treat!" He was dressed in sunglasses, a ball cap, a plaid shirt, and jeans hanging low on his hips.

"Clem," she said, "it's February. You're four months late."

"I'm dressed up as a contractor. They're always four months late."

"Well, then, I suppose I can give you a piece of candy."

"There were some expenses not in my original estimate. You owe me ten more pieces of candy."

◆ - - ◆

(b) Express the same argument under §§ 241 and 242 of the Restatement.

It's even harder to make the argument under the Restatement.

Under section 241:

(1) *The client isn't being deprived of the benefit he expected. The benefit is the project as a whole. I'd make the argument that the benefit is on-time completion, but if I were a judge I wouldn't buy it.*

(2) *The client can argue that because it can't prove with certainty the sales that will be lost because the project came on the market late, it can't be compensated for the loss. The counter-argument is that it should be able to get a substitute painter in and deduct the cost as damages without it being a material breach that would justify withholding 8 times the cost of the painting.*

(3) *If the breach allows the client to withhold 8 times the cost of the painting, that would probably constitute a forfeiture. I'd argue that Construction Company got 75% of the contract price even though it screwed up, but that, too, would probably be a loser. They might, of course, be able to recover on quantum meruit, and if they could, that would cut into my client's windfall, as I would explain to him most forcefully.*

(4) *Here I'd pull out all the evidence I could find of Construction Company making promises in the past and then failing to perform them. There are usually plenty of those in every construction project.*

(5) *The problem doesn't give any indication of bad faith, but I'd certainly see if I could find any. Unfortunately (or maybe fortunately for the sake of justice) it looks like all the bad faith is on the client's side.*

Under section 242: I'd argue that you can't separate the client's right to replace Construction Company (which arguably it is entitled to do) from its right to terminate its duty to make any future payments (which seems quite unfair). Arguably it takes a total breach to allow the client to terminate Construction Company's right to finish the job and that same total breach terminates their right to receive any further payment (except for quantum meruit).

(c) Suppose that instead of saying "Time is of the essence," the contract had said, "Completion by March 1, 2002 of all work to be completed hereunder shall be a condition precedent to Developer's duty to pay any outstanding sums due and failure to complete all work by March 1, 2002 shall entitle Developer to terminate this contract and recover damages."

(i) Would this improve Developer's position?

Is this just form over substance? Or is it better drafting: posturing the term as a clear condition precedent tied to the consequences of the failure to satisfy the condition?

(ii) Would you expect a contractor to sign a contract with a provision like this?

This would of course make it much more likely that the court would deny Construction Company any further recovery. Moreover, the fact that the client could have bargained for such a clause makes it unlikely that the court would reach the harsh result the client wants without it. Under normal circumstances, a contractor would not be likely to agree to such a clause. But if the retainage was small, the deadline looked easy to meet, and the contractor expected a decent profit on the job, it might well agree to such a provision.

This is a chance to remind the students that a party (including your own clients) will often agree to a one-sided provision if the overall deal looks good. If the client wants to agree to a bad legal deal that he thinks is a good business deal, don't be a deal-killing lawyer. Just write a CYA letter or otherwise document your cautionary advice on the matter. On the other hand, if the other side is agreeing too readily to the tough protections you drafted for your client, you'd better think about what you (or the client) has overlooked on other aspects of the deal.

♦ - - ♦

PLAYING IN THE BAND: CONSTRUCTIVE CONDITIONS, SUBSTANTIAL PERFORMANCE, AND MATERIAL BREACH

♦ - - ♦

PROBLEM 24-2

Homer and Marge ("H&M") entered into a contract with Builder, who was to build a home for them. Because H&M are now getting a million dollars an episode, it was to be quite a place. The contract provided for progress payments to be made as construction progressed. The last payment of $100,000 was to be made when construction was completed. The house was finished two months late. When it was finally done, H&M went for their last walk-through and discovered that the painting in the living room was so badly done that the room would have to be repainted. Builder refused to do the repainting and H&M hired a painter to do it at a cost of $2,000. H&M also incurred additional rent of $5,000 because construction was late. H&M are now living in the house. They haven't paid Builder the last $100,000.

(a) If Builder's breach was a total breach, what are H&M's rights and obligations?

Don't have to pay the last $100,000.
Builder may be able to recover in quantum meruit.

This problem is just to make sure the weakest students in the class haven't missed the forest for all the trees. If the breach was a total breach, they can stop paying and keep the $100,000. If it was not a material breach, they can only get the damages that they can prove. In fact, they may be in breach themselves for withholding more than they were entitled to.

(b) If Builder's breach was not a material breach, what are H&M's rights and obligations?

They can recover $7,000 in damages.

◆ - - ◆

K & G Construction Co. v. Harris
Court of Appeals of Maryland
223 Md. 305, 164 A.2d 457 (1960)

Bench Trial below: "Does a contractor, damaged by a sub-contractor's failure to perform a portion of his work in a workmanlike manner, have a right, under the circumstances of this case, to withhold, in partial satisfaction of said damages, an installment payment, which, under the terms of the contract, was due the subcontractor, unless the negligent performance of his work excused its payment?"

Paragraphs 7-9 contain a nice statement of the law of implied conditions.

Note the horrible sentence structure and comment re: same.

The answer is Yes.

1. What happened? Sub knocked down a wall of the contractor's house with a bulldozer. (This is a breach of the covenant to do work in a workmanlike manner and in accordance with best practices.) It cost $450 more than the contract price to obtain substitute performance.

2. Review law re: dependent and independent conditions [para. 16]. The presumption is that conditions are mutually dependent, so excuse performance. When the subcontractor negligently knocked down the house, he breached his covenant of workmanlike performance, and this was a material breach, excusing counter performance (payment).

319

3. Notions of Setoff and Recoupment (discuss and differentiate – set off requires mutuality of the parties, recoupment is the extra element of "same transaction," which is very flexible, especially in Medicare cases).

◆ - - ◆

Britton v. Turner
Superior Court of Judicature of New Hampshire
6 N.H. 481 (1834)

Plaintiff can't recover under contract as they did not labor for the whole year and that was a condition of counter performance. Can they recover in Quantum Meruit anyway?

Maybe.

"In the case of a failure to perform such special contract, by the default of the party contracting to do the service, if the money is not due by the terms of the special agreement he is not entitled to recover for his labor, or for the materials furnished, unless the other party receives what has been done, or furnished, and upon the whole case derives a benefit from it."

NET benefit will be payable, capped by contract price for labor.

◆ - - ◆

PROBLEM 24-3

Owner and Roofer enter into a contract for the re-roofing of Owner's home. The contract provides that the price will be $4,000. Roofer spends $3,000 doing the job. Owner claims the roof is the wrong color. She refuses to pay, and gets another roofer to re-roof the house. She pays the second roofer $4,200. Owner sues and it is determined that Roofer committed a total breach of the contract by putting on the wrong color of shingles. It is also determined that the value of the work done by Roofer was $3,500. Case law in the jurisdiction provides that in the proper circumstances a party who has committed a total breach can recover under quantum meruit. **How much is Roofer entitled to recover from Owner?** (Owner has, to date, made no payments to Roofer.)

   a. $4,000

   b. $3,500

   c. $3,000

   d. Nothing

Answer is "d" as there was a total breach and no benefit at all was received by Owner. No recovery under contract because of material breach. No quantum meruit recovery as the whole job had to be redone. No benefit had been conferred.

PROBLEM 24-4

Contractor and Sub entered into a contract under the terms of which Sub was to do part of the construction on a dam project for a price of $2.5 million. There was a great deal of friction on the project. Contractor claimed that Sub's work did not meet specifications. Sub countered that its work did meet specifications and even if it did not, it was the fault of Contractor for furnishing defective plans, failing to properly prepare the site, and denying it access to the project at certain times.

Finally, Contractor and Sub got into a major dispute, and Contractor threw Sub off the job. Contractor got another sub to finish the job for $500,000. At the time it left the job, Sub had spent $2.8 million, and it would have had to spend another $400,000 to complete the job. It had been paid $1.5 million. The court found as a fact that the value of the work Sub had done prior to its dismissal was $3.2 million.

(a)   How much is Sub entitled to recover if it is determined that Sub was the party who committed the first total breach?

(*The answer is in* Britton v. Turner *[para. 14]: Reasonable worth of benefit received less payments made less other party's damages. Here: $3.2 million less 1.5 million less $0 [or -0.5 million]= $1.5 million, [para 18]: but this is capped by the unpaid contract price of $1 million, less the damages of cover price, $500,000= $500,000.*)

(b)   How much is Sub entitled to recover if it is determined that Contractor was the party who committed the first total breach?

(*See* Southern Painting Co. *in Chapter 18. If subcontractor were to not be the breaching party, the contract price limitations are removed and we are left with reasonable value of benefit conferred less amounts paid, here 3.2 million less 1.5 million, or 1.7 million.) Do you see why, in a messy contract dispute, it is important to make a sufficient record showing that your client is not the first to breach?*

◆ -- ◆

NOTE

Because the law of implied conditions is so fuzzy, good contracts use Events of Default, Declarations of Default, Opportunities to Cure, and Specifications of Remedies to address the situation. *Every contract carries within it the implied covenant by each party to provide a remedy to the other in case of breach. The parties are free, however, to make this covenant express and use conditions to do so. It is far superior to provide for a detailed remedies section in the contract rather than leave the matter wholly to the common law, the statutes, and the courts.*

For example, in a secured loan agreement, the following could be events of default:

- breach of warranty
- failure to pay on time
- failure to perform any other obligation in a timely manner
- grant of a subordinate security interest in the collateral
- sale of the collateral w/o paying over the proceeds or lender consent
- material impairment of the value of the collateral
- violation of financial covenants

If an event of default occurs, the lender can choose to declare a default, or it may be automatic. In truth, some sort of notice will always be required, even for automatic defaults.

There may be a cure period for the event, usually triggered by notice from the lender. Some lenders don't like to grant cure periods and just like to convince borrowers that they won't default them for minor problems – this gives them the whip hand if they need it – and remember, while the friendly loan officer selling you the loan may be someone that you would trust with a
whip, her buddy in collections may be someone that you would not want to meet in a dark alley!

Specified remedies can include: ceasing future advances of funds, accelerating obligations, obtaining possession of collateral, requiring the debtor to assemble collateral, allowing for inspections, conducting an auction (that shall be deemed commercially reasonable). *Can you think of what remedies could be provided for in a real property lease? A personal property lease? An intellectual property license? A franchise agreement?*

CHAPTER 25

SALES: CONTRACT FORMATION AND PERFORMANCE UNDER THE UNIFORM COMMERCIAL CODE

— ◆ —

A. THE PERFECT TENDER RULE

Bullet point list of what is important to emphasize at the beginning of class:

- Review cure, perfect tender rule, rejection, revocation,
- The Perfect Tender Rule requires that the goods conform to the contract.
- Acceptance changes the burden of proof.

PROBLEM 25-1

Kent, a wealthy lawyer, contracts with Jacob & Youngs Mobile Homes, Inc. to have two mobile homes custom built. One is to be airlifted to a remote area of the Adirondack Mountains, where Kent plans to use it as a hunting and fishing retreat. The other is to be transported to a remote island in the Caribbean, where Kent plans to use it as a winter hideaway. The contract provides that all pipe used in the mobile homes "must be well galvanized, lap welded pipe of the grade known as 'standard pipe' of Reading Manufacturer."

When the mobile homes are completed, Kent goes to the factory to inspect them prior to having them transported to their sites by another contractor. He discovers that they conform to the contract in every respect except that one home has about half the plumbing done with pipe manufactured by the Cohoes Pipe Company rather than with pipe manufactured by the Reading Pipe Company.

1. Does Article 2 apply to this transaction? Isn't building a structure like this a service rather than a sale? Aren't these houses real estate rather than goods? (Regardless of how you come out on this point, assume for the questions that follow that Article 2 does apply.)

Under § 2-105, goods are "all things (including specially manufactured goods) which are movable at the time of identification to the contract for sale other than the money in which the price is to be paid, investment securities (Article 8) and things in action . . . ." Uninstalled mobile homes would seem to fit the definition pretty clearly.

2. Which of the following courses of action are open to Kent?

(i)   accept both homes

(ii)   reject both homes

(iii)   accept the home with the conforming pipe and reject the one with the non-conforming

(iv)   accept the home with the non-conforming pipe and reject the one with the conforming

(v)   reject the non-conforming pipe and accept both homes otherwise

All of these courses of action are available to Kent. The first three are pretty straightforward applications of the statute. The fourth one is helped by the third sentence of comment 1: "Partial acceptance is permitted whether the part of the goods accepted conforms or not."

     3.   Read § 2-714(1). **May Kent accept the homes and then sue for damages?**

Yes. § 2-714(1) expressly so provides. But he may have a hard time proving damages under § 2-714(2).

     4. Refresh your recollection of Jacob & Youngs v. Kent, 230 N.Y. 239, 129 N.E. 889 (1921), from Chapter 24, above. **Does the UCC change the result? How?**

In Jacob & Youngs v. Kent, Justice Cardozo excused what he and the rest of the majority believed was a trivial and innocent variance from the detailed building specifications in the contract. If you take § 2-601 at its word, then there is a perfect tender rule, and Mr. Kent would be able to reject the goods even if the variance from the specifications was "trivial and innocent."

PROBLEM 25-2

     The Mad Hatter ordered 100 yards of gray wool felt from Black Sheep Wool Products, LLC. It was to be delivered in one shipment on September 1. When the wool was delivered, Mr. Hatter discovered that about 10 yards of it was of a slightly darker color than called for by the contract specifications. He can reject the wool felt (choose one):

(1)   only if the discrepancy constitutes a material (no pun intended) breach of the contract.

(2)   only if the discrepancy substantially impairs the value of the felt to him.

(3)   **as long as the goods failed to conform to the contract in any way and he acted in good faith.**

(4)   under no circumstances. There's no way he can reject the felt on the basis of such a minor discrepancy.

The answer is "3" – a duty of good faith is implied into all contracts by the UCC under § 1-304, and good faith is defined in § 2-103 as "honestly in fact and the observance of reasonable commercial standards of fair dealing in the trade" for merchants, and in § 1-201(a)(20) as "honesty in fact and the observance of reasonable commercial standards of fair dealing."

PROBLEM 25-3

Suppose the Mad Hatter in problem 25-2 wanted to keep the 90 yards that had the right color and reject the off-color 10 yards. **Could he do that?**

Yes, if a yard or 10 yards is a "commercial unit or units" – the point is to prevent him from impairing the seller's goods that are returned. § 2-601(c).

PROBLEM 25-4

Black Sheep Wool Products LLC learned its lesson. It made sure the wool in the next shipment was perfect in every way. (Of course, it also charged the Mad Hatter a little extra to make up for the increased costs of additional quality control inspectors. Everything has a price.)

The contract called for the felt to be delivered on November 1, but it was a few days late. **Can the Mad Hatter use the perfect tender rule of section 2-601 to reject the felt on the ground that the delivery was late?**

In thinking about this problem, consider Harlow & Jones, Inc. v. Advance Steel Co., 424 F. Supp. 770 (E.D. Mich. 1976), which presented interesting issues about the perfect tender rule. Harlow was an importer of steel. It entered into an oral contract to sell Advance 1,000 tons of cold-rolled German steel. The contract provided that the steel was to be shipped from European ports during September—October, 1974. Harlow's confirmation form had a provision that stated: "All delivery dates are approximate and not guaranteed." It also had *force majeure* clauses which provided that Harlow was not responsible for delays beyond its control.

The steel was shipped from Europe in three shipments. The first shipment was shipped in September and arrived in October. The second was shipped in October and arrived in early November. The third was shipped in mid-November and arrived in late November. Advance rejected the last shipment because of late delivery. Harlow sued, claiming the delivery was not late. The court rejected Harlow's argument that the terms in its confirmation form were controlling, holding that under UCC § 2-207 they did not become part of the contract. The court did, however, hold that the last shipment conformed to the contract terms because "according to an accepted steel importing trade usage, shipment in September - October means delivery in October - November." Thus, because the last of the steel had been delivered before the end of November it conformed to the contract.

The case illustrates a couple of important points about the perfect tender rule. First, the perfect tender rule is a default rule. Where the parties would prefer that there be a less strict standard, they can agree to that. In this case, the seller wanted a less strict standard, but it didn't want it enough to insist on it as a condition to the formation of a contract. The second point is that even though the perfect tender rule requires strict compliance with the terms of the contract, the terms of the contract may be something other than what a person who is not in the business would expect from a literal reading. So a lawyer who gets involved in a sales contract has to make sure she understands all the trade usages. This often means grilling the client on all the trade usages that they take for granted.

So, what result does that imply for the Mad Hatter and the right to reject the felt because it was a few days late?

Maybe. The question, as the note that follows the problem suggests, is whether there is a usage of trade or course of dealing between the parties that would suggest that the literal language of the contract was not to be strictly applied. Otherwise, the delayed arrival is an imperfect tender and may be rejected under § 2-601.

B. CURE

PROBLEM 25-5

Simple Simon operates a chain of organic coffee houses. They serve only food grown without the use of pesticides. Simon's usual pie supplier is closed by a strike, so Simon places and order for "100 pies, assorted flavors" with The Pieman, LLC. The contract provides that all of the pies are to be made from ingredients grown without pesticides. It also provides that delivery is to be made prior to 10 a.m. on Friday the 13th.

The Pieman is unable to obtain organic raspberries, so it includes in the shipment 10 pies made with raspberries grown using pesticides. The rest of the pies are all made entirely from organic ingredients. The pies are delivered at 8:30, and when Simon learns about the raspberries (the pies were accompanied by a letter explaining about the raspberry problem), he telephones The Pieman LLC and demands that it send someone to "pick up all of your poisonous pies before we throw them in the dumpster!"

The Pieman responds by saying, "Before 10 am we'll deliver 10 organic apple pies to replace the raspberry." Simon doesn't think this is fair. He wants your advice as to whether he has to accept this tender of The Pieman's wares.

What do you tell him? *See* section 2-508(1).

326

If Pieman LLC gets the conforming pies to Simon at or before 10 a.m., under § 2-508. Simon must accept them.

PROBLEM 25-6

The farmer's wife damaged her butcher knife while defending herself from three vision-impaired rodents. So she goes to the Sonoma-Williams website and checks out the model 1682 butcher knife. The site informs her that the model 1682 ships within 24 hours. In reliance on that assurance, Ms. Farmer places an order for a model 1682. She pays extra for expedited shipping because she fears that further rodent attacks may be imminent.

The knife arrives two days later, no rodent attacks having occurred in the interim. When Ms. Farmer examines the knife, she discovers that it is a model 1870, rather than the model 1682 that she had ordered. She calls Sonoma-Williams, and they tell her that because of a shortage of model 1682 knives, they have been shipping model 1870 knives, which are actually a more expensive model at no additional charge. When Ms. Farmer insists that she wants a model 1682, the customer service associate is very apologetic.

The customer service associate tells her that a model 1682 will be shipped that day and that she can use the model 1870 to defend herself against any rodent attacks that occur prior to the delivery of the model 1682. "Just be sure to wipe any blood off before you return it," he tells her. "The people in the returns department don't have a sense of humor." Ms. Farmer says she'll think about it. After some discussions with her daughter, who is active in the animal rights movement, Ms. Farmer decides she really doesn't want a new butcher knife. She'll try reasoning with the creatures instead.

She wants advice on her rights. *See* section 2-508(2). **Which of these pieces of advice would you give her?**

(1) Actually, if they had insisted on your accepting a model 1870, you would have been stuck. Consider yourself lucky you're going to get a model 1682.

(2) The seller has a right to cure, so you have to accept the model 1682 they've offered.

(3) Under the facts you've related to me, the seller has no right to cure and you don't have to accept the model 1682.

(4) **If the seller had reasonable grounds to believe that the model 1870 would be acceptable, you have to take the model 1682 if they get it to you within a reasonable time.**

The answer is "4" based upon the wording of § 2-508(2).

♦ -- ♦

Transcontinental Refrigeration Co. v. Figgins
Supreme Court of Montana
585 P.2d 1301 (1978)

Meat market display cases supplied under a financing lease—how do we know it is a financing lease? He gets to keep the cases at the end of the lease term. So, how can the "lessor" protect itself from a later bankruptcy of the meat market? File a UCC-1 on this equipment.

Mid-August, the customer wanted a "3000" unit with wood grained sides. Signs lease. Next day, sales person tells Figgins that the company told him that the 3000 model did not come with wood grain. The only model that did is an MD-8, so they change the order and the MD-8s arrive and are installed. Figgins wants to use his own compressor, so the units were shipped without compressors. But they dry out his meat. The 3000 models use a passive gravity coil system and no fans, the MD's blow air over the meat with three fans.

Manufacturer's attempts at cure are weak—condensation pans to boost humidity. Doesn't work. He contacts an attorney, puts the cases in storage and sends a formal notice of cancellation and rescission to Transcontinental.

Some 6 months later, Transcontinental sues him. He counterclaims and wins in the trial court. Rescission granted and damages awarded. And this court affirms. Reasonable opportunity to cure was had—the situation just could not go on like it was.

NOTES AND QUESTIONS

1. **Was the seller's right to cure governed by § 2-508(1) or § 2-508(2)? Which do you think? Which does the court think? Does it matter in this case?**

(The court thinks it is (2)—that it was not a question of a little fix, but replacement of the cooling system). Does it matter?

2. Suppose the lease was silent as to the date the display cases were to be delivered. **How long would the lessor have to affect a cure?** *See* § 2-309(1).

A reasonable time [under all the facts and circumstances].

3. **How diligent was the lessor about curing the defect?** *Not very.* **Should this be a factor in determining how much time it has to cure?** *Discuss.*

♦ -- ♦

Zabriskie Chevrolet, Inc. v. Smith
New Jersey Superior Court, Law Division
240 A.2d 195 (1968)

Seller sells buyer a real lemon of a car. Won't take back and give credit for money paid. Wants to swap out the transmission and "fix" the problem. The customer was really buying a new car and not a new car with a "used" transmission. Court will have none of it.

C. ACCEPTANCE, REJECTION, REVOCATION OF ACCEPTANCE

The theme of this section is the shifting of the burden of proof from Seller to Buyer as time passes and the transaction "matures."

◆ -- ◆

PROBLEM 25-7

On February 1, the Mad Hatter received another shipment of felt. This time the color was off on the entire shipment. Because he was in the middle of a large order, he put the shipment aside, intending to ship it back to Black Sheep Wool Products LLC by return post.

By this time, however, the mercury nitrate used in the felt and hat production process had affected his brain, and he forgot about rejecting the wool until February 21, when he sent the wool back along with the a nasty letter telling Black Sheep Wool Products LLC that just because they could sell inferior products to the little boy who cries in the lane didn't mean they could deal so cavalierly with "a person of my stature."

Does Black Sheep Wool Products have to take the wool back? *See* UCC § 2-602(1) and UCC § 2-606.

§ 2-602(1) says rejection must be within a reasonable time, and § 2-606(1)9b) provides that "Acceptance of goods occurs when the buyer . . . (b) fails to make an effective rejection (subsection (1) of Section 2-602), but such acceptance does not occur until the buyer has had a reasonable opportunity to inspect them." So, the question is whether a 20 day delay is a "reasonable time or not." Reasonable minds can differ on this. Don't forget industry custom and course of dealing.

PROBLEM 25-8

Suppose Mr. Hatter's rejection is not effective. **Then what happens?** *See* UCC § 2-607(1) and UCC § 2-714.

If the Hatter's rejection is not effective and he has accepted under § 2-606(1)(b), then under § 2-607(1) he must pay for the goods, but, under § 2-714 he can recover damages for any non-conformity of the tender, as determined in a reasonable manner. Essentially, at this point the Hatter is stuck with the same result as the common law rule of substantial performance and immaterial breach.

PROBLEM 25-9

Hi-Ho Dairy Stores placed an order with In The Dells Farms, Inc. for a thousand gallons of fat-free skim milk. When the milk was delivered, the manager of Hi-Ho's packaging facility asked the driver of the tank truck: "Are you sure this is fat-free skim milk? It smells like one percent to me."

The driver, Simon Simple, an authorized agent of In The Dells Farms, Inc., assured the manager that it was. On that basis, the manager said that Hi-Ho Dairy Stores would accept the milk and told Mr. Simple to pump the milk into one of Hi-Ho's empty tanks.

Believing it now to be one percent milk, Hi-Ho Dairy Stores would like to revoke its acceptance of the milk. It can use the milk because it sells one percent milk as well as fat-free skim, but it would like to revoke the acceptance "to teach those corporate agri-business people a lesson."

Assuming that it accepted the milk, can Hi-Ho Dairy Stores revoke its acceptance? *See § 2-608.*

Under § 2-608(1), Hi-Ho is authorized to revoke the acceptance on these facts under subsection (b), as long as the "non-conformity substantially impairs its value" to it. This is the question posed by the secret motives of Hi-Ho to teach them a lesson.

PROBLEM 25-10

Big City Edison ("Big Ed") contracts to buy 500,000 barrels of fuel oil from Abdul, an oil broker operating in the "spot market." The contract requires that the oil have a maximum sulfur content of 0.50%. Big Ed notifies Abdul it will not accept delivery of oil with a sulfur content in excess of 0.50%. When he bought the oil, Abdul received a certificate from a reputable independent testing laboratory showing that the sulfur content of the oil was 0.48%. The contract calls for delivery on or before June 1. The oil is actually delivered and pumped into Big Ed's tanks on May 30. On June 4, a test by Big Ed's chemist shows a sulfur content of 0.53%. This is confirmed by independent laboratories.

1. Does Big Ed have to accept the oil? *See UCC § 2-601.*

He can reject it under the perfect tender rule, § 2-601.

2. Does Abdul have a right to cure under UCC § 2-508(2)?

Under § 2-508(1), the time for performance has passed and thus Abdul cannot claim a right to cure under § 2-508(1), given the specific notice that Ed will

330

not accept oil with a sulfur content of over 50%, it looks like § 2-508(2) is not going to provide Abdul with a right to cure unless he can show that he had "reasonable grounds to believe" the oil would be acceptable (things like past course of dealing and the like).

3. Suppose that Big Ed mixes 100,000 barrels of the oil delivered by Abdul with oil having a higher sulfur content. Can it reject (i) all 500,000 barrels, (ii) 400,000 barrels or (iii) none? *See* §§ 2-601, 2-606, and 2-607(2). **Would it matter whether the oil was mixed before or after Big Ed received its lab results?**

It appears that (ii)—reject 400,000 barrels—is the best response. Answer (iii)—none—is eliminated by § 2-601(c) which allows acceptance of any commercial unit and rejection of the balance. Gallons or barrels appear to be the commercial units in question. Answer (i) is problematic as Bid Ed has mixed the oil, which appears to be acceptance for purposes of § 2-606(1)(c) (act inconsistent with seller's ownership) and § 2-607(2) (provides that once there has been acceptance of the goods, rejection is precluded although revocation of acceptance may be possible). It does matter if Ed knew about the non-conformity as, if so, revocation of acceptance will be banned.

4. Suppose that Big Ed fails to notify Abdul of its rejection until June 10. **Would it matter that the world oil price had fallen between June 1 and June 10?** *See* UCC § 2-602.

The market price of oil, or more particularly, its volatility, would be a factor to be considered, along with others, including the speed with which testing results would be available, in determining whether 10 days was a reasonable time under § 2-602(1).

5. Suppose that Big Ed accepted the oil on the basis of the test results from the independent laboratory. **Could it revoke its acceptance when it gets its own lab results? Would it matter whether it got the independent lab's report (a) from Abdul, as part of Abdul's effort to induce it to accept the oil and pay for it, or (b) directly from the independent lab, paying the independent lab a separate fee as part of Big Ed's acceptance, verification and quality control procedure?** *See* UCC § 2-608.

Yes, as long as he has not mixed the oil. It would not matter whether facts (a) or (b) were present, either fact scenario meets the test of § 2-608(1)(b), although fact set (b) is stronger and more compelling.

6. **Would it matter to your answer to question (5) whether federal regulations prohibited Big Ed from burning oil with a sulfur content greater than 0.50? Would that fact matter to your answer to question (1)?**

If there is a government regulation preventing burning the oil, this makes the case for revocation under § 2-608 even stronger as the non-conformity now even more substantially impairs the oil's value to Big Ed. This additional fact, however, does not make a difference to the response to question number 1.

7. Can acceptance be revoked as to the 100,000 barrels mixed with the high sulfur oil?

No. § 2-606(1)(c) act inconsistent with the seller's ownership = mixing the oil with higher sulfur oil = acceptance. § 2-608(2) revocation of acceptance must occur within a reasonable time and before any substantial change in the condition of the goods.

PROBLEM 25-11

Ahmed contracts to deliver one 50,000 barrel shipment to Golf Oil each month for 2 years. The contract calls for oil with a sulfur content not to exceed 0.90%.

1. Ahmed's second shipment has a sulfur content of 0.96%. The oil is less valuable than it would be if it conformed to the contract, but Golf can still use it. **Can it nevertheless reject the shipment?** *See* UCC § 2-612.

Under § 2-612(2), the question is whether or not the second shipment's quality "substantially impairs" its value, even though it can still be used. Because this is an installment contract, the perfect tender rule doesn't apply.

2. **Ahmed's first shipment and his third through eighth shipments have sulfur contents of less than 0.90%, but his ninth shipment has a sulfur content so high Golf can't use the oil. Can Golf reject the shipment? Can it cancel the contract? Would it affect your answer if the high sulfur oil had been shipped in the first shipment rather than the ninth?**

If Golf can't use the oil in the 9th shipment at all, that may "substantially impair the value of the whole contract" (§ 2-612(3)), which would constitute a breach of the whole contract. Given that it was only 1/12th of the contract, it is going to be a tough sell. Whether it was in the first shipment or the ninth should not affect the analysis, but it could be used to argue, at the time of the first shipment, that 100% of the accrued contract value was lost, making the impairment more substantial.

Comment 6 to § 2-612 precludes the argument that substantial defects in the first shipment justifies cancellation of the contract because it means the buyer can't rely on the seller to supply conforming goods.

♦ -- ♦

Keen v. Modern Trailer Sales, Inc.
Colorado Court of Appeals
578 P.2d 668 (1978)

The Keens bought a trailer home. They were told it was 14x70 feet long (980 sq. feet), but it was really only 64 feet long (thus lacking 84 sq. feet). It drifts off its foundations and that is when they discover it. Grounds: § 2-608(1)(b) revocation of acceptance. Trial court finds against them on the grounds that there was no substantial impairment of value, this court reverses and remands for new findings of fact.

The court's standard is one that is both subjective and objective (and confusing in the abstract). "This section creates a subjective test in the sense that the requirements of the particular buyer must be examined and deferred to. Yet, since the rationale of the substantial impairment requisite is to bar revocation for trivial defects or defects which may be easily corrected, the impairment of the buyer's requirements must be substantial in objective terms."

What does this mean? What would you do on remand if you were the trial court? Why?

QUESTION

Could the Keens have argued they had rejected the mobile home? If they had, how would it have changed the burden of proof? *See* UCC § 2-607(4).

If they have accepted, the burden of proof is on the buyer. Under § 2-607(3), they can reject after accepting tender of the goods if they notify the seller within a reasonable time of when they learn or should have learned of the breach. That would leave them with the seller holding the burden of proof as to performance of the contract. The mobile home slid off its piers within a month of installation, which seems like a short time. On the other hand, if the piers were set out, would measurements not have been taken then to see how long it was? How substantial was the shortfall?

♦ -- ♦

Hemmert Agricultural Aviation, Inc. v. Mid-Continent Aircraft Corp.
United States District Court, District of Kansas
663 F. Supp. 1546 (1987)

Super B Spray Plane Sale. Plaintiff seeks to revoke acceptance under § 2-608. Court quotes statute and states "To revoke acceptance is to refuse the delivered goods after they have been accepted and after the time for their rejection has run. While a buyer may nominally reject for any defect, acceptance cannot be revoked absent a substantial non-conformity."

"Typically, the notice of revocation will be given after the general notice of breach required under 2-607(3)(a), as the purchaser's wish to revoke is frequently the last resort after the seller's attempts to cure have failed. Because one purpose behind the notice provisions is to allow the seller the chance to cure, the outer limits of the reasonable time period should be flexible to encourage both the buyer and seller to cooperate in an effort to cure [Cmt 4]. Similarly, if the seller continuously assures the buyer that defects will be remedied, the notice provision should be accordingly suspended."

Under 2-608, the buyer has the burden to prove:

(1) The nonconformity of the machine to the needs and circumstances of the purchaser when the purchase was made;

(2) That such nonconformity in fact *substantially impaired* the value of the machine to the purchaser, and

(3) That the purchaser accepted the machine under circumstances which bring him within either paragraph (1)(a), reasonable assumption of cure, or paragraph (1)(b), difficulty of discovery.

Court finds that the shaken faith doctrine applies and value was substantially impaired. What about the warranty disclaimers? No integration, so no parole evidence rule bar to other evidence. Court finds warranty in advertising and salesperson statements.

Remedy. When a buyer rightfully revokes his acceptance he may recover pursuant to UCC § 2-711 a refund of the purchase price paid and incidental and consequential damages, which may include expenses reasonably incurred in inspection, receipt, transportation and care and custody of goods, and any other commercially reasonable charge or expense in effecting cover or caused by delay or other breach. The buyer is also entitled to prejudgment interest from the date that revocation is attempted.

As an aside, the Super B appears to have been a successful product. Lloyd's Internet search reveals no adverse comments.

CHAPTER 26

ANTICIPATORY REPUDIATION

— ♦ —

The issue here is when is an early statement or action that suggests that a contract will be breached enough to constitute a current breach even when the time for performance has not yet arrived. Present the R2d standard from § 250; cover the UCC's detailed regime of UCC §§ 2-609, 2-610, 2-611 (Kuney does this using two overheads of each section, the first clean and the second marked to show the areas that are uncertain or fact-intensive). Stress how important it is to be the non-breaching, non-repudiating party.

♦ - - ♦

In the next case, *Hochster v. De La Tour*, the plaintiff had been engaged to act as a "courier" to accompany the defendant on what was then known as "the grand tour." This was a tour of Continental Europe that was considered the capstone of an English gentleman's education. The courier's job was roughly the equivalent of that of a modern musician's road manager. The courier handled the logistics (meals, lodging, transportation, baggage, etc.) for the client's entire entourage, which would include several servants and possibly even a tutor. Adam Smith, the father of modern economics, supplemented his meager academic income by accompanying young gentlemen as a tutor on the grand tour.

♦ - - ♦

Hochster v. De La Tour
Queen's Bench
2 El. & Bl. 678, 118 Eng. Rep. 922 (1853)

Agreement between A and B for A to work as B's "courier" on the grand tour of Europe starting on a certain date in the future and, before that day, B renounces that agreement. Can A sue and recover damages from B prior to the time of performance?

Yes. This requires more than a passing intention on the part of the defendant that he might repent of. Rather, it requires, as here, an utter renouncement of the contract or the doing of some act that renders it impossible to perform the contract.

If so, then there is no point in requiring the plaintiff to remain idle and pretend like the contract is going to be performed. Rather, she can start to mitigate her damages immediately and arrange for substitute performance and sue for damages (note that this is expressed as an option – can always wait for eventual breach or performance).

Court provides some examples:

If a man promises to marry a woman on a future day and, before that day, marries another, he is instantly liable for breach of promise of marriage. *(Could always get divorced or the wife could die prior – but is that the same quality of performance? No. Perception of "damaged" goods or at least something different than what was contracted for . . .).*

If a man promises to lease certain premises for a particular term and, before that, leases them to another, he is instantly liable for the breach. *(Could still buy out the lessee . . .).*

If a man contracts to sell specific goods in the future and, before that day, sells them to another, he is instantly liable for the breach. *(Could still buy back . . .).*

Reasons for this are:

Has rendered it impossible to perform – but not really (see italicized text above).

By contracting you create a relationship and that relationship impliedly promises that in the meantime neither will do anything to the prejudice of the other inconsistent with that relationship. *(This explains why the italicized text comments above are not applicable – and it smacks of the duty of good faith and fair dealing that we will come to soon . . .).*

NOTES AND QUESTIONS

1. The *Hochster* opinion, among other things, should make it plain how important paragraphs and headings can be in making text easily readable. The opinion featured neither and is not. Remember that when writing exams.

2. *Hochster v. De La Tour* is considered the seminal or ovular case for the doctrine of anticipatory repudiation. **What two things does it allow a party to a contract to do upon the other party's repudiation?** *Suspend performance and seek adequate assurances.*

3. At the time this case was decided, it was well accepted that courts didn't make law; they found it among the already-established rules. **How does this court explain that anticipatory repudiation is not really a new rule, but just an application of well-established rules?** *Analogizing prior authorities, other contexts.*

♦ - - ♦

AMF, Inc. v. McDonald's Corp.
United States Court of Appeals, Seventh Circuit
536 F.2d 1167 (1976)

AMF seeks damages from alleged wrongful cancellation and repudiation of contract for supply of computerized cash registers.

Trial court for McDonalds and this court affirms.

The cash registers never really worked out and the prototype was not working either. Bleeding edge technology, here. Always dangerous for the seller to contract to develop and supply, and always dangerous for the buyer to rely upon timely delivery of first generation technology in properly working form.

Interrelationship of UCC § 2-610 and UCC § 2-609. Anticipatory repudiation and right to adequate assurance of future performance. (Put up on Board and discuss).

Back to *AMF v. McDonalds* – discuss facts under the UCC sections. What about the need for a writing (This court is liberal and excuses this – most do not! See notes on page 684)?

NOTES AND QUESTIONS

1. The R2d contains a provision similar to UCC § 2–609, R2d § 251, as does the CISG, article 71(3), and UNDROIT, article 7.3.4. These authorities do NOT require the demand for assurances to be in writing as the UCC does.

2. Not all courts are this liberal when confronted with the explicit statutory requirement of a writing contained in UCC § 2–609. In fact most are not, as many lawyers who have failed to follow the statutory requirements have found. Eastern Airlines won a $25 million judgment against McDonnell–Douglas on account of late deliveries of airplanes that put Eastern at a severe competitive disadvantage. The judgment was reversed because Eastern had not followed all the statutory formalities in giving McDonnell–Douglas notice that they had defaulted. Eastern Air Lines v. McDonnell Douglas Corp., 532 F.2d 957 (5th Cir. 1976). On the specific question of whether a demand for adequate assurance under Article 2 must be in writing, the majority of the courts that have addressed the issue have held that it must. The Illinois Appellate Court said: "The record contains no indication that [the buyer] at any time placed a demand for assurances of future performance on the part of [the seller] in writing, and a demand for assurances of future performance is ineffectual unless placed in writing." Bodine Sewer, Inc. v. Eastern Illinois Precast, Inc., 143 Ill. App. 3d 920, 97 Ill. Dec. 898, 493 N.E.2d 705, 1 UCC Rep. Serv. 2d 1480, 1489 (1986). UCC § 2–609 is very explicit and should be followed mechanically in <u>every case</u>; unfortunately, commercial lawyers and clients, like police required to "Mirrandize" their suspects, all too often fail to do so properly, with serious results.

◆ - - ◆

Drake v. Wickwire
Supreme Court of Alaska
795 P.2d 195 (1990)

Malpractice action against attorney for advising client to break an earnest money sales agreement.

Drake is the seller.

Hosley is the broker (according to the majority, the seller's – Drake's – agent for limited time).

Wickwire is Drake's attorney (seller's agent – sort of).

Buyers are Goldsmith, Hofshulte, and Nystrum.

Closing to occur within 10 days of clear title – on 4/3 preliminary title report – PTR – comes back with a judgment lien in favor of Drake's ex-wife – they will solve that by cashing her out at closing and they negotiate a discounted payoff – DPO – (what is that? How common?) due on April 11. But the obligation to close looks like it is for April 13.

Buyers' broker realizes that DPO may lapse prior to close and calls attorney for the ex-wife – DPO payoff has been extended to the end of April.

Do we have clear title yet? Is that a condition to closing? If so, what of it?

On April 11, Wickwire calls Hosley to set up the closing – Hosley says buyers don't have the money and would not have it before May 1 – they are "resisting pressure to close" (What does this mean? Who is Hosley working for? In law or in fact? Perhaps he was working with the buyers to cut price? Who knows – real estate transactions make for strange bedfellows). Some would claim that a broker is only serving "the deal" – not the parties, or either of them. Can this be true? How? Can it be "right"? In what sense?

Wickwire sends letter saying that Drake's offer to sell was withdrawn – letter to Hosley – Hosley shows up the next day with 10% down payment – refused as already sold to another on advice of counsel (Wickwire).

Court holds this *per se* negligent as a matter of law – looks to Restatement sections [paras. 9-11] requiring repudiation to be reasonably clear (and finds this one to be ambiguous) – does not mention that it is coming from Hosley and is part of a game of telephone.

Points out that under R2d, could ask for assurance of performance and did not do so. Big mistake. Make a record.

Rabinowitz, dissenting – genuine issues of material fact should prevent a summary judgment and this should go back on remand for trial.

NOTES AND QUESTIONS

1. The court seems to think that the contract called for the closing to occur on April 12 or April 13. **What is the basis for this belief?** *April 3, preliminary title report (PTR) received showing clear title, earnest money receipt from March 23 stated closing "within 10 days of clear title" and "ASAP" (time is of the essence?).* **Are there alternative interpretations of the contractual language?** *Of course. Title was not shown "clear" on the PTR – there was the lien in favor of the wife. Potentially, clear title only shown once she agrees to the DPO, two or three days later – or arguably later as, if "clear title" is a condition precedent to closing, and that could require wife's conditional tender of a release of her lien to escrow before we could say that title was clear.*

2. **According to the majority, whose agent was Hosley (the broker)?** *Drake.* **If this is correct (it probably is) what does that do to the dissent's argument?** *Defeats it. The fact that the seller's agent tells another seller's agent that the other side will not perform would seem to fall short of R2d § 251's standard. Perhaps it would have been a good idea to request adequate assurance of future performance ala the UCC, even if not required, in order to create a proper record? A good record protects the attorney as well as the party.*

3. **What was the effect of Wickwire's letter to Hosley, dated April 11, stating that Drake's offer to sell was withdrawn? What does Wickwire's phraseology and choice of addressee say about his legal knowledge?** *It appears imprecise at best, although this may also be use of an appropriate legal terminology in a convincing fashion to muddy the record. There was no "offer;" there was a contract. And writing to another agent of the seller is an odd, scrambled way to communicate withdrawal of an offer or termination of a contract for failure of a condition precedent.*

◆ - - ◆

Hope's Architectural Products, Inc. v. Lundy's Construction, Inc.
United States District Court, Kansas
781 F. Supp. 711 (1991)

Construction Contract – Litigation that is all or nothing means settlement is tough if neither side believes it is at risk (or does not care). Uncertainty breeds settlement (as does lack of wild cards like punitive damages).

Hope's makes and delivers windows.

Lundy's is building a school for the state.

Bank IV is the performance bonder (no materialman's lien for state jobs, so bond them).

Hope's is late with the windows and Lundy's apparently threatened to invoke a non-existent liquidated damages provision or back charge them (what is a back charge? – not a forward charge on a cost plus contract – take it out on the sub, not the owner).

So, Hope's, in writing, suspends delivery of the windows until there are assurances of no back charge – same day that it is received by Lundy's, a Hope's rep. tells Lundy's that it needs full prepayment or it won't deliver. They go elsewhere.

Hope's says it is availing itself of its § 2-609 request for adequate assurance of performance rights – but the big problem is that it is already in breach! Those rights are for non-breachers. So what it really did was a breach of the contract (why is it not an anticipatory repudiation? Because the time for performance had already come and gone!).

Hopes makes weak excuses about force majeure – but that is for things outside of its control – not problems with its own bonderizing process – and, even allowing for those, they would have been late (Wait for next chapter on impossibility and impracticability for more on this sort of thing).

And *Quantum Meruit* – NO WAY! Yes, you can get costs of preparation to perform as well as performance in the appropriate case – but the touchstone is "benefit conferred" – none conferred here.

Note: These are tough calls. Yes – but think about what is driving the employee actions. Fear. Hope for a bonus. Desire to not lose commissions. Agency problems are everywhere.

◆ - - ◆

NOTES AND QUESTIONS

1. Re-read the first paragraph of the opinion. As it indicates, situations very similar to that presented by the case are likely to come up in *your* practice.

2. **What would have been the effect of the October 14 letter discussed in paragraph 7 if: (a) the contract did not require Hope's to meet those deadlines or (b) the contract did require Hope's to meet them?** *This bears on whether substantial performance or perfect performance was the intent of the parties.*

◆ - - ◆

One can do problem 26-1 in class and, in the end, put § 2-611 on the board. *Discuss.*

◆ - - ◆

PROBLEM 26-1

Grower had a contract to deliver carrots to Soup Company for $300 a ton. Because of a drought, Grower's crop was much smaller than usual. He still had enough carrots to perform his contract with Soup Company, but he didn't have many left over to sell on the open market. As a result, it looked as if he was going to suffer a loss for the year. Because of the drought, the market price for this type of carrot was $450 a ton. If he could sell the carrots for $450 a ton, he could make enough of a profit to keep his daughter in law school. He consulted with his daughter, who told him that the doctrine of impracticability relieved him of his obligations under the contract. Unfortunately, the daughter, who had apparently been drinking something other than carrot juice when she was studying contracts, was (as we'll learn in the next chapter) wrong when she told her father he could get out of the contract.

Grower called Soup Company's purchasing manager and told her that "on advice of counsel," he didn't have to perform, and he wouldn't perform if she didn't agree to amend the contract to raise the price to $400 a ton.

The purchasing manager told him, "We expect your carrots to be delivered in accordance with our contract. If not, we'll see you in court."

(a) Did Grower's threat constitute a repudiation?

Carrots are goods, so UCC applies. UCC definition of repudiation not clear, although the comments to UCC § 2-610 are helpful, especially comment 2.

(b) Does Soup Company have to take steps to mitigate its damages, or can it just wait to see if Grower delivers his carrots?

Either if commercially reasonable; UCC § 2-610.

(c) If there are no further communications between Grower and Soup Company and Grower delivers the carrots the day before the last day for performance under the contract, can Soup Company refuse to accept them?

No, unless Soup Co. can show that it materially changed its position; UCC § 2-611.

(d) If the purchasing manager decided that Grower probably wasn't going to perform and purchased substitute carrots from a farm in Brazil, is there any need to give Grower notice of this fact?

> *See UCC § 2-611, where it would seem the answer was "no" – but prudent practice*
may dictate otherwise. Make your record.

CHAPTER 27

IMPOSSIBILITY, IMPRACTICABILITY, AND FRUSTRATION OF PURPOSE

— ♦ —

Taylor v. Caldwell
King's Bench
122 Eng. Rep. 309 (1863)

Lease or license to use a music hall (A distinction with a difference? Probably. Property law concept of lease was rooted in obsolete duty to pay rent in the form of an independent covenant; a license could easily be seen as a contract with mutual, dependent covenants). Post contract but pre-performance the hall was destroyed by fire.

Excuse of performance or breach? Tease that out.

Paragraph 4 - "There seems no doubt that where there is a positive contract to do a thing, not in itself unlawful, the contractor must perform it or pay damages for not doing it, although in consequences of unforeseen accidents, the performance of his contract has become unexpectedly burthensome or even impossible."

"But this rule is only applicable when the contract is positive and absolute, and not subject to any condition either express or implied" [and here is the hook – treat the existence of the subject matter of the contract – here the hall and gardens – as a condition precedent to the duties under the contract.]

Impossibility (something not arising from the actions of one of the parties – Q: what would we call that? A: Voluntary disablement and anticipatory repudiation) excuses performance.

"The principle seems to be that, in contracts in which the performance depends on the continued existence of a given person or thing, a condition is implied that the impossibility of performance arising from the perishing of the person or thing shall excuse the performance." Note that you could change this rule by express allocation of the risk in the contract.

♦ - - ♦

Mineral Park Land Co. v. Howard
Supreme Court of California
172 Cal. 289, 156 P. 458 (1916)

Defendants are building a bridge across Arroyo Seco and contract with plaintiffs to take all the sand and gravel that they need for the job from plaintiffs' land.

Estimated amount needed is 114,000 cubic yards. Payment to be 5 cents per cubic yard for the first 80,000, the next 10,000 yards are to be given free of charge, and the balance was to be paid at 5 cents per cubic yard. This is a *requirements contract*.

Defendant used about 101,000 cubic yards, of which 50,869 came from somewhere else. Although plaintiff's land had more gravel than this, no greater quantity could be taken "by ordinary means" as it was a wet year and the arroyo was full (would have needed a steam dredge and drying the material first – impracticable).

The single question is whether the facts justify defendants in not taking all their earth and gravel from plaintiff's land.

Trial court – nope, no excuse.

This court – reverse. Excuse of impracticability.

Mining cases – where you contract to take out a quantity and pay a royalty on that amount, you are not bound to take it out and pay the royalty if it is not there. And in figuring out "if it is not there" or if it is "available" we view the circumstances in a practical and reasonable way. Here, the contract was for removal of gravel from a historically dry ravine/riverbed, and it was a wet year.

Impracticability and allocating risk – The parties can do so explicitly in the contract, or the court may when they don't and it makes or does not make a finding of impracticability.

Note on perspective: The rains involved were an extremely unusual occurrence. Southern California, as any Northern Californian will tell you, is a desert. "Arroyo Seco" means "dry ravine." From 1962 to 2006, there were only 17 rainouts at Dodger Stadium.

♦ -- ♦

American Trading and Production Corp. v. Shell Intl. Marine Ltd.
United States Court of Appeals for the Second Circuit
453 F.2d 939 (1972)

1 voyage charter, priced by long ton at $417,327.36, in advance.

Suez Canal closed due to war; charter diverts around Cape of Good Hope. Owner claims the canal was the route and its elimination made the contract legally unenforceable, seeks $131,978.44 in additional fees (*quantum meruit*).

Trial Court: Dismissed.

Appellate Court: Affirmed. Not legally impossible. Canal was probably contemplated but was not contracted for as the exclusive route. ". . . [t]he implied expectation that the route would be via Suez is hardly adequate proof of an allocation to the promisee of the risk of closure" [para. 5].

Also, not commercially impracticable. Extra cost less than 1/3 of contract price. Among other things, the master was on warning when passing Gibraltar that the canal was threatened and could have headed for the Cape then, saving the cost of crossing the Mediterranean and turning around and coming back.

Contrast with a wet Arroyo Seco – are these cases consistent? Discuss.

♦ - - ♦

Publicker Industries v. Union Carbide Corp.
United States District Court, Eastern District, Pennsylvania
17 U.C.C. Rep. Serv. (Callaghan) 989 (1975)

Contract for 3 year supply of "Spirit Grade Ethenol." Impracticability defense to price escalator provision in the face of the 1st oil shock of 1973-74. Not effective.

Union Carbide had claimed (1) force majure and (2) impracticable.

Force majure – the clause was express and referenced occurrences beyond Carbide's reasonable control, including shortages. Similar protection from non-occurrence of basic assumption on which the contract was made under UCC 2-615.

Court looks at both force majure and impracticability at once and notes (1) cost alone is usually not enough, (2) certainly not enough when it is less than a 100% increase.

Here the parties had allocated the risk with the escalator clause, and the court was willing to honor their bargain.

Note the use of the escalator clause – it is like an adjustable rate mortgage (ARM) home loan – and the dangers of working with "standard forms" when you don't think through the clauses like you should and adopt an allocation of risk that you do not intend.

♦ - - ♦

United States v. Wegematic Corp.
United States Court of Appeals, Second Circuit
360 F.2d 674 (1966)

Bid for a computer system for the Federal Reserve Bank – the invitation to bid or request for proposals (RFP) emphasizes the importance for early delivery as a consideration (this is good lawyering – it sets up enforcement of the liquidated damages provision as an allocation of the risk that was intended by the parties).

Wegematic submits the winning bid and contracts for delivery 9 months out, purchase price of $231,800, liquidated damages of $100 per day for late delivery. If Wegematic failed to comply with "any provision" of the agreement "the Board may procure the services described in the contract from other sources and hold the Contractor responsible for any excess cost occasioned thereby." (Again, good lawyering, but maybe too excessive – the "any provision" sweeps rather widely – not advisable to trigger the remedy with a little thing – document the problem before going to defcon 4.)

Wegematic is behind schedule and writes the Board asking for additional time (extension from June 30 to October 30) and a waiver of the $100 a day "penalty." (Lloyd thinks it is too cute to use the penalty language in a set up letter; Kuney is not too sure – might work and what is the down side?) Board takes request under advisement. (Was this anticipatory repudiation? A: No.).

Could they have terminated right then and invoked their remedy of cover and charged for the price differential? Maybe, but.... – certainly grounds for reasonable insecurity and request for adequate assurances of future performance.)

Finally, in October, Wegematic claims impracticability and asks for cancellation of the contract without damages. (They must be kidding).

Government sues to recover $235,806 with interest. Wins at trial court. This court affirms.

The claim of impracticability based upon "basic engineering difficulties" that would cost $1 to $1.5 million and had taken 2 years to perform with success not guaranteed is not sufficient. Back to UCC 2-615 and looking at the last part to see how much risk the parties had assumed. Here, pretty clear it was all on Wegematic.

NOTES AND QUESTIONS

2. The UNIDROIT principles address impracticability in articles 6.2.2 and 6.2.3, which establish a renegotiation process prior to commencement of court action. **What do you think of this procedure and the standards enunciated?**

Seems pretty reasonable and civilized. Almost a "lite" version of pre-suit mediation or negotiation.

◆ - - ◆

PROBLEM 27-1

In 1965, Amalgamated Edison ("AmEd") was planning to build a new generating plant. Choosing between a nuclear plant and a fossil-fuel plant, it was leaning toward a fossil-fuel plant. As its CEO told representatives of Eastinghouse, which was trying to sell it a nuclear plant, "We are concerned that as more utilities start building nuclear plants, the price of nuclear fuels will go up more quickly than will the prices of fossil fuels." To get the sale, Eastinghouse agreed to sell AmEd all the fuel it needed to run its plant at a price equal to (a) the 1965 price multiplied by (b) the ratio of (i) the Producer Price Index for the year in which the fuel was to be delivered to (ii) the Producer Price Index for the year 1965. (The Producer Price Index is measure of inflation similar to the Consumer Price Index but based on the price of raw materials rather than the price of goods and services used by consumers.)

Things went well until 1976, when inspired by the success of the Organization of Petroleum Exporting Countries ("OPEC"), the countries where uranium was mined formed a cartel, and the price of nuclear fuel quadrupled. Eastinghouse refused to honor its contract with AmEd, claiming that the formation of the cartel made performance under the terms of its contract impracticable.

It is 1976. You are a clerk to a United States District Judge. Eastinghouse has filed in your court a declaratory judgment action seeking to have the court declare that Eastinghouse is not bound to perform under the terms of its contract.

Advise the judge as to the way she should rule on the issue of whether UCC Section 2-615 relieves Eastinghouse of its obligation to supply fuel at the contract price.

This problem is based on the famous Westinghouse Uranium Contracts Litigation. The case was settled before there was a decision on the merits, but most commentators believe Westinghouse had no basis for its impracticability argument. The facts, which we've embellished some (but not all that much), make it pretty clear there was a conscious allocation of the risk to Westinghouse.

347

(a) Farmer and Broker enter into a contract under the terms of which Farmer agreed to sell and Broker agreed to buy 100,000 bushels of wheat at a price of $3.00 per bushel. Some time thereafter, Farmer's crop was wiped out by a dust storm, something that had never before happened in that area. Farmer did not deliver the wheat even though wheat was available on the open market at a price of $3.50 per bushel. Farmer claims that the doctrine of impracticability relieved her of her obligation to deliver the wheat. **Is she correct?**

It's not impracticable for Farmer to sell Broker the wheat. He can go into the market and buy it. Some courts have taken this approach and held the seller to her contract. Other courts have said that the parties understood the contract was for wheat grown on the seller's farm and have therefore said her performance was impracticable.

(b) Suppose that when broker offered Farmer the contract, Farmer had asked to have it changed so that instead of "100,000 bushels of wheat," it read "100,000 bushels of wheat grown by Farmer on her land." **How would that affect the outcome?**

Now, that would make it clearly impracticable. This question was asked in class by a student who grew up on a wheat farm. He said that in the area where his family farms, farmers sometimes ask to have this language inserted and the grain elevators always refuse. It seems to us that in this circumstance the parties have allocated the risk to the farmer. The question illustrates the need to keep a record of the course of negotiations. Of course, anyone sophisticated enough to do that is probably sophisticated enough to go one step further and expressly allocate the risk in the contract.

◆ -- ◆

Krell v. Henry
Court of Appeal
2 K.B. 740 (1903)

Henry arranges to rent a room from Krell for the purpose, not stated in the contract, of watching a coronation. He agrees to pay 75£ in rent and makes a down payment of 25£ before the announcement that the coronation for the days in question has been cancelled.

Relying on *Taylor v. Caldwell*, where we began the chapter, the trial court held that the occurrence of the coronation was an implied condition of the contract and, since the event that was the subject of the condition did not occur, the condition was not satisfied. As a result, judgment was entered for the defendant (Henry) on the plaintiff's claim for the balance of the rental amount and on the defendant's counterclaim for refund of the rent already paid.

The appellate court affirms in what is recognized as *the* classic frustration of purpose case. Quote from the middle of paragraph 4, just before the reference to the "two letters of June 20": "I think that you first have to ascertain inferences, drawn from surrounding circumstances recognized by both contracting parties, what is the substance of the contract, and then to ask the question whether that substantial contract needs for its foundation the assumption of the general words, and in such case, if the contract becomes impossible of performance by reason of the nonexistence of the state of things assumed by both contracting parties as the foundation of the contract, there will be no breach of the contract this limited."

Excuse of performance because of impracticability or failure of the essential basis of the contract is not limited to impossibility. "The test seems to be whether the event which causes the impossibility was or might have been anticipated and guarded against."

Note remedies sought. The landlord was seeking the additional 50£ over and above the 25£ deposit. Defendant had originally sought return of the deposit, but had dropped the claim. How does that play into your perception of the right result?

♦ - - ♦

Lloyd v. Murphy
Supreme Court of California
25 Cal. 2d 48, 153 P.2d 47 (1944)

August 4, 1941, lease of a car lot on Wilshire Boulevard. There is a use restriction clause that limits it to new car sales, service and repairs of cars, selling gas, and to make occasional used car sales.

In 1942, the Federal Government orders that sales of new cars be discontinued, then subjected them to rationing by the end of January (look how fast this happened – December 7, 1941 was Pearl Harbor).

Plaintiff landlords offered to waive restrictions on use and subletting but Defendant abandons the premises anyway. Plaintiffs rent out land to another to mitigate.

Defendant took the position that he could not make a go of it in that location with automobiles.

Trial court: No excuse of performance.

This court: Affirms.

Doctrine of frustration of purpose and impossibility are related in their development but are not the same.

Impossibility includes impracticability.

Frustration of purpose goes to whether there has been an unanticipated circumstance, the risk of which should not be fairly thrown on the promissor, which has made performance vitally different from what was reasonably to be expected.

Here, the war appeared imminent at the time of contracting and the defendant can be fairly said to have assumed the risk. Has also not proven that the lease is worthless.

(Note how the plaintiffs acted reasonably or at least made a record of doing so – very useful for winning in court later.)

NOTES AND QUESTIONS

1. In paragraphs [2] and [3] the court addresses the question of whether the doctrine of frustration of purpose applies to leases. **What was the basis for thinking that it might not?**

The migration of contract principles into lease law softening the absolute duties of the traditional common law lease laws. Discuss the interplay and historical separation of contract and lease law and its erosion over time. Draw on the implied covenant of habitability from Property, which many of them have already had.

Historically, a lease was treated as a conveyance in land, rather than a contract. Thus, there was a question whether it was proper to apply an emerging contract principle to leases simply because it applied to contracts generally. It is now well established that a lease combines elements of contracting with elements of conveyancing and that contract law should apply to the contract elements and real property law to the conveyancing aspects.

◆ - - ◆

PROBLEM 27-3

Farmer and Ginning Company entered into a contract under the terms of which Farmer agreed to sell, and Ginning Company agreed to buy, 100,000 pounds of cotton at a price of 65 cents per pound. After the contract was made, India and Pakistan got into a war and India's cotton fields were destroyed. Then most of the American cotton crop was destroyed by a newly-mutated insecticide-resistant boll weevil. Farmer, who expected to be able to harvest 400,000 pounds of cotton on her land, was only able to harvest 100,000 pounds.

There is a silver lining to all this, however. Because cotton is in extremely short supply and because the tense international situation has caused the military to order much more cotton for uniforms, the market price of cotton has gone from 65 cents a pound to $3.00 a pound. Farmer has asked your opinion as to whether she can get out of her contract with Broker on the basis of (i) impracticability or (ii) frustration of purpose. Assume it is clear that no one could have foreseen the war, the boll weevil, or the increased demand for cotton. Note, also, that there is another fact you need to get from Farmer. *See* UCC § 2-615(b).

There have been many cases with similar (though obviously less extreme) facts. The courts have uniformly held that there was neither impracticability nor frustration of purpose. If the farmer can meet his commitments, there's no impracticability, even though he suffers a loss on his operations as a whole. Similarly, the fact that he is not making a profit doesn't constitute frustration of purpose. "Making a profit" is not the sort of purpose that the doctrine of frustration applies to.

This problem is based on a series of real cases. The facts weren't quite so extreme, but there was a bad cotton crop in India and a closure of the Suez Canal. The farmers uniformly lost. There was no frustration of purpose. The farmers' purpose was to sell cotton, and they weren't prevented from doing that. All they were prevented from doing was making a windfall on the sale in question in order to make up for the losses resulting from having a smaller than expected crop. It's well understood that even though one's real purpose in most business transactions is to make money, frustration of that purpose doesn't excuse contract performance.

Similarly, impracticability doesn't work as long as the farmer can perform and has no other calls on her output. Farmer does have a limited way out. Section 2-615(b) allows the farmer to allocate among her customers. So if she has contracts for any of the other 300,000 pounds she expected to sell, she can pro rate among those with whom she has contracts. And § 2-615(b) allows her to go even further and sell some of the cotton to "regular customers" with whom she has no contract. This leaves open the question of what it takes to be a "regular customer" and whether she can sell three quarters of the cotton at $3.00 a pound. Comment 11 indicates that she can sell to other regular customers at the "advanced price." But it still leaves open the question of who qualifies and how much they should get. The comment says "the seller should exercise real care in making his allocations." There's no case law on the subject, but White & Summers have an extensive discussion in their multi-volume practitioner's edition. Their conclusion is that the courts should give deference to sellers' allocations because the need to maintain good relations with customers will normally be sufficient to deter opportunistic behavior. White & Summers Practitioner's Edition, § 3-10 g.

CHAPTER 28

GOOD FAITH

— ♦ —

The trend has been to find the existence of the covenant since at least the 1970s, for litigation for breach of the covenant to expand (wildly) through the 1980s and early 1990s, and to be shut down or substantially contained (except in the case of insurance bad faith denial of coverage cases) in the late 1990s and 2000s. Differentiate between straight tort suits for breach of covenant of good faith and fair dealing and its use as a contractual claim or defense in larger litigation, which is more viable in most jurisdictions.

A Few Rules About Good Faith

1. There is a general obligation of good faith that applies to all contracts.

2. A party to a contract has a duty to avoid doing anything that will injure the ability of the other party to receive the contemplated benefits.

3. It is impossible to say exactly what good faith is, but it consists of avoiding conduct that does not conform to accepted norms of decency, fairness, and reasonableness.

4. Good faith means avoiding "opportunistic behavior," which, in turn, is defined as using a contract term to get an unbargained for advantage, usually because of circumstances not contemplated when the contract was made.

5. The obligation of good faith does not override the express terms of the contract.

6. The obligation of good faith should not be used to protect parties from things they should have protected themselves from when they negotiated and documented the deal.

♦ - - ♦

Schoolcraft v. Ross
Court of Appeal of California
81 Cal. App. 3d 75, 146 Cal. Rptr. 57 (1978)

The right of a beneficiary to apply insurance proceeds to the balance of a note secured by a deed of trust must be performed in good faith and with fair dealing and that, to the extent the security is not impaired, the beneficiary must permit those proceeds to be used for the cost of rebuilding.

Ross sold the Schoolcraft's a home for $14,500, seller took back financing (looks like 100% financing). 10 months later, home totally destroyed by fire with $13,585 outstanding note balance.

Insurance policy will either pay Actual Cash Value, here $8,250 (note that this does not include the land value), or rebuilding funds of up to $14,100.

The Schoolcrafts opt to rebuild, Company cuts joint check, Ross won't sign over proceeds and applies them to the note (so, now there is a $5,335 outstanding balance). The Schoolcrafts cannot both rent a place and make $100/month payments, so Ross forecloses out the deed of trust, purchases the property on the courthouse steps for $600, which she sells for $6,000, i.e. for $5,400 profit (which is just enough to cover the outstanding balance on the note if attorney fees were not too high. Note that Ross is not making huge profits on this deal and explain the process of foreclosure and credit bidding).

Trial Court: Breach of obligation of good faith and fair dealing. Award damages of $4,500.

Court of Appeals: Affirms. Rule in second sentence of paragraph 1. Then at the end – last sentence of paragraph 16: "The covenant in this case does not mean good faith in the abstract, but, instead, refers to the purpose of the particular contract. To reiterate: To the extent the security was not impaired, defendant Ross had no right to the funds." The beneficiary must exercise the option under the policy reasonably and to claim the money only to the extent of impairment of security.

What is "impairment of security" – here, Kuney discusses a lender's adequate protection and the notion of an equity cushion. Questions of value are tough and very important; absent actual exposure to a market, valuation is always an estimate, even if dressed up as based upon comparables, the income approach, the cost to replace approach, or some combination of these methods. Everything in business is cash flow streams. Don't you want a little cash flow stream from something other than your job? You may aspire to get beyond your day-job W-2 status. Do you want to be a K-1, or maybe a 1099?

NOTES AND QUESTIONS

1. If your house burned down and you went to the bank to borrow money to rebuild it, they wouldn't give you the money all at once. They would give you enough to clear away the rubble and rebuild the foundation. When that was done, an inspector would come around and look at the property. If she was satisfied that the work so far had been up to standards, she would report that fact to the bank and they would give you the money for the next phase of construction. The process would be repeated (four or five times in the case of a small house, many more times in the case of a larger project) until construction was complete. The purpose is to keep the bank from giving out all the money and finding that

what they have for security is a half-built house (construction projects are notorious for going over budget) or one that is shoddily built. **How could Ms. Ross protect herself against these risks?**

Point out how construction lending is really largely disbursement of funds administration and not traditional lending. Generally construction financing consists of short term loans that are converted or taken out once construction is complete and sell out or rental operation occurs. They are generally replaced by traditional longer term loans. Ms. Ross could set up a similar process perhaps using an escrow facility.

2. As you can imagine, *Schoolcraft* caused considerable consternation among California lawyers who represented lenders. They pulled out their standard trust deed forms and started drafting. **What would you say in such a document to be sure your lender client was protected?**

What would you do to react to the Schoolcraft case? What is the "draft around"? How about providing in the loan agreement that the lender had sole discretion to apply proceeds of insurance to pay off the note or allow rebuilding. Should a later court faced with that sort of a provision and the Schoolcraft case enforce the provision? Why or why not?

♦ - - ♦

Don King Productions v. Douglas
United States District Court, Southern District of New York
742 F. Supp. 741 (1990)

Don King is a promoter for both Douglas and Tyson, boxers. (Note the inherent potential or actual conflict of interest. Are lawyers allowed to serve the plaintiff and defendant? Are real estate brokers? Why or why not? Does a promoter "represent" either fighter? Or does he or she merely promote the event (and its integrity)? Perhaps the fighter's managers more clearly "represent" the fighters?)

Feb. 10 fight in Japan, Douglas was knocked down in the 8th round but got up before the 10 count had expired.

King protests at the end of the 8th round that there had been a long or slow count.

Then in the 10th round, Douglas knocks out Tyson.

Post-fight airing of slow count objection and challenges are filed to the fight and its results in Japanese Boxing Commission.

King claims he acted moderately – but that is not the Don King we know and love. (For more information on Don King and a hair raising picture or two, Google or otherwise search the web for "Don King Productions." Like most masters of promotion, he doesn't hide!). The court seems to be making fun of him on that score in the text and the footnotes.

Held: King breached his duty of good faith and fair dealing.

Three big statements in paragraphs 12-13:

The covenant is violated when a party to a contract acts in a manner that, although not expressly forbidden by any contractual provision, would deprive the other of the right to receive the benefits under the agreement [para. 12].

The implied covenant does not, however, operate to create new contractual rights; it simply "ensures that parties to a contract perform the substantive, bargained for terms of their agreement" and that parties are not unfairly denied "express, explicitly bargained-for benefits" [para. 13].

. . . it seems doubtful that the covenant of good faith– even as informed by industry customs– permits a promoter, who has contracted to advance the fortunes of two fighters who compete in the same class, both of whom the promoter has under exclusive contract, actively to further one fight outcome over another.

This is not a big stretch.

◆ - - ◆

Market Street Assocs. Ltd. Partnership v. Frey
United States Court of Appeals for the Seventh Circuit
941 F.2d 588 (1991)

1968, Sale/Leaseback deal between J.C. Penny and General Electric Pension Trust ("GEPT"). Discuss sale/leaseback deals and tax advantages of rent as expense over capital ownership and the business advantages of liquidity to finance growth. Also discuss capital appreciation and the great increase in real estate values in the latter half of the 20th century, which is the driver behind MSA's conduct in this case.

GEPT may finance improvements to properties of $250,000 or more. J.C. Penny to request, GEPT to give reasonable consideration to the financing, parties to negotiate, if no agreement, Penney gets to buy back the property at purchase price + 6% per year. Why? If GEPT doesn't finance, nobody is going to finance a leasehold tenant like this, must regain fee ownership. Penny later assigns the lease to Market Street Associates (MSA), the plaintiff.

1987, MSA has possible subtenant that wants to build (or have built) a drugstore. MSA triggers the finance or repurchase offer ($1 million for a $3 million property due to the real estate market run-up of 1968-1987). See paragraphs 3-5 for details.

Trial Court: Grant SJ for GEPT based on failure of MSA to reference the specific provision in the lease so that GEPT would know the penalty for not negotiating, which was creation of a purchase option in favor of MSA.

Appellate Court, per Posner: Reverse. Not ripe for summary judgment. Lengthy discussion of good faith and contrast of it to fraud and a possible duty of candor in paragraphs 10-20. Since GFFD is a state of mind determination, trial is necessary.

NOTES AND QUESTIONS

1. On remand, Judge Reynolds conducted a bench trial and took testimony. After considering all the evidence, he entered findings of fact and conclusions of law substantially identical to those in his original decision of the summary judgment motion that the Posner panel of the 7th Circuit had reversed. *See* Market Street Assocs. Ltd. P'ship. v. Frey, 817 F. Supp. 784 (E.D. Wis. 1993). On appeal, again, the trial court's decision stood. *See* Market Street Assocs. v. Frey, 21 F.3d 782 (7th Cir. 1994). Judge Posner had laid out the legal standard in the first appeal and remanded the case for a "do over," which the trial court had documented in application at trial, and, faced with a fully developed factual record on the second appeal, which is reviewed on an abuse of discretion standard, the Seventh Circuit affirmed.

2. **If you were counsel for Market Street Associates, upon discovering the paragraph 34 option, how would you go about triggering it so as to maximize the chances that GEPT would refuse to negotiate while still meeting or exceeding the basic standards of good faith and fair dealing as described by Judge Posner?**

Open discussion of creative lawyering tactics.

◆ - - ◆

Centronics Corporation v. Genicom Corp.
Supreme Court of New Hampshire
132 N.H. 133, 562 A.2d 187 (1989)

Note that it's not really clear who gets the interest on the $5 million in escrow. By saying that Centronics would have a claim for the time value of money, Souter seems to be saying Genicom got it, but things he says later imply the contrary. (Parenthetical at end of paragraph [11] says Centronics is making a claim for interest). Most students don't think of that and it's a good illustration of the time value of money.

Centronics is the plaintiff-seller.

Genicom is the defendant-buyer.

Purchase price is consolidated closing net book value (CCNBV) + $4 million.

Began by calculating Consolidated book value as of Sept 28.

Centronics would then revise through the closing date—unaudited w/ help of Coopers & Lybrand's Boston office.

Coopers & Lybrand's Richmond office would review for Genicom and propose adjustments.

In the event of a dispute, NY accounting firm would arbitrate.

Genicom would pay at the closing the purchase price (based on Sept 28 financials) less $5 million and put the $5 million into escrow. Escrow would be increased if Centronics showed an increase based on the operations from Sept 28 to the closing.

On closing, Genicom paid $71.5 million and put $5 million into the escrow.

Centronics said the book value went up by $10.9 million. Genicom put $10.9 million into the escrow. (Now have $15.9 million in the escrow.)

Genicom suggested $10.2 million in downward adjustments.

In the summer of 1987, Centronics says: Give us the $5.7 million you admit we're entitled to.

This has gone on for two years. At six percent, two years interest on $5 MM is $600,000.

Note that this was a very detailed agreement, including with respect to payment out of the escrow. Court talks about "detailed instructions for payment out of escrow."

The summer of 1987 request makes sense, right? If a portion of the funds are not in dispute, why not release them? Or is this about creating leverage by locking up the whole? Perhaps that is an integral part of the dispute resolution process. Explore structuring dispute resolution procedures and provisions to control and influence the parties' relationship even (perhaps most importantly) when it is falling apart or otherwise in trouble.

Trial court for Buyer (no breach of GFFD) as just enforcing the contract. This court affirms.

Lengthy discussion that divides GFFD into three contexts [para. 16]:

A. *GFFD at contract formation* ("traditional duties of care to refrain from misrepresentation and to correct subsequently discovered error, insofar as any representation is intended to induce, and is material to, another party's decision

to enter into a contract in justifiable reliance upon it;" court notes a dicta statement in prior case linking GFFD breach of
an implied representation of full disclosure (no unfair surprise) to voidability of a contract on grounds of unconscionability) [para. 17].

B. *GFFD in termination of at-will employment contracts* ("employer violates an implied term of a contract for employment at will by firing an employee out of malice or bad faith in retaliation for action taken or refused by the employee in consonance with public policy" – like whistle blowers) [para. 18].

C. *GFFD in limits on discretion in performance* (here, look at contract, prior dealings, context to determine if conduct is within the reasonable mutual intentions of both parties – note the structure of this opinion, the serial case analysis build up and then synthesized into 4 questions (below)) [paras. 20 to 28].

The four questions for category 3 (can be developed as a flow chart) [para. 28].

1. *Discretion?* Does the agreement ostensibly allow or confer upon the defendant a degree of discretion in performance tantamount to a power to deprive the plaintiff of a substantial proportion of the agreement's value?

2. *Intent to be bound?* If the ostensible discretion is of that requisite scope, does competent evidence indicate that the parties intended by their agreement to make a legally enforceable contract?

3. *Exercise of discretion unreasonable?* Assuming an intent to be bound, has the defendant's exercise of discretion exceeded the limits of reasonableness?

4. *Causation?* Is the cause of the damage complained of the defendant's abuse of discretion or does it result from events beyond the control of either party, against which the defendant has no obligation to protect the plaintiff?

If all the answers are yes, then liability will lie.

The court's analysis is broken down to the point of absurdity.

Here, the first question does it. There is no discretion. The contract does not say you can release the undisputed funds. End of story. (So, are all the other questions "mere dicta?"– If so, what is the use or importance of mere dicta from the Supreme Court of a state?)

♦ - - ♦

Taylor Equipment, Inc. v. John Deere Co.
United States Court of Appeals, Eighth Circuit
98 F.3d 1028 (1996)

Jury found that Deere had breached implied covenant of good faith and fair dealing when it refused to allow Midcon to assign its dealership and Midcon had to sell the business to others for $1.7 million less.

Deere terminated Midcon for selling out of trust. Gave them 18 months to find a buyer. Midcon entered into a contract to sell the dealerships to Interstate. Deere had previously approved purchases of other dealerships by Interstate, but it refused to approve this one unless Interstate put in additional equity capital. Interstate refused to do this. Midcon's owners (the Taylors) ended up selling the assets to two different buyers. The contract provided that Midcon could not assign its dealership "without the prior written consent of [Deere]."

According to the court, the jury in the trial court believed that the additional equity capital requirement was a pretext, and Deere was really trying make them sell to the dealers they ultimately sold to in order to reduce the number of dealers it had to deal with. Jury found for Midcon.

Court says there's an implied covenant of good faith in every contract, but the remedy is strictly contract— no tort recovery.

The Eighth Circuit Court of Appeals reverses. Court quotes a 7th Circuit opinion saying that good faith is merely a "gap filler." It does not affect the negotiated terms of the contract.

Court notes that a 10th Circuit case held that with no assignment-without-consent clause the implied covenant of good faith meant that consent could not be withheld unreasonably. Court says that makes no sense. It means you have to affirmatively say you can be unreasonable, which poisons the negotiation process.

Held: Because the implied covenant of good faith and fair dealing cannot override an express term of the contract – here that Midcon could not assign its dealership without the prior written consent of Deere – and there is no showing that Deere failed to exercise "honesty in fact," the court reverses the judgment against Deere.

Does the UCC apply to the sale of a John Deere tractor? (Yes.) How about to a contract about sales of John Deere tractors? (Yes.) Dealership agreements? (Here the majority position is "no" the UCC does not apply to dealership or franchise agreements – contracts to make contract for the sale of goods – but this is somewhat illusory as some courts will analyze by analogy to UCC principles under these agreements even if UCC is not directly applicable.) The majority seems to think so.

Language taken from Great American Chocolate Chip Cookie Co.: Contract law does not impose a duty to be reasonable but to avoid taking advantage of gaps in a contract in order to exploit the vulnerabilities that arise when contractual performance is sequential rather than simultaneous [para. 17].

Dissent (omitted in the text): Since this is state, not federal, law – need to look searchingly to predict what the South Dakota Supreme Court (SDSC) would do. This judge is convinced that the court would look to the Restatement § 205, which uses the Prof. Summers standard of bad faith = violating community standards of decency, fairness, or reasonableness. Comment [e] to the Restatement makes it clear that breach extends to dealing that is "candid but unfair" such as taking advantage of folks.

NOTES

♦ -- ♦

Industrial Representatives, Inc. v. CP Clare
United States Court of Appeals, Seventh Circuit
74 F.3d 128 (1996)

CP Clare contracted with Industrial Representatives, Inc. ("IRI") to sell CP Clare's products. After CP Clare grows, it decides to terminate the relationship and gives more than the required 30 days notice. IRI sues on basis of the duty of GFFD and the obligation to avoid opportunistic advantage-taking. Both trial court and appellate court dismissed the claim.

Easterbrook states IRI "got what it bargained for" [para. 4] and discusses allocation of risk.

QUESTIONS

1. **Why does Judge Easterbrook mention the fact that CP Clare gave IRI 42 days' notice when the contract required only 30?**

Makes it look even more fair and reasonable, right? Perhaps the results of good pre-termination lawyering on the part of CP Clare.

2. **Consider what Judge Easterbrook meant when he said:**

The idea that favoring one side or the other in a class of contract disputes can redistribute wealth is one of the most persistent illusions of judicial power. It comes from failing to consider the full consequences of legal decisions. Courts deciding contract cases cannot durably shift the balance of advantages to the weaker side of the market. They can only make contracts more costly to that side in the future, because [the other side] will demand compensation for bearing onerous terms.

Original Great American Chocolate Chip Cookie Co. v. River Valley Cookies, Ltd., 970 F.2d 273, 282 (7th Cir.1992) (internal citations omitted). Discuss.

◆ - - ◆

PROBLEM 28-1

Pat O'Reilly operated the most popular pizza parlor in Smalltown. Pat's place was so popular that nobody wanted to go into competition with him. When he turned 65, Pat decided to sell his place to Marcia Smith. Neither Marcia nor Pat was represented in the transaction by a lawyer, and the contract that they signed did not contain a "non-compete," a clause common in business sales whereby the seller agrees not to go into competition with the buyer. After a couple of years, Pat grew bored with retirement and decided to open up a new pizza parlor across the street from Marcia's place. Marcia comes to you and wants to know if she can sue Pat. **What do you tell her?**

Like many of the problems in this book, this one is based on a real deal. It wasn't a pizza parlor in Smalltown, but a sandwich shop in Los Angeles that supplied the sandwiches lawyers choked on while they argued whether the condition was "in Buyer's reasonable discretion," or "in Buyer's sole and absolute discretion, exercised in good faith."

Usually, if you don't get a non-compete, the court isn't going to write one in for you. There are a lot of famous examples. The water sports enthusiasts among your students will be familiar with O'Brien, the company that makes wakeboards, water skis, and other things students use when they ought to be studying. The company was founded by Herb O'Brien, who invented the first practical fiberglass water ski. When things weren't going well for the company, the directors and bankers forced Herb out and sold the company to Coleman, the folks who make Coleman stoves and other camping equipment. Coleman didn't get a non-compete, and Herb went out and started HO (for Herb O'Brien) Sports, which now sells more skis and wakeboards than his old company.

A similar thing happened when James A. Ryder was forced out as head of Ryder Truck Rental, which he had founded. He started a competing company under the name JarTran (for James A. Ryder Transportation). Unlike HO, it was not successful and was liquidated after a few years of operation after going through two chapter 11 cases.

But these are just fun facts. The main point of the problem is to see what arguments the students can make on the basis of the cases they've read. Under Schoolcraft's principle that there is an implied covenant "that neither party will do anything that injures the right of the other party to receive the benefits of the agreement," it would seem that Pat is liable (and enjoinable). Justice Souter (Centronics) would seem likely to take the position that the parties must have contemplated this possibility and chosen not to include a non-compete. But it's also likely that Centronics is distinguishable because the parties in that case were sophisticated and were represented by counsel. Judge Easterbrook would likely say this does not fit into the definition of "opportunistic behavior" because it could have been contemplated at the time the parties entered into the contract. (We think this is the real meaning of Centronics as well.)

PROBLEM 28-2

Mohammad Habib is an immigrant from Egypt. He holds a Ph.D. in history from the University of Cairo, and he is fluent in English, but he is not familiar with the American legal system, nor does he have any experience in business, either in Egypt or the United States. Unable to find a satisfactory teaching job in the United States, he took his $25,000 savings, borrowed an additional $75,000 from friends and relatives and purchased a Shamrock Pizza franchise. He was not represented by a lawyer in the transaction.

On the whole, the Shamrock franchise agreement is fairer to the franchisee than are most similar agreements, but it does lack one protection common in franchise agreements—it doesn't contain any territorial protection, i.e., there is nothing to prevent Shamrock from opening another restaurant right across the street. Shamrock's standard form franchise agreement has written across the top in large letters: "CONSULT A LAWYER BEFORE SIGNING THIS AGREEMENT" but Mr. Habib signed the agreement during his initial interview with the Shamrock salesperson who neither encouraged him to consult a lawyer nor discouraged him from doing so.

For the first two years, Mr. Habib did reasonably well, netting about $65,000 a year before taxes for six ten-hour days a week. In the third year, Shamrock decided that Mr. Habib's location was in fact a truly prime location and Mr. Habib's failure to earn large profits was due to his introverted personality and his failure to deal forcefully with a group of disreputable-looking (but actually quite harmless) teenagers who frequented his restaurant and detracted from its otherwise upscale (for a pizza restaurant) atmosphere. Shamrock officials therefore decided to open a "company store" (a restaurant owned by Shamrock itself, rather than by a franchisee) directly across the street from Mr. Habib's restaurant. Mr. Habib's net immediately dropped almost to zero, and he consulted you. **Can you successfully argue that Shamrock breached the implied covenant of good faith and fair dealing?**

This problem was inspired by the practices of one particular fast food franchisor who shall remain unnamed. There have been a number of suits brought by its franchisees, but the franchise agreement has a so-far bulletproof arbitration clause, so there aren't any reported decisions on the merits.

♦ - - ♦

Requirements contract for propane entered into by the parties when American Bakeries is contemplating conversion of its fleet of trucks to propane fuel. Then American Bakeries decides not to convert its fleet of trucks to propane and doesn't purchase any.

Empire Gas sues for expected profits. Wins over $3.5 million at trial.

Court examines and construes UCC § 2-306, holding that "seller assumes the risk of all good faith variations in the buyer's requirements even to the extent of a determination to liquidate or discontinue the business" [para. 9].

Supporting reasoning. Paragraphs 9-14 provide an excellent example of statutory interpretation, whether one thinks it is the product of inductive or deductive reasoning. As is the dissent.

Judgment affirmed.

CHAPTER 29

NON-PARTY RIGHTS: ASSIGNMENT, DELEGATION, NOVATION, AND THIRD PARTY BENEFICIARIES

— ♦ —

A. ASSIGNMENT AND DELEGATION

Shoreline Communications, Inc. v. Norwich Taxi, LLC
Appellate Court of Connecticut
70 Conn. App. 60, 797 A.2d 1165 (2002)

A basic assignment and delegation case illustrating that the assignee stands in the shoes of the assignor and, when an assignee takes an assignment unconditionally, it will be held to have assumed the risk that the assigned contract may not suit its needs.

Unilateral mistake will not excuse performance [paras. 12 et seq.].

Nor is that result unconscionable [paras. 21 et seq.].

Nor will the non-assigning party's right to look to the assignor for performance (absent a novation) excuse the assignee from the consequences of its assignment or justify a rescission [paras. 35 et seq.].

NOTES AND QUESTIONS

♦ -- ♦

Transportation & Transit Associates, Inc. v. Morrison Knudsen Corp.
United States Court of Appeals for the Seventh Circuit
255 F.3d 397 (2001)

Transportation and Transit Associates ("TTA") was a subcontractor for Morrison Knudsen Corp. ("MKC") in the railcar business. Settlement gave TTA $15 million in business over 5 years and "most preferred vendor" (i.e., most favored nation) terms. Probe and explain.

MKC divests itself of its railcar operations, to Amerail, which took on the settlement obligations by delegation. Amerail does not perform, and TTA does not get as much work as the settlement requires.

TTA, near end of term, sues both MKC and Amerail.

Trial Court: Summary Judgment for TTA, approximately $900,000 in damages.

Appellate Court, per Easterbrook, C.J.: Affirm. No Novation.

NOTES AND QUESTIONS

◆ -- ◆

Fanucchi & Limi Farms v. United Agri Products
United States Court of Appeals for the Ninth Circuit
414 F. 3d 1075 (2005)

Fanucchi Farms, Financed by United.

1994 original documents - go over nature and purpose of each one and discuss the nature of financing document package [para. 3].

1994 documents include an all-amendments-in-writing clause.

1995 - Crop failure and workout discussions. United to subordinate to new crop financing, split profit 60/40 between United and other creditors, pay down to $300k or $400k and United will forgive the balance. (Disputed) Oral agreement.

1998 - Workout officer leaves United [para. 6]. No more willingness to subordinate to family creditors. Fanucchi Farms fails.

Trial Court - No breach by United, S.J. for United.

Appellate Court - Reverse in part and remand.

- Affirm on the no modification based upon Cal. Civ. Code § 1698(c).

- Reverse on Novation theory; very fact intensive. Instead of modifying, did the discussions substitute a new agreement?

- Distinction between modification, novation, and accord without satisfaction is discussed to preempt dissent [paras. 22-34].

◆ -- ◆

Ilkhchooyi v. Best
Court of Appeal of California
37 Cal. App. 4th 395, 45 Cal. Rptr. 2d 766 (1995)

1984. Lease with Landlord (Westar) consent to assignment and 50/50 profit sharing clause for bonus rent.

1987. Original Tenant (Rosenblatts) subleases to plaintiff in sublease approved by landlord that provides sublease terminates if original lease terminates.

1988. Tenants (Rosenblatts) file bankruptcy petition.

1989. Discharge granted, Westar takes position that lease, and thus sublease, have terminated and offers to negotiate new lease with subtenant. Messy negotiations, but new lease does get executed.

1990. Subtenant (now tenant) contracts to sell business for $120,000, consisting of $80,000 for fixtures and equipment and $40,000 for a covenant not to compete. They take the position that the lease is over market and adds no value.

When Landlord's assent to assignment of the lease is sought, Landlord points to the 3/4-of-all-amounts-in-excess-of-future-rents-go-to-landlord clause and claims 3/4 of the covenant-not-to-compete value ($30,000) [para. 7].

Things get messy and go to trial, [paras. 8-15] with judgment against landlord on all causes of action, awarding $40k as general damages and $30k as punitive (note the interference w/economic advantages tort).

Held: Affirmed, except for the tort claim, strike punitive damages.

    1. Legislative analysis of Civ. Code § 1995.240, *Kendall*. Limits "consideration" in the statute to the appreciated value of the *lease*, not the business. Thus, lease clause here is too broad.

    2. Unconscionability analysis, sliding scale approach that combines procedural and substantive unconscionability.

NOTES AND QUESTIONS

    1. *Ilkhchooyi v. Best*, in addition to addressing conditional assignment provisions and the public policy implications that they present, highlights the importance of bonus rent in the leasing community. Bonus rent clauses are a method by which the parties allocate the potential upside of an appreciating market between them. In cases like this, as opposed to when the lessee is a major department store, the landlord has the upper hand. Here the landlord went too far.

    2. If the landlord cannot use a percentage-of-the-non-compete clause to capture the bonus value above and beyond bonus rent, what sort of alternate measures are available, if any? How would you try to draft around this decision if your client asked you to? What are the ethical implications of such a request, if any?

Open discussion.

3. The next case considers, among other things, whether certain rights are of a nature that they cannot be assigned as a matter of law. Traditionally, this has been stated as an exception to the broad rule of free assignability and alienation. Often used examples of contracts that cannot be assigned include contracts by famous opera singers to perform, expert doctors to operate, and the like. This case examines the issue in a more commercially relevant context: real estate development. It also illustrates the interrelationship between contract and property law.

♦ - - ♦

Beattie v. State of Oklahoma, ex Rel Grand River Dam Authority
Supreme Court of Oklahoma
2002 OK 3, 41 P.3d 377 (2002)

Plaintiffs took land by quitclaim deed from U.S. government. The land is subject to a number of easements for power transmission from Dam Authority, each had relocation or removal provisions running in favor of the U.S.

Plaintiffs want to develop water front property and invoke relocation and removal provisions. Dam authority refuses.

General rule of free assignability [para. 9], and exception for personal duty contracts [para. 10], requiring exercise of knowledge, judgment, or skill.

Reverse and remand.

B. THIRD - PARTY BENEFICIARY CONTRACTS

Lawrence v. Fox
Court of Appeals of New York
20 N.Y. 268 (1859)

Historical development of 3rd Party Beneficiary law.

Holly (promisee and not a party to the lawsuit) loaned Lawrence (Defendant/Promisor) $300 and Lawrence agreed to pay the $300 to Fox (Plaintiff/ 3PB) for a debt that Holly owed to Fox.

Issue: Whether privity of contract must exist between the Defendant and the Plaintiff in order for the Plaintiff to recover.

Holding: No

Where one person makes a promise to another for the benefit of a third person, the third person may maintain an action upon that promise.

Court Rationale: The promise was made to Holly and not expressly to the plaintiff, but in this case the defendant received consideration for his promise to pay his debt to the plaintiff. "That a promise made to one for the benefit of another, he for whose benefit it is made may bring an action for his breach," had been applied to trust cases. The plaintiff did not release the defendant from his promise.

Formalist dissent: The plaintiff had nothing to do with the promise, it was not made to him, nor did the consideration proceed from him. There must be privity of contract. The party who sues upon a promise must be the promisee, or he must have some legal interest in the undertaking.

◆ - - ◆

PROBLEM 29-1

Old Nettie, in the belief that she was dying, asks her husband Albert to draft her a will. When she reviews it she is unhappy because it does not provide that her house should go to her favorite niece, Marion. Instead, under the will, it goes to Albert during life and then to a charity. Albert offers to write a new will, but Nettie thinks that her time is drawing near and there is no time to lose. So Nettie has Albert promise her that if she signs the will as drafted, he will modify his own will to take care of Marion.

As you by now expect, when Albert dies, shortly after Nettie, his will makes no provision for Marion whatsoever.

Can Marion enforce the agreement between Nettie and Albert against Albert's estate?

See Seaver v. Ransom, 120 N.E. 639 (N.Y. 1918) *(yes)*.

◆ - - ◆

NOTES AND QUESTIONS

1. **Who was the promisor, the promisee, and the third party beneficiary?**

Promisor – Lawrence; Promisee – Holly; 3PB – Fox.

2. **Who could have sued and recovered against whom under the contract? Why?**

Promisee, Holly under basic contract law; Fox as a 3PB under this and like decisions.

3. The court discusses "privity" and "privity of contract." Privity is an older, formalist notion of a direct, in this case contractual, relationship between

369

the parties that gave rise to the right to sue to enforce the contract. Although notions of privity are still in use, the modern trend is to avoid or gloss over the concept in performing third party beneficiary analysis. It is still useful, however, especially in understanding where the rules in this area began — as exceptions to the strict requirement of privity. Although formalists would differ, privity is more a conclusion than a fact.

♦ -- ♦

Schauer v. Mandarin Gems of California, Inc.
Court of Appeal of California
125 Cal. App. 4th 949, 23 Cal. Rptr. 3d 233 (2005)

Divorced woman brings, inter alia, a breach of warranty action against the jeweler that sold her former husband the engagement ring he had given her. It was of lesser quality than as warranted. (How rare do you think this is?)

Trial Court: dismissed.

Appellant Court: Reverse on breach of warranty action. She is and was an intended third party beneficiary of the sale.

Note [para. 25] that in California, 3PB can only enforce the contract. The option of rescission is not available to her.

NOTES

The next case illustrates the evolution of third party beneficiary law in the context of multiparty commercial agreements that are meant to provide for mutual cooperation and benefit in order to avoid the "tragedy of the commons."

The "tragedy of the commons" describes what is otherwise known as the public goods problem: It is hard to coordinate and pay for public goods, i.e., those that are owned or used collectively. Think of the "commons" as a pasture owned by the community and used by a group. Each user owns sheep and has the incentive to put more and more sheep on the pasture to gain, privately. The overall effect of many individuals doing this overwhelms the carrying capacity of the pasture and the sheep cannot all survive. In the case that follows, a group of food vendors has banded together to assess fees to clean and maintain the common food court area. One of the vendors was not happy with the method of allocating fees between the businesses.

♦ -- ♦

Gourmet Lane, Inc. v. Keller
Court of Appeal of California
222 Cal. App. 2d 701, 35 Cal. Rptr. 398 (1963)

Food Court Association required by the terms of the Landlord's lease of space to the tenants. First organized as unincorporated association, later incorporated.

Dispute over allocation method for expenses: Dish count or ratio of taxable sales; dispute over minimum charge, etc. Finally, defendant just stops paying [para. 8].

Lease provision held to create a joint and several liability in and between the several tenants to form, join and obey the association.

NOTES AND QUESTIONS

1. Note how California's statute on third party beneficiary status (quoted in paragraph 12) makes no explicit mention of creditor and donee beneficiaries or the distinction between intended or incidental beneficiaries. Those distinctions are supplied by the courts in that state. This provides a good example of the continued common law tradition of judge-made law based upon and elaborating upon statutes that purport to codify the law in a quasi-civil law format.

2. Review R2d section 133. **In applying the standard of this section to the facts of the case, do you think that the court in *Gourmet Lane* got it right? Why or why not?**

3. In the next case, the R2d's categorization of purported beneficiaries into intended and incidental beneficiaries is applied.

◆ - - ◆

BIS Computer Solutions, Inc. v. Richmond, Virginia
United States Court of Appeals for the Fourth Circuit
122 Fed. Appx. 608 (2005)

Subcontractor attempts to sue "around" the prime contractor, who was acquiescing in the prime contract's termination; software designed for Richmond's police department.

Trial Court: 3PB status available. Awards damages.

Appellate Court: Reverse. No 3PB standing. Applies the "did the contracting parties clearly and definitely intend to confer a benefit upon the third party?" test.

India.com, Inc. v. Dalal
United States Court of Appeals for the Second Circuit
412 F.3d 315 (2005)

Is Sandeep Dalal a third party beneficiary of a stock purchase agreement between Easy-Link (his former employer) and Business India Publication Limited ("BI")?

Trial Court: Yes.

Appellate Court: No. Reverse and remand re: intentional frustration and avoidance of commission.

Trial Court had found that specifying Dalal in the contract overcame the negating clause, which it dismissed as "mere boilerplate" [para. 14].

Appellate Court literally applies the negating clause [paras. 22-25].

♦ -- ♦

End of Casebook

QUESTION COVERING ACCEPTANCE AND UCC §§ 2-201 AND 2-207

(40 minutes)

Bertha Lundquist had retired as owner and operator of Bertha's Kitty Boutique, a small store which sold pet accessories. She worked three afternoons a week as secretary of the Lake Woebegon Lutheran Church, which had a congregation of 250 souls. Every year, the church held a traditional Scandinavian Christmas Eve supper featuring lutefisk (cod cured in lye), boiled potatoes, and cream gravy.

On November 20, Bertha telephoned Arne Olafssen, owner of The Scandinavian Smorgasbord, and offered to buy all of the food for the supper from him if he would agree to furnish it for a price of $5.00 per person. (It is undisputed that Bertha's proposal was an offer.) Arne asked how many people Bertha expected to have, and Bertha said "Between 80 and 120. I'll give you an exact head count by the end of the day on December 22." (Even though Karl Llewellyn will roll over in his grave when he reads this question, this transaction IS a sale of goods).

Arne told Bertha he would think about it and would "get something to you pretty soon." Bertha told him, "that would be fine."

On November 25, Bertha was getting anxious to get the food for the supper lined up. She called Arne's restaurant and heard a message on the machine that said the restaurant was closed indefinitely. Bertha called several people in the congregation to try to learn why the restaurant was closed. Nobody knew for sure, but several people said that Arne had a bad heart (Scandinavian food doesn't have much flavor, but it has a lot of saturated fat) and they thought there was a good chance he'd had a heart attack. The third time Bertha heard this surmise, she called the Chatterbox Café and entered into a contract with them to buy pot roast for the supper
for $5.50 a person.

It turned out that Arne hadn't had a heart attack. On November 24, he'd had chest pains and Doc Hansen had sent him to a specialist in St. Paul. "Drive him right to St. Paul," Doc Hansen had told Arne's daughter. "Don't even stop at home to pick up a toothbrush."

The folks in the big hospital in St. Paul did a catheterization on November 25, and Arne arrived home in Lake Woebegon early in the afternoon of November 27. (His doctor thought he should stay in the hospital longer, but the HMO wouldn't allow it.) Arne immediately wrote Bertha a note telling her that he accepted her offer to supply the food for the supper. But his letter included the following: "I understand the number of guests will be not more than 120 nor less than 80. I must have an exact head count by Monday, December 20. This shouldn't be a problem. In prior years you've posted sign-up sheets in the church on Sunday and given me a head count on Monday morning."

Arne signed the note, put it in an envelope addressed to Bertha, and put the envelope in his mailbox. Because he didn't have a stamp, he put the envelope in his mailbox without one. This was something he often did. He lived out in the country and the mail carrier knew him well. When Arne didn't put stamps on his letters, the mail carrier did it for him and Arne repaid her by giving her an occasional free lunch at the Scandinavian Smorgasbord. (The mail carrier paid for the stamps out of her own pocket. No criminal law issues in this question.) This time, however, the mail carrier stuck the envelope in her pocket, planning on putting a stamp on it later, and forgot about it until December 6, when she found the letter in her pocket. She was so embarrassed about it that as soon as she finished her appointed rounds that day (in a snowstorm, of course) she drove over to the church and hand-delivered the letter to Bertha.

Pastor Johanssen, who used to be an executive at Enron before she went into the ministry, has sought your advice. Because the church has a contract with the Chatterbox Café, she would rather serve pot roast ("after all, our ancestors used to have to eat that stuff when they were raiding England") than have to buy lutefisk from Arne.

Discuss completely the answers to the following questions,

(a)   Does the church have to purchase lutefisk from Arne?

(b)   If the church does have to purchase lutefisk from Arne, when does it have to tell him how many people he will be supplying with this wonder of Scandinavian cuisine?

ANALYSIS

No contract was formed if Arne failed to accept the offer. Arne's letter changed the date for the exact count, but because this is a sale of goods, UCC 2-207(1) would apply and the letter would still function as an acceptance.

A more important problem is that the letter may not have been timely. An offer that does not state a time for acceptance expires after a reasonable time. To determine whether the reasonable time elapsed before the offer was accepted, it would make sense to begin by looking at when Arne's acceptance letter became effective.

Normally an acceptance by mail is effective when it is posted. This is subject, however, to limitations. First, the mail must be a reasonable means of communicating the acceptance. Here, given the time constraints and the fact that the offer was made by telephone, it could be argued that acceptance by mail was not reasonable. However, Arne's statement that he would "get something to you" could be interpreted as a proposal to put his acceptance in writing, and Bertha's statement that "that would be fine" could be her agreement that a written acceptance was appropriate. Moreover, the possible need to satisfy the statute of frauds (if these people worried about such things) could also argue for the appropriateness of a reply via the postal service, especially because there is no indication these people used e-mail regularly.

If snail mail was a reasonable means of acceptance, there is the issue of whether the letter was properly posted. Application of the mailbox rule requires that the sender do what is ordinarily done make sure it reaches its destination. Arne will argue that since he took what are normal precautions, he has complied. The church can argue that it should not suffer because Arne's informal arrangement with the mail carrier didn't work out on this occasion. If a lawyer's letter went astray because her secretary failed to put a stamp on it, we'd all say that the mailbox rule didn't apply there. Arne's situation is different because the mail carrier isn't his employee, but I would argue that the analogy still applies because she is working on his behalf.

Bertha can also make an argument that the mailbox rule doesn't apply because Arne's statement that he would "get something to you" and her saying that was fine was an agreement that he had to "get something" to her for the acceptance to be effective. I wouldn't buy that argument because I think it is reading too much into casual statements, but I think the argument is worth making.

Because it is not clear whether or not the mailbox rule applies, we have to consider both November 27 and December 6 as possible dates for effectiveness of Arne's acceptance. Arne said he would get something to Bertha "pretty soon" and Bertha said that would be fine, so the parties may have agreed that the acceptance would be effective if it were given "pretty soon." Here, again, it may be reading too much into a casual statement. Also, "pretty soon" may be so imprecise that it may not differ from the default standard of "within a reasonable time."

In determining what is a reasonable time (or "pretty soon"), do we take into account Arne's medical problems? I think not. I think we have to look at it from what the parties knew at the time the offer was made. Moreover, we have to look at time from the position of the offeror. The offeror has to know when it is no longer bound by its offer.

Looking at November 27 as the date of the acceptance, it could be argued that this was late because Christmas was getting close (the supper was less than 4 weeks away) and the church needed time to line up an alternate source of food if Arne rejected the offer. Moreover, since this answer assumes that the mailbox rule applies, there would be an additional delay in getting the letter to her, even if things had gone smoothly. Nevertheless, it was only a week after Bertha had first made the offer. Her lateness in making the offer and her failure to specify the need for a fast reply argue against the response being late. I would conclude that the offer had not expired before November 27.

If the acceptance was effective on December 3, the acceptance is more likely to be late. It's only three weeks from the date of the supper, and it might be hard to line up a substitute for Christmas Eve on such short notice. Moreover, it's 13 days after Bertha made the offer. I would conclude that an acceptance made on December 3 is not effective.

Because there is an issue as to whether the acceptance was effective, we have to deal with the issue of whether the statute of frauds precludes enforcement of the contract. I was surprised how few people saw that issue. Maybe it was because I haven't asked a statute of frauds question lately. UCC Section 2-201 applies to contracts for the sale of goods for the price of $500 or more. Here, the quantity has been left somewhat open and the total price may or may not be $500 or more. I don't know what you do in a situation like this. The one-year rule provides that a contract is within the statute of frauds only if performance cannot be completed within a year. By analogy, it could be argued that a contract for an indeterminate amount of goods is within the statute only if the price *must* exceed $500. Given the judicial hostility to the statute of frauds, that argument seems likely to prevail.

If the contract is within the statute of frauds, Arne's letter may bind the church under subsection (2) of section 2-201. This would apply only if the church is a merchant. As we discussed in class, whether the church is a merchant should depend, not on whether they sell a lot of food, but whether they are the type of organization that should know about things like the need to respond to mail from suppliers. Section 2-204(1) defines a "merchant" to include someone who holds himself out as having knowledge of the practices involved in the transaction.

Many people properly noted that Bertha's prior experience in business should be a factor here, but nobody mentioned the pastor's business experience. Even though the pastor wasn't directly involved in the transaction, she would be responsible for the church's general procedures.

Most people did well on the 2-207 issue, except that too many people failed to discuss whether the change in dates would materially alter the contract. I assume that was because they were tired and short on time.

QUESTION COVERING CONSIDERATION AND PROMISSORY ESTOPPEL

(30 minutes)

Rachel was the star programmer at Bill's Software. In May, Rachel worked three weekends in a row finishing up the programming for the company's newest product. On the Friday before the fourth weekend, Rachel's part of the project was finished and Rachel was looking forward to a weekend of rock-climbing. Then she heard the weather report. The funny-looking dude on the Weather Channel said there would be two inches of rain on Saturday. That meant the rocks would be too wet for climbing all weekend. Rachel was wandering around the office complaining to anyone who would listen about her lousy lot in life. "One weekend all month I get off, and what does it do? It ____ing rains."

Bill heard Rachel complaining and was disturbed. He wanted her to be happy and productive. But more than that, he wanted her to shut up and stop ruining the morale of the rest of the troops. He said to her: "I'll make you a deal. I'll pay you ten thousand dollars if it rains this weekend. That ought to pay for a nice vacation somewhere where it won't rain."

"You've got yourself a deal," said Rachel.

Things went pretty much as expected, at least for a while. Rachel shut up and went back to work. It rained on Saturday.

Rachel didn't quit the company. Before Bill made his promise, she had been receiving calls from headhunters about once a month on the average. Most of the jobs they wanted her to interview for were substantially comparable to her job at Bill's, so she never pursued them because she wanted to spend her limited free time rock climbing, not sneaking around to be interviewed by Bill's competitors. After Bill made his ten thousand dollar promise, Rachel continued to turn down the headhunters, but she says (and for purposes of this question the court will accept it as true) that if it hadn't been for Bill's promise, she might have pursued some of the job leads to try to find a job that would give her more free time.

Unfortunately, the software for which Rachel sacrificed three weekends didn't sell. Because it didn't sell, Bill's Software had some financial problems, and Bill was forced to lay Rachel off. He never paid her the ten thousand dollars.

Rachel had sued Bill for the ten thousand dollars. Discuss the issue (or issues) the court will have to decide in order to resolve the case.

ANALYSIS OF QUESTION

Consideration

There doesn't seem to be any consideration for Bill's promise to pay the ten grand. He didn't bargain for anything in return. His promise was subject to the condition that it rain, but he certainly wasn't bargaining for that. It wasn't a promise or performance that she could give.

It might be argued that there was an implied condition that she stop complaining or that she remain employed with the company for a certain period. I think that's a tough argument. If the promise were otherwise enforceable, it would be hard for Bill to argue that he had put these conditions on the promise and not told Rachel about them.

Promissory Estoppel

In order to recover under promissory estoppel, Rachel must show (1) Bill made a promise, (2) Bill should reasonably have expected that it would induce action or forbearance on Rachel's part, (3) it did induce such action or forbearance, and (4) injustice can be avoided only by enforcement of the promise.

Bill certainly made a promise. As to elements (2) and (3) there are several actions or forbearances involved. The one that Bill should reasonably have expected (since he sought to induce it) is forbearance from complaining. That forbearance, the question tells us, was actually
induced. Is this enough to say that injustice can be avoided only by enforcing the promise? On one hand, it can be argued that Bill got the benefit he wanted, and he ought to pay for it. He shouldn't be able to get away without paying simply because the promise doesn't quite meet the
requirements for bargained-for consideration. Moreover, because Rachel is unemployed, she may need the money, although it is not clear whether this sympathy issue ought to enter into the calculation. If it does, Bill can argue that he needs the money too, because his company is in such bad shape that it had to lay off Rachel, whom the question characterizes as his "star programmer." Moreover, Bill can argue that with respect to the forbearance from complaining (leaving aside for now the forbearance from quitting her job), ten thousand dollars is a lot of money and the restatement says that "the remedy granted for breach may be limited as justice
requires." So maybe Rachel should only get part of the ten grand.

There is also the fact that because of the promise, Rachel forbore from looking for other jobs. There is no direct indication that Bill should reasonably have expected that his promise would induce this. But on the other hand, he runs a software company. He probably is aware that headhunters are contacting his programmers, particularly "star programmers" like Rachel. He also knew that Rachel was unhappy (unless he thought that programmers, like sailors, are only happy when they're complaining). So it can be argued that he should have put two and two and two more together and have reasonably foreseen that his promise would cause Rachel to stay on her job when she might otherwise have left. From this perspective, reliance on Bill's promise has cost Rachel a period of unemployment which she might have avoided if she had jumped off Bill's ship before it began to sink. Because of the inherent injustice in allowing Bill to avoid a promise from which he seems to have received a benefit (Rachel's continued employment and the productivity resulting from her better morale), I believe the court would enforce Bill's promise.

QUESTION COVERING MISTAKE, MISREPRESENTATION, AND UNCONSICIONABILITY IN THE CONTEXT OF LAWYERING SKILLS

(15 minutes)

You are general counsel for an insurance company. The company's standard-form release to be signed by people whom the company has compensated for injuries allegedly caused by its insured reads:

Releasor hereby releases, acquits and forever discharges Releasee and any other persons and entities of and from any and all actions, causes of action, claims, demands, damages, costs, loss of services, expenses and compensation on account of or in any way growing out of any and all known and unknown personal injuries resulting or to result from the accident that occurred on or about [date and time], at or about [location].

In spite of the language of the release, which you think is pretty clear, a number of courts have held that it does NOT release claims for injuries that the signer does not know she has when she signs the release and accepts the money.

You have been asked to re-write the release to make it more likely that courts will interpret it to release claims for injuries not known at the time the release is signed. Explain what you would do. You may either explain it in general language or give specific examples. (If you have time, you can do both.)

NOTE: Don't worry about the strange law in California. You will have local counsel draft a California-specific release that will satisfy the wackos out there in Schwarzenegger land. You will also, of course, have a law clerk do research to see if there are other states that have unusual requirements. But your job here is just to draft a basic release that will do the job in the ordinary run-of-the-mill red state.

GOOD STUDENT ANSWERS

To avoid mistake:

I would add a provision that states that the releasor has agreed to assume any risk that there are unknown injuries. I would also add that the releasor has limited knowledge regarding any potential unknown injuries. I would also add a provision that states that the release is not being signed under any assumptions regarding the unknown injuries.

To avoid misrepresentation:

I would add that the releasor agrees that the release has made no representations about any possible unknown injuries. I would add that the releasor has not relied on the releaser in any way regarding the unknown injuries.

<u>To avoid unconscionability:</u>

I would clearly print across the top of the document something to the effect of: "THIS IS A LEGAL DOCUMENT WITH LEGAL CONSEQUENCES." I would also add something to the effect that the releasor understands that seeking legal advice before signing the document is the prudent thing to do. I would add that the releasor considers the release to be a fair and equitable release. I would also instruct whoever is handling the signing process to point each provision of the release out to the releasor and explain it to them.

This answer is shorter than I would like, but it still got a relatively good score because it covered the most important points clearly and concisely:

I would include a specific stipulation that the release is applicable to injuries not known at the time of the release. I would put this sentence in big bold letters, possibly at the beginning of the document. I would use plain as language as possible so that a lay person would understand it. I would also put in a sentence in big bold letters at the top of the document that the person must read the document before signing it or it is not valid and require the insurance agent to make the person read it.

QUESTION COVERING PROMISSORY ESTOPPEL

(30 minutes)

One night, when Kelli was 17, her family was invited to Grandmother's house for dinner. Kelli wanted to go out with her friends instead, but her father insisted that she go to Grandmother's. To show what she thought of the whole deal, Kelli lit up a cigarette at dinner. This upset Grandmother because Grandfather, a heavy smoker, had died of lung cancer.

"Kelli," said Grandmother, "it has always been my intention to give you and your cousins each $25,000 when you graduate from college. But I've decided to change the deal a little bit. I'm going to deduct $100 for each cigarette you smoke between now and your twenty-first birthday."

"Like, how you going to know how many I smoke?" asked Kelli.

"I'll trust you to keep track. In spite of what all my friends who voted for George W. Bush tell me, I think one can trust a person with pierced tongue."

"This one count?"

"This one counts."

"How 'bout, you know, if I like stub it out now?"

"It doesn't count," said Grandmother, smiling.

"It doesn't count," said Kelli stubbing out the cigarette with a noncommittal look on her face.

Kelli immediately gave up her habit. This caused her some discomfort, but not too much. Because her parents didn't allow her to smoke in the house, she hadn't become as addicted as she otherwise might have been.

From then on, Kelli was pretty much clean. On a few occasions, when she'd had too much to drink, she had a cigarette, but the next morning she dutifully recorded the cigarette in her PDA. When Kelli graduated from college with a degree in public health administration, she estimated she had smoked 32 cigarettes. Because there were a few times she had imprecise recollections of the night before and a couple of times when PDAs had been lost without the files backed up, she may have been a little off, but she thought 32 was a pretty good estimate. Maybe she'd even given Grandmother the benefit of the doubt.

Shortly before Kelli's graduation, Grandmother died. She left half of her estate to People Against Hunger, an organization that teaches efficient farming techniques to people in poor countries and provides them with genetically-modified seed and genetically-modified livestock to make their farming more efficient. The other half of her estate, she left to the unemployed male model she had married shortly before her death.

Kelli graduated from college and shortly thereafter, she joined a religious cult that believes: (1) genetic modification is the work of the Devil, (2) all the traits of individual plants, animals, and humans are determined by The Big Dice In The Sky, and (3) Fox News is fair and balanced. As a condition to joining the cult, the cult required that Kelli promise to give the cult any earthly possessions she acquires while a member of the cult (this would of course include any money she received from Grandmother's estate).

The executor of grandmother's estate has refused to pay Kelli the money she claims is owed her. Kelli has sued to enforce Grandmother's promise. If Kelli wins, the amount she wins will be deducted half from the amount that would otherwise go to People Against Hunger and half from the amount that would go to her male model widower. Discuss the issues the court will have to decide. ASSUME THERE ARE NO STATUTE OF FRAUDS ISSUES. Assume also that there was no federal, state, or local law that would have prohibited Kelli from smoking.

ANALYSIS

One way to look at this transaction is to say that it is a unilateral contract. If Kelli smokes fewer than 250 cigarettes before she turns 21, she gets some money, the exact amount to be determined by the number of cigarettes she smoked. Grandmother's characterization of it as "a deal" lends credence to this interpretation. On the other hand, Grandmother has also characterized the transaction as merely adding a new wrinkle to a long-planned gift. Moreover, courts are reluctant to find contracts in informal, non-business family transactions like this. Nevertheless, I believe the transaction should be characterized as a unilateral contract under the terms of which Grandmother will pay Kelli if she smokes fewer than 250 cigarettes.

If the transaction is characterized in this way, there is the question of whether she also has to graduate from college to complete her performance under the contract. Under the traditional common law rule, an offer for a unilateral contract can be revoked at any time before performance is complete, and Grandmother's death would constitute a revocation of the offer. Therefore, Grandmother's death would revoke the offer and Kelli could not recover, *if graduation from college was required in order to complete performance.* Another interpretation would be that Grandmother's reference to Kelli's college graduation meant only that the payment would be made at that time, and that graduation itself was not required in order for Kelli to complete performance of the contract. I favor this interpretation because I think that if Grandmother had intended that to be a requirement she would have said so more explicitly, but there's really not much evidence one way or the other. Under the Second Restatement, the beginning of performance makes the offer irrevocable, so this would not be an issue. But under the common law, it is. Interestingly, the class was pretty well split between those who *assumed* that she had to graduate from college to complete performance and those who *assumed* that she did not. Very few people saw this as an *issue* that could be resolved either way.

If the transaction is a gratuitous promise rather than an offer for a unilateral contract, Kelli may still be able to recover under a theory of promissory estoppel. Grandmother made a promise. It's pretty clear that she should reasonably have expected the promise to induce action or forbearance on the part of Kelli. That was the reason she made the promise. And the promise did of course induce the forbearance she intended.

The difficult issue is whether injustice can be avoided only by enforcing the promise. On one hand, Kelli is probably better off having curtailed her smoking. The fact that she gave up a legal right would be sufficient if the issue were consideration, but giving up a bare legal right is not the sort of detriment normally required for promissory estoppel. One perfectly proper response would be: "Tough cookies. Grandma tricked you, but you're better off than if she hadn't. You're not entitled to come into court and waste public resources crying about it. Promissory estoppel is for people who suffer serious harm from relying on a promise. On the other hand, it could be argued that Kelli has denied herself the pleasure she would have derived from smoking and that her non-smoking may have imposed on her certain social costs, including a loss of her social standing among her pierced-tongue friends. But (switching sides again) it can also be argued that when the Restatement says "injustice can be avoided *only* by enforcement of the promise" (emphasis added), it means that there needs to be a clear case of injustice, not some speculative and intangible potential loss like Kelli claims to have suffered.

I don't know to what extent it's appropriate to consider the fact that Grandmother would not have wanted the money to go to an organization that opposes genetically-modified food. The Restatement gives no guidance to how we determine what constitutes "injustice." On one hand it can be argued that injustice is limited to questions of the amount of detriment suffered by the person relying on the statement. This would be in keeping with Professor Gilmore 's characterization of promissory estoppel as being very much like a tort. On the other hand, it can be argued that promissory estoppel is essentially a vehicle to allow the court to do "justice" as whatever fashion the court believes is appropriate under the circumstances and that justice in that case should include such things as the wishes of the promisor and who would get the money if it is not given to the promisee. In this case we can presume that because Grandma left half her estate to an organization that is attempting to encourage the use of genetically-modified food, she would not want her money going to a cult that opposes it. Her remarks about pierced tongues could be taken as an indication she does not share the cult's faith in Fox News, but the statement that she has friends who watch it could be taken as an indication she has no problems with Fox News. In any event, a court would likely be reluctant to get into that sort of political issue. But if the court did choose to do so, it might need more evidence to determine what
Grandmother thought about Fox News.

One final point: Many people confused principles of consideration with those of promissory estoppel. In particular, a lot of people seemed to think the promisee's reliance was a factor in determining whether there was consideration.

QUESTION COVERING UCC SECTION 2-207

(20 minutes)

Buyer called Seller and asked: "What's your best price for Grade 2 stainless Steel?

Seller replied: "Seven hundred twenty-three dollars a gross."

Buyer: "If you can go seven hundred, I'll take ten gross."

Seller: "Sold. Ten gross of stainless steel doomaflaches at seven hundred dollars a gross."

Buyer: "It's a deal. I'll send you a confirmation."

Buyer sent Seller the following note:

This will confirm our purchase of ten gross of Grade 2 stainless steel doomaflaches at $700.00 per gross, total price $7,000.00. This order is expressly made conditional on your assent to our requirement that the doomaflaches be individually boxed for resale. If you fail to assent to this requirement, this order will be null and void.

Seller normally sold doomaflaches boxed twelve to a box, and he shipped them to Buyer that way. When the doomaflaches arrived, Buyer was in desperate need of doomaflaches to fill orders from his customers, so at considerable expense, he had the doomaflaches boxed one to a box and resold them.

Buyer has sued Seller for breach of contract. **It has been determined that if the contract does not provide otherwise, doomaflaches may be shipped twelve to a box.** How should the court decide the case between Buyer and Seller? Explain your reasoning. **DOOMAFLACHES ARE "GOODS" AS THAT TERM IS DEFINED IN THE UCC.**

ANALYSIS

What most people didn't seem to realize is that there was an oral contract formed over the telephone. I tried to make this beyond dispute by having Buyer make what was clearly an offer, having Seller accept it, and then having Buyer say "it's a deal." Thus, the note that Buyer sent Seller is not a "definite and seasonable expression of acceptance" but instead "a written confirmation" under 2-207(1). Once these guys have a deal, the "null and void" language in the confirmation can't change this. Most people, however, didn't think carefully about *what was really going on*. They saw the confirmation as an acceptance "expressly made conditional," and on that basis they threw the deal into subsection (3). If that were possible, no one could ever depend on an oral contract.

Because we have a confirmation, we have to look at the packaging term under 2-207(2). The first question is whether the packaging term is an "additional term" or a "different term." One could argue that it's a "different term" because the original oral contract, by default provided for boxing 12 to a box. I think, however, it's an additional term because it wasn't expressly addressed in the oral contract. Any contract covers all issues not addressed with default terms, so if this were a "different term," there would never be any "additional" terms.

No matter whether you consider it an additional term or a different term, you need to consider whether it materially alters the contract. I think it does. There would seem to be a lot work involved in re-boxing items, and in fact the question says that the re-boxing was done "at considerable expense." Moreover, the fact that Buyer considered it so important seems to indicate that it is material.

I didn't say whether these guys were merchants and I guess I should have. But it seems pretty apparent from the facts that they were. It says that Seller normally sold doomaflaches boxed twelve to a box. The fact that he *normally* sold them would certainly make him a merchant. The fact that Buyer was buying for resale would make him a merchant.

QUESTION COVERING PROMISSORY ESTOPPEL

Note: Some of you may find a lot to write about on this question. Don't let your enthusiasm mess you up for Questions Two and Three. Make the best arguments you can in the time allotted and move on.

Pamela grew up on a farm. After college, she became an elementary school teacher. She loved the kids but she hated her job because of the frustration of dealing with the bureaucracy. So she decided to find a new career.

She found a building that would make a wonderful day care center. The price was $100,000. On February 20, she told her father of her desire to own her own day care center, and her father said: "I was proud to have a teacher in the family, but I'd be even prouder if you were a successful businesswoman. To get you started, I'm going to give you the $20,000 you'll need for a down payment. This is, of course, dependent on my not having a bad crop year next year." Dad didn't say what he meant by "a bad crop year," but Pamela remembered that when she was growing up, there had been two years (out of the 18 years she was living at home) when her father had complained about there being "a bad crop year." In those years, the family spent their vacation visiting relatives instead of skiing in Colorado, kept the house a little cooler in winter and did other things to economize.

Pamela was so happy that her father was supporting her effort that she immediately entered into a contract to buy the property. She didn't try to bargain the price down.

On March 1, Dad called and told Pamela that he and Pamela's mother were getting a divorce. This upset Pamela, and she avoided thinking about it by throwing herself into preparations for starting the day care center. The next day she spent $2,000 buying supplies and doing some preliminary advertising.

On March 17, Dad called and said that he wasn't sure, but he was afraid the expenses of the divorce would keep him from giving Pamela the $20,000 he had promised her. Pamela responded: "But Daddy, you promised. You always told us promises are sacred."

"I know, Honey, I'll do my best, " he said.

The next day, Pamela resigned her teaching position. She decided she was committed to the day care center, come hell or high water, and besides, when her father had said he would do something, he always came through. She e-mailed her father, telling him that she needed the $20,000 by April 1, or she would default on the contract to buy the property. He responded that he would do his best.

On March 28, Dad called and told Pamela that he would not be able to give her the $20,000 because of the expenses of the divorce. Pamela tried borrowing the money from friends, but she couldn't come up with it. As a result, she lost the chance to start the day care center, and she was liable for $10,000 in damages for breaching the contract to buy the property. If she had negotiated the price down, as she could have done had she not let her enthusiasm get the best of her, she would have been liable for only $5,000 in damages. Pamela wasn't able to get her teaching job back, but she was able to get another teaching job in a different school district. It paid $3,000 a year less than her old job, but it shortened her commute from 30 minutes each way to 15 minutes each way. Otherwise, the job was pretty much the same.

Subsequently, Pamela learned the reason Dad's divorce had been so expensive. Mom found out that Dad had taken his girlfriend to Las Vegas for Valentine's Day. Dad had said he was going hunting with the guys, but Mom's lawyer found out the truth. The theretofore amicable divorce turned bitter and the attorney fees went up several fold. Dad had the better lawyer, though. He got the farm and Mom got a less-than-generous settlement.

Pamela is pissed. She has sued Dad for the $20,000 he promised to give her. After paying off the $10,000 judgment against her, she plans to give the rest to Mom to make her life a little better. She's given up on the idea of running a day care center or doing anything else useful. She thinks that maybe in a couple of years she'll try law school.

Discuss the likely outcome of her suit against Dad. Explain the issues the court will have to decide, developing the arguments as fully as you can **within the time allotted.**

ANALYSIS

Most people did reasonably well on this question. I gave a lot of facts that could be used to argue both sides of whether Dad should be liable under a theory of promissory estoppel and, if so, for how much. Many people did a good job, given the time constraints, of using these facts to develop good arguments.

The first challenge I put into the question was the conditional nature of Dad's promise. We had never seen a promissory estoppel case where the promise was conditional. Some people questioned whether that kept it from being a "promise" for purposes of the first element. Generally, they concluded, correctly I think, that because a conditional promise is still a promise for consideration purposes, it's also a promise for promissory estoppel. Still, it's a point worth raising–should the boundaries of what qualifies as a "promise" be different depending on whether we're analyzing consideration or promissory estoppel?

The element of "the promisor should reasonably expect" the promise to induce action or forbearance is where I really expected the conditional nature of the promise to become an issue. While I was writing the question, I played around with the ratio of "bad crop years" to good years in order to make it such that everyone should see that there was some risk involved but no one would decide it was so risky that it was clear there was no reliance and thereby foreclose discussion of the rest of the issues. It worked out pretty well. Most people were able to see issues on both sides of the expectation of reliance issue.

Many people discussed whether there was a conventional contract–offer, acceptance, consideration. I didn't intend that to be an issue. In fact, I intentionally made the facts similar to *Ricketts v. Scothorn* and Problem 5-5. In both of those, we summarily decided there was no consideration. Dad never overtly bargained for anything, and it's hard to find anything that could be an implied promise. Still, I can't fault people who mentioned these points quickly to make sure they covered everything. But if you went on at length about offer, acceptance, unilateral and bilateral contracts, and the like, you wasted a lot of time on what was clearly a promissory estoppel question.

The three big issues were (1) whether and to what extent the promise could be relied upon, (2) whether injustice could be avoided only by enforcing the promise, and (3) to what extent the remedy should be limited. The three issues are intertwined, so it really didn't matter which of the specific facts of the case you discussed under which issue. What was important was how you used the facts to analyze the extent to which Pamela should be allowed to recover.

In class, we looked at several cases where a timeline made the analysis easier. This was certainly such a situation.

Feb 14	Dad takes girlfriend to Vegas
Feb. 20	Dad promises to give Pam $20,000
Immediately thereafter	Pam enters into contract
Mar 1	Dad tells of impending divorce
Mar 2	Pam spends money on supplies
Mar 17	Dad indicates he may not be able to keep promise
Mar 18	Pamela quits teaching job

In Contracts II, you'll learn rules for damages for breach of contract. Obviously, I wasn't looking for you to use them in your answer. I don't think they would apply in this situation anyway. The real questions are to what extent Pamela can rely and what is just. Under these facts, I don't think there are any clear answers.

Most people thought that Pamela was justified in relying initially because there had only been two bad crop years out of 18, but others made good arguments to the contrary.

In some ways, it seems fair that Dad should have to pay Pamela the money she lost on the building because she entered into the contract in her initial burst of enthusiasm after Dad made his promise. But was she going to have to buy a building anyway? Maybe would have to, but maybe she would have been able to rent space. Should Dad have to pay the whole $10,000, or just the $5,000 Pamela would have had to pay if she had bargained the price down? I don't think there are clear answers for these questions. The important thing was that you saw that the questions were there.

Should Dad have to pay for the $2,000 Pamela spent after Dad told her he was getting a divorce? On one hand, Dad hadn't yet said anything that directly indicated that he would not pay Pamela the $20,000. On the other, Pamela should have known divorces were expensive, and Dad doesn't seem to have had much of a cushion. Otherwise he wouldn't have needed to condition his promise on not having a bad crop year. Moreover, because Pamela was already committed to starting a day care center, she would have had to buy supplies even if Dad hadn't promised to give her the money. Interestingly, we're not told why Pamela gave up her plan to start a day care center. If she wasn't really that serious about it until Dad made his promise, that would be an argument for favoring her on some of the close issues. The fact that she hadn't resigned her teaching job before Dad made his promise but did so as soon as the promise was made indicates she's relying pretty heavily on his promise.

The fact that Pamela is going to use part of her recovery from this case to right what she perceives to be the wrong of the divorce raises an interesting issue. Can a court take this into account in determining whether "injustice can be avoided only by the enforcement of the promise" or if "justice requires" that the breach be limited? I don't think so, but I don't know of any rule about it. Even if the court does take this into account, which way should it cut? Dad looks like a bad guy, but if the court orders him to give the money to Pamela, knowing that she's going to give it to Mom, is this court then, in effect, second-guessing the divorce court?

This raises another interesting issue. Dad is trying to get out of his promise (or part of it) by pleading poverty. Is it legitimate to take into account his financial situation in determining whether and to what extent justice requires the promise to be enforced? I think it probably does, although we haven't seen any case that said so directly. If so, is it fair to take into account the fact that Dad had money for trips to Vegas but now can't find the money to make good on his promise to his daughter? These are all interesting questions for which I don't think there is a legal rule. Some people made very clever arguments on one side or the other of these questions.

Many people discussed misrepresentation. I can't see a misrepresentation issue. We discussed misrepresentation as a way to *avoid* a contract, but people tried to use it to get Dad *into* a contract. Almost no one who discussed misrepresentation saw this anomaly.

QUESTION COVERING MISREPRESENTATION

(30 minutes)

Slumlord owned an old house near a large university. He had divided the house into apartments for students and other undesirables who couldn't afford to live elsewhere. Developer approached Slumlord and told him she was interested in buying the house because she heard there was a lot of money to be made renting to students. In fact, Developer wasn't interested in renting to students. She was interested in *selling* to students (or their parents). She was planning a condominium project. She had secretly obtained options on the houses on both sides of Slumlord's property, and she needed Slumlord's property in order to have the three contiguous parcels she needed to make the project viable.

Developer had been pretty tricky in this deal. She knew that Slumlord was a hard bargainer. She also knew that if she told him she was buying the land for a condominium project, he would ask for much more than the property was worth as rental housing. To make her job even more difficult, she had to make sure she got all three of the properties or none at all, because she needed all three to do the condo project and she didn't want to get stuck owning rental property in the Fort. So she first approached the property owners on either side of Slumlord's property and purchased options to buy their properties at prices higher than what they would otherwise be able to get for them. The property owners knew that if they told Slumlord what was going on, he would hold out for a high price, and it might kill the deal for all of them, so they kept their mouths shut.

When Developer talked to Slumlord about Slumlord's property, she pretended to be concerned about whether the building had termites. This was part of the scheme to keep Slumlord from realizing Developer's plan and holding out for a higher price.

Slumlord knew there were termites in the building, but he also knew that the termite infestation and damage was in a place where it was very hard to detect. In addition, he knew that people who buy old buildings in the Fort are usually too cheap to shell out for a sophisticated termite inspection. So when Developer asked if the building had ever had termites, Slumlord told her: "I keep a close eye out for termites. This building has never had them."

After some hard negotiating, the parties agreed on a price of $200,000 for the property. A written contract satisfying the statute of frauds was signed by both parties.

After the contract was signed, but before the price was to be paid and the deed delivered, it was announced that another condominium complex, as well as a huge apartment complex, were going to be built in the neighborhood. Hearing this news, the bank that had been going to finance Developer's project backed out. Developer wasn't able to come up with the $200,000 to buy the house (and she wouldn't have wanted to even if she could, given the market conditions).

Developer did NOT have a provision in the contract allowing her to get out of her obligation to buy if she couldn't get financing.

Slumlord sued for breach of contract. While preparing for trial, Developer's attorney discovered that the building had termites. Developer now seeks to avoid the contract on the basis of misrepresentation. At trial, it was shown that (1) because of the importance of the property to Developer's plans, she would have been willing to pay up to $250,000 to get it, (2) if Developer had known about the termites, she probably would have been able to negotiate the price down to $185,000.

Discuss the arguments that both sides will make as to whether Developer should be allowed to void the contract on the basis of misrepresentation. **DO NOT** discuss whether Developer is entitled to money damages. That's a question for Contracts II. In this course, we've limited our discussion of misrepresentation to whether the misrepresentation allows the recipient of the misrepresentation to void the contract. Also, **DO NOT** discuss mistake. It might be possible to make some mistake arguments, but we didn't go into enough detail about unilateral mistake.

ANALYSIS

Slumlord made a fraudulent misrepresentation. He knew there were termites in the building and he told Developer otherwise in order to induce Developer to enter into the contract. Because a contract is voidable if the misrepresentation is *either* fraudulent *or* material, it wasn't necessary to discuss whether the misrepresentation was material. It was fine to say something about it briefly in order to make sure you had covered all the bases, but if you discussed it at length, you were spending time that could have been better used elsewhere.

The only real issue in the case is whether the misrepresentation induced Developer to enter into the contract. Most people saw this issue and concluded that because Developer didn't care about the termites and was going to buy the property anyway, the misrepresentation shouldn't allow Developer to void the contract.

A more sophisticated analysis asks whether the issue should be (1) did the misrepresentation induce Developer to enter into *a* contract to buy the property or (2) did it induce Developer to enter into *this* contract to buy the property *at this price*?

As far as I know, there is no case law on this point. The reason there is no case law is that principles of contract law and tort law allow persons in Developer's position to, in effect, get a reduction of the price in the amount of the loss they suffered on account of the misrepresentation. You'll learn about these principles in Contracts II and Torts II. They don't apply in this situation because (a) Developer needs to get out of the contract entirely, not just get some money back, and (b) you're not supposed to know about them yet.

So I don't know whether Developer should get out of the contract or not. In the closest analogous case I know of, the court held that the person in Developer's position should lose. I criticized the decision in an article I wrote, but that probably doesn't matter. My wife and kid don't listen to me (nor does the guinea pig), so why should the courts be different?

There are a couple of additional factors that cut against Developer, although I don't know exactly how they fit into the rules we're applying. First, it can be argued that Developer was the one who made the first misrepresentation. She deliberately misled Slumlord as to her intentions. It's hard to see how this helps Slumlord, though because Slumlord isn't the one trying to get out of the contract. It's a little like the situation where one football player punches another and the second one punches him back, only to get penalized because the referee didn't see the first punch.

Also, if we let Developer out of the contract, she's getting a windfall. She made a strategic decision that turned out to be a bad one. Now she's getting out of the contract on a basis totally unrelated to any of her concerns.

Some people suggested that Developer should be allowed to void the contract under the principle "fraud vitiates all." (As you may recall the dissenting opinion in one of our cases made a big issue of this principle.) Given all the anomalies of this case, maybe that's what we should ultimately conclude.

QUESTION COVERING UCC § 2-207

(40 minutes)

Ridgeway's Feed and Seed Store ("Buyer") placed an order for 10,000 pounds of sunflower seeds with Upper Midwest Distributing Company ("Seller"). The purchase order form that Buyer sent Seller provided that Buyer would have 60 days to make claims on account of defective seeds shipped by Seller. Seller responded with a form which was headed "Acknowledgment" and began "We have entered your order for 10,000 pounds of sunflower seeds." On the back of the form were seventeen numbered provisions, including: "3. All claims for defective goods must be made within 10 days after receipt of the goods. NO EXCEPTIONS."

Buyer did not respond to the form. Seller shipped the sunflower seeds. Buyer paid for them and then discovered a problem with them. Buyer notified Seller of the problem, and when Seller refused to remedy the problem, Buyer sued Seller. The outcome of the case will depend on whether Buyer made a timely claim on account of the defective goods. Article 2 of the UCC provides that if the parties do not agree otherwise, all claims for defective goods must be made with a reasonable time.

The case was filed in the United States District Court. Because there is no case law governing these issues in the state whose law controls, the federal court has certified to the state supreme court the question of how long the buyer has to

make claims. You are a clerk for a judge on the state supreme court. She has asked you to prepare a memorandum covering the
following points:

A. How have courts in other jurisdictions decided these issues, and what was their reasoning?

B. Which of these alternatives should this state adopt, and what are your reasons for this choice?

QUESTION THREE

(20 minutes)

Your real estate developer client has entered into an oral agreement to purchase a piece of land from Lem Williams for a price of $400,000. Under the county land use (zoning) laws now in effect, this land may be used only for farming. As farmland, the property is worth at most $200,000. Your client believes that he can get the land use laws changed so that they will allow the land to be used as a shopping center. Your client believes that if the land use laws are changed, the property will be worth more than a million dollars.

Lem is 75 years old. He dropped out of school in the ninth grade and speaks as if he had lived in the hills all his life. People who know him only casually think of him as a "nice old man." Those who have dealt with him in business know that he is very smart and not very ethical. Although he has more money than he'll ever be able to spend, he's ruthless in the pursuit of more. You've heard it said "he'd run over his grandmother for a dime." Lem is a very experienced real estate trader. Among other things, he is a major slumlord in the university town, the outskirts of which are rapidly expanding toward the subject property.

Lem is aware that the property will become more valuable if the land use laws are changed, but he apparently doesn't share your client's optimism as to how much more valuable it will become. Otherwise, he would be asking more money for the property. Also your client has some ideas for changing the law, ideas that probably haven't occurred to Lem. Lem is too cheap to hire lawyers. Your client, on the other hand, after he learned some expensive lessons trying to do his own legal work, sees the need for our profession and gives you a lot of work. (But he still complains about your bills). He hired you to look into the possibility that the law prohibiting the use of the property as a shopping center could be invalidated on constitutional grounds. You told him: "There's a good possibility, probably less than 50-50, but still a good possibility." If that fails, there is a fallback plan. There is a pro-development movement in the county and the leaders of this movement plan an all-out campaign to elect a majority of pro-development commissioners to the county commission at the next election. A group of real estate developers, led by your client, plan to contribute large amounts of money to the campaigns of the pro-development candidates. If the election goes the way your client hopes, the commission will probably change the law so that the shopping center can be built.

Lem probably has no idea the land use law is vulnerable to constitutional attack. He thinks the constitution is "something sleazy lawyers use to keep drug dealers out of jail." You expect that he's generally aware of the pro-development movement, but he's probably not aware of how hard its leaders plan to work to capture the county commission.

You have been asked to prepare a written contract between your client and Lem for the purchase and sale of the land. You expect that if the land use laws are changed in the way your client hopes, Lem will try to get out of the contract on the basis of mistake, misrepresentation, and unconscionability. He might even break with tradition and hire a lawyer to help him do so. (But he won't hire a lawyer to represent him in the negotiation of the initial contract.) Explain what provisions you would put into the contract to maximize the likelihood that your client will be able to defeat these while paying your litigation partners a minimum of fees.

FOR PURPOSES OF THIS QUESTION, ASSUME THAT YOUR CLIENT HAS NO LEGAL OR ETHICAL OBLIGATION TO DISCLOSE TO LEM ANY OF THE ABOVE FACTS.

ANALYSIS

I asked this question because I've been trying to teach the practical aspects of contract law. A number of people didn't answer the question, but instead told me why Lem should lose if he sues. That wasn't what the question asked. I emphasized in class that it isn't enough to have your client win on appeal. You have to try to prevent litigation, and if you can't prevent it, you try to make sure that the documentation is so clear that your client wins on a summary judgment. In the land of Perfect everyone remembers what was said and testifies truthfully about it. Courts find the facts as they actually occurred, and even trial courts apply the law correctly. Cases are decided quickly and economically. But we don't live in Perfect. That's why lawyers have to think about legal rules in a practical way. If your client loses her butt on a business deal because you didn't cover all the bases, she's not going to be mollified by the fact that you can recite the elements of misrepresentation.

This answer is much longer and more detailed than you could write in the time I gave, but I wrote it to show how much of the material we discussed in class could be worked into this question. I could have given more time to answer the question, but, because I had not asked a question like this recently and I felt some people might be surprised by it, I wanted to keep it from having too much weight in proportion to the more traditional questions.

Because I want to keep my client from getting tied up in litigation and running up large legal bills, I would like to write the contract in such a way that

Lem's suit can be disposed of on a 12(b)(6) motion for summary judgment. This will be difficult because mistake, misrepresentation, and unconscionability involve the kind of fact questions that will be difficult to resolve prior to trial. I need to make sure the client understands this and is willing to go into the deal on this basis. Lem's willingness to lie will also make it more difficult to get a summary judgment because Lem may submit perjured affidavits. I don't know for sure that Lem will lie. He may be an honest slumlord. But I want to make sure that the client knows that Lem's willingness to lie under oath affects the client's risk.

My client also needs to know that the more specific language I put into the document to protect him, the more likely it is that Lem will back out of the deal, either because the language alerts him that the likelihood of the law change is higher than he thinks or because he just doesn't like long contracts that seem to give all the advantages to the other party.

In making an unconscionability argument, Lem's lawyer will undoubtedly argue that Lem is a poor, uneducated farmer (combining Jeffersonian virtues with the *Williams v. Walker-Thomas* sympathy aspect) who was taken advantage of by a real estate developer (a class that judges and jurors generally dislike). It would therefore be nice to be able to show in the document I draft that Lem is a sophisticated real estate operator. We discussed in class a case in which a party claiming he was not a "merchant" for UCC purposes "forgot" to disclose that he held an MBA from Harvard. I would therefore like to have in the document a very clear statement that Lem is a sophisticated real estate investor and have in the document as much factual support as possible. The problem with this, of course, is that if we say this clearly, it will probably tip our hand. So I would want to work this into the document in an innocuous way.

One way we could do this would be to say something like "Both parties acknowledge that they are experienced in real estate transactions and have had an opportunity to seek legal advice with respect to this transaction." In *Zapatha* we saw that access to legal advice was a factor in the court's upholding the contract, so this provision would help to cover that base as well. To make it clearer that Lem had a chance to seek legal counsel, I could send a draft of the agreement to him with a request that he tell me the name of his lawyer so that I could send him/her a copy of the draft. This does two things in addition to showing that Lem had an opportunity to seek counsel. It shows that he had the document to read and think about. This was one basis on which we distinguished *Zapatha* from *Weaver*. Also, by indicating that the document is a draft, we show that the contract was not offered on a take-it-or-leave-it basis. This not only protects us against an unconscionability argument, but it also should cause the court to give greater weight to the self-serving provisions we include to protect against mistake and misrepresentation attacks.

We saw in *Quickie Aircraft* how a provision that the UCC says is prima facie unconscionable was upheld because (among other reasons) the contract spelled out the reason the provision was fair under the circumstances of *this* deal. Ideally, I would like to set out in the document the fact that the sale price is greater than the price of the land as farmland and that this reflects the fact that there is a chance the land may become suitable for development.

Similarly, I would like to preclude claims of mistake by stating in the document that the parties have conducted their own investigations of the property and the transaction and that they assume the risk of any facts relating to the transaction being different from what they believe them to be. This is of course a two-edged sword. Lem knows a lot about the property that my client doesn't, so this might preclude some mistake or misrepresentation claims that my client would otherwise be able to make. I could of course make this provision apply only to Lem, but this would increase the likelihood that Lem would object and also make the document look more one-sided to a court.

Along the same lines, we had read two cases in which courts upheld contracts against misrepresentation claims because they contained statements that the party making the claim had relied on no representations of the other party except for those expressly set forth in the document. In one case, the court even held that the party seeking to avoid the contract could not claim that he had been induced to execute the document by fraud because the allegedly fraudulent misrepresentations concerned fraud, and the document specifically stated that the other party had made no representations as to the specific issues in question. I would therefore like to include in the document a provision stating that the parties are making no representations as any possible changes in the law relating to the use of the land, that any such representations made during the course of negotiations may not be relied on, and that the parties have no duties to disclose any knowledge that they have concerning such possible changes. Practically, however, it might be necessary to tone down this language in order to avoid raising too much of a red flag.

QUESTION COVERING EXPRESS CONDITIONS

(25 minutes)

On April 1, 2004, Buyer and Seller entered into a contract for the purchase and sale of Seller's home. The contract contained the following provisions:

This contract is subject to Buyer's ability to sell Buyer's existing home.

The closing shall occur on July 1, 2004, subject to any necessary extensions not to exceed 60 days.

Immediately upon entering into the contract, Buyer contacted a real estate broker who advised Buyer that she should list home at $300,000 and expect to sell it for between $250,000 and $275,000. Buyer decided to save the real estate broker's commission and sell the home herself. She thought the home was worth about $275,000 but she thought it would make sense to try and sell it for $350,000. "After all," she said to her friends, "you never know who might be out there willing to pay more for a house they really fell in love with." So she made

$350,000 her asking price. She put a sign on the lawn and advertised it in the local newspaper. She held an open house with wine and cheese every second Sunday.

During the period of April 1 through June 25, Buyer received offers of $295,000, $280,000, $278,000 and $275,000. She rejected them all. On June 26, she told Seller: "I need that 60 day extension."

Seller responded: "You can have the extension, but only if you agree to lower the asking price to $300,000 and accept any reasonable offer over $280,000."

"In that case," said Buyer, "the deal is off." Buyer followed this with a letter from her lawyer saying that Buyer had terminated her obligations under the contract.

A lawsuit followed, with both Buyer and Seller claiming the other had breached the contract.

A. Explain how the court should decide the case.

B. Explain how the contract should have been drafted to avoid this problem. It is not necessary to draft actual language (although you can give it a try if you want). You just need to tell what issues needed to be addressed and in general terms tell how they might have been addressed.

QUESTION COVERING IMPRACTICABILITY, FRUSTRATION OF PURPOSE, AND DAMAGES

(35 minutes)

Note: Take some time to think about this question. Once you've understood what's going on, you won't have to write a long answer.

In April 2000, the Eastern States Waste Management Association ("Eastern") entered into a contract with the Surfrider Hotel ("Hotel") for a convention to be held at Hotel's property in Hawaii during February, 2002. The contract provided that Hotel would reserve 200 rooms for convention delegates and their spouses (and bodyguards and mistresses) at a special convention rate of $500 per night for the 5 nights of the convention. (The normal rate for the rooms was $750 per night at that time of the year). It also provided that Eastern would pay for any of the rooms not occupied by convention guests at the rate of $500 per night unless Eastern notified Hotel at least 90 days prior to the start of the convention that it would not need the rooms and granted Hotel permission to release the rooms for the use of its other guests.

After the events of September 11, 2001, Americans (even waste management consultants) were reluctant to travel by air. In early October, Eastern hired a group of professional travel consultants to advise them whether to cancel the convention. The consultants advised that travel would quickly rebound and that Eastern should not cancel the convention. In late December, when it became obvious that the consultants were wrong and that travel would not rebound for some time, the consultants changed their minds and advised Eastern to cancel the convention. The consultants determined that if it had not been for September 11, Eastern would have made a profit of $50,000 on the convention. (The main purpose of the convention was not to earn money but to bring the members of the organization together and to strengthen their ties to the organization). After September 11, it appeared to the consultants that Eastern would lose $50,000 if it canceled the convention immediately (in late December) and would lose $350,000 if it went ahead and held the convention. (The $50,000 loss from immediate cancellation did **NOT** take into account any potential liability to Hotel). Upon receiving this advice, Eastern notified Hotel that it was canceling the convention. This was less than 90 days advance notice required by the contract.

At the time it received Eastern's cancellation notice, Hotel, which had a total of 400 rooms (200 rooms reserved for the convention and an additional 200 rooms available for other guests), had only 100 of its other rooms booked for the 5 nights of the convention. Normally, it would have had all 400 rooms booked those 5 nights. Experts attributed the decrease in reservations solely to September 11. Hotel made demand on Eastern for payment for the rooms in accordance with the contract. Eastern claimed that the events of September 11 has excused its compliance with the contract. To mitigate its damages, Hotel cut its prices dramatically. As a result, 150 of the 300 rooms that had not been booked at the time the convention was canceled were booked for the 5 nights in question (i.e., the nights when the convention would have had them) at a rate of $250 a night. (Hotel did not reduce the prices for the guests that had previously booked the 100 rooms at $750 a night. After all, a deal is a deal).

Hotel sued Eastern States, asking not only for the $500,000 (200 rooms at $500 a night for 5 nights) Eastern had promised to pay if it did not use the rooms, but also for $200,000 in consequential damages. The $200,000 in consequential damages was based on studies done by Hotel's marketing department before the contract was entered into. These studies showed: (1) on the average, Hotel earned a profit of $100 per room per night on (a) purchases made by guests from the dining room, bar, room service, minibars, and the like, (b) rake-off from telephone charges, (c) Internet access charges, (d) any other rip-offs management could think of; and (2) because waste management consultants liked to throw money around, Hotel could expect to earn $200 per room per night on these things from the convention guests. (These profits were **in addition to** $500 per night occupancy charges for the rooms.) At the end of the presentation of evidence, the court ruled that these consequential damages **were** foreseeable, but that they **had not** proven with sufficient certainty and therefore could **not** be recovered as consequential damages.

The parties have stipulated (so you can take it as a given) that if the events of September 11 had not occurred, the hotel would have had all 400 of its rooms reserved at the time of the convention and that the guests in the rooms not reserved for the convention would have been paying $750 per night.

A. Explain how the court should rule on the liability issue (i.e., is Eastern liable for breach of contract or did the events of September 11 excuse its performance?). In addition to any other principles that might apply, discuss impracticability and frustration of purpose.

B. If Eastern is liable for breach of contract, how much should the court award as damages? (Note: You can express the damages in terms of dollars per room per night, e.g., "the damages are $125 per room per night." You don't have to multiply it out.) As always, I am not particularly interested in your final number. What I am interested in is what things the court should take into account **and why**, and what things the court should not take into account **and why**.

QUESTION COVERING WAIVER, BREACH, REQUESTS FOR ASSURANCES, AND ANTICIPATORY REPUDIATION

(45 minutes)

The Hotel California is located in Key Largo, Florida. In 2011, the hotel's owners, who had long been stuck in a 1970s mind set, decided that it was time they had a web site. Their occupancy rates had been falling slowly for several years, and they had hired a business consultant to advise them on how to deal with this problem. The consultant told them the
reason for the decline in business was that their competitors had web sites which allowed potential customers to see pictures of the property, determine the availability of particular rooms on particular dates, and make reservations on line.

Hotel California hired Hospitality Hosting, a company that specialized in hosting web sites for hotels, to design, build, and host a web site similar to those of Hotel California's competitors.

The contract that the parties signed provided that Hospitality Hosting would set up a web site for Hotel California (including graphic design, art, and programming) at a total cost of $30,000. The contract contained the following provisions:

The price for the web site design shall be $30,000. It shall be paid as follows:

(1) The sum of $5,000 shall be paid immediately upon the execution of this contract;

(2) The sum of $5,000 shall be paid when Hotel California has approved the preliminary design concept;

(3) The sum of $15,000 shall be paid when the project is substantially completed; and

(4) The sum of $5,000 shall be paid when the site is fully operational and functioning to the satisfaction of Hotel California.

Completion of the project shall proceed on the following timetable:

Hospitality Hosting shall begin work no later than May 1, 2011.

Hospitality Hosting shall submit a preliminary design concept to Hotel California no later than June 1, 2011.

A test version of the site shall be available on Hospitality Hosting's server no later than August 1, 2011.

The final version of the site shall be available for use by Hotel California's customers no later than September 1, 2004.

Except as set forth above, the contract contained no express conditions. It had been prepared by the parties from a standard form promulgated by an organization of web site designers. Hospitality Hosting didn't belong to the organization, but Mick Fleetwood, Hospitality Hosting's president, had scrounged the form from an old girlfriend who was a member. The contract was two single-spaced pages in length. It did NOT have a merger clause, and it did NOT provide that time was of the essence.

The contract was signed on April 15, and Hotel California made the initial payment of $5,000 on that day. On May 5, Hospitality Hosting asked Hotel California for an advance of an additional $2,000 so that it could begin work. Hotel California gave them the two grand. Hospitality Hosting got the preliminary design concept to Hotel California on June 15 and asked for an additional $5,000. Hotel California reminded them of the $2,000 advance and paid them $3,000. Mr. Fleetwood apologized for the delays and Don Henley, the president of Hotel California, told him: "No problemo, Dude. We're laid-back guys – that's why we left our jobs in L.A. to run a low-budget hotel."

Hospitality Hosting got the test version of the site working on August 15. At this point the Hotel California folks realized that the delays were going to cost them money. It is widely known in the hotel business that customers begin making reservations for winter vacations (the big season for Florida hotels) immediately after September 1 and that not having the site operational by early September would cost them money.

What was more, the test version of the site had a problem: It required that customers wait 90 seconds to see if their reservation had been accepted. When the Hotel California people pointed out this problem to Mr. Fleetwood, he said, "No big deal. It's just a little glitch. We can fix it just by adding a few lines of code.

We'll get it straightened out as soon as you pay that fifteen grand, which, by the way, we really need in order to pay our programmers."

By the fifteen grand, Mr. Fleetwood meant the payment required under the contract when the project was substantially completed. Hotel California refused to make the payment. First, they said that the project was not substantially completed because the "glitch" really was a major problem, and because the site was not available to potential customers but was still a test version. Moreover, they said (in writing) that they would make no more payments until "you provide us with assurances that you will be able to provide us with a fully-functioning web site in a timely manner as set forth in the contract dated April 15, 2011." Hospitality Hosting responded by giving Hotel California the names of two customers for whom they had set up web sites and who would confirm that Hospitality Hosting had done satisfactory and timely work. Hotel California responded to this by saying that they would make the $15,000 payment only when Hospitality Hosting either (1) completed the project to Hotel California's satisfaction or (2) provided a complete list of Hospitality Hosting's customers so that Hotel California could survey customers at random to see if there were some unhappy customers out there. Hospitality Hosting thereupon said that it would neither provide the customer list nor do any more work on the project until Hotel California made the $15,000 payment. On August 25, Hotel California informed Hospitality Hosting it was terminating the contract. Shortly thereafter, Hotel California sued for breach. Hospitality Hosting counterclaimed, alleging that it was Hotel California who breached.

Discuss the issues the court must address in order to decide who is liable for breach. Do **NOT** discuss damages. The contract is **NOT** subject to Article 2 of the UCC.

QUESTION COVERING EXPRESS CONDITIONS

(20 minutes)

Your client is a trade organization of building contractors. You have been hired to draft a standard-form contract that contractors and their customers will use on building projects that are too small to make it economical for the each of the parties to hire a lawyer to negotiate and draft on their behalf. The contract is to be between the owner and the contractor and is to cover such things as when various phases of the work are to be completed and when progress payments are to be made. The standard form contract has to be fairly evenhanded (i.e., it can't give the contractor an unfair advantage) because the people the contractors will be dealing with are sophisticated enough that they will not sign a one-sided contract.

Explain how you would use **express conditions** to limit the risks the parties will be exposed to. **Limit your discussion to express conditions.** There are a lot of things you would want to cover in such a contract, some of which we discussed in this course and some we didn't, but all this question is asking is what you learned in this course about express conditions. **Take time to** think. **You don't need to write a lot on this question.** Your answer can be fairly general, but feel free to use specific examples if that will help.

ANALYSIS

A major problem in construction contracts is determining when a party's duty of performance becomes due. This becomes especially difficult if the other party's performance has been less than perfect. The law attempts to deal with this problem through the device of constructive conditions and the concept of material breach. This is an imperfect device for a number of reasons. First, constructive conditions are very general and are not tailored to the specific needs of the contract. For example, the default rule is that the contractor must complete the entire project before the owner is obligated to pay anything. This would obviously place too much of a risk on my contractor clients.

To use conditions to protect my clients, I would provide that receipt of a payment of a certain percentage of the contract price was a condition precedent to start work. I would then provide that when the work progressed to a certain point, say completion of the foundation, a second payment was due. I would expressly provide that satisfactory completion of the work to that point was a condition precedent to the owner's obligation to make that payment and that the owner making that payment was a condition precedent to the contractor's obligation to do any further work. I would have a series of such payments as work progressed, each of them structured conditions in the same way.

To reduce the likelihood of disputes slowing the work, I would try to make the conditions as objectively-verifiable as possible. Because there will always be some disputes, however, I would provide a mechanism for resolving these quickly and inexpensively. In some of the cases we read, satisfactory completion had to be certified by the architect or engineer on the project. Because this contract will be used on small projects, there probably will not be an architect or engineer, but I would provide for someone with similar credentials (or maybe just another contractor that they both trust) to resolve disputes. I would provide that this person's decision on whether conditions had been satisfied was to be final and not subject to appeal to the courts or otherwise. As we saw in one of the cases, most courts will honor such provisions.

QUESTION COVERING PAROL EVIDENCE RULE, INTERPRETATION, DAMAGE PRINCIPLES, LIQUIDATED DAMAGES

(60 minutes)

Owner and Contractor had conversations concerning the remodeling of Owner's motel. In their conversations, they always talked about the remodeling being done "during the spring" of the following year (2004). Early in January 2004, Owner heard that there was to be a major water ski tournament in town during the first week of June. She called Contractor and left the following message on Contractor's voice mail: "We need to finalize things for the remodeling. Be here at 2:30 and bring a contract." Contractor arrived at 3:45

(which is pretty good for a contractor). He had with him a standard from contract with all the blanks filled in. The form had been prepared by a professional association to which Contractor belonged and was intended (as was clear from a reading of it) to cover all aspects of a construction project. It did not, however, address the question of damages for breach the contract. Also, it did **not** have a merger (integration) clause, but it did have a provision which read: "See attached sheets for additional terms and conditions. If no additional sheets are attached, check here and initial." Contractor had already checked the box. The form had a provision which read: "Construction shall be completed by." This was followed by a blank space. In the blank space, Contractor had filled in "end of spring, 2004."

Owner looked over the form and said: "Everything looks OK, except I need construction finished by the middle of May. That'll give us two weeks to get ready for the water ski tournament."

"No sweat," said Contractor. "I'll agree that 'the end of spring' is May 15. That's when summer starts around here anyhow. What's more, if I'm not finished by the time the tournament starts, I'll pay five thousand dollars for every night you're not open during the tournament week. That's more than you'll ever lose if I'm late."

"If that's the deal, I'll sign," said Owner, and she signed the document and initialed the space next to the check box for no additional sheets attached. Contractor then signed and initialed as well.

Contractor of course finished the remodeling the day **after** the tournament ended, and Owner did what every red-blooded American does when things don't work out. She sued. At trial she showed the following:

(1) Prior to the remodeling, average revenues during May and June were $1,500 per night.

(2) After the remodeling, average revenues during May and June were $2,500 per night: Of the $1,000 per night increase in revenues, $700 per night was due to the increased room rates that were charged because the place looker better. The other $300 of the increase was due to an increase in the number of customers. Since other motels in the area did not see a similar increase in the number of customers, it was assumed that this increase was due to the fact the place looked better.

(3) During the week of the tournament, each of the fourteen motels in town was full.

(4) If Owner had had the motel open the week of the tournament, revenues would have been $4,000 per night during that week.

(5) Because Contractor did not complete construction by May 15, Owner lost 14 days of non-tournament-week (a total of $35,000) revenues and 7 days of tournament-week revenues ($28,000).

(6) Each day that the motel was closed, Owner saved $500 in operating expenses.

You are a law clerk for the trial judge, and she has asked you to write her a memorandum addressing the following questions:

A. How should she deal with the testimony concerning the agreement that the "end of spring" means May 15?

B. Assuming Owner is successful in establishing that construction was to be completed by May 15, what effect should be given to Contractor's agreement to pay $5,000 per night for every night the motel was not open during tournament week?

C. Assuming Owner is successful in establishing that construction was to be completed by May 15, what damages is Owner entitled to?

(i) if Contractor is **NOT** held to his agreement to pay $5,000 per night for every night the motel was not open during tournament week?

(ii) if Contractor is held to his agreement to pay $5,000 per night for every night the motel was not open during tournament week?

QUESTION COVERING EXPRESS CONDITIONS AND DAMAGES

(25 minutes)

Argus Corporation is a business that makes money by acquiring other businesses for less than they are worth. Argus analysts found a small oil company, Target Oil Company, which had developed a new process for making hydrogen from oil. The process could become extremely valuable, but it would become valuable only if (1) hydrogen fuel cells became an important source of power for automobiles and (2) nobody developed a better process before the owner of Target's process made its money from the process. This was a long shot, but Argus's analysts determined that the process was worth $30 million to Argus. This was based on the supposition that if the conditions listed above were to occur, Argus might earn several hundred million dollars from the process.

Target Oil had a second asset, oil rights to a tract of land known as the Trango Field. The Trango Field was estimated to contain a million barrels of light, sweet oil. At the time, the market price for light, sweet oil was $20 a barrel, and it was estimated it would cost $5 a barrel to bring the oil to market.

All of the stock of Target Oil was owned by the Target Family Trust. Control of the trust resided in the company's founder, Barbara "Big Babs" Target, a former professional wrestler turned businesswoman.

Argus decided to attempt to buy all of the stock of Target Oil for $30 million. As noted above, Argus's analysts believed Target Oil to be worth $45 million–$30 million for the process and $15 million for the Trango Field. But Argus's management thought they could get all of the stock of Target Oil for a mere $30 million because (1) other potential buyers had not done the analysis, (2) the Target family was particularly anxious to sell to Argus because Argus was known for paying all cash for its acquisitions and for allowing the old management to continue to run the company, and (3) there were few other buyers who could afford to take a big loss if the process turned out to be worthless. (The process probably would turn out to be worthless, but if it didn't, the payoff would be spectacular. It was like buying a very expensive lottery ticket.)

Argus approached Big Babs with an offer to buy the company for $30 million, and Big Babs negotiated the price up to $35 million. They agreed on that price, and the lawyers spent the first week of May cooped up in a conference room writing a contract for the sale of all the stock of Target Oil to Argus. The contract they agreed upon contained the following provisions:

Article 5: Warranties. The Target Family Trust makes the following warranties:

* * *

D. The Process [this was a defined term for the process from making hydrogen from crude oil] is covered by the United States and foreign patents listed in Schedule 9 hereto, all of which patents are properly registered and have not been contested.

E. The Trango Field contains no less than 800,000 barrels of light, sweet oil.

* * *

Article 6: Conditions. Argus Corporation's duty to perform its obligations under this agreement, including but not limited to its obligation to purchase the stock of Target Oil Company and pay the consideration therefor, is subject to the following conditions precedent:

* * *

J. No suit shall have been filed contesting the validity of the patents covering the Process.

* * *

M. The Target Family Trust shall employ an independent consulting geologist acceptable to Argus in its sole and absolute discretion (exercised in good faith), and such geologist shall supply Argus Corporation with a report stating that the Trango Field contains not less than 800,000 barrels of light, sweet oil.

* * *

The conditions in this Article 6 are for the sole benefit of Argus Corporation and may be waived by Argus Corporation, but only in a writing signed by an authorized officer of Argus Corporation and referring specifically to this Agreement.

The closing (the meeting at which Argus was to pay the money and the trust was to deliver the stock) was originally scheduled for May 1, and the parties found a geologist who said she could render the required report by April 15. On April 3, the geologist informed the parties that because of "unexpected difficulties" she would not be able to deliver her report until "late May at the earliest." Argus was willing to wait for the report, but Big Babs explained that the trust had committed itself to some obligations that required it to have the money by May 15.

To maintain its reputation for being easy to deal with (and therefore its ability to buy other companies on the cheap), Argus waived the requirement for the geologist's report. It executed (i.e., caused an authorized officer to sign) a document which stated:

Argus Corporation waives the requirement for a geologist's report as contained in Paragraph M of Article 6 of the Agreement dated as of February 14, 2004 by and between Argus Corporation and the Target Family Trust. This waiver is not a waiver of any other rights of Argus Corporation under the Agreement.

Big Babs was suitably grateful, and the Argus officers accepted her thanks without telling her that it really wasn't any big deal because Argus was really interested in the Process, not the oil.

The closing occurred as scheduled. Argus paid the trust $35 million and the trust transferred to Argus the ownership of Target Oil Company. Several months later, after the trust had its money and Argus had owned Target Oil Company for a while, it was discovered that the Trango Field contained only 700,000 barrels of oil. Because of this discovery, Argus has sued the trust for damages. Since the suit was filed, the price of oil has risen substantially, and Argus was able to sell the Process for $100 million.

Explain whether the trust is liable for damages. **Your answer need not be long, but you should explain your reasoning fully.** *If* you think the answer is clear, it is *not* necessary to argue both sides. Do **not** discuss the **amount** of damages, the parties have stipulated as to the amount. Just discuss whether the trust is liable for any damages at all and why this result follows from the facts and the applicable law.

ANALYSIS

The trust is liable for damages if there is a breach of the contract. The non-occurrence of a condition is not a breach, so the failure to deliver the geologist's report would not have been a breach, even if it had not been waived.

The untruthfulness of a warranty is a breach, however, and any breach, even one that is not material, gives rise to a claim for damages. The contract contains a warranty that the Trango Field contained at least 800,000 barrels. Because the Trango Field contained less oil, the warranty was breached, and the Trust is liable for damages.

The waiver of the condition is not a waiver of the warranty. The effect of the waiver is simply to allow the transaction to close. (In technical Contracts II language, its effect is to cause Argus's obligations under the contract, in particular the obligation to pay the purchase price, to become due.) This would be true even if the document had not specifically stated that it was not a waiver of any other rights.

The fact that Argus was only interested in the Process and that it would have bought Target Oil even if it had known the Trango Field contained only 700,000 barrels is not relevant. The fact is that if the contract had been performed, Argus would have had 800,000 barrels, and it is entitled to be placed in the position that it would have been in if the contract had been performed (i.e., if the warranty had been true).

Similarly, the fact that Argus made even more money than they expected does not change the result. Their entitlement to damages does not depend on whether they made more money than they expected or less money than they expected. It depends on whether they got what they were promised, and here they did not.

QUESTION TWO

(60 minutes)

Developer and Contractor entered into a written contract for the construction of an office building on land owned by Developer. The contract contained the following provision:

> 14. As soon as practicable after the first day of each month, but in no event later than the tenth day of the month, Developer shall pay Contractor for the work done during the previous month as certified in writing by Architect. It shall be a condition precedent to any such payment that Contractor shall have delivered to Developer lien releases signed by all subcontractors who have

worked on the Project at any time prior to the end of the month for which payment is to be made.

Persons who work on a construction project, including subcontractors, are entitled to file what are called "mechanics' liens" against the project if they are not paid. These liens give the holder the right to foreclose on the property and have it sold to pay the money owed to the holder. In practice, these liens are almost never foreclosed upon because somebody (usually the owner or the holder of a mortgage) pays the lienholder what it is owed. Nevertheless, the existence of the lien allows the holder to be sure that it will get paid. If the subcontractor is not paid, it can still file a lien, even if the general contractor has been paid for the work that sub has done. This means that if the owner pays the general contractor and the general contractor goes bankrupt (or goes to the Cayman Islands) without paying the subcontractors, the owner can end up having to pay twice. To avoid this, smart owners (like Developer) get lien releases from the subs before they pay the general contractor. Lien releases are documents in which the subcontractor gives up its right to file a mechanics' lien for the work done to date.

Construction started in March. On April 1, Contractor brought Developer a certificate from the architect ("Architect") attesting to the amount of work done during March along with lien releases from all of the subs who had worked on the project during that month. Developer paid Contractor on April 5.

On May 2, Contractor again brought Developer what appeared to be the right paperwork, and Developer paid Contractor on May 6. On May 11, Architect was looking at the paperwork, and she discovered that there were two subcontractors who had worked on the project during April and for whom Contractor had supplied no lien releases. Developer called Contractor, and Contractor said he would get right on it. In two days, Contractor had supplied the lien release from one of the subs. The other sub had finished her work on the project, and was not easy to reach. She and Contractor exchanged phone calls (neither was very prompt about returning calls and neither bothered to give the other the number of their cell phone) for a couple of weeks until Contractor, knowing he might not get the next payment if he didn't get that lien release, sent someone to the job where the sub was working and got her to sign a lien release.

On June 1, Contractor brought Developer a certificate from Architect attesting to the amount of work done during May along with lien releases from all but two of the subs who had worked on the project during that month. Both of the subs had done less than $1,000 worth of work on the project during the month. Developer paid Contractor on June 4. He said, "What I'm really concerned with is releases from the subs who've done $10,000 or more worth of work during the month."

On July 3, Developer paid Contractor, even though Contractor had not supplied Developer with lien releases from 6 of the subs, one of whom had done $50,000 worth of work and the rest of whom had done less than $10,000 worth of work.

On July 8, Developer and Contractor got into an argument. Developer made Contractor tear out some work that he had done and rebuild it. Developer claimed the reason he did that was that the work had not conformed to the drawings that were part of the construction contract between Contractor and Developer (i.e., the contract required Contractor to build according to the drawings and it did not require him to do any construction beyond that). Contractor's position was that his original work (the part Developer made him tear out) was in conformance with the drawings and that he should be paid extra for tearing it out and rebuilding it.

The issue was not resolved on August 1 when Contractor presented Developer with his bill for July. The bill included the disputed amount attributable to the tearing out and rebuilding required by Developer. It was accompanied by all of the required lien waivers **except for** (1) the waiver from the sub who had done $50,000 worth of work in June (i.e., the waiver that should have been delivered to get the previous payment) and (2) waivers from two subs who had done less than $10,000 work, all of the work of these two subs being done in July. There was also missing the certificate from Architect. Architect had left on July 25 for two weeks in her mountain cabin.

When Contractor presented the bill to Developer, Developer refused to pay it, saying he wouldn't pay without Architect's certification. Contractor called Architect, who had taken her cell phone with her but left word she didn't want to be called "unless the end of the world is imminent." Contractor put Developer on the phone and Architect told Developer that all the work through July 24 had been completed in accordance with the plans and that she would orally certify that. Developer told Contractor that wasn't enough. He would not pay without a written certification from Architect and lien releases from all of the subs, including the sub who had done $50,000 worth of work in June and had not yet given a waiver covering that work. "You can get it whenever you want, and when all the paperwork is in order, I'll pay you," Developer said.

Contractor got Developer to agree that he would accept a certification by Architect if it were sent by fax. But when Contractor asked her to drive into town to fax a certification, Architect said, "You've been a pain in the butt all through this job. You've never done one thing I asked without giving me grief about it. I'll be damned if I'll mess up my vacation to accommodate a jerk like you."

Contractor pleaded with Architect to fax the certification. He explained that he desperately needed the money from this job to pay his employees, subs, and suppliers on another job. If he didn't get the money right away, his employees and subs would walk off the job, his suppliers would cut him off, and he would default. This would make him liable for substantial damages. Architect would not relent.

Overhearing this, Developer offered to waive the requirement for Architect's certification if Contractor dropped his claim for the work that he'd been required to tear out and rebuild. At this, Contractor became irate. He threw his Palm Pilot across the room, destroying it and putting a dent in the wall. He said, "I'm off this job. I'm going to pull my subs off the job and I'll see your miserable, cheating butt in court." He stomped out of Developer's office. This all occurred at approximately 4 PM.

Contractor went home and tossed back some tequila. In the morning, he realized that he had no choice but to deal with Developer. He called Developer, intending to apologize, but Developer told him he was so angry over the outburst in his office that he had ordered Contractor's employees and subs off the job. He said that he didn't feel he had deal with "people who behave like that," and that he was going to hire a new general contractor for the job.

At trial, it was determined (1) that Contractor had been told several weeks ahead of time about Architect's vacation plans and (2) that the work which Contractor was required to tear out and rebuild was originally built in accordance with the plans and specifications and therefore under the contract Contractor was entitled to additional compensation for the cost of tearing it out and rebuilding it. The amount of additional compensation that Contractor was entitled to on account of the work torn out and rebuilt was approximately $40,000. The total price for the entire job was $2,000,000.

Between Contractor and Developer, who committed the first material breach of the contract? Assume that Architect is totally independent of both parties and that neither Developer nor Contractor is responsible for her acts.

QUESTION COVERING CONSTRUCTIVE CONDITIONS AND ANTICIPATORY REPUDIATION

(30 minutes)

Owner and Roofer enter into a contract for the re-roofing of a portion of Owner's store. In the contract, which contains no express conditions, Roofer promises that "the shingles used will match exactly the shingles used on the remainder of the building [i.e., that part of the building that is not being re-roofed]." When Roofer goes to purchase materials for the job, however, she discovers that the shingles used for the rest of the roof are no longer manufactured. She can get the shingles manufactured specially, but it will cost $2,500 to have matching shingles manufactured. This will mean she will lose money on the job. The contract price for the job was $3,000. Roofer had estimated that she would have $1,000 in materials cost, $1,600 in labor cost and $400 profit. Distressed over the prospect of losing money on the job, she calls Owner and tells him: "I won't be able to match the shingles exactly."

"Just what do you mean by that?" asks Owner.

"It won't be quite the same," says Roofer, "but don't worry. A person will have to look very closely to see the difference."

"Listen," says Owner. "If you can't get an exact match, don't even bother showing up."

"Tell you what," says Roofer. "If you'll accept what I can do at a reasonable cost, a good but not exact match, I'll forego my profit. I'll do the job for $2,700, but if you want an exact match, I'll have to charge you $4,500."

"The devil you will," says Owner. "If you don't promise me that you'll give me an exact match for $3,000, you can forget about the job."

"Don't hold your breath," says Roofer.

"I'll give you three days to assure me you'll do exactly what the contract says," replies Owner. "Otherwise I'm going to hire somebody else to do the job."

"You do and I'll sue," says Roofer.

Owner does (i.e., he finds another roofer) and Roofer sues (i.e., she finds a lawyer, which is a lot easier than finding a roofer).

Discuss the issues the court will have to decide in order to determine whether Roofer or Owner is entitled to damages for breach of contract. Do not discuss issues relating to the amount of damages, just tell who should win and why.

QUESTION COVERING DAMAGES

(20 minutes)

Alarmed by reports that potato blight is spreading across the country, Greasy Foods, Inc. ("GFI") calls Broker and asks her to enter into a contract to supply GFI with 100 tons of potatoes. Broker has also heard of the potato blight, so before she agrees to a contract with GFI, she gets a contract to buy the potatoes from Farmer. Broker's contract with Farmer calls for Farmer to sell the potatoes to Broker at a price of $40 a ton. The contract calls for Broker to pick up the potatoes at Farmer's farm.

Broker then enters into a contract to re-sell the potatoes to GFI at a price of $50 a ton. This contract calls for Broker to deliver the potatoes to GFI's plant. Broker can get a trucking company to pick up the potatoes at Farmer's farm and deliver them to GFI's plant for $4 a ton To protect herself further, Broker has the following provision inserted into the contract between herself and GFI.

> If Farmer shall fail to deliver the potatoes to be delivered by Farmer under that certain "Potato Agreement" dated March 21, 1998, Broker's obligation to deliver potatoes to GFI hereunder shall be discharged."

As feared, the potato blight wipes out Farmer's crop (as well as those of lots of other people). As a result of the blight, the price of potatoes goes up. On the date Farmer is to deliver his potatoes to Broker, the market price for potatoes in

Farmer's locality is $100 per ton. On the date Broker is to deliver the potatoes to GFI, the market price for potatoes in GFI's locality is $110 per ton.

GFI sues Broker for breach of contract, and Broker sues Farmer for breach of contract. Because of the condition in the Broker-GFI contract, Broker is able to get GFI's suit dismissed. Farmer raises a defense of impracticability in the suit by Broker, but the court finds that the potato blight was foreseeable at the time that Broker and Farmer entered into the contract.

Discuss the amount of damages that should be awarded to Broker in Broker's suit against Farmer. (Discuss it on a **per ton** basis. It makes the math a lot easier.)

QUESTION COVERING IMPRACTICABILITY AND LIQUIDATED DAMAGES

(55 minutes)

Contractor and Owner agree that Contractor will build an airstrip on Owner's ranch. The contract contains the following provisions, among others:

(1) The total price for construction of the airstrip according to the plans and specifications described in this agreement shall be $500,000.

(2) Construction shall be completed and the airstrip ready for use by turbojet aircraft with a gross takeoff weight of 25,000 pounds by August 15, 1999.

(3) If construction is completed and the airstrip is ready for use by a turbojet aircraft with a gross takeoff weight of 25,000 pounds by August 15, 1999, Owner shall pay to Contractor a bonus of $10,000 per day for each day prior to August 15, 1999 that the airstrip is completed, with a maximum bonus of $100,000."

(4) If construction is not completed by August 15, 1999, Contractor shall pay to Owner as liquidated damages the sum of $100,000 and if construction is not completed by September 15, 1999, Contractor shall pay to Owner as additional liquidated damages the additional sum of $100,000.

(5) "This document expresses the entire agreement of the parties and supersedes all prior agreements, oral or written.

On July 15, the airstrip is within 10 days of completion when an unusually heavy rain causes delays in construction. Construction is delayed for several weeks, and the airstrip is fully completed on September 18.

Meanwhile, on June 1, the county in which the ranch is located passes an ordinance, effective September 1, prohibiting the takeoff and landing of turbojet aircraft from airports not in operation prior to the effective date of the ordinance (September 1).

After the airstrip is completed, Contractor, who was paid a total of $300,000 in progress payments during the construction, sues Owner for the remaining $200,000 due on the $500,000 contract price and the $100,000 bonus to which he would have been entitled if the rains had not come. Owner sues for the return of the $300,000 paid to date and for additional damages due to the loss of the right to operate a jet from her ranch.

(a) Discuss the issues the court should address in determining who wins the lawsuit.

(b) Discuss the damages that should be awarded to Owner if Owner wins the lawsuit.

(c) Discuss the damages that should be awarded to Contractor if Contractor wins the lawsuit.

QUESTION COVERING UCC DAMAGES

(30 minutes)

Mary Nevershow, a home remodeling contractor, entered into a contract with Martin Stewpot, a wealthy lawyer. The contract called for Ms. Nevershow to remodel Mr. Stewpot's gourmet kitchen for a price of $50,000. The major items to be installed in the kitchen were a range with a retail price of $8,000, a refrigerator with the retail price of $4,000, imported Italian quarry tile with a retail price of $3,500, cabinets and countertops with a total retail price of $12,000, and lighting fixtures with a total retail price of $4,000. The total retail price of all these items was $31,500. Using the various discounts available to her, Ms. Nevershow expected to be able to obtain these items for a total price of $27,000. She anticipated that other materials would cost her $3,000, and that labor of her employees and subcontractors (including the touch-up painting described below) would cost her $12,000 and that she would make a "profit" of $8,000 on the job. Some of this profit would of course be attributable to her own labor and the overhead of operating her business.

When the job was almost completed Mr. Stewpot and Ms. Nevershow got into a fight over whether the refrigerator was the "right" shade of avocado. Mr. Stewpot threw Ms. Nevershow off the job. At that time, Ms. Nevershow had installed all of the items listed above except for the refrigerator. Most of the other work (painting, carpentry, plumbing, etc.) had also been done. The costs she incurred were the costs she anticipated, as described above, except that she saved $200 because she didn't have to have her painter do the touch-up painting, and she saved $400 because there was a light fixture she didn't install. There would also have been some clean-up, which she would have done herself. At the time

Ms. Nevershow and Mr. Stewpot got into their little tiff, Mr. Stewpot had already paid Ms. Nevershow a total of $30,000 in progress payments.

Ms. Nevershow attempted to return the refrigerator to the manufacturer, but the manufacturer refused to take it back because it was a custom color. She then attempted to sell it to several appliance dealers, one of whom said "Avocado has been out of style for decades, dearie. Maybe you can find somebody who's stuck in the Sixties." The others didn't say it as colorfully, but the message was the same. Ms. Nevershow thereupon sent Mr. Stewpot a letter informing him that she was going to sell the refrigerator, and a reasonable time thereafter she put an ad in the classified section of the local newspaper saying the refrigerator was for sale for "$2,500 or best offer." The first two days the refrigerator was advertised there were no responses to the ad. On the third day, a man with long sideburns and bell-bottom trousers offered Ms. Nevershow $900 for "that groovy refrigerator." She took the offer without attempting to negotiate.

At trial, it was determined that Mr. Stewpot totally breached the contract when he threw Ms. Nevershow off the job. It was also determined that the refrigerator had a retail value of $4,000 and a wholesale value of $3,000. How much should Ms. Nevershow recover in damages? Discuss the issues involved and calculate the damages.

QUESTION ON CONSTRUCTIVE CONDITIONS, DAMAGES, AND LIQUIDATED DAMAGES

(60 minutes)

Jennifer was a partner in a small (but very profitable) investment banking firm. It had become the fashionable thing among her set to buy a cottage in a certain small fishing village in Maine. (Actually it wasn't a real fishing village any more. The real fish were long gone from the area. They had been replaced by investment bankers and plastic surgeons.) It was also the fashionable thing to have your house painted by Bert, who was an old-time Yankee house painter. He dressed like one, talked like one and added a lot of charm to the town, even though (unknown to most everyone in town) he was actually a former screenwriter from California. He had fled California after successful rehabilitation from alcoholism, and he earned most of his income by writing romance novels under the nom de plume *Paulette Passion*. He painted houses in part to keep him away from the temptations of alcohol that sometimes still gnawed at him when he was home alone writing. But he also liked house painting and the money it earned him.

Because all the wealthy investment bankers wanted to have Bert paint their cottages, he could charge ridiculously high prices. Even better, he could make a royal pain in the butt of himself, and the young investment bankers just lapped it up because he was a colorful character and his antics gave them good stories to tell at business lunches.

413

The general contractor that Jennifer hired to build the cottage refused to deal with Bert, so Jennifer entered into a general contract that called for the cottage to be left unpainted. Then she went to Bert and told him: "I'll pay you $6,000 to paint my cottage, inside and out."

"Waal," said Bert, "that there's a heap o' money fer a small cottage like that. What's the catch?"

"The catch," said Jennifer, "is that there's a penalty provision. For every day you're late, I deduct a hundred bucks."

"Waal," said Bert, "you just write up a contract and maybe I'll sign it."

Jennifer wrote up a contract with the following provisions:

> **The total price for the job shall be $6,000. Three thousand dollars shall be paid when the painting of the interior of the cottage is completed and three thousand dollars shall be paid when the exterior painting is completed.**

> **Painting of the interior of the cottage shall be completed no later than June 1, 1998 and painting of the exterior shall be completed no later than July 1, 1998. For each day that completion is delayed beyond these dates, Contractor shall pay Owner, as liquidated damages and not as a penalty, the sum of $100.**

> **This document constitutes the entire agreement of the parties with respect to the subject matter hereof, and no prior agreement written or oral, shall be of any force or effect.**

"Why'd you say the first of June and the first of July, when you ain't comin' up here till August?" asked Bert when he saw the document.

"Because I know how unreliable you are, and I want to make sure I have plenty of time to get things squared away before you mess up my vacation. You can think of the hundred dollars a day as compensation to me for having to deal with an ornery cuss like you."

"You city folks sure are strange," said Bert. "But I reckon anybody pays me $6,000 to paint a little bitty cottage like this here, I can put up with a bit of foolishness." He thereupon signed the document.

On June 10, Bert sent Jennifer the following e-mail message:

Finished the interior yesterday. Could have done it by June the first, but I figured you'd rather I waited. The last week in May was pretty damp. Paint that dries when it's damp doesn't last as long as paint that dries when the humidity is low. Had some real low humidity here last week, unusual this time of the year, and you got yourself a real nice coat of paint. Soon as you send me that check for $3,000, I'll get started on the exterior.

On June 18, Jennifer sent Bert an e-mail message that said:

I'm mailing you a check for $2,500. According to our agreement, I could have deducted $900, but because it seems as if you were looking out for my interests in your own misguided way, I only deducted $500.

She didn't actually get around to mailing the check that day, however.

On June 19, Jennifer sent Bert the following e-mail:

Get right to work on the exterior. A friend of mine in Hollywood got me a deal. They're looking for a location for a made-for-TV movie. They'll pay $30,000 for the month of July, but the place has to be ready by July 1.

Bert responded by e-mail:

No way I'm going to start on the exterior until I have your check and your promise that if the exterior is done by July 1, you'll pay me the full $6,000.

On June 20, after spending a sleepless night berating herself for dealing with Bert, Jennifer wrote him the following e-mail message:

You win. I'm putting that $2,500 check in the mail today. If the exterior is finished by July 1, I'll send you a check for $3,500, the balance of the $6,000 we originally agreed to. But I reserve the right to sue to recover any damages I'm entitled to.

She did mail the check on the twentieth, and it reached Bert on the 25th. Bert couldn't start work immediately because it was raining on the 25th. As soon as it became dry enough (in Bert's judgment) he started painting. He painted eight hours a day, but he wasn't able to finish until July 3, and the movie company found another cottage to use.

Bert admits that most other painters wouldn't have waited as long for the cottage to dry before they started to paint, but he puts it this way:

I'm an old-fashioned Maine craftsman. I'm not just in it for the money like them kids. That's why folks hire me. Why if I'd started painting while it was still damp, two years from now the paint would start blistering and peeling. Then folks would be saying "Look at that Jennifer's cottage. Old Bert did that and it just didn't hold up worth a hoot." If folks was saying that about me I couldn't stand living in this town. So I do things right.

Jennifer refused to pay the rest of the $6,000, so Bert went out and got himself a lawyer (a good local feller). Jennifer found out about the royalties from those romance novels and decided to go after Bert with both barrels. She got herself a big-city firm from Bangor and they cross-complained, asking for, among other things, the thirty grand Jennifer lost on the movie deal.

Explain how the court should decide the case, including the amount of damages that should be awarded. It has been stipulated that the fair market value of painting the interior of the cottage is $2,000 and the fair market value of painting the exterior is $1,500.

POLICY QUESTION

(20 minutes)

You are chief of staff (and policy guru) for a member of Congress from a heavily-agricultural district. A bill has been introduced providing that a farmer has the option to rescind (i.e., get out of) a contract to sell his/her crops or livestock (or any part of his/her crops or livestock) any time the market price of the goods to be sold rises above 110% of the price called for in the contract (in other words, whenever the market price increases by more than 10%). The proposed law would apply only to farms owned and operated by individuals and families. It would not apply to corporate agribusinesses. Also, it would apply only to Americans. It would not apply to foreigners selling agricultural products in the United States.

Advise your boss as to the effect of this bill on American farmers.

QUESTION COVERING CONSTRUCTIVE CONDITIONS, ANTICIPATORY REPUDIATION AND GOOD FAITH

(60 minutes)

In 2001 a group of young people who had made hundreds of millions in electronic commerce decided to start a new football league that would play in the spring. They hoped to attract fans who had become bored with hoops. They were aware of the fact that several similar ventures had failed in the past, but having succeeded in e-commerce, the founders of the new league felt that they had the business acumen to overcome the obstacles that had stopped the other leagues.

L.X. Wormwood was a back-up defensive tackle for the Pittsburgh Steelers. In the fall of 2000, he played out the last year of his one-year, $600,000 contract. Wanting a chance to be a starter, Mr. Wormwood, on January 15, 2001 signed a contract with Palo Alto Nerds, Incorporated, a corporation. The contract called for Mr. Wormwood to play for the Palo Alto Nerds of the Millennium Football League. The contract called for him to play for the Nerds during the 2002 and 2003 seasons at salary of $800,000 per year. It further provided that "salary payments to Player [Mr. Wormwood] are dependent upon Player's making such promotional appearances on behalf of the Palo Alto Nerds and the Millennium Football League as officials of the team and/or the league shall reasonably request."

The contract also required Mr. Wormwood to refrain from playing for other professional sports teams during the period covered by the contract. This meant that Mr. Wormwood had to sit out the fall 2001 NFL season. During that fall, Mr. Wormwood began to have second thoughts about his decision to become a Nerd. He began to miss his friends in the NFL. When he did try to hang out with them, they dismissed him as a "minor leaguer." Even more troubling, Mr. Wormwood began to get indications the new league would never begin play. He learned that many of the owners in the league (although not the owners of the Nerds) had lost interest in football and had moved on to yacht racing. Their teams were undercapitalized. Two had had their stadium leases canceled for failure to make payments on time and one had had its weight-training equipment repossessed. When Mr. Wormwood was asked about this on a television program, he said: "I'm beginning to think the people who run the Millennium Football League are a bunch of flakes. If they don't get their act together, I'm going back to the NFL."

Mr. Wormwood's remarks gained national attention. When the Nerds' management heard about them they had their lawyer contact Mr. Wormwood's lawyer and demand a retraction. Mr. Wormwood's attorney responded with a letter in which he said: "Demand is hereby made for assurance that the Millennium Football League will play its schedule during the Spring 2002 and Spring 2003 seasons and that the Palo Alto Nerds will honor their financial obligations to Mr. Wormwood. If satisfactory assurance is not forthcoming within seven (7) days, Mr. Wormwood will treat your failure to provide such assurance as a repudiation of your obligations under his contract and will enter into a contract to play in the National Football League."

The attorney for the Nerds responded 10 days later with a letter which stated that $800,000 representing Mr. Wormwood's salary would be placed in escrow in an account at a bank of Mr. Wormwood's choice within 30 days. The escrow instructions to the bank would provide that the money was to be paid out to Mr. Wormwood in accordance with the schedule for payments under the contract during the 2002 season. The letter from the Nerds' attorney further stated that if the league failed to play its 2002 schedule, Mr. Wormwood would be given his choice of being released from the remaining year of the contract or acting as a celebrity spokesperson for the other businesses operated by the team's owners. The letter went on to say that the deposit of the money in escrow was conditioned upon "Mr. Wormwood publicly stating his belief in the continued viability of the Millennium Football League."

Neither Mr. Wormwood nor his attorney responded to the team's letter. Forty-five days after Mr. Wormwood's attorney sent his letter, Mr. Wormwood signed a contract to play in the National Football League during the 2002 season. The contract prohibited him from playing in the Millennium Football League.

As you can imagine, there was a lawsuit in which the Nerds claimed Mr. Wormwood was in breach of his contract and Mr. Wormwood claimed it was the Nerds who breached. Discuss who should prevail in the lawsuit and explain in detail the issues the court will have to address. Do **NOT** discuss damage issues.

You may assume that all acts taken by attorneys in connection with the transactions described above were authorized by their clients and that their legal effect is exactly as if the clients had taken the acts themselves.

ANALYSIS

Mr. Wormwood's attorney's letter is a demand for assurances coupled with a threat not to perform his duties if the assurances are not given. It should first be noted that this is not a contract to which Article 2 of the UCC applies. Thus, it is not clear whether a party who deems himself insecure is entitled to demand assurances. Section 251 of the Restatement (Second) provides that a party who has reasonable grounds for insecurity may demand that the other party supply adequate assurances of due performance and may treat the failure to supply such assurances within a reasonable time as a repudiation. Some jurisdictions, however, do not recognize this right, so the problem must be analyzed both under the rule of section 251 and under the law of those jurisdictions that do not recognize section 251.

First, if section 251 applies, Mr. Wormwood may not be entitled to take advantage of it because a party who is himself in breach is not entitled to assurances from the other party. Arguably, Mr. Wormwood breached the contract when he made his statement about the people who run the league being flakes. It could be argued that a statement such as this violates the implied covenant of good faith and fair dealing that is inherent in every contract. There are several responses to this. One is that some jurisdictions have not recognized the implied covenant of good faith and fair dealing. Another is that it does not cover this situation because the team's lawyer could have, if she wished to impose a duty not to make statements derogatory to the league, provided in the contract that Mr. Wormwood could not make such statements. On the other hand, Mr. Wormwood's conduct seems very similar to that of Don King. But even in that case, the court said that Mr. King's conduct, which was more extreme than that of Mr. Wormwood, would not constitute a breach of the implied covenant of good faith and fair dealing if the standards of the boxing business permitted such conduct. In this case, Mr. Wormwood can argue that the standards of pro football allow a player to bad-mouth his team and league from time to time. Moreover, Mr. Wormwood's contract is with the team, and that is to whom he owes the duty of good faith. His remarks appear to have been directed not at the team but at the league in general. On the other hand, anything that is bad for the league is also bad for the team. Nevertheless, I would conclude that Mr. Wormwood did not

418

breach the covenant of good faith and fair dealing, at least not in such a way as to constitute a material breach of the contract.

Assuming that Mr. Wormwood did not materially breach the contract by his remarks, he is, if he has reasonable grounds to deem himself insecure, entitled to adequate assurance of due performance. The question then arises, what is he entitled to assurance of, only that he would be paid or that he would also have an opportunity to play football in a viable league. Exactly what this "due performance" that he is entitled to assurance of may depend on the language of his contract or the court's interpretation of the parties' intent.

Mr. Wormwood's lawyer's letter contains a threat to enter into a contract to play in the NFL if assurance is not received within 15 days. This may itself be a repudiation. Because a contract to play in the NFL is apparently inconsistent with playing in the MFL, signing such a contract would be a total breach of his contract to play for the Nerds. If a person threatens to breach a contract unless he is given something to which he is not entitled, that threat is a repudiation. Thus, the lawyer's letter is a repudiation unless Mr. Wormwood is entitled to the assurances demanded. He may not be entitled to the assurance because (as discussed above) he may not have grounds for insecurity, or he may not be entitled to demand that the assurance be given within seven days. Seven days appears to be a short time. On the other hand, all that needs to be done is to give the assurance. It should not take a long time to do that. Resolution of this issue will probably come down to a question of whether Mr. Wormwood is himself under any time constraints. If he has some deadline for making a decision about his future plans, seven days may be reasonable. If he is not, it is probably not a reasonable time.

If Mr. Wormwood was not entitled to demand the assurance he did, either because the law in the jurisdiction does not give parties the right to make such demands or because his demands were excessive, the threat to play in the NFL unless the demands were met would itself be a repudiation and Mr. Wormwood would be liable for damages for total breach. If Mr. Wormwood were entitled to make the demands he did, then we must determine whether the team provided him with adequate assurance. It can be argued that the placing of the money in escrow would constitute adequate assurance that Mr. Wormwood would get paid for both years of his contract. For one thing, if the owners can come up with the money for the first season, it is a good indication that they will be able to come up with the money for the second. In addition, we are told they and their fellow owners made "hundreds of millions of dollars" in electronic commerce. Moreover, if the league goes under after the first year, Mr. Wormwood will be able to protect himself against further loss by joining an NFL team at that time. On the other hand, Mr. Wormwood can argue that it has only been shown that the owners were rich. It has not been shown that the team itself had assets sufficient to pay his salary. What is more important, he can argue that his purpose in entering the contract is not just to make money. He can do that in the NFL. He wants to be a starter and he can't be a starter if there is no one to play. Thus, he is entitled to assurance that the league will play its schedule, and that he has not been given.

Arguably the team's response is inadequate because it was not given within the seven days called for by Mr. Wormwood's letter. I don't think a court would buy such an argument, however, because (1) the seven days was a short time to begin with, and (2) the team's response was received long before Mr. Wormwood took any action.

If this assurance is inadequate, does Mr. Wormwood have to give the owners an opportunity to provide better assurance? Taken literally, the Restatement seems to indicate that he could just treat the failure to provide assurance as a breach. Common sense and the obligation of good faith and fair dealing, however, would argue that where they have attempted to give assurances but misunderstood what he was looking for, he should tell them why their assurance is inadequate and give them another chance to provide adequate assurance.

Arguably the assurance may also be inadequate in that the deposit in escrow is conditioned on Mr. Wormwood publicly stating his belief in the continued viability of the league. On one hand, it may be argued that there is nothing in the case law or the Restatement that authorizes a party to condition their assurance on some performance by the other party. On the other hand, it may be argued that all Mr. Wormwood is being asked to do is to rectify his prior breach of the contract, a breach that could well keep him from being entitled to any assurance in the first place.

In summary then, Mr. Wormwood was entitled to treat the team's failure to provide adequate assurance as a repudiation if (1) he was not in material breach because of his remarks, (2) the case law in the jurisdiction allows a person to demand assurance, (3) he had reasonable grounds to believe the team would commit a breach, (4) his demand was reasonable, and (5) the team's response was not adequate. If any of these conditions was not fulfilled, he is himself in breach on account of his signing with the NFL. As discussed above, I believe that some of these conditions were not fulfilled and that Mr. Wormwood is therefore in breach.

QUESTION COVERING CONSTRUCTIVE CONDITIONS, ANTICIPATORY REPUDIATION, AND DAMAGES

(45 minutes)

Owner and Contractor entered into a contract which called for Contractor to build a swimming pool in Owner's yard for a price of $40,000. The contract contained a promise that the pool would be completed by June 15. The contract did **not** have a liquidated damages clause and did **not** provide that time was of the essence. Completion by a certain date was **not** an express condition to any performance under the contract.

On June 2, work seemed to be proceeding on schedule, but on that day Owner heard one of Contractor's employees complaining that she hadn't been paid the previous Friday as she was supposed to be. Owner thereupon telephoned Contractor and demanded that Contractor assure him (Owner) that the pool

420

would be completed by June 20 at the latest because Owner had a big party scheduled for June 25 when his son was graduating from divinity school, "and I don't want the yard all torn up then."

Contract said he wished Owner had told him that before. "If you'd have told me that a month ago I could have made sure it was finished by the 15th. But now I got myself over committed and it doesn't look like I'll be able to get it done before the first week in July. But I know you're in a bind, so I'll do my best to get it done by the 24th. And I might even cut a little off the price if I'm late. But if you want to be absolutely sure it's done on time, you'll have to pay me an extra $5,000. That'll make the price $45,000. That way I'll be able to pay my crew overtime."

Owner told Contractor, "If that's the way you feel about it, you can just get your crap off my property and I'll get a reputable contractor to finish the job."

Owner then called seven other contractors. Three of them wouldn't even look at the job. One looked at it and said she didn't want any part of it. One offered to finish it for $23,000 but said he wouldn't be able to get to it until July. Another offered to finish it for $25,000 but said it would be August "at the earliest." The seventh, hearing of Owner's plight, said that because Owner's son was going to be a preacher he'd get the pool finished by June 20, but he would "have to charge $32,000."

Owner agreed to pay the $32,000, and the pool was finished in time for the party.

Prior to the time he kicked Contractor off the job, Owner had paid Contractor $20,000 in progress payments.

    A. Who committed the first total (or material) breach of the contract?

    B. If Contractor committed the first total breach of the contract, what damages is Owner entitled to?

ANALYSIS

Part A

Owner has made a demand for assurances and Contractor has given assurances that apparently were not adequate in Owner's eyes. Under the Second Restatement, when there are reasonable grounds to believe that one party will commit a total breach, the other party may demand adequate assurance of due performance. Arguably the employee's statement that she had not been paid would give such reasonable grounds. If the employees aren't getting paid, they aren't going to work and it is going to be hard to find new employees. On the other hand, this was only one employee, and there might be a legitimate reason she was not paid.

In response, Owner demands assurances that the job will be completed on time. This is arguably not an appropriate demand where the cause of the insecurity is an indication that the contractor may be going broke. The demand deals with time of completion whereas the solvency issue goes to whether the job will be completed at all. But Owner can argue that the two are related in that a cash flow problem could delay completion until Contractor found more money.

Assuming that Owner was entitled to make the demand that he did, there is the question of whether Contractor's assurances were adequate. Contractor stated that the pool probably would not be completed by the date promised but that it would be completed within approximately three weeks thereafter. Neither the Restatement nor the cases we have read makes it clear whether the assurances are to be that the party's promises will be fully performed or that they will be substantially performed. From the reference in section 251 to "total breach," however, it seems that the party only has to give assurances of substantial performance. Common sense indicates the same thing, since few contracts are fully performed. There are always some minor discrepancies.

Given that Contractor had only to give assurances of substantial performance, the question is whether late completion would constitute a total breach. To determine this, we look at the factors listed in section 241.

(a) To what extent will the injured party be deprived of the benefit which he reasonably expected? Owner will argue that the benefit he reasonably expected was having a swimming pool for the party and having his yard put back together by that time. The better view, however, is that the benefit is having the swimming pool for the next 20 years (or however long a swimming pool lasts). That this is the proper view is reinforced by the fact that nothing was said at the time of contracting about the party. Thus Owner is not really being deprived of a substantial part of the benefit.

(b) To what extent can the injured party be adequately compensated? owner can't be adequately compensated because his claim for damages for his party being messed up will fail for certainty and foreseeability.

(c) To what extent will the party failing to perform suffer forfeiture? Contractor probably won't suffer a substantial forfeiture because most jurisdictions allow quantum merit recovery by a party in breach. He will suffer some losses, however, because switching contractors will increase the cost of the project, and he will be required to bear that cost.

(d) To what extent will he cure his failure? If the failure is late completion, it won't be cured.

(e) To what extent does his behavior comport with standards of good faith and fair dealing? A lot of people said in a conclusory

422

fashion that Contractor's asking for more money to assure on time completion was bad faith. I don't think it's so simple. He indicated that he wasn't trying to make an additional profit, but rather that he was going to use the money to pay his crew overtime. In fact, he said that he might reduce the price if the job was completed late. That doesn't sound like bad faith. What might be bad faith, however, would be his getting over committed. If he's just bad at estimating how long jobs will take, that is all right, but if he intentionally took on more work than he could handle, knowing that it would make this job late, that might be bad faith.

Coupling these factors with the fact that a short delay in completion of a construction contract is generally deemed not to be a material breach, I would conclude that Contractor has not failed to give adequate assurances.

If Contractor has not failed to give adequate assurances, then Owner breached the contract by throwing Contractor off the job.

If it is determined that Owner was entitled to demand adequate assurances and that Contractor failed to give those assurances, then there is the question of whether Contractor was given a reasonable time to give those assurances. In this case I believe he was because he stated his position and did not indicate he needed more time to consider the matter further. In this case, Contractor would be in reach for failure to provide adequate assurances. This would be true, however, only if the jurisdiction followed the Restatement rule. Under the common law, there is no duty to provide assurances, so Owner could not treat Contractor's failure to provide assurances as a repudiation, and Owner would be in breach.

Part B

The simple analysis is that Owner's damages are $12,000. His loss in value was $32,000 because the work that Contractor failed to complete cost $32,000 to get done. He had no compensable "other loss," and he avoided a cost of $20,000 (the remainder of the payment to be made to Contractor under the contract).

A more sophisticated analysis would consider whether he should have taken the $23,000 bid. Our principle of mitigation would say that his damages should be based on that bid unless taking it would result in undue risk, burden, or humiliation. Arguably, having the yard torn up at the time of his son's graduation when he was planning to have a pool ready would constitute that sort of burden or humiliation. (Those terms weren't intended to be read narrowly.) But on the other hand, allowing Owner to take the party into account in getting substitute performance is inconsistent with the idea that only foreseeable damages can be recovered. We wouldn't give him money to compensate him for the pool not being ready for the party because that was not something Contractor could have foreseen at the time the contract was entered into. But if we make

Contractor liable for the extra cost Owner paid to get the pool finished in time for the party, we're doing the same thing in an indirect way.

QUESTION PAROL EVIDENCE RULE, EXPRESS CONDITIONS AND GOOD FAITH

(30 minutes)

Buyer and Seller entered into a contract for the purchase and sale of Seller's home. The contract contained the following provision:

> Buyer's obligation to purchase is subject to the condition precedent that Buyer enters into a contract to sell her present home prior to July 1, 2001.

Prior to the time they signed the contract, Buyer had told Seller, "I'm only going to sell if I can sell it at a reasonable price."

"What would you consider a reasonable price?" asked Seller.

"I need to get at least $300,000," said Buyer.

There is a dispute as to what was said after that. Seller testified he said, "That sounds awfully high" and that nothing more was said about the matter until after the contract was signed.

Buyer denied that Seller said "that sounds awfully high." Buyer claims Seller said instead, "I can live with that."

Buyer put her old house on the market for $350,000 (to give herself room to negotiate). She got no offers, and after a month she reduced the asking price to $300,000. When she went another month without receiving any offers, she told Seller the deal to purchase Seller's house was off.

Seller sued. The case was tried without a jury. Based upon expert testimony by real estate appraisers, the trial judge determined that the value of Buyer's old home at all relevant times was $225,000. She now wants to know whether she has to figure out whose version of the conversation is correct or whether she can decide the case without getting into this messy factual issue.

Answer **the following specific question** for the judge: "If I decide I believe Buyer's version of the conversation, is Buyer in breach of the contract,

      (i) if I find that the written agreement is a fully integrated agreement; or

      (ii) if I find that the written agreement is a partially integrated agreement?"